Praise for *Public Intellectual*

"This intimate and penetrating account of a remarkable life is rich in insights about topics ranging from the academic world to global affairs to prospects for a livable society. A gripping story, with many lessons for a troubled world."
—NOAM CHOMSKY

"Richard Falk is one of the few great public intellectuals and citizen pilgrims who has preserved his integrity and consistency in our dark and decadent times. This wise and powerful memoir is a gift that bestows us with a tear-soaked truth and blood-stained hope."
—DR. CORNEL WEST

"Richard Falk's *Public Intellectual* is a citizen pilgrim's journey across the world , over nearly a century, contributing to peace in Vietnam, Iran, Palestine . . . . Through his life and ideas he invites us to imagine and shape the 'politics of impossibility' to heal our 'endangered planet' and our fractured societies. Whether you are a peace activist or researcher, or you care about the earth and fellow human beings, *Public Intellectual* will enrich you intellectually and politically."
—DR. VANDANA SHIVA

"Richard Falk recounts a life well spent trying to bend the arc of international law toward global justice. A Don Quixote tilting nobly at real dragons. His culminating vision of a better or even livable future—a 'necessary utopia'—evokes with current urgency the slogan of Paris, May 1968: 'Be realistic: demand the impossible.'"
—DANIEL ELLSBERG

PUBLIC INTELLECTUAL

The Life of a Citizen Pilgrim

Richard Falk

Clarity Press, Inc.

In-house editor: Diana G. Collier
Cover design: R. Jordan Santos
Cover photo: Dante's Lantern by el grillo

"As one who, walking by night
carries a light behind him and not for his own benefit
But to make wise those who come after him…"
—DANTE, Purgatorio, *Divine Comedy*

Library of Congress Control Number: 2020952167

Clarity Press, Inc.
2625 Piedmont Rd. NE, Ste. 56
Atlanta, GA 30324, USA
https://www.claritypress.com

For Hilal

TABLE OF CONTENTS

Acknowledgements

More than with earlier writing, I have leaned on others in the course of writing this memoir. It is not only that I know less about my life than about my researched intellectual pursuits. I am also inevitably biased, and so sought readers who saw aspects of my experiences and character with different eyes. Beyond this, I touched on many areas of public concern, and wanted to do my best to avoid mistakes of fact and distorted remembrances.

No one I approached declined, and many gave me valuable feedback that I did my best to incorporate in a seemingly never-ending series of revisions that have made my life miserable well before the COVID pandemic elevated my private woes to a planetary level.

I needed encouragement early on, and received it from several trusted, cherished friends, including Victoria Brittain, David and Carolee Krieger, Tom Plate, James Kavanagh, Avery Gordon, Nora Gallagher, Maivan Lam, Mark Bruzonsky, Lisa Hajjar, Phyllis Bennis, Radmila Nakarada, and Virginia Tilley. Our Geneva lunch group, a source of unrelenting stimulation over the last decade, consisting of Eugene Shulman, Daniel Warner, and Matthew Stevenson, administered constant injections of self-belief when I needed them most to get this wingless project off the ground. It is with sadness that I note the death of Gene, who provided much of the glue that kept us together over the years, and although championing a cynical worldview, he was always emphatically and lovingly supportive in personal relations.

Our lovely adopted 'daughter,' Huyen Giap Mitchell, and my longtime anti-war collaborator, Cora Weiss, helped me with the Vietnam chapters, as did Vida Samiaan, Sasan Fayazmanesh, Nader Hashemi, and Behrooz Ghamari with the Iran chapter, and Hilal Elver with the Turkish chapter. It seems odd that the only chapter for which I was willing to rely solely on myself was the most controversial one, on Israel/Palestine.

I am particularly grateful to Susan Abulhawa, Rich Appelbaum, Ceylan Orhun, and Paul Wapner for detailed comments on early chapters that saved me, especially, from overly long sentences, some snide reflections on friends who chose differently on sensitive issues, and kept my spirits high enough to keep from abandoning the project midway. I owe Vincent Stanley a special debt of gratitude for stealing time from his own busy schedule to read and comment constructively on the whole manuscript when it was much longer than the present version, and hope he recognizes the impact that his feedback had on this final version.

I was touched by the willingness of our children, Dimitri Falk and Zeynep Zileli, to read parts of the manuscript, and not only read, but make important helpful suggestions that are incorporated in the final text. This was also true for Hilal who relied on her gifts of generosity to overlook aspects of my blemished past, and offered valuable ideas about structuring my unruly life in more palatable forms.

Above all, I owe heaps of gratitude to Diana Collier who went far beyond the normal role of editor/publisher to offer criticism, commentary, and indispensable encouragement. I have published many books during the last 60 or so years, but have never previously had such a benevolent interactive publishing experience as with Clarity Press.

My longtime intellectual comrade, friend, and talented digital artist, el grillo, contributed the mysteriously appropriate cover, and endured unanticipated technical obstacles while arranging the complicated transition from computer print to book. If I had known in advance that such difficulties were present, I would have lacked the courage to approach him. Indeed, ignorance can be bliss, allowing me the special pleasure of having el grillo so closely associated with this rendering of my life.

Martha Hughes, a skilled professional editor, did her best to improve an early draft, and helped me persist against my better judgment. Every author should be so lucky as to have such expert advice.

Hilal, my life partner for more than the past 25 years, not only kept our life together and flourishing in Santa Barbara, Yalikavak, and Istanbul, but also took her own challenging journey to new heights by serving with such dedication and skill as UN Special Rapporteur for the Right to Food during the entire ordeal of producing this memoir. Her love, and that of our children, Noah, Dimitri, and Zeynep, and our amazing granddaughter Juliet, helped sustain us, bringing us the joys and challenges of intimacy through good times and bad. There are many others who helped make my life what it became, and I would mention particularly my previous wife, Florence Falk, the mother of Noah and Dimitri, a warm friend to Hilal and myself.

This is the first time I have leaned so heavily on friends in the course of producing a book, and not surprisingly, I turned to others because of my feelings of falling short in expressing my life experience in a readable way that compromises with truthfulness as little as possible. It was not only a matter of appealing for help, but I have come to admit, pleas for reassurance. So often during the last three years I have been ready to discard the project as beyond my capabilities, but somehow, I had just enough belief and support to keep me going until I staggered across the finish line.

There were many who were crucial to me at different stages of my life, as friends, relatives, romantic partners, political allies, and intellectual gurus whose influence has lingered but whose presence in the pages of this memoir is ether minimized or even excluded due to length restriction and sensitivity inhibitions. I hope they know who they are, and do not mind, maybe even welcome, this shadowy anonymous acknowledgement.

After this elaborate demonstration it should be obvious that a work of this kind cannot avoid being in subtle senses 'collaborative,' making mandatory the habitual acceptance of responsibility for the errors and infelicities that remain.

PART ONE
BEGINNINGS

CHAPTER 1
A Reluctant Chronicler

"Don't look for anything but this.
If you point your cart north
When you want to go south,
How will you ever arrive?"

—Ryōkan (1758–1831) (translated by John Stevens)

I have long hesitated before embarking on this impossible journey and would recommend against it, had I known. I wondered whether I had the perseverance needed to go from start to finish, or whether I will even survive long enough to see, much less cross, the finish line. I also wondered whether I started too late, being 90. In tandem, I wondered whether I should not devote my remaining time to doing what I have been doing for the past 60 or so years, writing topically and responsively, even journalistically and by way of a blog, on many of the global political issues of the day, as well as their deeper meanings as viewed through my highly personalized and normative optic that is unabashedly progressive, which means it is left of liberal and addresses such underlying structural issues as capitalism, consumerism, and militarism.

Writing this memoir has been as much about *discovering* my story, that is, myself as it is about *telling* it.

Defending Progressivism

There is much commentary these days about the obsolescence of left/right descriptions of political life. The left has never recovered its confidence or a coherent grasp of contemporary realities after the collapse of the Soviet Union, the ideological retreat of China, and the dehumanizing impacts of predatory neoliberal globalization.

The right in America has, until the advent of Trump, somewhat masked its readiness to accommodate, if not endorse, racism and plutocracy. Trump and Trumpism has encouraged the right to reemerge in a crude and overtly reactionary manner, comfortable beneath the banner of the alt-right worldview, a version of pre-fascism. For me personally, politics has never been reducible to a coherent ideology as represented by a political party or ideological dogma. My politics are issue- and personality-governed, often problem-generated. They reflect a sustained inclination to take the suffering of others seriously, to identify with the underdog in conflicts, to worry during my professional lifetime about world order, nuclear weaponry, and threat diplomacy, and to believe that most of what is politically desirable is not permanently beyond human reach, even if seemingly unattainable at present.

I have long been intrigued by how to explain the occurrence throughout history of 'the impossible,' that is, occurrences seen by the mainstream as so unlikely to happen as to be unworthy of responsible discourse, dismissed as 'utopian' or 'doomsday alarmism.' My previous hopeful worldview always reflected a refusal to accept the status quo realism of influential pundits.

I admit that my earlier hopefulness has been increasingly challenged by an avalanche of discouraging developments. A variety of concrete circumstances in the last decade has made me increasingly skeptical about human survival and a humane future. Perhaps, most telling of all, is the mounting evidence of our failures of ecological responsibility, most pointedly evident in the pallid responses to climate change. The contrast between the world according to Greta Thunberg and that of Donald Trump depicts two kinds of future for humanity. I have come to question whether the human species has a *collective* will to survive because it has turned its back on such convincing evidence of impending apocalyptic catastrophe. I feel misgivings about the destiny we seem to be imposing on future generations. Such a destiny encompasses the lives of my own grandchildren. As I see it, we have yet to acknowledge this overwhelming threat to the human future, and until a real acknowledgment is made, there will be a continuing dynamic of denial, escapism, and blinding extremism as the bio-ethical crisis intensifies.

Beyond Liberalism

I have long been dissatisfied with shallow approaches to existing social wounds and their root causes. Without the transformation of underlying structures, crises will recur, and broader social and political systems will at some point disintegrate or experience catastrophic breakdowns. We need to respond to the urgencies of the moment, but connect crises with deficiencies of structures, identities, priorities, and values. In this regard, I am sympathetic to revolutionary impulses, although suspicious of revolutionary practice given the disappointing record of performance of many successful revolutions once power was achieved. Such was the experience of the French, Russian, Chinese, and Iranian revolutions, as well as the nationalist victories over European colonialism during the last half of the 20th century, change often achieved at great cost to the native population only to be hijacked by competition for leadership and the play of antagonistic social forces once empowered. We can only hope, and hope fervently, that the present ferment in the United States is prefiguring a revolutionary upheaval that will be responsive to ecological challenges, and also to the failure to produce social, economic, and climate justice for Americans. Recent lapses in the constructive global leadership of the United State have weakened the problem-solving capacities of the present world order, and must be corrected if the mounting challenges are to find solutions.

Perhaps, also, I have at times been too dismissive of the incremental advances made through the dedicated efforts of 'good liberals' who are guided by the dual logics of private self-interest, often reducible to the security of their bourgeois lifeworld, and their belief in the political as the art of the feasible, that is, what seems presently achievable.

My point of departure is that we are experiencing a widening gap between the feasible and the necessary. This is perhaps most easily illustrated by the failure to reduce greenhouse gas emissions in accord with the scientific consensus on climate change and is also apparent in the many dysfunctional responses to the Coronavirus pandemic. We are also experiencing the two destructive standard ways of coping with this gap, which is itself rarely acknowledged as such. Prevalent patterns of denialism and shifting blame are evident if we pause to reflect on what we are doing individually and collectively.

The gap between the feasible and the necessary is already leading to *denialism, extremism,* and in their wake, almost certainly, *catastrophe.* These ways of reacting without responding meaningfully deepen the crisis. The only positive response is by way of pursuing with all available energy what is *desirable,* however improbable, a willed posture best understood as a *necessary utopianism.* Such is my interpretation of the contemporary predicament, currents of thought that weigh heavily on how I view past, present, and future. In the end my story is of someone living, loving, and learning mostly in America, themes that inform and pervade all that follows. The learning part reflects more than 60 years of teaching, reading, and academic writing, while the living and loving parts are accounts of my struggle to be an engaged citizen, a satisfying partner, and a decent parent.

In other words, the personal has become acutely politicized in my life, while the political has become intensely personalized. So *my* private story is a miniaturized version of *the* public story, or so I like to think. In this regard, my present angle of vision is impeded by menacing storm clouds that affect interpretations of what is past and what is to come, although always accompanied by glimmers of hope. If a positive future unfolds it will come together as a result of an almost sacred appreciation of the preciousness of life and the moral imperative to preserve it, and a restored political will to make it happen.

I seek a deeper understanding of landing where I did, privately, politically, and spiritually, and in so doing, am depicting the public intellectual I have become while my life as a citizen pilgrim unfolded. This requires explaining as best I can why I chose paths that were professionally, politically, and I guess personally, quite different from those of almost all others with whom I shared similar pasts and starting positions. More concretely, what deep roots can help explain why my ambitions veered off normal career paths and conventional middle-class family life? Although I paid a price for doing so, I have rarely had regrets.

CHAPTER 2
Childhood Revisited

"We are all born ignorant,
but to remain ignorant is a choice."

—Chinese proverb

Not as It Was, but as I Remember:
The Relevance of My Childhood at Age 90

I will make no attempt to paint a series of portraits of my childhood at various stages, especially as it unfolded and was experienced. I am looking back at these first years through a blurry rearview mirror to pick up hints of relevance to who, how, and what I have become eight decades later. I have no assurance that my memory serves me well. I actually don't know whether the most important clues from this distant past have been forgotten, suppressed, unnoticed, or lurk somewhere in the denial bin we all use to dispose of unwanted and humbling memories. I recall during my early teen years feeling impatient to get beyond the constraints of childhood, yearning for the unrestrained freedoms I then foolishly associated with being an adult, not realizing back then that adult responsibilities would at first weigh me down far more than the absence of parental constraint would set me free. Above all, while young I had no real comprehension of how I had been scarred and influenced by the pains I experienced in relation to my parents and sister, as well as the unusual character of what 'family' meant to me during these formative years.

I remember rather vividly a walk in a Stockholm suburb on a country road with a well-known Swedish psychiatrist, who doubled as a Strindberg literary critic, in which we agreed 30 years ago that each successive decade of our life up until that point had been more satisfying than the preceding one. We were both approaching 60 at the time, but this way of affirming life as I grow older has continued to sustain me, despite my curtailed sports life, limited mobility, assorted aches and pains, and a demoralizing feeling that the tides of history, especially as playing out in America, and also the world, have turned mainly against my hopes, values, and expectations. I also face the unwelcome reality of declining sexual capacity, somewhat aggravated by an undiminished erotic imagination. Such tensions between capabilities and their imagined fulfillment were not experienced until the curtain of old age dropped from the great beyond, with the odd effect of stimulating the re-experiencing of those life's joys that remained accessible. Yeats did this kind of exploring in some of his late poems and so did Gabriel Garcia Marquez in *Memories of my Melancholy Whores,* a novel about the asexual yet sensual relationship between a man in his 90s and his favorite prostitutes.

Early Life without a Mother

Not really, nor literally, yet almost. Maybe I am being callous by even daring to complain about the torments of my childhood when I pause to realize how privileged my upbringing was compared to those many children orphaned by misfortune, war, racism, extreme poverty, and famine. Yet while quite young, under 10, my normally sensitive, tender father let me know, perhaps in one of those thoughtless moments we all experience from time to time, that before they agreed to marry, my mother insisted on the condition that they not have children. Her desire to avoid motherhood was not primarily a career decision although my mother, Hélène Pollak, at the time had been a nationally ranked tennis player for fifteen years, starting in the early 1920s. There likely would have been some tension in trying to be a mother while competing at the highest levels and traveling the world. I have come to believe that a more satisfactory explanation for obtaining such an unusual pre-nuptial pledge was her awareness of her absence of maternal motivations, perhaps somehow connected with her own unpleasant experience as the child of frosty and socially ambitious parents.

This maternal reluctance was undoubtedly strongly reinforced by her traumatic failures of childrearing when trying to be a mother for my sister, Joan, who was born more than seven years before me. Joan, who was loving and lovable, spent most of her life in mental institutions, undergoing for decades the ordeal of 'treatments' relied upon in the 1930s and 1940s that resembled torture more than therapeutic responses to mental disorder. I never did discover whether these widely separated births of my sister and myself occurred as two accidents or resulted from temporary suspensions of this commitment to a childless marriage. Unlike property arrangements I assume that this pre-nuptial pledge was informal, unwritten, and reversible, and for me, best of all, that it was happily ignored on at least two occasions.

In retrospect, even without the pledge, I would have supposed that the traumatizing ordeal associated with my sister, who was periodically difficult, divisive, as well as disturbed, would have made even family-oriented adults hesitate before embarking on the uncertainties of a second child. By the time I was born, Joan was already showing telltale signs of what would later be clinically described as a 'psychopathic personality with psychotic episodes.' From this perspective, the mere fact of my existence is in this trivial sense 'miraculous,' although what I am pompously calling a miracle maybe nothing more than the unintended, and even unwanted, outcome of a ribald night of forgetfulness with consequences difficult to undo. Abortions at that time were unlawful, dangerous, and expensive, and not so common, or else I might not be alive to offer conjectures as to why I was born.

In any event, I was begotten and born, and have rarely contemplated this unusual form of contingency: that is, I exist only because for some unknown and now unknowable reason my parents, both long deceased, broke their promise to one another. I never asked my mother about her recollections. I wish I had, but knowing her lack of self-esteem, I doubt that I would have received an honest response even if she had agreed to talk about such deep and awkward feelings. She never wanted to accept responsibility for what went wrong with Joan. She regarded my sister's mental disorders as purely genetic and aggravated by my father's failure to take action that would protect the family from disorders arising from their supposedly damaging side effects. My father, in an equally self-serving manner, was inclined to attribute Joan's condition to her clashes with my mother or as temporary growing pains that could have been overcome by love, time, and possibly, psychiatric treatment.

Disturbingly, I realize that I loved Joan more during the years she was confined to mental hospitals, one after another, than after she was declared fit to live in society after the 'cure' of mind-dulling lobotomy. Joan was a vivid and lovable presence, if impulsive and sometimes disruptive, before she was 'fixed.' Her post-lobotomy self was a cardboard image that lost the vitality that had earlier made her a formidable social force with an infectious smile and a playful disposition.

When Joan died in 1973, I was appalled by my mother's response. She failed to attend the funeral, which was perhaps understandable as she was living in California, in a fine house atop the La Jolla bluffs. What I found embarrassingly distasteful was her crassly insensitive materialism. My mother phoned to ask if I could arrange to send several fur coats that Joan had accumulated as a result of gifts from her maternal grandmother. This struck me as more than peculiar, a bit eerie. Who wears fur coats in La Jolla? Even elsewhere such attire was becoming politically incorrect. Mother made no pretense of sadness, or even a show of sentimentality, to this premature death at 56 of her daughter. It reinforced my own sense of being essentially unwanted, and unloved by her. While growing up, I withheld judgment, and accepted what she offered, not being attuned to what was being withheld. As an adult I became more confident, and hence more judgmental.

Worse was to come. My mother's second husband, Detmar Walter, or Det, a greedy gambler of fascist disposition, contacted me a few days after Joan's death to ask whether I would forego my inheritance as the beneficiary of a trust set up by her rich grandparents (my mother's parents) to handle her special needs as someone permanently dependent. I found this to be a totally inappropriate request. Its brashness struck me as jaw-droppingly surrealistic. I had struggled for twenty years after my father's death in 1956 to manage Joan's accounts and any issues that arose bearing on her wellbeing. I accepted without complaint the realization that my mother was totally unwilling to play any parental role. So I made clear that I was not at all inclined to give up any part of the inherited sum. I never had second thoughts, but it permanently soured my relationship with Det, and he made sure that it would break the formally correct yet rather frigid relationship I had fashioned over the years with my mother. I paid a financial price. My mother, who died less than a decade later, disinherited me. But that mattered far less than the emotional price.

The money I did inherit under Joan's will helped ease financial pressures later on. It may have been this margin of economic privilege that indirectly subsidized my activist and controversial politics. In this sense, my mother's family, without any intention to do so, turned out to be a crucial benefactor that enabled me to live my middle and later years with less stress and more feelings of financial security. Without savings of my own I nonetheless escaped my father's financial worries in the latter stages of his life. My experience suggests that a modest inheritance enhances life if well spent, while a large inheritance is almost always ruinous, and should be disallowed.

I have come to realize that from childhood I tried to understand my mother, viewing her actions from her standpoint, doing my best to avoid feelings of bitterness and resentment. Although she never bestowed affection or showed much concern with whether I rose or fell in life, she did try before moving to California and remarrying to be a friend of sorts, giving advice, and keeping minimal contact. She had some qualities that impressed me favorably, including offering emotional shelter to gay men at a time when this was not commonly done even in New York City. Perhaps, I would have never developed impulses and skills of public empathy if my mother, never 'my Mom,' had loved me. What I struggled to achieve all along was the capacity to live in relative sympathy with a mother who refused to act as or pretend to be a Mom. Increasingly, I have come to believe that this struggle, carried on without much awareness on my part, also had major impacts on how I deal outwardly and inwardly with my deepest feelings, projecting an outward appearance of serenity and clarity without ever overcoming inner struggles with turmoil, self-doubt, and distrust.

If a Love Child

I have occasionally wondered if my life would have been different if I had thought of myself as a wanted child, especially a love child, or had experienced the normal quantum of maternal affection as an infant. Likely, yes, to some uncertain extent. I would then have had the benefits of a mother's love and affection, maybe making me more trusting of emotional attachments as I grew older. Yet if she had remained unhappy and duty bound as wife and mother, I might have suffered even more than I did from her detachment and departure, and maybe from the absence of a surrogate female presence while growing up as Dad never remarried. He settled for a series of short-term romantic attachments that never reached the stage of altering the nature of our male household.

Even during early childhood, I never consciously regretted Mother's departure, or absence from my life. Of course, reflections on what might have been are totally irrelevant to what I became, and are in any event, mostly unreliable musings. Maybe the most discernible impact of this maternal void was that I was to go through life with feelings of being unwanted, lacking entitlement. I tried to insulate myself from the risks and hurts of anticipated rejections and abandonments as I never felt I deserved the love of others. In effect, I have not been able to trust fully, and hence to be entirely trustworthy in that regard. I have over the years sometimes kept default options in reserve should my core relationship fall apart. Only during these last 25 years of a happy marriage with Hilal have I gradually learned to accept the vulnerability that must accompany an unconditional commitment to another person, an understanding of life's unavoidable contingent nature that Buddhism elevates to a first principle, that of detachment. Hilal raises the stress level of attachment by viewing my occasionally flirtatious style as a litmus test of the quality of our marriage, even drawing into question my love for her, and feeling justified in punishing me by her own emotional withdrawal from time to time.

Aside from making it hard for me to trust the love and loyalty of women, the main legacy of this childhood deprivation was to leave me without lofty expectations for myself, a trait I view as both good and bad. I have tended throughout my life to treat my rejections and disappointments as deserved, or at least understandable, not worth complaining about, much less resisting, but helpful to comprehend, and then move on and try again.

I was occasionally challenged, and not just by women, who speculated that I was scared of commitment, even intimacy, because of my experience of childhood hurt and neglect. I was even accused in midlife of being 'a serial killer,' in the sense of leaving behind what my female assailant called 'a trail of broken hearts.' I found this allegation melodramatic because it claimed I caused distress of magnitudes beyond the reality. I don't believe I have left behind feelings of deep resentment or lingering hurt, although some of my more mature relationships did end with rough landings. Later, with the passage of time, friendship was restored, and positive memories crowded out whatever pains associated with the breakup still remained. As far as I am aware, despite three former wives and several close partners, I have yet to experience long-term repudiation by any woman I once loved. Yet I confess that I often had trouble satisfying expectations of sustained emotional and erotic closeness and was criticized—with reason—for being unwilling to do the 'work' needed to build sustainable relationships. Only when I might be too old for it to matter, do I acknowledge this necessity, and do my best. Earlier I had the idea that if core relationships required heavy lifting they had already failed. Now, at least, I know better: no love relationship with a partner can be sustained without a conscious, sometimes anguishing effort that centers on self-criticism and refrains from shifting blame from oneself.

Early Life with a Disappointed Father

My dad was exceptionally tender, loving, loyal. He was unconditionally supportive throughout my growing years, offsetting the negative
effect of an absent and unaffectionate mother. His affirmation of who I
was and what I did was especially helpful to me during adolescence when
I was such a dismal dullard in my own eyes and an eclipsed presence in
the eyes of most others. This sense of being supported allowed me to
tread water without drowning during my bland and banal childhood and
early adolescence. I write thus in retrospect. While I was growing up, I
was clueless about such matters, although I envied those who seemed
smarter, more composed and better liked.

Dad's own life was marred by many bumps in the road, especially
during the last twenty years of his life. He was conventionally patriotic,
loved the U.S. Navy, disapproved of the New Deal, and would have
neither understood nor endorsed the rise of 'identity politics.' His views
on several litmus test social issues would be regarded as decidedly unfashionable according to current liberal standards. Despite this, I believe
he would have detested the Trump presidency as much as I do.

Dad subscribed to negative stereotypes that exhibited the standard cultural prejudices of the time against gays, women, and African
Americans. He affirmed by attitudes of respect and affection the America
crafted by white Anglo-Saxon Protestants (familiarly known as WASPS).
His law practice did not bring him much satisfaction or the material rewards he felt were his due. His day job as a lawyer provided an abundant
source of close friendships, including with several glamorous clients
over the years, most notably Claudette Colbert and Zsa Zsa Gabor. His
passion for the navy, deriving from his role at a member of the small staff
of the Admiral of the Atlantic Fleet in World War I, never dissipated.
This position on the staff of an admiral whom he greatly admired seemed
the peak experience of his life. For him it was comparable to being a star
quarterback for a winning college team or, if a girl, being homecoming
queen of a Midwestern university. With this devotion and great discipline, he managed to write several respected books on naval history in
his spare time, which meant he was mainly at home in the evening after
a day at the office. He even found first-rate publishers, and once received
a review on the front page of the *New York Times* Sunday Book Review
section for his book on the rise of Japanese sea power.

Dad has exerted several strong influences, positive and negative,
over my life from its beginning all the way to the present. It took me
many years to find my own moral and political compass, and shake free

from his conservative, militarist tendencies and strident anti-Communist beliefs. I long had trouble reconciling his personal warmth, kindness, and empathy with his lack of public compassion, regressive stereotypes, and reactionary politics.

He held views of the U.S. Constitution and the role of courts that were roughly along the lines so influentially championed recently by Anthony Scalia. Dad wrote a book length manuscript that never found a publisher opposing FDR's plans for expanding the U.S. Supreme Court. Roosevelt, frustrated by the Court's refusal to uphold his welfare legislation, controversially decided in the 1930s to expand the number of judges on the Court so that he might appoint several who would be sympathetic to his welfare policies being judicially blocked. Constitutional conservatives were up in arms by what they viewed as a threat to the political independence of the judiciary. FDR's plan was labeled the 'Court packing plan' by its critics. Such a shift in the judicial balance would have given Congress a freer hand in legislating more benign social and economic policies. FDR's benevolent intention was to lessen the Great Depression's hardships on workers and the poor. Such legislative and executive initiatives went against the grain of constitutional republicanism. Critics charged that such tampering would weaken the Constitutional design of government based on checks and balances. For constitutional purists like my father these distinct branches of government deserved respect and adherence even in crisis situations when pressures to be expedient and compassionate mounted. These are recurring challenges to republicanism and are again putting the Court in the line of fire. It is always risky to circumvent constitutional constraints to achieve short-term results that purport to serve 'the public interest.' Yet to have government paralyzed by such a stalemate between branches of government at a time of socio-economic crisis is also untenable, as seemed the case to the majority of American citizens during the Great Depression. If hard economic times come again, similar tensions are likely to reemerge.

After Trump became president with scant respect for the rule of law or even constitutional forms of governance, robust checks on the exercise of executive power seem wise, sensible, and yet exceedingly fragile if and when the country falls sway to unscrupulous leadership and irresponsibly compliant behavior of coordinate branches of government. Trump has at least produced a renewed appreciation of the 'republican' features of creative tension introduced into the U.S. Constitution almost 250 years ago. Yet these virtues are themselves contingent. Relying on law and the good conscience of its interpreters to prevent tyrannical abuses of presidential authority only succeeds if the cognate branches of government remain principled and sufficiently sensitized to the benefits of constitutional government, including the rule of law and traditions of restraint. Avoiding a consolidation of power by an aspiring demagogue depends on a mobilized opposition in the citizenry as well as a conscientious Congress and Supreme Court. As the legalism of Nazi Germany or the Soviet Union demonstrated, law without ethics and political independence is just one more mechanism used by the state to deny justice and oppress the citizenry. It may be helpful to realize that autocrats love law more than do democrats.

Yet if law does not yield to pressures for change and is tied rigidly to a past that no longer serves the people, it will function as an instrument of reactionary politics. It will produce human tragedy and political crisis. Yet legal opportunism can also be damaging to a system of constitutional integrity as was the case when at the outset of World War II Japanese-Americans, including citizens, were sent to internment camps for alleged security reasons for the duration of the war, a position endorsed by the Supreme Court. These two instances led me to understand that grave harm can equally result when law operates to block paths to social and economic justice as when it opens gates that allow claims of security to take precedence over basic human rights.

It was in the context of the Great Depression that I recall being taken by my father to Washington for a visit to the Supreme Court at the age of 8 or 9. He went to enlist support for his efforts to oppose FDR's 'Court Packing Plan.' Dad brought me along, I now suppose, to share the experience of visiting this eminent institution of American government. At the time I felt as if we were going to spend the day at a famous zoo to visit rarely seen animals such as snow leopards. Dad met individually with a series of justices who years later I realized were then the most celebrated of jurists in the country: Louis Brandeis, Harlan Fiske Stone (my father's law school teacher and friend), and Felix Frankfurter.

It was a hot June day in Washington, and I remember three things: Stone showing me that a bookcase behind his desk obscured a hidden door opening onto a living room, a kind of hidden private chamber that appealed to my childish attraction for secret hideouts; Brandeis holding my hand as we crossed one of those broad Washington avenues to find a restaurant for lunch; and at the end of it all, my fatigue after such a series of meetings during which I tried rather vainly not to display boredom. I remember confiding to Dad, 'I am judge-sick.' I remember having the vague sense at the time that the purpose of these meetings was to secure support for his view that FDR posed an existential threat to the authority and independence of the judiciary, and specifically the Supreme Court. Those with whom we met seemed sympathetic with his concerns.

Dad suffered from several serious health issues, endured romantic disappointments, and was always beset by financial worries. He died at the age of 62 in 1956. The negativity he experienced during my childhood and adolescence taught me lessons that I have used to guide my behavior in different directions. I have tried to avoid these particular pitfalls of his as best I could. So far, I have been fortunate in these respects, although my early romantic experiences all ended badly, yet without bitterness or any haunting sense of failure on my part. I did not pursue, nor was more than ever momentarily tempted by unattainable trophy females, as Dad had been in the period after his divorce from my mother.

My realistic appreciation of these limits was faintly tested, and perhaps established, by Zsa Zsa Gabor, whom I adored. Her impact started in my early teen years and lasted for more than a decade. Her radiant sexuality and energetically joyful engagement with life attracted me deeply, but I was not so out of touch. I knew that however much she seemed to enjoy my company, Zsa Zsa was well beyond my reach, besides being thirteen years older. It was pleasure enough for me to have the chance to experience her embodiment of feminine charms mixed with a bit of wizardry. Now that I am free to engage a fantasy—I confess that had I known of Emmanuel Macron's pursuit of Brigette when he was fifteen and she was forty, I might have mustered the courage to make a fool of myself. Zsa Zsa was always warm and forthcoming with me, and we laughed a lot. She taught me to curse in Hungarian. I showed off this bit of Budapest street talk to a bunch of kids on a train going to Maine for summer camp, then was taken aback when an older woman across the aisle chastised me for 'gutter talk.' Momentarily, I felt cornered by the omnipresence of Hungarians, and never again cursed in Hungarian, at least not until 20 years later when I was retaught while married to an irreverent Hungarian. Such are the strange patterns we call 'life.'

Nannys, Maids, Minders, and Servants

It was a common middle-class practice in Manhattan in the 1930s, even for those living on the upper West Side with moderate financial means and some worries, to employ live-in help. Apartments were large, and in a concession to my passions of the time, we even had a ping pong table in what in most city residences would serve as the room set aside for dinner parties. I mention this as a way of signaling that my rather extreme attachment to sports started early, and even now remains a part of my life, as I am still enjoying tennis and ping-pong.

I recall my mother invoking the popular cliché of this pre-Spock era—'children are to be seen but nor heard,' and it seemed, in my case, also 'and seen as little as possible.' At the same time, on the few occasions when we met after she left home, Mother treated me as an adult more than did Dad, perhaps not burdened by the sense that there was something special about a mother/son relationship. I rather enjoyed this. In this spirit, she conveyed to me one time that her wealthy father once told her that he would hire the best lawyer in the country if she wanted to gain custody of me. She claimed that she didn't accept this offer because she was sure that it would produce a lengthy ugly fight with Dad that would not be good for me. I doubted even at the time that this was her true motive for forbearance.

Later on, I remember that we had a Hungarian cook and an Irish immigrant maid/minder, Bridie Horan Leary, who took care of me from, say, age five to twelve. Bridie was affectionate and my friend as much as my governess and always a good companion. She took me quite often to a Catholic Church, St. Paul's, within easy walking distance from our Manhattan apartment. This allowed her to attend mass and take communion. I listened and watched, somewhat entranced by the mysteries of the church rituals. Since the mass was then recited in Latin, I had no idea what was being said or done during its performance, and Bridie never tried to explain. Yet, this exposure to religious practice made me envy the sense of community and belonging shared by those regularly attending church services. Looking back, I believed I missed then and since feelings of community and spirituality that seemed present in this, or almost any, religious surrounding. I had the misleading belief that I have never entirely lost, that religion was *necessarily* a call to nurture our better selves. Later as a student I became fascinated by comparative religion. I never developed a lasting institutional attachment to any particular religion, although because of my early experiences of being in church I felt less connected to Judaism than Christianity during childhood.

Later, I became curious about all religions, with an ecumenical readiness to dabble in any faith tradition. And yet throughout my life I have been unwilling to commit to any organized religion except in a superficial manner that exhibited curiosity more than commitment. Only once in my late 20s did I came close to an actual affiliation. Even this short-lived resolve was suspect, being intertwined with a romantic involvement. I fancied myself in love with a devout Catholic woman who was herself a converted Catholic. She let me know that she would take my affections seriously if I first embraced Catholicism. I knew at the time that an institutional affiliation and an emotional attachment should be kept separate, but in my state of confusion the two realities became fused. In the end, hours before my scheduled baptism, with pangs of conscience, I withdrew.

Bridie was succeeded by Willis Mosely, the first African American who entered my life in a strong personal way. Willis was originally from Kansas City, Missouri. When he came to work for us, he had recently graduated Phi Beta Kappa from UCLA. Willis was then about 28, striking me as already a fully formed adult. He was tall (6'3"), slender, and well-spoken. This job was supposed to be a temporary stop on his quest for a career in theater. Why this never materialized, I still do not comprehend, although it seems likely that racism played a part. Willis possessed a commanding voice and was strikingly intelligent. To top it off, he had the most infectious laugh I have ever encountered. Willis was brilliant and charming, with a comic gift, unabashedly gay, and with it all, charismatic.

Willis' flamboyant identity bothered my father who was mildly racist and somewhat homophobic—although being 'bothered' was not at all the same in his case as 'rejecting.' My father came to appreciate Willis' many endearing qualities, and despite their vast differences, they came to share an affection and respect for each other that moved me. Despite stereotyping his approach to Willis, Dad displayed a redeeming willingness to make exceptions—some of his closest friends were overtly gay. Just as family servants had more impact on me than their masters, gay men probably opened my eyes to the joys and travails of life more than did straight folk. During my teen years and early college experience Willis introduced me to his wide multi-ethnic circle of friends, many of whom were involved in the arts, and took me with him to gay parties. Again, as with church, I keenly observed the gay scene without passing judgment when witnessing men physically intimate with one another. I felt no attraction, or even ambivalence, keeping a social distance in the hope of avoiding awkward encounters. Only once, days after my father's death, did Willis seek some kind of physical intimacy with me by jumping into my bed while I was lying down. When I clearly withdrew, he withdrew without diminishing what had by then become a warm friendship. I remember that my only feeling afterwards was the hope that Willis was not hurt by my rejection. As far as I could tell, he wasn't. Only years later did I realize that there was undoubtedly a racial aspect, as well: when a white boy rejects a black man's advance it must have intense racial undertones even if innocently motivated.

The residue of these childhood encounters influenced who I later became, inculcating a steadfast refusal to judge the lifestyle choices of others. This remained so even though I pursued a rather conventional path. I was delighted that my high school and college friends congregated around Willis in our kitchen where he held court with composure, charm, and enthralling wit. Only my poor, mentally disturbed, yet loving, lively, and sweet sister, Joan, was comparably attractive within the confines of our apartment. She and Willis had magnetic impacts on my friends.

We All Need Role Models

Willis and my sister were each, despite their own formidable difficulties, positive role models for me, as well as making me aware of my own shortcoming. Willis as a brilliant, kind, funny, decent, gay African American undoubtedly helped me see people as they were, and not through the prejudicial filters constructed by white racism and classist self-segregation that pervaded the social mores of the self-satisfied North. Sadly, Willis never found success in theater, his dream, but despite disappointments and constraints, he remained a vivid and lovable personality. Is there a greater achievement in life than this?

While I was an adolescent, my father was put under some pressure by his largely bourgeois friends to 'let Willis go,' as the Manhattan privileged class liked to express their discretionary control over the destiny of others less fortunate. The reason given: to protect me from becoming gay and dissolute, especially absent the guidance of a woman in the home. Fortunately, I was consulted, pleaded with my father not to heed such unwelcome and unnecessary advice, and my plea succeeded.

Willis remained a fixture in our family until Dad died. This was a characteristically impressive display of Dad's willingness to depart from even the regressive conventions he embraced if this was what was called for to give way to those he loved. Willis had a serious drinking problem, was detained by police on several occasions for soliciting sexual partners on NYC streets at a time when homophobic and racist attitudes prevailed, especially among the police. Despite decades of supposed progress in overcoming ingrained racism, I doubt that Willis would have done better in the present atmosphere.

Law and Life

My Dad was a lawyer who thought less about law and more about forging lasting friendships with many of his clients. He seemed somewhat dazzled by his several celebrity clients. He never pushed me to follow his professional path, yet it was the only path I came to know as an adolescent.

I lacked a clear idea about what a lawyer does, beyond carrying around lots of thick documents in heavy brief cases, befriending clients, and hoping for the kind of lucrative settlements that in Dad's case were more imagined than real. He had tales of near misses that he would recount quite often to explain his current economic distress. He partly blamed the refusal of his law partners to accept contingency fees from the venture capitalists who were among his clients. According to his narrative, several became big successes, and had his partners been more patient they could have all become relatively rich. I listened to this tale of missed opportunities, being neither convinced nor doubting his words.

I developed two somewhat contradictory ideas during those years, neither entirely accurate. First, lawyers are always bored by their work. Secondly, that the legal profession is a reasonably smooth path to social respectability and economic security in American society. Law offers a Plan B & C for those, like myself, who display neither scientific nor artistic talent, and have no appetite for business or medicine, nor have an awareness that a life of public service might be an option.

Later when I entered law school without the slightest idea of what kind of career to pursue, I felt ready to drift to wherever the current eventually deposited me. To end up in academic life was then as far from my expectations about my future as becoming an astronaut or piano tuner. In those years, I was pushed forward by the nervous feeling that I must prepare myself for some sort of career or else I would sink to the bottom of the sea. I had some interest in expressing my ideas through speech and writing, but not by way of lawyering. It early seemed to me that the successful lawyers I knew as a child were either helping the rich become richer or seeking to minimize the pain of wealthy clients who were doing bad things. Later on, I came to appreciate that some lawyers were heroic and others were living exciting lives, especially pro bono and progressively oriented lawyers. I was especially influenced by my strong friendship with Leonard Boudin, a talented left pedigree lawyer who liked to hang out at the Harvard Club, and was as proud of his Harvard Law degree as my father was of being on the staff of a U.S. Navy admiral.

I approached the challenges of adulthood with feelings that earning a law degree was a respectable way to postpone life choices, creating an option that would allow me to knock on many doors once I earned the degree. Also, I learned from my father a reverence for the written and spoken word, and did aspire to see my name someday on a printed page. I also fantasized about stirring large crowds to frenzy as I spoke from a balcony hovering above a large plaza filled with an impassioned and responsive crowd hanging on my every word. I sometimes teased myself to sleep play acting these demagogic phantasies.

Despite a humiliating late life dependence on my 'devices' (laptop, I-pad, I-phone), I have never lost this Gutenberg affinity for the printed word, and hope to die before I do. And as for speaking, I developed with lots of practice a non-charismatic ability to express ideas and sentiments with credible passion and some clarity. I think I exceeded what might have been expected in my youth. I had been humbled by receiving a 'C' in an undergraduate public speaking class. My performances as a speaker were also marred by an awkward public shyness that has been my lifelong companion. Despite thousands of public talks, I have never lost the existential fear of seeming foolish in the eyes of those I respect or care about.

Sports and Games

I cannot remember the origins of my love of sports and games, but it started early, and has remained with me throughout life, adapting over the decades to facilities of place and the constraints of age.

I learned to play baseball when 8 or 9 and was hit in the head by a pitch one time, but ping pong became my main early 'sport.' Tennis, squash, basketball, even football all came later. My sports life climaxed in my non-sports minded high school where I was able to play on the basketball, baseball, and tennis varsity teams. I also played American Legion baseball in Van Cortland Park, and had the good luck of having my best day at bat when a major league baseball scout happened to be watching the team practice. I was both startled and excited to receive an invitation for a major league tryout at the Polo Grounds where the New York Giants played prior to their move to San Francisco. I was nervous when my great day came, and intimidated when batting against an array of wild young pitchers who were throwing from a high big league mound. I had never experienced anything like this before. I know that I would have happily gone off to the lowest level farm club of the NY Giants had I been recruited. Fortunately for me, neither my hitting nor running showed sufficient promise, only my throw from third base gave a slight hint that I might someday have big league potential. This was not enough for the scouts. I was given a pink slip and a friendly smile.

I learned chess at the end of grammar school, played competently at an amateur level, only studying the game in a fitful, superficial manner. Chess remains an activity that brings pleasure, but I never had steady chess friends. I have always enjoyed learning more about the game by playing better players. I minded losing only when I made blunders below my skill level, allowing weaker opponents to prevail, which probably is also a clue to a character trait that manifests itself in many competitive settings. I have played from time to time with my son, Dimitri, who is thoughtful, patient, and methodical, which is not at all the way he otherwise thinks or lives his life.

I continue to play chess, but in recent years almost exclusively with a software computer opponent that boasts the skills of a grandmaster and proves it by beating me consistently. Against ChessPro I have never won. Sometimes, I reach the endgame on a par, but quickly get outmaneuvered. I realize that I do not have the motivation or knowledge to achieve my full chess potential but remain satisfied by a competent level of play. This same lack of serious dedication limited my tennis game.

While at Princeton several of my closest and abiding friendships were with squash and tennis regular opponents. I played daily, sacrificing lunch and the more academic network building that went with such meals. I enjoyed the competitiveness of the squash league and did pretty well. In ping pong I fared better over the years, usually winning tournaments in college and law school. My ping pong peak was reached at the 1955 national table tennis championship. I reached the third round, but at the cost of failing the NY Bar on my first try.

Entering college, poker almost immediately became my thing, casting a dark, near fatal, pall over my freshman year at Penn. I played almost nightly, won consistently, and was only weakly motivated to complete my course assignments or get enough rest to be attentive at lectures. Toward the end of the academic year I was made to realize the cost of these antics, but was slow to mend my wayward ways, although eventually I did, mainly from fear.

I also managed almost to earn a place on the much-heralded Penn freshman basketball squad, surviving until the last cut, and did play singles for the freshman tennis team. In this role, I visited Princeton for the first time and lost to my opponent after choking, blowing an easy match point at net that I can remember as if it occurred yesterday. Over the years I remain more in touch with my failures than my successes.

My sports and games life never entirely vanished. I was moderately successful over the years in poker, chess, pool, and checkers, and a tolerable 'club player' in ping pong, bowling, tennis, squash. I might have done somewhat better had I taken lessons, worked harder on my own, but I never mobilized the energy or possessed enough ambition, and so remained content with competing with those more or less at my level. Even if I tried harder to reach my potential, the difference likely would not have been significant. I lacked the physical and mental endowments needed for real excellence in either sports or games.

At the same time my engagement with sports and games bestowed benefits that have endured as my life evolved through its various stages. I attribute my good mental and physical health as an adult to this devotion to sports and games. It remains my therapy, and as I liked to explain, I found such 'play' more effective, far cheaper, and more fulfilling than what I learned from my three experiences with professional therapists. These diversions provided a sense of balance, offering a satisfying place of refuge when things went badly at home or work. My regular tennis and squash players became and remain true off-court friends.

Both of my sons, Dimitri and Noah, were more gifted athletically than I, eventually beating me even at ping pong and tennis, and my third son, Chris, dominated me in squash forty or so years ago when I was still playing at my highest level. To be in my own family the third best in tennis and ping pong and second best (out of two) in squash does not suggest Olympic potential. Yet, acknowledging mediocrity never dimmed my enjoyment of sports even after my sports-afflicted knees reduced my mobility to near zero. Sports served also as a source of strong bonding with my male children that has persisted even as they have become middle-aged, and even more so with Hilal, who also turns out to be gifted in the sports that depend on eye/ball coordination.

I have sometimes wondered whether my middling achievements as an athlete and game player are not also features of my professional career as teacher and writer. In my most self-critical moments, I attribute my professional success to persistence rather than talent. I take James Baldwin at his word when he wrote, 'Beyond talent, lie all the usual words: discipline, love, luck, but most of all, endurance.' At other times, I feel that I have a somewhat special ability to analyze and think through difficult political and legal issues, as well as to define my intellectual identity in ways that sympathetic others find authentic, somewhat innovative, and far enough from the mainstream to be both progressive and challenging. This combination has brought me gains and a few losses at every stage of my life.

Classical Culture Came Later

I grew up surrounded by sophisticated New Yorkers, yet strangely without much highbrow contact with the cultural life of the city that surrounded me. Classical music, opera, museums, even jazz, dance, poetry, and serious films played no part in my upbringing. I was exposed to middle-brow offerings, such as Broadway musicals (*South Pacific, Kiss Me Kate, Guys and Dolls,* and a bit of Shakespeare), but not much else. In his younger years Dad was drawn to serious literature in the classic mode, but he rejected the contemporary art/literature scene, rejected abstract art and stream-of-consciousness writing and long sentences (Joyce, Faulkner). Ironically, this was precisely what I later came to love.

I never had the torment, opportunity, and discipline of piano or dance lessons. I was only rarely exposed to other ways to deepen my relationship to cultural activities, despite living at the epicenter of the greatest contemporary mecca of culture in the world. It was somewhat ironic to live a block away from Lincoln Center during my first twenty-four years on the planet, yet never once attend a ballet, opera, or concert performance so close by.

By some unrecollected quirk we visited the home and studio of Jackson Pollock when I was twelve or thirteen. Pollack was already a celebrated contemporary painter living and working in the Hamptons. He was notorious for avoiding art critics and interpreters of his work, and yet he invited me to come to his studio across the lawn to look at some of his work-in-progress. I had never before seen paintings done in the controversial drip style painting that he perfected. I felt flattered by this attention from someone I knew was a famous artist. I listened closely and looked at his work with rapt attention as he patiently explained why he developed a calligraphic style as a path to beauty and rapture, thereby overcoming what he believed to be the exhausted legacy of figurative or representative art. It was an experience that has stayed with me, recalled every time I see a Pollock hanging on a museum wall.

It was only later in my last undergraduate years that I began to be exposed to these dimensions of culture, and tried to learn as much as possible about religion, art, philosophy, and non-Western civilizations as I knew about sports. I wanted to be involved with people, especially girls, who were culturally engaged and sensuously alive.

As sports continued to enthrall me throughout my life, so has culture, where I am open to a wide range of artistic avenues of expression, especially poetry, film, literature, painting, and to a lesser extent, music, dance, opera, theater. This love of culture, high as well as popular, not only enriched my life experience, but also softened the sharp edges of my political beliefs and careerist ambitions.

While married to Florence, my third wife and mother of my sons, Dimitri and Noah, I did enjoy and respond favorably to experimental theater, known in NYC as 'off-off-Broadway.' We often ventured to the city to sit in uncomfortable seats to watch a Richard Foreman, Robert Wilson, Jerzy Grotowski theater work or often seeing whatever was being featured at La Mama, the Public Theater, or the Brooklyn Academy. Again, despite an eagerness to be culturally connected, I seldom made friends with creative artistic personalities unless there was a romantic sub-text.

I have written poetry since my late 20s, publishing a few pieces during the 1970s, but never believed in myself as a 'real' poet except occasionally in solitude when I sometimes marveled at my own poems. Finally, at 85, I self-published a collection of poems under the title *Waiting for Rainbows*. It has been warmly praised, but only by friends and relatives, curbing false pride. At the same time some of this positive feedback came from readers who themselves had poetic credentials and fine aesthetic gifts of discernment, making me hope and sometimes believe that they wouldn't compliment my poetry without meaning it.

I will remain in 'the closet' as a poet for the rest of my life unless someone 'outs' me, for which I will be undoubtedly grateful. From time to time I am tempted to submit stuff to poetry magazines to see whether I could have a more visible presence. This ambivalence toward my own work remains unresolved. I remain disinclined to take myself more seriously if it requires me to spend time and energy.

I recognize something peculiar. I am timid about rejection, yet bold about opposing what I do not believe. I do not mind being seen as wrong, leftist, utopian, or whatever, if the concerns involve deeply held views on public issues. I have never liked debating my views, finding the experience polarizing and unrewarding, but welcome civil conversations and dialogue, including with those with whom I disagree—sometimes especially with them. Not surprisingly, I have found that I often learn more from sophisticated opponents than allies. My attitudes on these matters have been tested on my blog, a way of communicating to a

largely unknown and unseen audience that I embarked upon just after
my 80th birthday.

Being Jewish

I learned early in life that being Jewish was a primary signifier in
American society, but beyond this I was never given the opportunity as a
child to become acquainted with Jewish traditions or religious practices.
At home I was not even exposed to such ethnic staples as 'bagels and
lox' on Sunday mornings, and was not taken to a synagogue on Jewish
high holidays. I do remember the pastrami and sauerkraut sandwiches
and divine cheesecake at Lindy's on Broadway or the Stage Deli on
Sixth Avenue. These iconic Jewish hangouts were both within walking
distance from our apartment. I experienced these hallowed food sites
more as part of the midtown Manhattan scene than as particularly Jewish
markers.

I have no memories of Dad speaking about Jewish persecution or
anti-Semitism or Israel either during or after World War II. The dominant source of his identity was his lifelong effort to be and be seen as a
full-fledged American. He was preoccupied during my childhood with
foreign threats to the American future posed by Germany, but even more
so by Japan. During my years up until college I was among the few Jews
in my school that had a student population of 90% Jewish students, maybe the only one, who was required to attend classes on Jewish holidays.

Dad was friendly with Edgar Nathan, a prominent conservative
New York lawyer, and orthodox Sephardic Jew, who became Manhattan
Borough President at one point and a close supporter of Thomas Dewey
when he ran for president as the Republican candidate against Harry
Truman. We were invited by Edgar to spend election night in 1948 at the
Dewey headquarters located at the New York City Bar Association on
44th Street. It was a memorable experience with a twist. A celebratory
atmosphere prevailed during the evening as it seemed clear from the
early results that Dewey was on his way to victory. This was before there
were exit interviews and scientific polls. Dewey left his headquarters
near midnight to get some sleep before delivering his expected victory
speech the following morning—which turned out to be a concession
statement. I was indifferent to the outcome of the election, although to
my embarrassment I had written a solicited editorial in my high school
newspaper in support of Dewey. This made me a reactionary outlier in
the overwhelmingly left liberal atmosphere of my NYC high school,
Fieldston.

Partly in furtherance of his own Navy dreams, my father sent me to Admiral Farragut, a pre-college naval academy in Toms River, New Jersey, for two summers. There I first encountered what I would call soft anti-Semitism. The sadistic discipline administered by the counselors was far worse. They wanted to make the lives of us interloping campers miserable, whether we were Jewish or not. We campers were viewed derisively by the staff as mere tourists peeking at the rigors of academy life. Our tormentors wanted to experience the bitter taste of hierarchy, discipline, and punishment that was apparently the signature features of their four-year student experience. We were made to wear uniforms and stand in formation at attention in the hot summer sun on the concrete surface of the parade ground. One time a frail boy near me fainted, and when I moved to help him, I was gruffly chastised, and then punished.

What it meant for me to be Jewish never became important during my childhood, but this never bothered me. My father was anti-religious, as well as anti-ethnic, subscribing to a rather militant version of the secular religion of nationalism fused with a rather incoherent humanistic code of personal ethics and an ethnically flattened identity. My mother was completely indifferent to religion, pragmatic and materialistic in her private dealings, and cut off even more than I was from her ethnic roots.

Her socially ambitious parents, my Grandpa Henry and Grandma Eva, never even told her as a child that she was Jewish. She only found out at the age of 18 or so when the U.S. Lawn Tennis Association rejected her application for membership. She never mentioned to me being Jewish or spoke of concerns related to the Holocaust or even the rise of Hitler. Her brother, a successful business man and moderate Republican, did belong for seemingly 'professional reasons' to Jewish social clubs in NYC and encouraged his children to participate in the Jewish version of debutante life, including ridiculous coming out black tie dance parties for juvenile elites, established and aspiring. For a while, I guess as a family courtesy, I was put on the list of invitees. Being so brought in from the cold didn't work well in my case.

I never got over feeling awkward. I was alienated by the pomp and artifice of these pretentious events at which I was assigned a stranger to escort from her apartment to the dance floor. I felt a crude misfit, and each time, I went through the whole miserable process of dressing and meeting my date, I vowed that this would be the last time. I admit to some contradictory feelings that arose from my feelings of social inadequacy clashing somewhat with my contempt for such empty rituals of elite grooming. Thinking back, the whole experience might have been entirely different if either of two things had occurred—had I been more confident on the dance floor I might have overcome my sense of social discomfort. As it was, my ineptitude as a dancer epitomized my sense of being out of place. The other possibility, which never happened, was to become romantically entranced. Maybe also there was a third possibility. If our family had been rich as was the case for my two older cousins who never seemed bothered by the benefits of their status. Everyone at these events seemed rich (or at least acted rich) and at ease in these surrounding, except for me.

In the end I opted out, but in a hurtful manner that shames me even decades later. I stood up my assigned partner for the evening, whom I was expected to pick up at her residence, bring to the dance, and take home afterwards unless she found a better option at the event. What I did was awful. I left her waiting in an evening dress without even taking the trouble to phone and feign sickness. She appropriately complained about my bad behavior, and I was blacklisted. Never again was I invited to a debutante ball for Jewish girls. I regret treating this girl whom I didn't know in such an uncourteous, and possibly hurtful manner. I should at least have had the decency to call, apologize, and somehow explain. This dismal sequence of events taught me where I didn't belong. I admit that after the fact a small part of me had regrets. Deep down I felt envious of these bland souls who so thoughtlessly looked forward to these gatherings. They looked forward to claiming their place in high society even if it was somewhat ethnically then limited to that small flourishing and apparently hermetic world of Jewish socialites in NYC. They didn't seem to mind that they were second best when it came to ascending the upper reaches of the social pyramid in America.

Growing up, I was neither ashamed nor proud of being Jewish, and not very concerned about its relevance to my life in those early years. Looking back at my late childhood feelings, I recognize that I came to hope that my specific religious identity would become less important with age. I was generally aware of whether my friends were Jewish or not, and early on, almost all were Jewish. The girls I liked best from third grade all through high school were mostly Jewish. It interests me now that the social dichotomy that engaged me was the binary of being either Jewish or non-Jewish; these were the seeming ethnic alternatives on the upper West Side of Manhattan. Other ethnic, social, and religious identities never intruded on my imaginaries. Of course, this reflected the reality that my neighborhood and school were predominantly Jewish even if our home social life happened to be more diverse, which was almost unique among my friends.

Despite this, even when young I was uncomfortable when Jewish friends proclaimed themselves 'a chosen people,' and tried to demonstrate the claim by reciting the Jewish survival of multiple persecutions and by reference to Jewish influence and achievements far exceeding their numbers. I never doubted that Jews had many achievements to their credit, but intuitively felt that such claims of exceptionalism had their dark sides. I reacted negatively to claims of Jewish superiority, especially if explained by evidence of prominence, wealth, and influence, feeling put off by the implicit racism before I was familiar with the concept. Somehow, I early escaped my father's negative stereotyping of African Americans, women, gays, even World War II refugees. From my earliest memories I wanted to accept people as individuals regardless of their race, religion, and class, and just maybe I found myself more attracted to the exotic than the familiar, which I associated with solidarity feelings. I identified myself as an outsider, and thus saw myself, however misleadingly, as a victim of discrimination. Perhaps, I confused being mildly victimized in my immediate family surroundings with the harsh social stigmas and exclusions visited upon women and African minorities.

It is tempting for others, especially those of Zionist persuasion, to connect my ambivalent attitudes and shallow experience of Jewishness with my critical stance toward Israel. Undoubtedly, there are some links, but I do not think this is the explanation of why I have become so committed to this particular controversial issue. I had stayed aloof from the debate on Israel and Zionism for a long time, although I was aware that support for Israel went virtually unquestioned within my circles, but not until many years later did I come to understand the issues well enough to have an independent opinion, much less engage actively. In the end, I believe that my critical stand toward Israel and Zionism reflects factual reality and should be judged from that perspective alone without reaching for psychological explanations.

On Being American

Unlike being Jewish, being American in my childhood was more an unthinking fact than sentiment, not unlike breathing oxygen. Except for my father's somewhat chauvinistic nationalism and confident patriotism, I took my American identity for granted in a mindless uncritical way. It took me years, for instance, to revise my untutored view of Columbus Day, and regard it as a day much better spent mourning the abuse of native Americans rather than celebrating the colonialist ocean navigator. Growing up I took pride in the victory achieved by the West in World War II, and definitely viewed the Allied victory as a just outcome of a major war that defeated evil enemies. At the same time the battlefields and existential traumas of combat remained abstractions and statistics for me. These events failed to evoke the sorrows that should certainly have informed a proper understanding of a devastating war that caused such acute and massive human suffering and devastation. My insensitivity extended to those among the defeated peoples who despite a large measure of complicity never deserved the horrors inflicted upon them. I became distressed while still a student, especially by the use of atomic bombs and by the strategic bombing campaigns waged by the victorious power, state terror on a grand scale. W.G. Sebald's extraordinary book, *On the Natural History of Destruction,* brilliantly analyzes how difficult it was for German intellectuals to cope with their devastating experiences of mass death and destruction arising from strategic bombing because of their unresolved agonistic difficulty in acknowledging in authentic ways the barbarisms of Auschwitz.

Traveling to Europe for the first time in the summer of 1954 I became conscious that others were perceiving me through the prism of my American identity. At first, I reacted defensively, fending off criticisms that struck me as superficial or plain wrong. For the first time I felt a genuine surge of patriotic and national pride rise to the surface from some hidden place in the depths of my consciousness. Despite this self-discovery of my Americanness, throughout my European travels that summer I was enchanted by the national differences I encountered and felt excited by these first direct exposures to foreign cultures while traveling on my own.

Despite this default nationalism my visit to Europe exerted a deep and lasting influence, inclining me toward a globalist outlook that superseded my American birthright. I viewed travel as an enriching and endlessly valuable aspect of my professional and personal life, and an essential dimension of my lifelong learning experience. International travel was both liberating from the discipline and tedious responsibilities of normal routine, but also gave rise to inspiration, friendship, encounters with the unexpected, and even adventure. And during my pre-Hilal years, travel sometimes offered me the pleasures of a romantic/erotic playground.

Political Seeds of Discontent

During the last years of childhood, let's say late teens, I remained completely unformed and uncommitted politically. I had not broken free from my father's influence, while disputing his outlook in many specific contexts, especially when we conversed alone. He was the lawyer and friend of some militant anti-Communists who in the 1940s and 1950s would sip scotch or bourbon while decrying the presence of 'parlor pinks' in government and Hollywood. The central figure in this group was Isaac Don Levine, a rather passionate Russian living in exile, who wrote books. Don, as he was called by friends, had supposedly attended Lenin's funeral before leaving Russia and becoming a bitter opponent of the aftermath of the Russian Revolution, and later of Stalinism. It was Don who brought Alexander Kerensky, briefly the Russian leader after the February Revolution drove the Czar from power in 1917, into our home in the early period of his American exile, who I think became my father's client for a while. He was mild and calm in social settings according to my recollections, but still preoccupied with raising the level of anti-Soviet activism in the United States.

I declared myself as apolitical throughout childhood, not only because I remained uninformed, but also, despite the tumultuous times, I was mindlessly disinterested. The big Western political presences in those years after FDR's death were Harry Truman, Churchill, and De Gaulle, cartoonish superheroes of a kind. Maybe Truman didn't deserve to be so considered. He seemed and was an accidental president who turned out to be a well-oiled tool of the emergent Cold War security establishment and the political leader unapologetically responsible for dropping atomic bombs on Japanese cities in 1945. Churchill, too, was a great war leader for Britain, but I later learned that his career was tainted by a white supremist worldview and a high profile early government career that included colonial era crimes against humanity, especially in Africa, but also Ireland. De Gaulle was also guilty of colonial wrongdoing but deserves credit for being a proud beacon of anti-fascist French unity while living in exile during World War II, as well as later finally bringing the bloody Algerian War to an end. DeGaulle later displayed exceptional gifts of national leadership that deserve credit for avoiding a feared civil war in France.

Several Shades of Grey

I guess my childhood was neither black nor white, nor green nor red, but several shades of grey whether measured by achievement, temperament, or ambition. I managed, and mainly coped. I lacked self-esteem, dreams, empathy, and inspiration.

I was even somewhat ashamed of my family circumstances, being embarrassed by the fact that my parents were divorced and my sister was an inmate in a mental hospital. Further, despite finding my mother and her parents cold and detached, I somewhat envied their wealth, and associated my father's economic troubles with his feelings of personal disappointment in love and career, producing a declining sense of his own self-worth. The Pollaks, mother's family, allowed me to feel tolerated, yet openly conferred on me the dubious distinction of being the black sheep of the family, and as such, to be kept out of sight most of the time. I was compared by my grandmother unfavorably to my male cousin, the only son of my mother's highly successful brother, Maurice. I seemed to be viewed as a pitiable lost boy, the hapless victim of a broken family and a struggling father.

I can point to no big moments of exaltation looking back on those childhood years. There were interludes of brightness and promise in which the greyness lightened to become almost white, but soon faded to grey again. One bright moment occurred when my friend, James Simon, and I, who both had a crush on the same girl, Paula Levin, decided to give her jointly a simple bracelet as a sixth-grade school graduation present. Paula sent us each a thank you note but on the reverse side of mine was written 'love, and I mean you,' words that kept resonating within me for years afterwards. I insisted on looking at the back of Jim's note, insensitively hoping that I would not find similar words. The page was blank, but I was then much too shy to seize the opening, and Paula went elsewhere. Another bright moment was my selection after a competitive audition to take the leading role in a sixth grade graduation play about the life of Simon Bolivar, the Latin American leader who freed the continent from Spanish colonial rule. This theater performance was the climax of my grammar school experience.

Looking back, I find only a few true continuities: an abiding love of sports, and the accompanying intensities of competition in all spheres. I sought to reach competence in whatever I undertook but failed to make the added effort to achieve excellence. I had no resentment toward those who did better. I now realize that I lacked the discipline to reach higher through coaching and concerted study. I think this casual attitude toward commitment and ambition shaped my future approach to work and play. My EQ was very low during these early years. My friends seemed to regard me as okay, nothing special, without promise or distinguishing features, a kind of gray presence, a dullness complemented by timidity and an acute fear of rejection. Being a boy without qualities made me indistinct in personality, and hardly memorable.

Looking back from the present, I am comfortable with what I later became and affirm the pursuit of progressive goals at the cost of diminished professional recognition and status. I also realize that after childhood I was the recipient of unusually good luck with regard to my professional life and health, as well as a beneficiary of abundant comradery, friendship, and emotional intimacy. An important turning point discussed in the next chapter came at Penn when a fear of imminent personal disaster prompted a transformative response for the better that changed me forever.

I only crossed the threshold between childhood and adulthood when two developments occurred: an embrace of cultural humanism and an accompanying rise in self-esteem that allowed my romantic fantasies to become actual relationships. In some respects, I never crossed the threshold into adulthood, as the child within continues to roam freely, allowing me to tease and be teased, a reality that Dimitri tapped into better than my other children who appeared to feel l that I was work addicted, both night and day. Hilal is not entirely comfortable with this surviving inner child, disliking its outward show, particularly when I tease pretty women. I became convinced that when I began without artifice to infuse my teaching with playful humor, only then did I become both well liked and appreciated as a professor who taught classes, wrote books, and spoke his mind in the public square.

Without Role Models

What I have learned by reflecting on my childhood is that my parents both contributed to my mature self as much by their failings as by their successes or involvements in my daily life. My father, although loving and admirable in so many ways, influenced me to try hard to avoid his disappointments and mistakes in political outlook, romance, and professional endeavors. I seem so far to have escaped the traps that ensnared him in the latter unhappy stages of his life. At the same time, I cherish my memories of his tenderness with people, his basic decency, and humility, as well as his lively appreciation of the ironies of life.

My mother, of course, was more problematic for me, yet I did learn not to reciprocate her lack of love for me, and began a lifelong practice of trying to see as others see, and thus not become so self-absorbed as to blind myself with resentment or project an all-knowing arrogance. This has enabled me in recent years to brush aside the smears of Zionist adversaries without wavering in my commitment or becoming pointlessly preoccupied with fashioning self-justifying aggressive counter-narratives.

Hilal and Richard in Vietnam

Hilal and Richard with Zeynep

Chris and Judy Falk

Florence

Dimitri Falk

Noah Falk

Adopted daughter Huyen and family in Vietnam

PART TWO
WITHIN THE ACADEMY

Although I longed for the freedom that came with being away from home, I soon discovered I couldn't handle it. I was thrilled at first, being able to do and not do exactly what I wanted in a permissive college environment. This tantalizing absence of supervision and structure led me to stumble badly, so badly that it might have easily become a life-changing fall if I had not sought and obtained a steadying discipline. After this near collapse a series of awakenings occurred at three Ivy League universities. It was a period of personal transition that led me at its end to choose, quite unexpectedly, an academic career, a choice I continue to affirm, despite a few disappointments and disillusionments along the way.

It was at Penn that I abandoned my alienated posture of getting by. I began to find excitement when encountering challenging ideas and discovering that I had a standpoint of my own. After four years as an undergraduate I emerged a very different person than who I was when I arrived on campus. I was still at a pre-political stage of personal development, but the building blocks for a productive future seemed to have been acquired. Inspiring professors at Penn were partly responsible for this late awakening, as well as several mentoring student friends. It was also at Penn that I first responded to serious poetry and commenced a lifelong love affair with lyrical ways of seeing, feeling, knowing, engaging, and expressing.

CHAPTER 3

Collapse and Recovery at Penn

An Academic Stumble

As a freshman at Penn I started out as a conscientious student, attending classes, doing assigned reading, and receiving decent grades during the first few months. But such study habits didn't last beyond the Christmas vacation, being superseded by gambling, playing poker almost nightly until well past midnight, and devoting many daytime hours to sports.

I judged myself in those first months as a shameful embodiment of pure sheepishness, even going meekly along with this uncongenial college ritual of fraternity 'rushing.' I was sufficiently insecure as to feel this need for an institutional certification of social acceptance. It didn't even bother me that it was ethnically and religiously bipolar, either Christian or Jewish. I was seeking to find some receptive niche with social expectations low enough to invite me to join. In this mindless quest, I was slyly hoping to be invited by a fraternity with campus prestige, however foolish and vain. Fraternities did have profiles (athletes, nerds, rich families) and reputations, and we students were all aware of which ones catered to these various images of winners and losers.

I recall the undisguised disappointment of a senior fraternity member who asked me if I was related to the Falks of Pittsburgh. When I said no, he responded in a solemn tone, 'Well, that's too bad.' I later discovered that the Falks he had in mind were prominent philanthropists and community leaders, a far cry from my financially cramped background. This concern with status and connections struck me even then as a typical exhibit of the distasteful sensibilities of socially ambitious fraternities.

As we walked together that first rushing night toward the fraternities, my basketball buddy from Indiana, Ed Grimm, said in a friendly voice 'Why don't we do this together?' I replied, 'We are going different

places. I am Jewish.' I am sorry. I didn't realize,' he replied. And maybe,
I am not sure, we hardly ever exchanged another word ever again. Our
friendship lapsed. We never recovered the casual rapport we enjoyed
during our first weeks on campus. Ed was a decent guy who was without
malice, but he had a raw rural background in the Midwest that including
subscribing to some rather crude negative Jewish tropes, and this likely
explains why our shared love of basketball was not enough to sustain
our friendship.

I guess, more than I realized growing up in New York City during
the 1930s and 1940s, Jews were negatively stereotyped in the hinterlands
of American society. Perhaps more than I have ever admitted even to
myself, I had in those years adopted my father's disposition to forego
challenging the *idées fixes* of the dominant strains of ethnic prejudice
in the country, allowing slurs to pass unanswered. I still feel ashamed
of my passivity when I was confronted by everyday manifestations of
anti-Semitism, even if, as in this instance, the animus was without hostile
intent.

Of course, I was aware of the establishment of Israel in 1948, a year
that coincided with my graduation from Fieldston. I remember being surprised by the military triumph of Jewish forces over several neighboring
Arab countries in Israel's war of 'independence,' but for decades these
events were remote abstractions for me. They took place 'over there,'
having no perceived bearing on my life. I admit that I noticed nothing
discordant about the Orwellian twist of terminology by which the heroic
sounding 'war of independence' was used to describe a conflict in which
an orchestrated movement of militarized foreign immigrants gained what
was being proclaimed as 'independence' in the course of dispossessing
the majority indigenous Arab residents of what had been their homeland in Palestine and then suppressing those left behind. As many as
750,000 were coercively dispossessed, or in today's language, ethnically
cleansed, during that early war, which meant 'independence' for Israel
and '*nakba*' for the Palestinians who were not only dispossessed, but
denied the option of *ever* returning to their homes and homeland.

Many wars, including the American war of independence, were
subject to a somewhat similar deconstruction, and most stories of violent
national origins were glorified by the victors while the suffering of the
losers is distorted or erased. The United States had celebrated its own
war of independence, and a similar inversion of the historical record,
if the experience of native Americans is taken into account. In my
experience, to this day their tragedy is viewed as a trivial misfortune

hardly worth noticing amidst the glories of the settler colonist revolt against British imperial rule. During my youth, I plead guilty to charges of civilizational insensitivity. Only much later did I begin to reinterpret such historical watersheds from the perspective of the victims, and form the sort of complex and nuanced understanding that gives rise to feelings of empathy and even shame, and an abstract willingness to redress past wrongdoing. Such sentiments until reinforced by concrete acts of redemption—reparations, museums, socio-economic adjustments—remain suspect, liberal gestures without behavioral impact.

The American war was mainly fought against the British Empire, the American Indians having already been mainly banished to what Thomas Jefferson called 'the briny deep' to make space for his vision of an 'empire of liberty.' So effective is our educational brainwashing that such ironies are never acknowledged or acted upon until it is much too late to do anything about them except shed a symbolic tear or two, appropriating part of *their* culture as if it were *our* hallowed heritage, and finally, after the damage has become irreversible, the victors manage to subsidize a museum or two to commemorate the earlier vibrant existence of such defeated and subjugated cultures. For those with a more universalist turn of mind, some remorse but no regret, and a belated soft power resistance emerges that is dedicated to obtaining some redress of historical grievances. Even after George Floyd's murder few liberals are willing to heed arguments about monetary reparations and systemic racism even if ready to admit gross past injustices to and criminal victimization of the ancestors of such claimants. Such dark deeds when acknowledged are generally disregarded as sins of the past, of fathers that should not be visited upon their sons and daughters, and certainly not on later generations of descendants.

On the night of fraternity rushing at Penn I went on my own to the Jewish fraternities to which I was invited—an initial invitation was needed to be 'rushed' by 'the brothers' of a particular frat house. This first exposure functioned as the anxious prelude to being accepted or rejected. If this semi-formal social segregation had not existed, I would have stuck with my Christian sports friend, never feeling any impulse to associate with Jews only, or with any tribe for that matter. During the rushing interval I was still a member of Penn's Freshman Basketball team, which for a Jew in those days was seen as a better frat credential than good looks, a winning personality, being a top student, having close connections with former frat members, and perhaps even than being the son of a wealthy and known Jewish family. As a result, despite my social awkwardness and lack of relevant connections (friends or relatives in a particular fraternity), I received several invitations, and chose Phi Epsilon Pi (Phi Ep), the Avis of Penn's several Jewish fraternities.

During my three subsequent years at Penn, I was a marginal fraternity presence, having occasional meals and some friends, notable only for winning yearly ping-pong tournaments, and being a loyal member of the fraternity bowling team that won the league championship one year against 26 other fraternity teams. I greatly enjoyed this experience both socially and athletically, and when our victory came it was sweetened by being a surprise upset of the former championship team.

My two college roommates were more socially and politically conscious than I was, were what I would later call 'good liberals,' and neither of them approved of the fraternity concept, declining to take part in rushing, and somewhat looking down on me for rushing and joining. Only later did I come to share their critical outlook, although instinctively I was made uncomfortable by the fraternity bonding rituals that made some intense inroads on the lives of a few college friends. I just went along to hide my insecurity under this thin cloud of institutional and social acceptance. I was never willing to indulge in heavy drinking or share the compulsively macho attitudes of my more ardent frat brothers around such issues as dating, sex, women, and cursing. Rather inconclusively, I removed myself from the party scene at the fraternity without withdrawing altogether. I was part of the outer layer, never more than partially in nor completely out, perhaps a metaphor for how I have navigated many of life's more daunting obstacle courses.

Prior to my final year at Penn I was somewhat surprisingly approached by a similarly alienated frat brother to run as a dissident candidate for fraternity president. My friend wanted to make the place more of a cultural center and less of a ribald party zone, and I was his chosen vehicle. I declined, playfully invoking a nightmare scenario of actually winning, although fully aware that for me to win such an election was too outlandish to contemplate. I was often teased by mainstream brothers about my absentee habits. Yet I admit that even after this long passage of time, I was back then flattered by the suggestion of challenging the system from within as a leader of a reform movement, even if I realized the suggestion was absurd as I would never have been elected, and would receive only votes from the tiny minority of disgruntled frat brothers.

Escaping Academic Doldrums

As previously mentioned, I mostly won at poker during my first year at Penn, and that was about all I had to boast about, and came close to causing my downfall. As a freshman student I fared badly, ending the year in the purgatory of 'academic probation.' I 'earned' a D in French, another D in Introductory Composition, and an F in Physics, the latter a result of sleeping through my shrieking alarm clock next to the bed and missing the final exam, a stunning display of my irresponsible life style, although to sleep that soundly was an achievement of sorts. This dire situation that I brought on myself was depressing and posed some dead-end risks that I fortunately found threatening enough to cause panic, leading me to seek a corrective path. I didn't use this life crisis to figure out who I was or what I wanted. Instead, I reacted tactically. It was a rescue operation.

I first changed my institutional affiliation at Penn, shifting from the College of Arts and Sciences to the Wharton School, somehow thinking that if I started over from near zero I might do better, erase the past, and move on. I felt humiliated, at first, to be enrolled in a business school, even one with the high reputation that Wharton enjoyed. It seemed a second defeat. Seeing myself through my father's eyes I had failed. He viewed university education through a classical optic, and was dismissive of all forms of vocational training, which included a business school degree, as essentially a waste of time, a position I came myself to share later. Dad valued little else in college education other than learning to read difficult texts in literature and philosophy, gaining composure to speak knowingly about the great Western classics of the past. He also saw a university education as an opportunity to develop fluency in abstract thought by the study of logic, philosophy, and math. In these respects, Wharton seemed a self-willed dumbing down for me that offered none of these more uplifting intellectual challenges.

Unexpectedly, I was asked by Alan Oser, who would go on to a successful journalistic career, becoming the Real Estate Editor of the *NY Times*, to become his roommate in the next academic year. Alan was from a middle class Jewish family in Forest Hills and became my de facto cultural mentor (especially, doing his best to acquaint me with the glories and complexities of classical music), and was himself studious, a gifted violinist, yet modest. I was surprised, yet puzzled, by Alan's invitation. Fearing he might change his mind, I accepted instantly without a second thought, and never regretted the decision. I considered the prospect of having such a studious roommate to be equivalent to signing up to live in a rehab facility for students on probation.

Due to my lack of self-confidence, and fear of overt rejection, I would never have dared approach Alan with the suggestion that we become apartment mates. We were at the time only casual acquaintances, and he was a solid student, well grounded, all that I wasn't. Our friendship flourished over the next three years, although it became a bit clouded at times by an unacknowledged rivalry, probably because I started to do better than he in several courses we took together. He married a Penn classmate, Janice, herself a star student of philosophy with twinkling eyes, and more gifted than either of us. Our third roommate, Bill Laufer, hailing from a Brooklyn working class family, was extremely likable yet a bit too sensible and down to earth to become a close friend. We lived together without big squabbles for the next three years in a student tenement style apartment with small separate rooms for each of us. I lacked any political edge in this period, did little to keep up with the news beyond reading headlines now and then, concentrating my energies on becoming culturally semi-literate, and finding erotically satisfying or romantically stimulating girlfriends, not yet hoping to discover such qualities fused in a single woman. I was quite aware of my own shabby attractiveness credentials. I had little to offer the sort of person that I dreamed of loving and being loved by.

Enjoying Life at Penn

The academic side of my life suddenly became not only manage-able, but engaging, even fun, and often exciting. An intellectual 'high' was enrolling with Alan in a graduate course in philosophy taught by the revered dean of the College, Glenn R. Morrow. The course work con-sisted of a single task, a close reading of the entire corpus of Aristotle's surviving writings that covered a wide range of philosophic fields. At the time as undergraduate students we were awed, believing Aristotle knew everything about all there was to know, and that Morrow knew all that Aristotle knew. I still tend to believe that for his day Aristotle was as omniscient as any god, while being more moderate and compassionate than most of the Greek gods wandering around in his ancient world.

Reading Aristotle was an intimidating challenge, especially at first, yet by the end of the semester it had become a highly satisfying experience. This particularly reflected Professor Morrow's exemplary guidance. Morrow was a professorial model of devotion and dedication to his chosen subject, knowledgeable about every nook and cranny of

Aristotle's thought, building his entire career around teaching classical Greek Philosophy. This meant for him Plato and Aristotle, with some appreciative nods to pre-Socratic thought. Morrow, soft spoken and a bit remote, dressed conservatively and seemed socially shy. He fit perfectly the Hollywood image of an academic dean of an Ivy League college. Despite this bland surface, Morrow delivered illuminating and learned lectures dedicated to the themes that animated Aristotle's incredibly wide-ranging thought. It was not surprising that for Aristotle the peak experience in life was a mysterious affirmation of 'unthought thought,' perhaps an irony for a philosopher that delved so deeply that centuries later his 'thought thoughts' continue to stimulate the brightest minds among us.

Sitting in this seminar room surrounded by articulate and sophisticated graduate philosophy students was equivalent to an infusion of pride and built a growing confidence in my ability to perform academically, leading me to work hard, and to absorb the material as best I could. Initially my only goal was to avert any repetition of the humbling academic outcomes of my freshman year. In the end I received a grade of 'A' as did Alan, leaving both of us elated, but also a bit surprised, and certainly relieved. Neither of us had ever before taken a graduate course, and we didn't have any idea about what to expect. We ended the course fearing the worst as the final exam was a big, big challenge. The exam asked us to appraise Aristotle's approach to an array of difficult topics, and we found such a task challenging in the best sense. The course was the kind of peak intellectual adventure that universities can provide on occasion.

I had other exciting academic experiences during my final two years at Penn, all, not so incidentally, outside the Wharton School. I should not reject the Wharton experience altogether. It served me well by restoring my academic confidence after my freshman stumble. It also gave me enough understanding of economics to avoid coming across as a complete idiot when later in life I would be confronted by the graphs, models, and stats that economists used to carry the day in framing public policy. At Penn, I took 17 economics courses and wrote a senior thesis on business cycles, helped greatly by receiving indispensable guidance from Irving Kravis, a world class economist. Now, if my life depended on it, I could not describe the argument of the thesis or a single conclusion I reached. Whatever I set forth to satisfy the thesis requirement remains forever locked in a black box.

Unquestionably, my peak student experience at Penn was three courses taken with Edward Aubrey, a demanding and highly respected, and somewhat intimidating professor of religious thought. This venture at its start was another joint undertaking with Alan, but I soldiered on while he dropped out after the first daunting offering.

My third and final course with Aubrey was the most difficult intellectual challenge I had ever faced. It consisted of developing the framework of a personal religion on broadly assigned themes that were to be addressed in papers with weekly deadlines throughout the semester. Aubrey was rigorous, without mercy, in making us think clearly and coherently about such daunting topics as God, human nature, purpose of life, religious institutions, ethics, knowledge, and mortality, giving us detailed comments on the papers we handed him when due. Aubrey's eye was sharply focused on the expectation that the draft papers should be revised and resubmitted for his further scrutiny. He wanted us to be as clear as possible in setting forth our views, addressing the shortcomings he found in whatever position we chose. He was non-judgmental, and never disclosed to us any institutional affiliation of his own when it came to beliefs and doubts, seemingly totally dedicated to his pedagogical mission, a lifelong model for me of an inspirational mentor/teacher.

Not only was Professor Aubrey noncommunicative about his own beliefs, but he also would not even affirm the minimal metaphysical construct of God. I regarded Aubrey then and now as an extraordinary exemplar of pedagogic excellence, scholarly depth, compassionate mentorship, personal detachment, exacting expectations, and dedicated teaching. As far as I know, he never published much, yet left an indelible impression on most students, motivated us to perform beyond our abilities and always listened intently to what we had to say. These exceptional courses in religious thought exposed me to many writers whose works affected me deeply at the time, and whose writings I continue to treasure. They include Martin Buber, Karl Jaspers, Søren Kierkegaard, Reinhold Niebuhr, and several others.

With Aubrey's encouragement I went to nearby Haverford College to attend two extraordinary lectures given by Buber, the great Jewish philosopher, who was visiting the campus for a week. A rather small audience of students sat beneath an oak tree in a half circle around this short, passionate, charismatic figure with a biblical length beard, whose oratorical style remains etched in my memory. Buber imparted the wisdom and unforgettable presence of a Jewish prophet who stepped directly from the pages of the Old Testament. When one among us bravely asked this larger-than-life personage a question, Buber rose from his seat and walked close to the student, establishing intense eye contact from arm's length before responding, looking directly at the person's face. This encounter created for all of us an appreciation of I/Thou moments of recognition, which were the famed touchstones of Buber's approach to living a religious life. Seventy years later I remain captivated by the vivid intensity of this human interaction, nor has such vividness ever been repeated, although almost so, by attending poetry readings of T.S. Eliot and Pablo Neruda. All three of these iconic cultural figures helped me understand that intensity and passion are as important, or more so, than reason, data, and information in the supreme moments of living, loving, and learning.

I also adored an advanced course on comparative literature taught by a brilliant lecturer named Adolph Klarmann, who was both inspiring and erudite. His interpretations of contemporary poets and novelists were my first experience of the wonders of the literary imagination. Leaving the class, I often felt dazed, half stimulated, half bewildered. When I started the course, I had never before seriously interpreted or contemplated a single poem. Our first assignment was to write an essay on Rainer Maria Rilke's *Duino Elegies,* a text that in English seemed only slightly more accessible to me than the original texts in German, a foreign language I had never studied. I struggled to comprehend Rilke's celebrated cycle of poems. My initial objective in the required paper was nothing more ambitious than to avoid embarrassment.

I recall my acute feelings of apprehension when the graded papers were distributed a couple of weeks later. Receiving an A+ left me stunned, truly on the verge of tears. Unlike Aubrey whose comments filled the margins, Klarmann's only mark on student papers was the simple letter grade. I still wonder whether the grade was deserved. In any event, it served as a glorious start for my enduring love affair with poetry, and more broadly, the aesthetics of language.

It was then and there I gave myself permission to become a closet poet, which probably helped guide my heart and soul toward a rapturous spiritual embrace, years later culminating in a strong romantic attachment to Sally Appleton, both a genuine poet and radiant being who crossed my path, and I, hers while I was teaching at Ohio State a decade later.

Here's another recollection from the Klarmann course related to our main semester assignment. We were to choose one writer who had been discussed in the lectures, read critically his entire literary production, and on this basis submit a long comprehensive paper assessing his contributions. In a cloud of unknowing I chose Franz Kafka, benefitting from a close reading of his novels and extraordinary short stories, and remembering my struggle to pull it all together with the entirely unrealistic hope of making my paper seem insightful and coherent without too obviously exhibiting myself as a literary novice. After my Rilke success, I remember feeling a tinge of disappointment when I only received a grade of 'A.' How expectations can change overnight!

I also recall my sense of being socially out of place in relation to the others in the course. It was one of those rare undergraduate courses where permission of the instructor was a prerequisite. Most of the class were stalwart members of the campus literati, forming a deliberately exclusive and self-satisfied micro-community, with membership only by invitation after extended scrutiny. I tried to hide feelings of being an intellectually clumsy and uncultured Wharton interloper who had stumbled by sheer accident into this rarefied academic atmosphere. I did my work in isolation, looking on enviously as others were congratulating one another on the brilliance of this or that. I was struck by this aura of pure intellectuality, wondering if I would ever achieve the composure and exalted sense of self to attract such brainy, erotically charged females whose passions mixed their love of knowledge and language with an apparent mastery of the mysteries of eros.

Another important part of my learning experience at Penn consisted of a series of audited art history courses, particularly the lectures of David M. Robb, an eminent writer on the history of Western art, and an acute interpreter of leading painters and their paintings, as well as sculpture and architecture. Despite his academic excellence, Robb was a lecture hall Nazi, humiliating students who arrived late, often having an assistant lock the door to the lecture hall, and treating the teaching hours as hallowed events occurring within an enclosed sacred space, which they often seemed to be. If I put aside his authoritarian manner, which I did, I found myself able to partake of Robb's enchantment. He was capable of exalted lectures that made the slides of the paintings he discussed come alive in ways that have affected how I have experienced artistic work throughout my life. Immersing myself in art history was also an expression of my new self. I was voluntarily imposing extra courses on myself from sheer cultural greed, auditing lectures three times a week on top of a crowded schedule of courses taken for credit.

A couple years later on my first trip to Europe, as I went through many famous churches and museums, I realized how much I had learned from Robb's lectures. It allowed me to appreciate more knowingly a variety of art and architectural works in Rome, Paris, London, Venice, and Florence. In this period, I discovered within myself this reverence for and enjoyment of high culture, which finally began to displace, although not entirely, my somewhat philistine upbringing.

While at Penn, I worked a couple of summers for the DuMont Television station in New York City, Channel 5. I was continuously challenged on the job, being without relevant experience, and yet assigned to assist on several prime-time programs, first, as a collector of props for the sets, quite soon as an assistant director. It was early television, everything was new, with lots of improvising and a workload greater than the staff could handle, constant pressure, quick friendships, stress and short tempers, rather banal programming, and good career opportunities. I was initially a courtesy hire because my father was the personal lawyer of Allen B. DuMont, the owner of the channel and inventor of the cathode-ray-tube adaptation that underpinned early TV technology. Mr. DuMont, whom I remember as a rather plain spoken and bland character, also launched several TV channels and started a production company. These ventures were at first were successful, but later either failed or were absorbed by established networks.

The several TV Directors for channel WABD, called 'New York's Window on the World' were stretched far too thin. As a result, I was given assignments that exceeded my capabilities and exposed me as a shy underdeveloped teenager. It was ridiculous to ask me to direct rehearsals of dramas with casts of veteran actors, but I did it. There was an atmosphere of excitement in the studio, frantic efforts to make things work, much socializing in whatever time was left over. I gained a bit of much desired and rather needed credibility with my high school classmates by recruiting them to perform as dance extras in a Latin American musical program entitled 'Miguelito Valdez and the Mambo' that began and ended its weekly shows with sequences of dancers happily doing the mambo on a crowded dance floor. Some of these dancers became my friends, grateful to me for enabling them to be seen by their families on TV, which was still new enough in the lives of most Americans to be thrilling, the experience further enhanced by earning union rates for doing what was fun.

During the years at Penn I also became friendly with Ray Greenblatt, a year behind me, who had been an All-American high school football player from Green Bay, Wisconsin. Ray had the intelligence and organizational capacity to compile a four-year academic record with only straight A-level grades, made even more impressive by a sprinkling of A+s, supposedly a grade reserved for truly exceptional work. To my regret we lost touch. Ray provided me with an unattainable standard of dedication to sustained academic excellence, setting sights so high as to be beyond the reach of ordinary mortals. Despite his stellar academic profile Ray seemed to lack those indefinable qualities of risk taking, stubborn independence, and originality that give rise to intellectual breakthroughs. Even these qualities probably are not enough. Also necessary is a contrarian streak that rebels against deference to current societal standards, scorns conventional wisdom, and can get along without mainstream approval. During my teaching career I had several superb students who later went on to have distinguished, productive, and even exemplary careers as scholars, teachers, and activists, but none of them managed to break sufficient fresh ground to achieve intellectual or societal breakthroughs. I have in mind breakthroughs of the sort achieved by such friends as Noam Chomsky, Edward Said, Dan Ellsberg, Graciela Chichilnisky, Mary Kaldor, Robert Jay Lifton, and Howard Zinn, each possessing a distinctive variant of a contrarian temperament combined with a sense of certitude about the rightness of their chosen path. This difference between academic excellence and a breakthrough based on innovativeness of thought and action has long intrigued me. I situate myself in the DMZ separating intellectual excellence from societal salience, neither reaping the rewards of academic achievement within my reach nor gaining the plaudits of a positive public notoriety, yet managing a respectable academic, ethical, and activist presence among those who shared my progressive political and ethical agenda.

CHAPTER 4

Growing at Yale Law School

Drifting Toward Law

Approaching the end of my four years at Penn I began thinking about what to do next. Despite my Wharton grades that put me third in the graduating class I was not tempted by lucrative opportunities in business or finance. I had no aptitude or preparation for science. I was still too conventionally minded to consider an academic career in the humanities via a PhD, although that was where I was then emotionally drawn, and too squeamish about blood and pain to consider medicine. In light of this, I envisioned my future as somehow circumscribed by law and government. At the same time, I wanted to avoid reproducing my father's life as a mostly discontented lawyer and had no idea what it might mean to work for the government, although I was not then troubled by issues of conscience or conviction that would arise a decade later. In the end, I sought entry to law school mainly as a default option, thinking it would at least kick the can of profession and career down the road for another three years, while allowing me the space to explore the cultural terrain that I found so stimulating during my final years at Penn.

I scored in the mid-90s on the Law School Aptitude Test, which led me, unlike in high school, to aim high. I applied to law schools at Harvard and Yale, was admitted to both, and paid $50 to give myself more time to reach a decision that seemed momentous at the time but rather inconsequential in retrospect. Yale Law School had a reputation for making the lawyers' role one of benevolent relevance to society, which meant giving rise to career alternatives other than settling for a Wall Street type practice in some large American city. I decided on Yale for this reason, although it meant giving up my wish to live in Cambridge. After I became a student at Yale, these virtues seemed to lose traction in my mind. I came to feel that my experience at YLS was more conventional than its promotional image that had attracted me to enroll.

I felt intimidated after attending an introductory session, learning that in our rather small Yale class of 120 or so, there were 44 among us who had been either valedictorians or finished first in their college ranking. It leads me now to recall Michelle Obama's question to herself at various stages of her life, as reported in her memoir, *Becoming*: 'Am I good enough?' Our first-year class consisted mainly of white men, with a few women, and one or two African Americans, and no Asians. Somewhat to my surprise, given my dismal social past, I began to make friends fairly easily. I became a friendly acquaintance of Pat Robertson, son of a Senator from West Virginia. Astonishingly, Pat later became prominent enough as a religious leader and TV host to run for president. While in law school Pat had quite a different identity. He was part of a Southern group of law students who were known for their parties, casual study habits, courtly manner, and heavy drinking. It is possible that these impressions were exaggerated, even wrong, reflecting envy more than observation. I played lots of ping-pong in the basement of the law school where my skills garnered far more admiration than did my classroom performance on the whys and ways of law.

The required first year curriculum at Yale involved a series of standard courses (contracts, torts, constitutional law, property, criminal law) in large classrooms big enough for at least half of the entire first year class. I worked moderately hard, as usual fearing the worst recalling my terrible record at the end of my initial year at Penn, but also sensing that I possessed a sufficient aptitude for solving complex legal puzzles to handle the Yale challenge. I felt confident with respect to legal analysis and the abstractions of conceptual thought. At the same time, I considered myself inferior to several gifted classmates. My grades were okay at the end of the first semester, but fell just short of the law journal cutoff, which was the litmus test of elite performance.

I was impressed by the high quality of faculty teaching. Each of my professors knew how to make law interesting and challenging, keeping the class attentive, even on edge, partly arousing fears of making a fool of oneself if called upon. Teaching was faithful to 'the Socratic method.' an interactive question and response kind of dialogue with the student respondent picked at random from a class roster. There were additional opportunities to volunteer when the question and answer routine bogged down or got stuck. I remember being told a couple of times during the first two months by the professor that I already sounded like a lawyer. This seemed intended as a compliment from these teachers, as well as providing occasions for gentle teasing by nervous classmates.

At Yale I remained shy, but less so, somewhat more adept in most social settings, yet happily far from being one of the boys. I rarely participated in the frequent male gatherings at Maury's, the famous campus hangout where the beer was plentiful, and the guy talk veered toward recounting sexual conquests. An unspoken rule existed that nothing of substance would ever be discussed. Alone, I daydreamed about making love to women I hardly knew and read poems by poets I barely understood.

I also wondered whether I should attach myself to some sort of religious community, attended several Quaker meetings, moved by the silence, but soon irritated by the mundaneness of what led some of the faithful to speak their minds. After all this passage of time I still recall my annoyance when a middle-aged woman encroached on the serene atmosphere of this austere Quaker meeting hall by voicing a complaint about her adolescent son who repeatedly failed his assigned chore of emptying the family garbage on a daily basis. I stopped attending, blaming my loss of interest on such banalities, but now suspect that deeper considerations were at play, especially my lifelong inability to sustain commitments to any organized community, even the Quakers, who prided themselves on being non-dogmatically constituted.

I am not sure why community and institutional participation never worked for me. I seemed unable to form attitudes of institutional loyalty or pride, even as an active alumnus or at least as someone feeling obliged to heed funding appeals. What I did feel, but almost never acted upon, was curiosity, bordering on nostalgia, especially for girls, about how the lives of those I once dreamt about later unfolded. Being busy myself, I never summoned the energy to find out, and so repeatedly lost touch, digging few deep roots.

While my family ties are shallow compared to those of Hilal, my longtime life partner, I have in recent years tried to keep contact with friends spread out around the planet, which the Internet and social media makes easier. I also try to stay connected with the still unfolding lives of my children. Each of my children would likely respond, not unfairly, that they learned the practices of detachment from me!

The Road Not Taken

Yale Law School boasted to the world that after the first year required curriculum students were free in the next two years to customize their academic program in light of their interests and career ambitions. Ninety percent of the students sensibly used this discretion to develop a technical specialty in law, like taxation or property rights, that would

entice Wall Street recruiters and build the foundation of a successful career. I exploited Yale's flexibility with a different set of goals—to ensure
that my transcript upon graduation would be so unattractive to prestige
law firms as to ensure that I would not receive any offers that might tempt
me to swim with the golden current. I pushed the system to its limits, or
maybe just beyond. I admit that I was not entirely conscious of what I
was doing until after it happened. At the time I was just following where
my interests led me, which were increasingly directed at affirming otherness and exoticism of all kinds, especially internationally, and digging
as deeply as I could into the wellsprings of humanistic knowledge. Even
with Yale Law School's pretension of being indifferent about preparing
its graduates for state bar exams and standard law careers, I felt that I had
to react against the vocational mainstream vectors that still shaped the
imaginaries and curricular choices of most classmates.

On the faculty of the law school was a philosopher, F.S.C.
Northrop, who wrote an influential book, *The Meeting of East and West*,
after World War II, that contrasted ideas toward law and dispute settlement in the West with those prevalent in Asia, particularly India. I took
his two courses, which despite their titles were really devoted to 'The
World According to Northrop,' a feast of ideas and brilliant philosophic
conjectures about reconciling diverse civilizations as a contribution to
sustained peace in the world. In retrospect, Northrop offered the world a
remarkably prophetic depiction of future international horizons decades
prior to Huntington's 'clash of civilizations.' Northrop anticipated the re-
active array of offsetting non-Western responses to the clash hypothesis
that evolved under the banner of 'alliance of civilizations.'

The idea of becoming a university faculty member was still completely absent from my imaginary as I continued to view my future as
dependent on effort rather than talent. Also, law teaching in those days
was something not normally done immediately after graduating. Regular
faculty appointments in law schools were unusual if not preceded by
several years of interim experience in 'the real world,' clerking for judges, working at a law firm, doing something in the government, preferably
in Washington. I approached my future with neither a plan nor a goal, not
even realizing that I was being irresponsible.

Instead, I devoted my energies to Indian legal jurisprudence, so
much so that I tried to enroll in first year Sanskrit so that I could better
understand Indian texts on law and philosophy that contained many un-
translated Sanskrit and Prakrit words and phrases. I timidly approached
the Sanskrit teacher at Yale with a request that I be allowed to join the

class two weeks after the course began. The professor, an eccentric individual, was from Vienna. When I sought enrollment, he told me in a
dry unwelcoming voice that I could join the class if I wished, but that
I would probably never catch up with the two students who started on
time. I asked how much I had missed. He opened the Sanskrit beginner's
text, and to my pleasant surprise, he pointed to the first paragraph on the
first page.

I foolishly replied, 'no problem.' It took me only a few days to
realize how wrong I was and how right he was. What explains this jolt to
my expectations was the focus during the initial daily class meetings on
how to read 'devanagari' script, a challenge I found devilishly difficult.
This difficulty meant that I was unable to complete the current assignments no matter how hard I tried. Nevertheless, overall studying Sanskrit
was a memorable experience; perhaps, with a touch of irony, it is what
I remember most vividly from law school, 60 years later. The three of
us in the class bonded, became friends, probably due to the intensity
of the shared experience that set us apart from everyone else we knew,
somewhat like membership in a secret society or sect.

An article in a Columbia University Law School newsletter devoted itself to exposing the frivolity of the Yale approach to legal education.
It chose to highlight my Sanskrit escapade, and the tuba playing of a
friend in a local band. The journalistic piece seemed designed to demean
the educational atmosphere of its Yale rival. The Columbia article was
seeking to demonstrate the superiority of a Columbia preparation for a
career in law, which missed the point that we were the exceptions at Yale.
Most of our classmates did fine for themselves on or near Wall Street
with what Yale provided. In fact, Yale climbed to the very top of law
school ranking, displacing Harvard, although admittedly not thanks to
my brand of unorthodoxy.

An even more enduring learning experience at Yale than these
exotic encounters with Northrop and Sanskrit was a result of studying under Myres McDougal, then co-teaching international law with
arguably the most influential social scientist of his generation, Harold
Lasswell. They were developing an epistemological framework that
sought to bring available knowledge to bear on the decision processes of
judges and policymakers that addressed questions arising at the interface
of law and policy, with particular reference to the international arena. It
was an approach to law and legal thinking that was context-oriented and
values driven rather than rule-based and precedent-confined, attempting
to bring American 'legal realism' into the modern age of science-based

knowledge. Such jurisprudence was at the opposite pole of legal interpretative design from the 'originalism' that was so hegemonic in conservative legal circles like the Federalist Society. The signature course
of McDougal and Lasswell, 'Law, Science, and Policy,' expressed an
outlook that claimed to rescue law from the subjectivities of individual
judgment and was intended to guide judges and government officials as
well as lawyers toward more enlightened and 'scientifically' grounded
legal outcomes. Their effort to blend social science with legal studies
was stimulating for me as a student, but far too cumbersome to achieve
its proclaimed mission of guiding overwrought lawmakers, judges,
and government officials to reach more informed and ethically infused
decisions.

The McDougal/Lasswell jurisprudential innovations were rooted
in the normative soil of democratic liberalism as tempered by a rather
confusing realist deference to the sources of 'effective power' as projected by the U.S. Government during the Cold War. According to their
theorizing, law was not stable or inherently clear, and at most, reflected
the outcome of a diligent search for 'reasonable expectations' generated
by norms, rules, and past behavior. These expectations could only be
reliably discerned after a comprehensive review of the context of a
decision that took account of expected inputs from and impacts upon
the wider social, economic, and cultural order as assessed through the
optic of social science. Of course, this made things appear 'scientific'
and made inquiry burdensome, and for many legal experts and academicians, needlessly complicated and obscure. McDougal championed his
own views with great bravado, exhibiting an unbounded confidence that
his approach to law identified the essential path to an enlightened free
society. Such grandiosity, if emanating from most others, would have
produced ironic smiles of disapproval if not outright derision. However,
McDougal was so warm, affectionate, and intensely loyal to students and
friends that his intellectual narcissism never seemed to bother anyone,
and oddly, even added to his magnetic charm. More than anyone I have
closely encountered, McDougal was in life a theater presence larger than
a playwriter's imaginary.

Mac was convinced and convincing that his work represented
a breakthrough in legal thinking that was the wave of the future, not
only in America, but throughout 'the free world' (in this period Cold
War consciousness prevailed in the academy). Mac was also a master
academic empire builder, networking globally before the Internet. He
was extremely effective in placing his beloved and loyal students in

universities, governments, and leading law firms throughout the world. It was an amazing experience for me to be intellectually and personally exposed to this tsunami of a man. He became a leader in national legal education as much by virtue of the strength of personality and charm as due to the influence of his innovative jurisprudence. There was no doubt that many who truly adored the man did so despite his jurisprudence, although his most devoted followers loved both. Mac also did not fit Vanity Fair's image of an eminent Ivy League professor. He was rather heavy set, always wearing dark dress pants held up too high on his body by suspenders, accompanied by a white shirt and colorless tie, with thick glasses, and usually a green eye shade: quaint, forbidding, and lovable, topped off by a booming voice and thunderous laugh, which overall produced a puzzling sensibility that seemed at once bewilderingly abstract, yet intensely personal.

I owe my academic career to Mac more than to anyone else. His influence and devotion continued over many years despite my rather strident public disagreements with his positions on controversial U.S. foreign policy issues. I felt that Mac was adept at finding ways to endorse whatever reprehensible things the U.S. was doing throughout the world while condemning everything the Soviet Union and its friends did, even if benevolent. He was an unabashed partisan of the Cold War, and because he valued personal rapport more than ideological conformity he would make a special effort to reassure me that whatever we disagreed about had no effect on his opinion of my professional worth. For my part, I didn't want to disappoint Mac or lose his support, yet I found myself unable to pretend to share his nationalistic worldview and agenda.

On more than one occasion when we were together at academic conferences, Mac would sternly denounce my approach to international law as totally wrong, and worse, politically irresponsible and ethically regressive. I remember a panel on Nicaragua in the mid-1980s at NYU at which I wholeheartedly supported the emergence of the Sandinista government, with Mac screaming at me from the podium for endorsing 'a Communist regime.' After the discussion period, a pragmatic and prominent Canadian professor of international law who was in the audience, approached me to say in a patronizing tone, 'Dick, don't you realize that you are biting the hand that feeds you?' Such worldly advice was lost on me as I felt that my identity was by then based on expressing my true thoughts as presented in a respectful manner and listening carefully to what others had to say in return. If that caused some adverse career blowback, which it probably did, although not with Mac, I was prepared to live with that.

Another time, I think at Yale, there was an event discussing modern trends in jurisprudence. I had by then enough composure to mount my own challenge, including the temerity to tell McDougal that he didn't fully grasp his own jurisprudence, which I argued was much more progressive in its proper applications to current events and foreign policy than he would admit. I argued that since the overriding commitment of his approach was to maximize 'the value of human dignity' this should lead McDougal to adopt a selectively critical approach to America's role in the Third World. To my pleasant surprise, Mac this time laughed rather than blowing off steam, responding by saying, 'I half agree with you!' I never explored the other half as I was so pleased with this good spirited concession that I never expected to receive.

What was so striking to me over the years, as with my father, was that Mac's personal loyalty and friendship never wavered, taking absolute priority over any differences of opinion about either law or policy. McDougal through the years was my staunchest supporter, and I was not alone. It was striking that his community of followers covered the ideological spectrum from hard right to hard left and included as many women as men, which was highly unusual at the time. It was without a doubt his ardent support for my work and academic promise that accounted for my early professional recognition and success.

Even his fiercest critics were usually pacified by Mac's distinctive version of southern charm and winning ways, that is, all except a few jurisprudential adversaries whom he had publicly demeaned were thrilled to be within his wide circle of friends and acquaintances. I was privileged to be admitted to an inner circle of protégés that he once listed in my presence as his favorite four: the others being Rosalyn Higgins (to become a ICJ judge), Burns Weston (stellar scholar of human rights), and Michael Reisman (Mac's faithful successor on the Yale Law faculty). Such a listing is undoubtedly unfair to many others, including his collaborating authors from around the world. Such outstanding legal scholars as Florentino Feliciano, B.S. Murty, Lung Chou Chen, William Burke, and others produced massive tomes on such topics as use of force, space, public order of the oceans, human rights, treaty interpretation, and constitutional order. It is no exaggeration to claim that Mac's fame as a scholar owed much to his talented engagement in collaborative scholarship, although for his chosen partner it meant uncritically working within his framework (as developed with Lasswell) of the relations between law, government, and society.

Although I wrote a paper or two under Mac's supervision, one on the extraterritorial reach of American antitrust laws, a hot topic at the time, I had the good fortune to never became a fulltime collaborator, or I might never have discovered my own legal persona. Mac did try to enlist me to undertake a book-long collaborative expansion of this international antitrust paper, but just at that time he suffered from detached retinas in both eyes, rendering him practically blind during the rest of my time at Yale.

I was saddened by Mac's serious impairment of vision, yet I admit feelings of relief alongside grief at the time, realizing that it would have been difficult and uncongenial for me to adapt any scholarly inquiry to this carefully elaborated law, science, and policy framework. It made me realize that if I did any writing later on, it would feel authentic only if it issued primarily from my own thought processes. I was not suited to be an academic protégé, although I was comfortable being a fellow traveler, fervent admirer, loyal student, and equal status collaborator. Of course, even as I became a senior scholar myself, I never overcame a sense of subservience to this great teacher and mentor, and looking back, think of Mac as almost a surrogate father, motivating me to do my best, bolstering my self-confidence, and being there for me at any moment of real need. We who enjoy the mentoring benefits of such a benign guardian angel are truly blessed, even if we only fully realize this years later.

One thing I failed to learn from Mac, maybe for the best, was his incredible belief in the unquestioned importance of his life's work and the value of his contributions to reconstructing international law. Mac never manifested self-doubt, while I am never entirely free from it. With humorous disdain for the work of others with whom he disagreed and a warm embrace of those he affirmed, he drew many former students and prominent persons into an enchanted circle of shared belief. Outside his presence, there were murmurs of disbelief, traditional international law voices complaining about the obscurity and unfathomable complexity of the approach, and occasional critical murmurs about its ideological bias. These hostile voices never seemed to bother Mac, who was a consummate self-promoter and quite oblivious to his detractors.

Even in the face of my growing *political* doubts, I intellectually supported the general jurisprudential strategy of the McDougal/Lasswell framework. I contributed a couple of articles to major international law journals, dubbing their scholarly orientation 'the New Haven approach,' a label that stuck.

He deeply believed that such academic luminaries as Lou Henkin at Columbia or Dick Baxter and Roger Fisher at Harvard were 'childish' in their approach to international law, and would be soon superseded in their work and influence by practitioners of the New Haven Approach.

My saddest reckoning at Yale involved Tom Friedman, a close friend from my undergraduate days, and a brilliant student. Tom was endearing and benign despite and maybe because of his eccentric manner. His walking and talking style reminded me of a lovable character that might have stepped from the pages of the *Wizard of Oz*. We had been comrades at Penn, both outsiders at the same fraternity, yet together as bowling teammates. Tom was admitted to Yale Law School, and intending to come, but suffered what was described to me by his parents as 'a nervous breakdown' shortly before classes were scheduled to begin. This was a personal disappointment as we expected to share an apartment after the first year of assigned dorm living. Tom was placed in a mental institution near his home in Bay City, Michigan, and I never saw or heard from him ever again. After a few weeks at Yale I was informed that Tom had died, whether from suicide or treatment, never became clear.

I graduated from Yale Law School, doing well enough to be admitted to the academic honor society, reserved for those whose grade average put them in the top 10% of the class. When called to the podium during the graduation ceremony in the law school courtyard as one of the top students, I embarrassed myself by failing the decorum test. Unhappily, I made myself the object of ridicule as I wore only the customary graduation hat, but without the accompanying gown. I looked and felt ridiculous, having thoughtlessly trivialized the occasion, and even provoked a ripple of audience laughter. The dean, Eugene V. Rostow, a former teacher of mine, and later a high-ranking conservative State Department official and ardent Zionist, was not amused.

It was hardly the worst moment for me during my three Yale years. Worse were the two times I was almost mugged while walking at night from the law school library to my rented room just off campus behind Hutchinson Gym. There was in that period fierce gown/town enmity in New Haven, later diminished by university land purchases and gentrifying developments that created a protective buffer zone that lessened eye contact between the urban poor and the campus rich without touching the underlying irritants of class and race.

Gene Rostow, who became dean at Yale Law School during my second year at law school, was brilliantly conventional, hackneyed in thought, fluent in expression, trusted by the establishment, and without fail, dressed and deployed body language as if the managing partner of a leading Wall Street or DC law firm or financial institution. Gene did his best to downplay Yale's reputation as a place to train pro bono lawyering and socially deviant thinking and devoted his energy to improving the prospects of Yale students to get the best jobs in Wall Street and Washington leading firms, or in government. He gained attention by seeming to outmaneuver Harvard in this perpetual prestige race among leading law schools. Harvard Law School was then belatedly moving in the opposite ideological direction under the influence of the Critical Legal Studies movement. Harvard no longer wanted to be primarily known for educating those trained to provide legal services to the rich WASP elites of the country. In this vein it celebrated such radical faculty members as Duncan Kennedy and the seminal Brazilian legal theorist, Roberto Mangabeira Unger, who later doubled as a consultant to aspiring Brazilian left politicians.

In the 1970s I heard Unger deliver a series of conceptually elaborate lectures to a faculty seminar at Princeton, speaking flawlessly without a single note. His presentations included complicated distinctions and long classificatory lists. I was never sure whether Unger's performance was the result of memorizing his written text or an astounding display of a well-ordered mind, or some mixture. Whatever the explanation, it was an impressive performance. It came to pass that Yale Law School was losing its reputation as a place where students nurtured their conscience as well as trained their mind. This reflected the Rostow Fix that gave priority to beating Harvard at the mainstream legal careerist game. Yale wrested from Harvard the top ranking among American law schools at the cost of tarnishing its image as the law laboratory for social change. My respect for YLS diminished, possibly unfairly. While I was a student Yale had been the one educational experience that had made me feel institutionally comfortable.

In a different way, the Unger seminar experience reminded me of Noam Chomsky's linguistic lectures at Princeton a decade or so earlier. A huge initial audience attended the opening lecture, but as the series unfolded, the audience dwindled to an obligatory few. Chomsky's presentations were obscure and technically unyielding. This may have been his wish, wittingly or unwittingly. I was never sure. In the lectures, Chomsky, credited with the development of 'structural linguistics,' was contrasting his ideas, which he called 'the standard view' with those of his critics whom he dismissed with an authoritativeness that left no doubt as to whom he believed was right and who was wrong. As with Mac, and despite his contrasting quiet and unemotional delivery, Noam never gave the slightest hint of self-doubt, but on the contrary, was so calmly self-assured as to inhibit hostile responses or challenges from all except highly self-confident critics. As Noam was my house guest and friend, I felt obliged to sit through three lectures I neither understood nor appreciated, while admiring his integrity and high-minded disregard of losing his audience.

Noam's linguistic presentations were very different than his political talks, where he went out of his way to be engaging for the entire audience, while exhibiting an astonishing mastery of a wide range of primary, secondary, and even tertiary materials. Illuminating political insights were distributed liberally throughout his comprehensive, caustic, and often satiric treatment of concrete issues of the political lifeworld at home and abroad. What was true, whether discussing linguistic theory or political realities, is that Noam conveyed a serene confidence in the correctness of his own views, perceptions, and explanations combined with a finely-honed ironic contempt, politely phrased, for those who dared disagree. Off camera Noam was diffident and sweet, likeable and gentle in an entirely different way from Mac, who publicly and privately came toward one with the force of hurricane winds.

Another part of my Yale experience concerned my continuing interest in religion and philosophy. I gathered the energy in my second year at Yale to go every Friday from New Haven to Columbia to audit a series of teaching sessions with the Japanese Zen master, D.T. Suzuki, who is credited with introducing the Zen approach to Buddhist thought to the West. At this point in his long life of study and reflection, Suzuki devoted the two hours to reading from Zen scriptures, the legacies of earlier masters, in a low barely discernible voice, little more than the gurgling of a country stream. Every so often there was a flash of insight that made the trip and experience seem valuable beyond the uplifting sense of lightly touching the living embodiment of a sacred tradition.

The occasions were quite ritualized at each Friday session. A few minutes before a diminutive Suzuki, wearing a Buddhist gown, appeared in the crowded seminar room, a young beautiful Japanese girl in traditional dress would enter the room with a bundle of scrolls wrapped in a colorful Japanese silk scarf. She deposited the scrolls on a table in front of where the master would be seated. I hate to admit 65 years later that fantasies inspired by this unwrapping ritual had more value for me more than the great Suzuki's semi-audible presentations.

Decades later as an original fellow of the Lindisfarne Association that met annually at the Zen Buddhist community facility at Green Gulch in Marin County near San Francisco, I had several opportunities to hear Richard Baker, the first American born Zen abbot, meditate aloud. Richard had that rare capacity to stir the soul with a purified language, striking me as somewhat analogous to the Japanese game of Go, at once beguilingly simple, yet extremely deep. I heard the Dalai Lama give talks in Oslo at a Nobel Peace Prize seminar in 1991, the year that Aung San Suu Kyi was awarded the prize. The Dalai Lama possessed a similar gift of sophisticated simplicity, relying on everyday metaphors to describe previously allusive aspects of human experience.

The Road Taken

I was slow to find my way throughout life, and usually envied, although occasionally pitied, those who blueprinted their future. Because of this embedded uncertainty, by habit and generally good fortune, I let my life unfold more or less spontaneously, going with the flow, and not feeling inclined to attain a career goal through a focused effort to reach beyond the present. So far, despite some minor disappointments, I am glad I let it happen.

I can also admire those who address their personal future more pro-actively. Recently I met a young woman of fifteen or so in Turkey about to finish college in Istanbul, who said that ever since she was eleven years old she wanted to be a filmmaker, and for several years was sure that the NYU Film Academy was the place for her to study on the path to realizing her dreams. I could only listen with concealed envy to this tale of such ardent clarity at an early age, accompanied by a disciplined focus as to how to control the future by following routes indicated by implanting maps in the mind. I have long been eager to heed Henry David Thoreau's advice to follow the arc of your dreams, but rarely had the requisite dreams and thus lived for a long time by drift and chance and whatever randomly slipped across the transom of my experience. Only recently, thanks to the mercies of age, has habit displaced drift as I navigate rocky shoals of work and play as my life journey continues under a darkening sky.

As my period at Yale Law School was drawing to a close my sense of a political self slowly began to take shape, forming also in response to the historical situation. The overall atmosphere was dominated by the strong anti-Communist attitudes carried to hysterical and repressive extremes by the exploits of Senator Joseph McCarthy of Wisconsin, who made his name and notorious reputation by accusing prominent Americans of being secret allies of the Soviet Union. Many honorable lives were ruined by such deplorable political tactics at odds with the American claim of being the central pillar of 'the free world.'

I remember 1955, my graduating year at Yale, for several reasons. It was during the McCarthy hearings in the U.S. Senate that were investigating alleged Communist penetration of the American armed forces. I was requested by a student friend to circulate an innocuous petition opposing McCarthyism among my fellow students. It was for me a learning experience that lasted a lifetime. I was taken aback by the unwillingness of most students to sign, including those with liberal views. They feared a career blacklist. Despite Yale's reputation as a comfort zone for radicals, by 1955 almost all of my fellow law graduates seemed eager not to endanger their employment prospects with prestigious law firms, which were assumed to be conservative, anti-activist, and unsympathetic with any public show of political sentiments that might be viewed as critical of the established order.

Only later did I decipher the experience. It was partly expressive of the timidity of liberal Americans in their role as citizens, despite the propaganda of the day stressing 'freedom,' and partly the dead weight of conformity imposed by elite career ambitions that usually were fulfilled in conservative surroundings. In the course of my experience these Yale perceptions were confirmed, not only regarding those who practiced law, but also about those of us entrusted with the education of young minds. It disappointed me that over the years I had had so few faculty colleagues who discouraged timidity and careerism, either within the classroom or by way of example. At root, the meaning of life in a democratic society was at stake, particularly the privileges and challenges of citizenship premised on the Jeffersonian conviction that elections and voting, although indispensable, will not by themselves sustain a flourishing democracy.

My other mild shock during that graduating year at Yale was the cancellation of a Fulbright Scholarship I had been awarded to spend a year in Lucknow, India to continue my studies of Indian law. India was being 'punished' because its government had failed to pay the U.S. Government for PL 480 wheat that it had received years earlier during a food emergency in the country. This personal disappointment began to attune me to the perverse, and often cruel ways of the sovereign state, including my own. Why punish India by denying her the benefits of the presence of Fulbright scholars, or more accurately and personally, why punish these Americans who had worked hard for this opportunity of a lifetime?

As so often happens, one closed door was unexpectedly replaced by an open one.

PART THREE
PROFESSIONAL LIFE

After finishing Yale Law School due to a series of accidents I was given an opportunity to teach law at Ohio State University for one year but ended up staying for six. I then left to visit Princeton for a year, ending up staying for 40, retiring in 2001. Since 2002 I have been attached in various limited ways to the Santa Barbara campus of the University of California, as well as teaching at other universities as a visiting professor, including several in Europe. As I write, being professionally oblivious to age, I have accepted a five-year partial appointment at Queen Mary University London as Chair of Global Law, a position shared with four other scholars.

CHAPTER 5

Awakenings at OSU

Serendipity Delivers

My unexpected turn toward an academic life occurred in Ohio only because of an implausible series of unlikely occurrences, which only later appeared coherent enough to be more portentously describable as 'destiny.' Again, I was all set to spend the year after graduating from Yale Law School as a Fulbright Scholar in India, when the arrangement abruptly collapsed. To accept this Fulbright Fellowship, I had cancelled my earlier acceptance of a clerkship with Jack Weinstein, an outstanding Federal judge in NYC. Judge Weinstein had the reputation of being one the best federal judges in the country and serving as his assistant for a year would have been an excellent transitional experience from law school to a conventional law career. I recall Judge Weinstein as proud, self-confident, and rather impersonal. He reacted rather testily to my decision, perhaps conveying the understandable, and probably correct, feeling that I was foregoing a great career opportunity for a rather flakey experience in India that would lead nowhere. In retrospect, if the clerkship had been at U.S. Supreme Court rather than a lower court, I doubt that I would have given up such a special opportunity, and likely, my life would have taken a quite different course.

My departure for Ohio State might easily have not happened. I was in New York City during the summer, haphazardly studying for the NY Bar and pondering my future, realizing that despite my efforts at Yale to disqualify myself for elite lawyering, I might now end up begging to be given a regular law job. The bar cram course struck me as a waste of time, and not even relevant to whether or not I would manage to pass this vocational rite of passage. I endured the sweaty humid heat of a Manhattan summer for one of the few times in my life, having been sent to camp or California throughout my adolescence except for the two summers I worked in TV, kept so happily busy that I didn't even notice the mostly unbearable weather.

While contemplating my horizonless future, I received an unexpected call from Myres McDougal, asking if I would be interested in teaching international law at Ohio State's College of Law. A one-year vacancy came into being due to the sudden illness of their faculty member teaching international law. Mac was ready to recommend me if I showed interest. In less than thirty seconds, I said 'sure,' and an interview was set for the following week with an OSU faculty member, Carl Fulda, who was coincidentally visiting NYC. Carl was an affable German refugee scholar specializing in private international law who later became a friend. It was one of those all too frequent occasions when I behaved like a hyena, and yet somehow managed to come across as a lamb.

I met Professor Fulda at the entrance of the NY City Bar Association, midtown Manhattan, on an unusually hot June day. Carl asked me where we could have a quiet lunch nearby, indicating that he didn't care about the food, but sought air conditioning to escape the sweltering heat. We were across the street from the Algonquin Hotel, hangout of *The New Yorker* crowd in those days, with its famous lobby. I made a point of saying to Carl that I knew the restaurant was air-conditioned but I had no idea about the price. Carl's response was a single, trusting word, 'fine.' To my everlasting anguish the head waitress seated us, and then turned to me saying in a surprisingly friendly, almost intimate, voice, 'How nice to see you back again so soon with us!'

I was thoroughly flustered by these words and sat in stony silence not knowing how to respond, feeling devastated. I immediately assumed my teaching days were over before they began, that I was fully exposed as a crafty liar, and certainly not endowed with a character fit to instruct aspiring lawyers.

Only years later when I was confident enough to confess my anguish during this first meeting, did Carl let me know that he was so nervous about his responsibility to pass judgment on whether someone so junior could handle teaching law students so soon after graduating from law school, that he never noticed this seeming character flaw, nor was he prescient enough to anticipate that I would fail the NY bar during my first semester teaching students how to obtain that vital credential that every young lawyer needs. Had he been aware, he would almost certainly have passed on me, as I would have done when later given the chance to pass judgment on applicants for faculty appointments. The fact that the Algonquin hostess was innocently mistaken was irrelevant. I had never before eaten a meal there precisely because it was so expensive, although often meeting friends in the lobby.

Years later while at Princeton, I was asked by the lawyer for members of the Baader Meinhof terrorist organization in Germany to help with the preparation of legal arguments to be made at the trial. We arranged to meet at the Algonquin lobby one autumn afternoon. As I entered a man on a couch rose to greet me. I sat down, and he indicated he would start 'the interview' in a few minutes. I noticed a youngish man sitting opposite staring at me whom I correctly presumed must be the person I had agreed to meet. I realized that the man who had welcomed me minutes earlier had mistaken my identity. He was waiting for was someone else. I went across the room to meet the lawyer waiting to meet me, leaving this brief mistaken encounter with an embarrassed laugh.

Embracing Ohio State

I quickly accepted the offer of a temporary position at OSU, arriving in Columbus with an infant son, Chris, and the tricky domestic challenges arising from a collapsing marriage. My first wife, Rene, was so enamored of my father that she told me she would never agree to a divorce as long as he was alive. I remember being moved by this sentiment, and it reinforced my sense that, if closer in age and with different circumstances, they might have been great together, mutually appreciative and harmoniously attuned. I respected Rene's attitude, and also wanted to avoid disappointing Dad, and yet it became even clearer that we were not meant to be life partners.

Despite friction at home, I immediately fell in love with my new life as a young professor, actually younger than most of my students, many of whom were attending law school after returning from military service in the Korean War. To my surprise, and despite my anxieties, university teaching immediately struck me as a dream job, almost a rehearsal for what I fervently hoped might become a dream career. I never have had second thoughts about choosing the academic life over possible fame and fortune that might have been available to me if I had landed a permanent job with a big city prestige law firm.

I soon became comfortable with the prospect of spending my entire life in Columbus as a member of the law faculty, which was at odds with the views of my OSU faculty friends, almost all outside the law school, who uniformly sought greener institutional pastures and urban playgrounds, complaining about the philistine atmosphere of a Big Ten sports crazy university, the thinness of cultural life in Columbus, and the barren character of campus life.

Almost all these faculty colleagues unhappy with Ohio State as an academic home did go on to receive offers from other universities, fulfilling their wish to be at what they envisioned as greener pastures in the form of a 'better' university, which generally meant one located on either of the two coasts. Those with whom I kept contact were often soon disillusioned in their new academic habitats, even admitting nostalgia for the carefree good times and vibrant intellectual community that flourished in Columbus. What Ohio State offered, which I never found at Princeton (despite the high-density per capita brilliance), was a multi-disciplinary intellectual and social environment that valued friendship, nourished liberal and left critical thought and action, and facilitated permissive living when it came to erotic entanglements and recreational drugs/ alcohol. I found my years in Columbus more professionally satisfying and fulfilling than anything that I had previously experienced. Of course, the novelty of being on my own, earning my living in a respectable way, and making friends with congenial intellectuals were integral elements of this happy chapter in my life.

The faculty, and the law school deans at OSU, were extremely friendly, making me feel 'at home' in that special Midwestern way, at once casual and genuine, yet not deep, and rarely intimate except in boy/ girl situations. Teaching at the outset was a daily challenge, especially as I was assigned Criminal Law, a first-year course that had about 200 students, as well as Federal Courts, a highly technical subject I had never myself studied while a law student. I managed to keep an assignment or two ahead of the class, but whether I understood more than 50% of the material well enough to instruct others is a question that will remain forever unanswered. More than ever in my future teaching experiences, these OSU students were warmly appreciative. When the ordeal of the course was over the class raised my spirits with a standing ovation, which is a step beyond the customary applause a teacher receives from students at the close of the final course meeting.

What surprised me, especially at first, was the quality of the law faculty at the OSU College of Law. From a student perspective, it was no less expert or pedagogically dedicated than what I had experienced at Yale, supposedly the premier law school in the country. The OSU faculty devoted its energies to teaching more than to scholarship, and to the petty policies of law school administration that seem to agitate my colleagues who were extremely smart but without much societal leverage or status.

I have noticed this administrative turn inward in all the academic institutions: heavy artillery of the mind brought to bear on miniscule targets, and disguised faculty rivalries hindering the objective assessment of qualifications of candidates for tenure and promotion, the only really important decisions entrusted to university faculties.

The OSU law faculty was less ideologically inclined and more focused on obtaining the best available legal minds than either Princeton or Yale, although the consensus as to what was 'best' often did not reflect my idea of who was most likely to make 'interesting' and 'creative' contributions to legal thought and practice. The emphasis of my OSU colleagues was on technical mastery and analytic precision, coupled with a condescending and cynical attitude toward social consciousness or citizen engagement, although there were some liberals here and there on the law faculty who at least shared my discomfort with valuing vocational craftsmanship above all else. I developed an instinctive distrust for a profession that, as a whole, appraised its performance by winning and losing, almost taking pride in its deliberate indifference to human suffering or injustice of various kinds. Fortunately, there were memorable exceptions.

My interest in international law deepened, but the subject was 'owned' at OSU by Roland Stanger, a fine person who quickly became a mentor along with his caring and affectionate Greek wife, Alexandra. I can only barely remember teaching 'Rolly's course' but must have managed okay. Unlike McDougal, Rolly was jurisprudentially conventional, becoming my life coach more than my academic inspiration. His blend of decency, humility, and intelligence, complemented by an engaging self-irony, blended harmoniously with his pleasing, warm, and affectionate manner. I became deeply appreciative of his benevolent guidance despite our differences in background and jurisprudential outlook. Rolly, like Mac, overrated my abilities and promise, and seemed more dedicated to advancing my professional career than I was. I felt he was overly impressed by my Ivy credentials, which he falsely regarded as virtually automatic gateways to wish fulfillment. Against this background it is not surprising, despite his closeness as a friend, that he (more than I) viewed my presence at OSU as a temporary way station en route to what the various college rankings convinced the public was the promised land of academic access to wealth and power in American society.

Rolly was strongly affirmed and appreciated by the law school community and highly respected locally, but without a broader reputation in the field, and resembled in many respects my father, although without his reactionary politics. They shared star struck reactions when it came to celebrities, although Rolly responded to the twinkle in the eyes of academic stars rather than to the sort of Hollywood, governmental, and corporate luminaries that so entranced Dad.

Beyond Career: On Caring, Loving, and Engaging

What made the difference at Ohio State in my life was a series of 'openings' to unexpected futures, politically, romantically, and professionally. Not long after coming to Columbus I came up against racism at the university in the form of housing discrimination against black students, who were denied convenient and affordable housing close to the campus, and forced to settle for inconvenient and inferior housing at higher rents. When we discovered that most of this discriminatory behavior was associated with property owned by members of the OSU Board of Trustees, it was too much to bear even for usually passive liberals, and so a few of us, non-tenured junior law faculty put together a legal brief alleging the unconstitutionality of this discriminatory pattern, intending to name members of the Board as defendants in a formal action. To our relief, and that of our timid colleagues, the property owners connected with the administration of OSU backed down, abandoned discrimination against African American renters, and we dropped the law suit, somewhat relieved that on this occasion we could safeguard our careers without compromising our conscience. We were at the same time disappointed because we were optimistic about the outcome of the lawsuit and relished the prospect of such a victory even if it meant a career backlash.

There were also the 'real world' lessons at OSU that I am still glad, even at 90, to have refused to learn. A wily, somewhat gruff, warmhearted senior adjunct member of the law faculty, Jeff Davies, locally admired for his success as a trial lawyer, wandered into my office at the law school one day. His purpose was to give me a short course in worldly wisdom. He began by asking me if I realized that I had given the son of one of the most prominent men in Ohio a course grade of 'D'? I acknowledged giving the grade, but also saying I had no idea about the lineage of this poor student, whereupon Jeff departed from his normally affable and somewhat folksy manner, making no effort to hide his anger and contempt, thundering: 'Grow up! Learn to live in the real world!' I listened without responding beyond a whimper or two to let him know I was listening. Jeff said that I could make amends by telling the grading registrar that I had made a technical error on my grade sheet. I stood my ground, declaring that I would never change a grade unless there was a proper reason to do so.

Without any further exchange Jeff stormed out of my office never to return. I assumed that most of my colleagues would have responded as I did, but I never tried to find out. In retrospect, I fault myself for not reporting the incident to the dean's office. The only comparable experience occurred years later at Princeton when a popular professor of sociology, a close confidant of the president of the university, William Bowen, made an unexpected office visit. He wanted to let me know that I had given a 'D' to the star of the Princeton basketball team, who even more relevantly was the son of a current nationally revered coach at Georgetown. He told me that my grade was a blow to sports at Princeton, and would I be willing to adjust the grade upwards. By this time, I neither cowered nor expressed self-righteous anger, but calmly told this institutional do-gooder, previously a friendly acquaintance, that I would not even consider doing such a thing. Unlike my OSU skirmish, this colleague silently left my office, undoubtedly conveying his disappointment with my 'immature rigidity' to the basketball coach, the justly admired Pete Carill, who was also my occasional tennis partner. This emissary of corruption quite likely informed the university president, also a friend and tennis/squash opponent. We rarely agreed on policy issues, and yet managed a casual friendship through the years. Bill Bowen was a gifted mainstream economist, specializing in labor and education, and became a widely admired university president who handled the contradictory stresses of the job with humane intelligence, and in accord with his conservative alignments and beliefs.

These experiences at OSU and Princeton could have been professionally fatal for me. But so far as I know there were never any ripples of discontent from either incident and I graded as before, refusing ever to depart from my assessments of a student's performance. While at Ohio State, despite my overall satisfaction with where I had landed, my inner life was primarily absorbed with self-questioning that I now realize were in many ways a manifestation of a lingering adolescence. For most persons such musings are done with when out in the world getting paid to make a go of life.

In contrast to the practicalities and fulfillments of adult life, I continued to interrogate myself, seeking to understand how to live *authentically*, which became a lifelong quest although I have long since stopped treating it as a chess problem. At Ohio State I filled my journal each night with reflections about the difficulties of living according to

my values. I was also trying to figure out how to live more authentically
without adopting the lifestyle of an ascetic, as austerity as a way of life
never appealed to me. It was too far removed from my prudent hedonism
ever to be a serious option. Yet I kept wrestling with such concerns,
finally saddling my compromises with the label 'sensible selfishness.'
Its modest moral ambition, not at all original, was 'to do no harm,' realistically, to do as little harm as possible. Except when subject to erotic
intoxications of one sort or another, I feel that I honored this pledge,
which was rather self-indulgent.

Among my closest friends at OSU were Robert and Mary Elliott.
They were a distinctly East Coast liberal couple, he an English professor
and she warmly supportive, treating me because of our age difference
with maternal warmth and fondness. Bob taught me squash on a handball
court, and this changed my life. Squash later became both my favorite
Winter therapy and a major source of friendship at Princeton.

Politically in Ohio I became alerted to the nastiness of right-wing
politics, John Birch Society style, by defamatory attacks on Bob Elliott
as a subversive, cast as a Communist sympathizer whom, his attackers
believed, should be driven from the university. At the height of this
witch-hunting crisis in Columbus I was asked to introduce Bob at a
public lecture on the defense of civil liberties in the midst of campus
turmoil created by Birch Society activism training its gun sights on
progressive professors. I used the occasion to celebrate our friendship
and to express my unconditional support for Bob's commitment to political freedoms, including the right to advocate dissenting views. This
well-attended lecture, due to Bob's popularity with students and faculty
colleagues, and his notoriety resulting from the local media coverage of
the Birch Society attack, had the effect of deepening and solidifying our
friendship, but it also 'outed' me as a left liberal willing to be exposed in
public space as 'controversial.'

It has been disillusioning for me over the years to acknowledge
that incredibly few in the academic community were willing to take even
such minimal risks of public exposure. They preferred to express any
controversial views they held in the private confines of cocktail parties
or over afternoon coffee. Some claimed that candor was more effective
if reserved for shielded situations where influence might achieve some
results. I regarded such discreetness as self-serving. I felt that the primary motivation of those with such links to power and the powerful was to
sustain those valued connections. Such an objective required avoiding

public provocations, including strong criticisms of existing government policies.

Of course, the publicity accompanying public controversy could have adverse consequences. I believed at the time, which borders on the paranoid, that this simple introduction of my friend and colleague might have ended any hope of my becoming a tenured university faculty member. Despite such forebodings, I never weakened my resolve to stand in public solidarity with a friend and uphold the values of a free society in concrete circumstances. Each time over the years I was given such an opportunity, it strengthened my commitment and built my confidence in the ethical imperative of *public* truth-telling and witnessing, requiring a willingness to put aside careerist considerations. This assurance has grown over time, and in the face of paying a growing price, especially if measured by many doors being closed and securely locked that would likely otherwise have been swung wide open if I had kept my mouth shut and plied my trade as an international law expert without making public waves or taking anti-establishment stands.

At Ohio State, I ran into a more unusual and unexpected institutional pushback for teaching beyond what was required. I had friends in the humanities who invited me to teach an introductory course in comparative literature, a course devoted to English translations of world literature, readings of great books. I was excited to be offered this opportunity, although I received no course credit or extra pay. Lacking normal credentials, I was undoubtedly invited to teach such a course because there was a shortage of qualified instructors, and I must have been perceived as literate enough to take on the challenge, as well as being available without seeking compensation. I gladly went across campus three times a week to talk about Homer, Goethe, Camus, Forester, and others. I enjoyed good rapport with the students. But there was fallout.

Word got back to the law school of my teaching comparative lit as a volunteer. This led the dean to summon me for 'a consultation.' The dean suggested in a fatherly tone that I should not again teach such 'an extra course.' He claimed that it would create the unwelcome impression that I was not being given enough to do by my employer, the law school, and indirectly, the state of Ohio. With genuine disappointment, I timidly followed this practical 'advice,' never being quite sure whether it was a recommendation or a command. It was not conveyed to me as 'a command,' but it made me wonder whether, if I had disregarded this 'friendly' advice, it would have classified me as not 'a team player.' Being reliable in such semi-formal situations always counts for a lot in

academic life where the most strategic concerns usually involve budget-
ary allotments and perceptions of political correctness.

At the same time, this voluntary teaching experience confirmed my
strong attachment to the humanities, especially literature and philosophy. This awareness gave rise to occasional feelings of regret that I had
not been mature early enough to orient my life toward ideas and poems
rather than law and politics. Later on, I became more positive about the
potential ethical and political relevance of law. Besides, being concerned
with law and society seemed to avoid the feelings of disutility afflicting several of my humanist friends who devoted their lives to telling
students about how to read culturally influential texts, while searching
themselves for ways to find societal relevance for these lifelong professional commitments.

A generation later there occurred a spontaneous revolt among humanities scholars staged to overcome this sense of societal irrelevance.
It led some of the most talented scholars to choose non-humanistic
topics for research and teaching that were of current societal importance,
although far from the traditional scholarly preoccupations associated
with their fields. I think of such friends as Elaine Scarry writing about
torture, 9/11, constitutional authority, and nuclearism, or Chris Newfield,
teaching science fiction in class while doing his main research on the
impending financial crises threatening quality public higher education in
the United States, or Elisabeth Weber exploring the philosophical depths
of counterterrorist responses to the 9/11 attacks rather than restricting
herself to the narrower channels of deep readings of intellectually demanding German texts for the rest of her academic career.

In any event, my teaching of literature, although satisfying, became nothing more than a dim memory I look back upon fondly. What
makes this humanistic venture worthy of recall is that together with my
religious concerns, it kept me from ever giving myself over entirely to
political affinities or library definitions of scholarship or unconditional
submission to careerism. It led me toward a hybridity of my own making
when it came to scholarship, activism, and most of all, sensibility. This
hybrid sensibility came to infuse my most serious scholarly efforts.

Maybe, less favorably, it also exposed a lifelong character weakness of mine—aspiring to be all things to all persons, lacking a clearly
defined 'self,' and hence continually groping for a better understanding
of this or that, which led harsh critics to dismiss my scholarship as amateurish or fanciful, at best, churlish alienation, or the work of a dilletante.
Happily for me, these criticisms were more than offset by praise from

the progressive scholarly community, especially leading non-Western scholars.

Covert Thought Control

There were other political side adventures, typical of the Cold War Era, which seem worth recalling. Perhaps the most deliciously revealing anecdote was an unusual private session at the request of the Dean of the Law School, Frank Strong, a middle-of-the-roader with sharply honed Midwest social skills. Thanks to these skills, abetted by self-deprecating humor, Frank was on top of the short list to become the next president of the university, which happened a few years later. Although the model of a laidback and friendly dean, Frank was careful and crafty, eager not to take faltering steps along his climb to the top of the academic adminis-trative pyramid. In an uncharacteristically strained voice, I interpreted at the time as due to his feeling of awkwardness about being a messenger entrusted with unwelcome news, Frank told me that he had been recently visited by members of the FBI who asked him whether he realized who was this 'Richard Falk' on the law school faculty.

The FBI informed Frank that I had been the director of a hypnosis institute in NYC that was being used as an active recruiting front for Communist Party activities during the 1940s, starting in 1942. When I told Frank that I would have been barely 12 years old at the time and had never heard of such an institute, Frank laughed genially and sighed with relief, saying he was glad he cleared the air, adding that he never really believed what the FBI warned him about. He concluded our conversation by saying that he felt obligated to be sure that there was no dormant red menace in the law school that might make his apolitical faculty the target of a witch hunt. The revealing takeaway from such an absurd incident is the extent to which Cold War raw nerves can harm private lives. It is possible that another dean, perhaps harboring suspicions of his own or disliking me, could have taken steps to make sure I never received a permanent appointment without my ever being informed of such a false allegation. Many good people were harmed in their careers and lives during this period of Cold War hysteria and not given a chance to explain or tell their side of the story.

Frank never brought this incident up again, nor did anyone else ever mention it to me. As suggested, there exists a rarely acknowledged dan-ger associated with this kind of covert back channel access to university administrators, although the inflammatory issues reflect shifting political concerns over time. During the last decade or so, I have experienced this kind of access being used against me for defamatory and repressive purposes. I have become quite aware of Zionist militants going back stage at North American and European universities to blacklist faculty appointments, cancel conferences, and discredit speakers thought to be critical of Israel.[i] Such critics are charged with anti-Semitism and those exerting pressure will often threaten the university with bad publicity and withholding of contributions to the university and its programs. Pressure is applied to block or cancel academic appointments and scheduled events including invited lectures and even large conferences. My personal experience suggests that these underhanded tactics often succeed because bureaucrats and university officials, almost without exception, are team players with concerns about what their administrative superiors would wish, and fear controversy and the kind of exposure that accompanies it, especially if negative funding implications are involved. Better safe than sorry.

True, more established, affluent universities are usually more self-confident, and fend off irresponsible critics and community pressures, including influence peddlers and rich donors, with gracious brushoffs like, 'I wish I could help, but academic freedom is valued in this place even for viewpoints that many of us detest.' Usually that is the end of it, although not really, as quietly, yet corrosively, the word goes forth to deans and department chairs that it is best to avoid events and speakers that are seen as controversial and provocative, making the typical *liberal* defense of academic freedom often a structural threat to the openness of debate and dialogue. I have found that many university administrators make a show of defending academic freedom in public while undermining or circumscribing such freedom in private, or indirectly, by pompously invoking considerations of civility and institutional decorum, and more concretely, by claiming an absence of funding as the reason to reject controversial conference proposals or invited faculty lectures. There is no way of counting how many controversial speakers are *not invited* or controversial younger faculty *not promoted* or *appointed*. Tacit forms of thought control and employment denials are far more insidious and certainly more prevalent than overt and crude forms.

---

i I know there are ideological orientations other than Zionist with backroom influence that have influenced academic recruitment procedures, but my own knowledge is limited to what I experienced.

When Friendships End

Why friendships end and don't end intrigues me. It can reflect emotional disappointments of one sort or another, but my few experiences of lapsed friendships have come about because of strong political involvements on one side of a struggle that is not shared. Even a friendship resting on a strong center of emotional gravity and shared experience can flounder under such circumstances. With Harry Frankfurt it was Zionism as related to Israel, with Fouad Ajami it was his swing to the right on all matters Middle Eastern, with Mansour Farhang it was my slowness to condemn the autocratic nature of the Islamic Republic of Iran, and with Peri Pamir and several other Turks, it was my lingering appreciation of the achievements of Erdogan and the AKP relating to developments in Turkey. I don't recall a friendship that ended during my adult life because of some personal falling out, although my closeness to John Sperling, the founder of Phoenix University, took a definite hit after I felt victimized by his pre-Trump penchant for transactional relations. It was trivial, yet for me subversive of the trust essential for real friendship. John overstated the price of coats he imported from Greece that he sold me and others while we shared an apartment in Columbus for a couple of years. Of course, friendships are different than romantic relationships and family in these regards. If friendships fail, it almost always involves single instances of personal disillusionment, and not matters of everyday trust and rapport. With romantic disenchantment, issues of physical and emotional infidelity are almost always paramount, although sometimes after the glow disappears, and routine takes over, the end is in sight. With close family, it is usually a sense of betrayal, deep cleavages of character, and disturbingly often, reflects property, money, and inheritance disputes.

Humanist Affinities

My awakenings during those Columbus years were intellectual as well as political and romantic. I became friends with Erich Kahler, a socialist intellectual emigré from Prague, author of *Man the Measure* and *The Tower and the Abyss,* a distinguished humanist by virtue of cultural erudition, linguistic skill, humanistic sensitivity, and scholarly reputation. His visiting appointment at OSU somehow produced a close intergenerational friendship that helped me shift my sensibility both leftwards and to the humanities once and for all. Erich was staunchly anti-militarist, anti-imperialist, and above all someone who believed with Hegelian certitude that ideas were empowering and capable of having transformational impacts. Erich also became a precious dimension of my then unimagined future at Princeton where he lived a quiet scholarly life without formal attachment to the university.

Erich had strong friendships with several of the most renowned European intellectual refugees, including Einstein, Thomas Mann, and Hermann Brock. He also converted his home in Princeton into a salon. It was my great joy to live for two years as a privileged tenant/friend in their home at One Evelyn Place, where he lived with his devoted companion, Lily. Lily was a dedicated and possessive Viennese lady with no humor, strong bourgeois ideals, and an intense drive to reform wayward characters like myself. Erich was her coveted acquisition, representing for her a valuable prize that conferred status and social acceptance upon her as well. She was jealous, resentful that even in his 70s Erich was attractive to younger women who responded to his Old World charm, while he made no secret of enjoying their companionship. It is only in my 80s that I learned for myself that erotic energies do not wane, at least in the mind, and their existence can be threatening, as well as annoying, to a devoted female partner. Hilal has been teaching me these 'truths' ever since we met, and although I have avoided deep entanglements, my learning curve has been slow and my impulsiveness sometimes difficult to restrain.

At Ohio State Erich was a novelty, an exemplary representative of European high culture. He was brought to the campus by Oskar Seidlin, an ultra-nationalist and somewhat effete, socially aristocratic German intellectual who scorned the Frankfurt School consisting of post-Marxist leftists. Oskar, with whom I was moderately friendly, ran the German Department as a fiefdom, yet he had a taste for talent and abundant confidence in his own judgment, allowing him to ignore normal academic guidelines. In this spirit, while teaching German at the blue-ribbon Middlebury summer language school, he discovered and greatly facilitated the professional rise and development of Sigurd Burckhardt, who later became my close friend. Sig, German by birth, a brilliant interpreter of literature, especially Shakespeare, was trying to refresh his German at the Middlebury summer immersion program when discovered by Seidlin, who was stunned by Sig's weekly assigned essays in German, identifying them as publishable works of literary criticism of the highest quality. Sig went on to vindicate, and more, this extraordinary recognition of the quality of his scholarship when he had yet to complete his graduate studies.

Sig was the most perfection-inclined person I have ever known well, which may have been his undoing. He was never satisfied with his work or life however much it was praised and admired by others. He probably needed the special privileged treatment he received from Seidlin, whose possessive attitude toward Sig raised suspicions that he may have been romantically attracted to this talented younger protégé that he had 'discovered.' If so, he never received any encouragement from Sig, who was ardently heterosexual. It was difficult to interpret Oskar's behavior, although he seemed to disapprove of Sig's affair and later marriage with the departmental secretary, and even more, Sig's 'disloyal' decision to leave Ohio State for UC San Diego. Sig's decision to leave Columbus seemed at least partly motivated by a desire to escape from the orbit of Oskar's influence, affections, and domineering manner. Accompanied by Peggy, his devoted second wife, he joined a group of friends that left Ohio State as a group to start the humanities program at UCSD, the newest campus of the then flourishing University of California system.

Not many years later, around the time of his 50th birthday, Sig committed suicide, possibly undone by his perfectionism.

The son of a liberal Protestant minister, Sig as a child had been sent to America to escape the Nazi years and never returned; his own outlook was deeply ethical and entirely principled, an admirable person who was as flawless as anyone I have ever known well. Perhaps for this reason he was unfit to endure the inevitable dilemmas and contradictory pulls of life on planet earth. I have found that you cannot hope to live happily without being something of a Hindu, that is, being relatively unperturbed by the contradictoriness of life experience and the inner coexistence of opposites. Sig seemed to lack that crucial willingness to acknowledge the need for a few dark corners where secrets can be kept even from those we love most, as on occasion, lie we must. We make fun of consistency, claiming that it is a demand of petty minds, but few in the West can get along without its appearance. Except aesthetically when viewing a painting or reading a novel, we rely on a logic that conflates rationality with consistency and deplore those who act irrationally and inconsistently.

A Psychedelic Moment

Sig was important to me in another way. While at Ohio State we were persuaded by a university psychologist, a friend studying changes in behavior under the influence of psychedelic drugs, to do a controlled experiment on perceptions of time. We agreed to do this in his modern house situated in a residential development planned by a local innovative architect. It was a strange and memorable experience. As I recall, it was suggested that I invite a friend to join me, and I managed to persuade Sig, somewhat against his better judgment. I went to the Ohio State Fair in the morning as I had been urged to prepare my mind for the experience by doing something that was not stressful. Nothing better dissipates tensions than a leisurely visit to the varied satisfactions of a Midwestern state fair.

We were given doses of the drug based on our weight, but somehow the doses got reversed. I was given too much and Sig too little, and this became quickly apparent in how we responded. The drug had multiple strong effects on me, and almost none on Sig, partly due to dosage and partly probably due to his mastery of Prussian virtues of self-control.

When I participate in experiences that some view as potentially transformative, or psychologically profound, I submit. I try to suspend any fears or suspicions, and submit as totally and fearlessly as I can, trusting my basic emotional resilience to protect me against calamity. Under the influence of this drug I did sense time as passing more slowly, heard music differently, saw the abstract paintings of our Austrian hostess in three-dimensional vivid color, suffered a scary memory loss, endured a paranoid interlude during which I thought that our somewhat peculiar hosts were moving about the house planning our execution, somewhat in the spirit of the horror movie *Get Out*.

While under the spell of the drug, I expressed my sense of this psychedelic moment in prose I thought at the time was electric with deep meanings. When rereading the next morning it had become mechanical prose drenched with clichés. I definitely experienced feelings of a dissolving self at the height of the drug's impact. It led me while under its influence to believe rather strongly that people should not risk such a mind warping chemical experience of this kind despite its exciting sensory disclosures. I was glad I did it once, but I knew that I never wanted to take such a risk again. I have used other non-psychedelic drugs from time to time, discovering that I react more strongly than most. My one-time encounter with Ecstasy was quite extreme, perhaps stoked by being coupled with weed, leading me to profess love to the near stranger in whose apartment the whole experience occurred while we were naked at her insistence. It was mentally enlivening, although with some effort I evaded the real-life consequences that were on the agenda of my pharmaceutically equipped seducer.

A Time for Exploration

As love, sex, and politics seem so often to be entwined in a variety of bewildering ways, my experiences in Columbus along these lines were probably less unusual than the way the elemental forces struck me. After a rather 'civilized' separation and divorce, which followed my father's death in November 1956, Rene left Columbus and resumed her life in Vancouver, raising our son, Chris, as a single mother. It was a friendly divorce, and I was dutiful and uncomplaining about sending support payments on a monthly basis and making annual and sometimes semi-annual visits. Chris grew up 'normal,' reflecting his mother's values and worldview, which meant being socially and politically conservative. Chris became a respected and upstanding member of the Canadian law fraternity and stayed well connected with Rene's wider family network. Through the years we managed a decent yet unspectacular father/son relationship. It has neither sharp edges of discontent nor strong bonds of attachment. It was a bit strained on both sides from time to time, with tensions often eased by our shared enjoyment of sports. And during the last twenty or so years our biological connection benefitted from the harmony of our wives, and some mutual appreciation of lives well lived.

In this period after my father's death and then the divorce, I was on my own, in an experimental mood, exploring relationships with a variety of young women, seeking a kind of sexual and erotic empowerment and liberation, but mostly consumed by a vain search for enduring love. Especially among PhD students and younger faculty there was a tendency at OSU to mingle sexual permissiveness with progressive political social gatherings, which tended to have a mildly socialist center of gravity, which although left of the Democrats was less dogmatic than most forms of Marxism or the rare outright embrace of Communism. My own development in this atmosphere was to shop around, neither standing apart nor embracing the consensus, still searching for an identity of my own, and somehow hoping that the right woman would grant me the emotional space to grow into myself. Only now do I wonder whether being stuck in this prolonged search mode was an unconscious attempt to fill the voids left by the absence and unloving nature of my mother.

Part of my search during this period involved what might be called the inner life, which I articulated to myself as spirituality, religion, and authenticity. It was definitely ecumenical in tone and substance, with an implicit anti-tribal animus. I increasingly thought of myself as 'human' rather than 'Jewish,' and felt more drawn to Buddhism and Christianity than to Judaism, or for that matter, atheism. This was partly because these other traditions were not my tribe, and partly because my education and experience were more closely linked to this religious 'otherness.' Also, my woefully superficial grasp of Judaism as uncongenially preoccupied with 'law, the Ten Commandments,' and ethnicity was a factor. In contrast I thought of Christianity as far more responsive to my spiritual yearnings for 'love,' anti-imperialism, and community and of Buddhism as focused on empathy, right action, as well as the middle path and mindfulness. I realize that these reductive images of complex religious worldviews amount to misleading over-simplifications based on selective interpretation, and yet that is what I then felt and thought.

Despite my anti-tribalism, also in relation to family and state, I felt somewhat isolated and metaphysically lonely, making the *idea* of joining a religious community appealing, although only in the abstract. The future would teach me that translating this religious impulse into an institutional reality, proved a mountain well beyond my climbing capacity. Unlike experiencing drugs or therapy I was unable and unwilling to check my mind at the institutional gateway through which one must pass. I was also unable to subscribe to metaphysical claims that collided with my rather pedestrian secular and rational epistemology. Despite seeking inspiration from the East, I never gave up my deeply entrenched Enlightenment worldview, which stressed the rational, the scientific, and the empirical. At the same time, my existential affirmations of spirituality have allowed me in the course of the ups and downs of life to remain receptive to religious and poetic ways of knowing. I find myself also impressed that even in the face of modernity so many persons otherwise consigned to lives of misery find a meaning for their life through their participation in an organized religion. In this regard, while Marx was right about religion as an opiate with respect to revolutionary consciousness, he was very wrong to overlook the relevance of religion to a fulfilled human life, especially for the many who are living materially deprived lives. Religion is a potent source of self-esteem, wellbeing, moderation, and community, yet certain religious postures and outlooks can mobilize followers to do terrible individual and collective harm. In other words, my political engagement, however much it informed my public persona, never extinguished a quest for spiritual wellbeing, while recognizing that in historical contexts religion in its manifold manifestations can work for or against such goals. I pride myself, perhaps without sufficient justification, on my ability to accept a non-polarized view of the relevance of religion to the human condition, without ever being wholly for nor fully against its influence and impact.

Maybe this helps explain why I never fit organizationally into any political movement nor felt at ease with the kind of New Age apolitical spirituality that took California by storm some fifty years ago. For better and worse, I could never free myself from this sort of hybridity with its pre-modern, modern, and postmodern overlapping of beliefs and commitments a blending of East and West. Standing apart often meant standing alone, which kept some at arms-length over the course of my life, yet fortunately, far from everyone.

CHAPTER 6

Experiencing Harvard

Harvard/Cambridge

I was fully content with my unfolding life in Columbus as a fledgling academic at Ohio State, and seemed accepted professionally as a teacher and personally as part of the wider intellectual community at the university. After a few years teaching at OSU, I received a one-year grant from the Ford Foundation in a program designed to nurture 'young law teachers' by funding them to spend a year studying, researching, and writing at any of the country's leading law schools. Without much hesitation, making up for my decision to choose Yale over Harvard five years earlier, I sought affiliation with Harvard Law School. In part, it was an opportunity to satisfy my earlier yearning to live in Cambridge and get a taste of its celebrated cultural milieu. I also looked forward to spending time at Harvard, which enjoyed a worldwide reputation as the world's greatest university.

Arriving at Harvard alone in the autumn of 1958, and with no close friends at the university was daunting at first, and complicated by the chilly reception I received from the formidable dean of the law school, Erwin Griswold. This man would later achieve national prominence as a fearless Solicitor General of the U.S. Government. It was my first brush with the Harvard version of Ivy League arrogance. Griswold, who had never previously dealt with a Ford Fellow in this program for young law faculty, frostily informed me that I could not just hang around the law school for a year. He insisted that I enroll in a degree program, displaying obvious impatience that my pleadings to the contrary were a waste of his precious time. It didn't take me long to figure out that the Master of Law option was a lose/lose proposition, involving mostly required courses and no professional benefits. This kind of master's program was mainly designed in the law school world as a cash cow to serve foreign lawyers seeking an introductory familiarity with the American legal system. I decided to enroll in the doctoral program leading to a juridical science degree, the JSD. This program was geared to serve aspiring foreign and domestic academicians, especially those seeking to escape from law schools without national reputations. It had far fewer course requirements, stressing instead a scholarly dissertation that was subject to rejection if not deemed 'a contribution to knowledge,' and was coupled at the end with an intimidating comprehensive oral exam conducted by a faculty committee entrusted with overseeing the thesis. The scope of the exam extended beyond what was submitted in the text to satisfy the thesis requirement. I was in residence at Harvard for only the 1958-59 academic year. I didn't manage to complete the dissertation until 1962, by then a member of the Princeton faculty without tenure, and somewhat fearful of what would happen if my work was rejected at Harvard.

Anxiety aside, the Harvard year was an exciting experience in many respects, although not because I learned very much of lasting value at the law school. What I did find permanently useful in my intellectual development was remote from my area of specialization, international law. The two leading international law professors at Harvard were Richard Baxter and Louis Sohn, whose courses I took more out of curiosity than real interest. Far more stimulating were several creative thinkers in residence at Harvard Law School including Kingman Brewster (later president of Yale University) and Roger Fisher (of 'getting to yes' fame). My informal relations with both Kingman and Roger as friends more than as teachers did deepen my understanding of international law, and law generally.

My most enduring memory of Roger, who on his way to 'yes' delivered long monologues devoted to his pet topics of how to solve the world's most daunting problems with boyish enthusiasm, is the time we were on the same ferry bound for Martha's Vineyard when the engine suddenly died, and the boat started rocking amid the ocean waves. It turned out that McGeorge Bundy was also on the ferry, and the three of us were together for some six hours until an engineer figured out what was wrong. Roger had a field day, giving Bundy an array of unsolicited solutions to the most pressing problems of the day. As was part of the Harvard ethos, power mattered more than sociability, and Roger spared me as what moved him was this rare opportunity to get his views across to Bundy, then a top White House advisor to the Kennedy presidency. I listened to what was almost a monologue as much as I could, and surprised myself by feeling sorry for Bundy, who was in Roger's line of fire for several hours, and evidently felt obliged to seem attentive, although I sensed that he was not very pleased with being told what to do in Washington to get things right by this brilliant Harvard clean shaven boy scout. Without doubt, Roger was talented, a clear thinker who used simple language to penetrate complex issues, but overbearing due to his belief that he had found answers that eluded others before requests seeking his wisdom had even been made. I preferred reading Roger than listening to him, a view that I suspect Bundy came to share after being a captive audience on the stalled ferry.

At Harvard, I was naturally, although somewhat misleadingly, cast as nothing more than another wayward intellectual protégé of McDougal and the misguided Yale approach to International Law. As a result, I was not particularly appreciated by these international law scholars who were unabashed legal positivists, regarding themselves as Harvard professors perched atop the academic hierarchy. They derisively dismissed the Yale approach to international law as 'politics' not 'law.' Although cordial personally, my interactions with HLS international law faculty occurred in an atmosphere of mutual disdain that never dissipated over the course of the year.

Despite doing my best to perform, the lowest grades on my Harvard transcript were in two courses on the law subjects where I had the most background, having taught international law the prior three years, and studied international law rather avidly while a law student. Such are the prejudices and hidden agendas of tenured professors at even the most esteemed centers of learning. Throughout the year I was challenged to cope with my strange dual identity at Harvard as an assistant professor on an American law faculty while at the same time being an enrolled graduate student subject to appraisal by eminent teachers with uncongenial jurisprudential approaches.

In the end, it worked out fine, and I was more than compensated by being overly appreciated by two other members of the law school faculty. One was Jack Dawson who did a course for a small number of students on judicial decision theory and the other was Lon Fuller, whose teaching featured a highly regarded large undergraduate law course in jurisprudence, a subject that interested me although I had never studied it while at Yale. The jurisprudence course included fascinating reflections by Fuller on his then recent celebrated debate with H.L.A. Hart of Oxford on whether or not Nazi governance was consistent with or, on the contrary, was the death knell of the German legal order. Fuller had been Richard Nixon's law teacher at Duke, and was seemingly somewhat out of character and miscast, a few years later, when he became part of Nixon's brain trust when he ran for president in 1960. Fuller believed that morality was necessarily embedded within the legal order in such a way as to make the Nazi invocation of legalism invalid and void. Hart, in contrast, adopted an intrepid neo-Kelsenite position in which the formalities of law-creation made irrelevant the moral outlook of a particular legal system. I later came to know Herbert Hart rather well during a week-long seminar on legal positivism at the Rockefeller Center at Bellagio, Italy, finding him a delightful person and much more approachable than Fuller, but in the epic debate on whether or not morality was embedded in law, I sided with Fuller.

In any event, I received the highest grade given that year in the Jurisprudence course, somewhat alleviating my anxiety, having feared being rated below the class majority of, Harvard's undergraduate law students, all bright aspiring lawyers. The jurisprudence exam was demanding, 48 hours to compose responses to several difficult theoretical questions. I completed my exam paper with enough time left over to help my beleaguered Indian girl-friend, who was a student in the master's program with an educational background in India that left her unequipped to handle these jurisprudential issues even had she been given a month in which to produce a credible set of responses. For years I pondered the ethics of this show of affection and empathy on my part, which would have been treated as a serious instance of 'cheating' if detected at the time. In a sense, she didn't deserve to pass the course, but she should never have been permitted by Harvard to enroll, given her lack of proper academic background. She was selling real estate in the Boston area when we met many years later. At Harvard I had enjoyed her warmth and emotional intimacy. She had an Indian charm that I found both playfully engaging and softly seductive.

It was for me a romantic adventure that seemed to be rather natural in the Harvard setting. Let me call her Ruti, a lovely young woman from the Parsi community of Bombay (now Mumbai), an Indian religious sect derivative from Zoroastrianism as once practiced in Iran. The Parsis were a small, very tight, affluent community accustomed to intermarriage, and my friend was expected to soon marry a Parsi judge who had himself done a law degree at Harvard several years earlier and encouraged her to follow suit. She came to Harvard with little money, but with several boxes filled with gold bracelets, which she sold whenever needing cash. We had a warm friendship with romantic overtones. At one point, Ruti seemed on the verge of abandoning her community back home if I was prepared to marry—which I wasn't. I felt affection and even love, but was not *in love*, and thought we could not be happy for very long when living together. Besides, after my divorce from Rene, I became more cautious, at least temporarily, becoming more responsible about distinguishing infatuations from long-term commitments. Admittedly, as it turned out, not nearly cautious enough.

At the end of the jurisprudence course, Ruti and her Indian girlfriend organized a small party of appreciation for Lon Fuller, with unspoken irony in gratitude for her passing grade. It turned out to be a snowy night, and I had my one and only automobile accident when I turned at a red light in Cambridge and was hit by a car unable to stop, which fortunately was driving slowly from the opposite direction. It slid slowly into my car causing no injury and only minor damage. It turned out to be 'a friendly accident.' The driver of the other car was also a Harvard student. We exchanged insurance information, and I never heard anything further, but it did delay my arrival at the party where I had agreed to be the co-host, and in those ancient days there were of course no cell phones, and no way of communicating my delay. Despite the weather and my mishaps, the evening ended happily. The rather uptight and socially conservative Lon Fuller seemed to enjoy immensely the attentions of these several attentive, lively, and laughing young Indian women, almost as much as I did.

Rawls and Tillich

As at Penn, my most exciting and influential academic experiences were outside my supposed area of concentration, mainly in philosophy, religion, and literature. I have always thought of my Harvard experience as combining law and philosophy. My thesis reflected this convergence of interests. I sat in on a famous course taught by John Rawls, who despite a rather intrusive stammer, delivered a series of stimulating presentations. We students were privileged to be listening to a reading of a rather advanced draft of what was published more than a decade later under the title *A Theory of Justice* (1971). The book, widely heralded in advance of publication, was received with great fanfare. It became the most influential and widely studied and discussed modern treatment of justice, and clearly the most debated philosophical work in the English language of the last half of the 20th century. What I remember best about this privileged intellectual experience was the exceptional conceptual precision of Rawls' text that disclosed an uncanny depth of understanding of how to frame philosophically cogent positions.

I also enjoyed and learned from William Earle's sprightly philosophical lectures on existentialism that offered ways of thinking that were responsive to the experiential realities of being in the contemporary lifeworld without the benefit of seemingly quaint metaphysical props. I found existentialism much more relevant to my concerns than the arid preoccupations of language philosophers and logicians that then dominated the Anglo-American scene. And for me, the existential worldview was more congenial than the pioneering work of Rawls on justice rooted in the mainstream liberal tradition of Anglo-American philosophy.

Undoubtedly, the best of my Harvard 'adventures in ideas' was exposure to the remarkable mind of Paul Tillich, the great Protestant theologian who brilliantly succeeded in bringing religious belief into harmony with science, art, modernity, and even the realities of trans-rational knowledge. Although in the twilight of his teaching career, Tillich still had a twinkle in his eyes coupled with gifts of extraordinary luminosity of expression that made his lectures, while systematic in thematic development and touching on many issues of contemporary concern, sources of arresting insights illuminating the darkest corners of knowledge. Tillich offered many interpretations of key issues, notable for their originality and clarity. I took two courses: one on the intellectual history of the Protestant Reformation and the other on Art and Religion.

I remember Tillich comparing Harvard with Union Theological Seminary where he had previously taught after retreating to the U.S. from Nazi Germany. While at Union Tillich was in contentious rivalry with the other great religious thinker of his generation, Reinhold Neibuhr, who also happened to be German. Tillich told us that Harvard was better at meeting his needs of creature comfort, but Union was more satisfying with respect to his spiritual aspirations. I understood this to mean that the intellectual and political challenges at Union had an uplifting effect, while Harvard offered a more harmonious and hedonistically pleasing environment that papered over bruising differences on matters of principle that arose with Niebuhr on matters of theology and politics. In subsequent reading, I learned from both of these towering figures, whose work was never confined by disciplinary boundaries. I felt more kinship with Tillich who distanced himself more from the domains of power politics, while Niebuhr's informed and insightful commentary on world issues added to his stature in the American public square.

ee cummings and Fidel Castro

Another experience during that year fulfilled my sense of why Harvard and Cambridge had such a magnetic appeal for those of us who were entranced by culture and politics. Perhaps the reason that this single year at Harvard remains so meaningful for me is that it put me in closer touch with the diverse pleasures of the mind off as well as on campus. One spring early evening I went to Sanders Theater to hear ee cummings read his poetry with a musical cadence that brought an excitement to his poems that I had not previously felt when reading them on my own. Poetry reading, especially of such a musically gifted poet as cummings, can be truly transformative, chilling the spine, awakening the soul, and above all, deepening a comprehension of the unspeakable. I remember as if yesterday cummings' reading of 'I Sing of Olaf' with its witty celebration of defiant anti-war pacifism.

Later that same evening I went to the Harvard outdoor field house by the Charles River to hear Fidel Castro give a rambling, fascinating talk. He was introduced by McGeorge Bundy of all people, then dean of the Harvard College. Castro spoke from the balcony of the field house high above the large audience gathered on the athletic field below. His guards were prowling around on an adjoining wall. Castro had been to the UN a few days earlier. This stop at Harvard was part of Castro's victory lap in the United States just after the takeover of the Cuban government, occurring before Washington had decided to brand him 'Enemy #1' in the Western Hemisphere.

The breaking point revealingly came not as a result of Castro's alignment with Moscow or adherence to Marxism. The break with the U.S. came because Castro nationalized the sugar industry, the backbone of the Cuban economy. The sugar industry had been heavily subsidized by the corrupt Batista dictatorship that had previously ruled Cuba as a gangster state with Washington's complicity. What Castro had done, undoubtedly with a delicious sense of irony, was to call attention to the injustices of the past as well as reassert Cuban sovereignty over its natural resources. He offered compensation to the expropriated foreign owners of sugar plantations and refining facilities for amounts based on the grossly deflated values of their assets that the investors, mostly Americans, had in the Batista period submitted to the Cuban government for tax purposes. These deeply corrupt tax records from the pre-Castro period, vastly understated business revenues and profits; if accepted, these valuations would have made foreign sugar investments almost worthless. Castro's approach exposed the manner in which foreign investors had been cheating the Cuban government and its people over the course of many years with the connivance of corrupt Cuban government officials. Should not past unjust enrichment be taken into account when evaluating the compensation owed these foreign investors who had long shamelessly benefitted from a corrupt Cuban leadership?

The later Cuban dependence on the Soviet Union was accentuated by Washington's febrile hostility, climaxing with the abortive Bay of Pigs intervention of CIA-backed Cuban exiles in 1961. JFK's refusal to provide air cover to the military operation was angrily blamed by conservatives for the failure of this anti-Communist mission and was thought by some conspiracy-minded analysts to be one of the motives for Kennedy's assassination two years later. Of course, much followed in ways that accentuated the malevolence and risks of the Cold War: the assassination with CIA help of Ché Guevara in Bolivia; the reported 50 CIA attempts to assassinate Castro, trying by every means, including providing the Cuban leader with exploding cigars and sneaking various poisons into his food. The harsh sanctions, continuing to this day, drove Castro into the ideologically rigid arms of the Soviet Union, and climaxed during the near apocalyptic Cuban Missile Crisis when many sane, informed persons were utterly convinced that nuclear war would occur due to the refusal of either Washington or Moscow to back down. As the Oliver Stone/Peter Kuznick TV documentary series on the Cold War shows convincingly, the prevention of a nuclear showdown occurred because a Soviet submarine commander refused to carry out an order to fire a nuclear torpedo at an American aircraft carrier. Even more authoritatively, Martin Sherwin demonstrates in *Gambling with Armageddon* (2020) that the avoidance of nuclear war in 1962 was sheer luck.

My personal connection with these events may have been unconsciously stirred by Castro's nationalist passions on display that evening in Cambridge.

Aside from writing academic articles upholding Cuba's right under international law to assert sovereignty over its national resources even if meant overriding foreign investors, a touchy issue that mingled Cold War concerns with the outreach of global capitalism, my contact with Cuba was sporadic. But many years after Castro's talk at Harvard I was asked to write the foreword to a book of essays by lawyers challenging the legality of economic sanctions imposed by the U.S. government on Cuba. I was told that Castro was pleased with the book, and this influenced a Cuban official to allow my son, Dimitri, to finish his excellent documentary film vividly exploring the pros and cons of life in

Cuba without insulting audiences with didactic messaging. The filming had been suspended at one stage because Cuban authorities discovered that their antipathy to homosexuality would be viewed critically in the movie. When Castro relented, a compromise on the film's content was reached, and the film went on to receive praise at festivals, including at Berlin being shown under the title *Midnight in Cuba* (1998). I was and am proud of Dimitri for doing the film. It took him six years, and along the way he was faced with funding challenges and travel obstacles, but he persisted and finished. What he achieved remains important for anyone who wants to understand the trials and tribulations of Cuba's extraordinary defiance of American hegemony in the Western Hemisphere sustained for decades in the face of high intensity geopolitical leverage exerted by the United States.

Encountering Ellsberg

During my Harvard year I had rented a nondescript apartment in Alston, a satellite town within greater Boston, not too far from campus, although on the other side of the Charles River. Alan Oser, my college roommate for three years at Penn, was living with his wife nearby in the town of Milton, and we saw each other from time to time. Alan was deeply impressed and attracted by a journalist, Brenda Murphy, who had an affiliation with Harvard for the year. Alan assumed I would be equally entranced by her intelligence and charm, and arranged a meeting that amounted to 'a blind date,' almost my only one ever. It was not a success. We had a forgettable conversation, both us seemed almost instantly aware that romantic chemistry was missing. Brenda was worldly, smart and rather 'cool' in ways that I was not. Instead of love at first sight, this was social distancing at first meeting in that pre-Tinder atmosphere.

Before parting that night, I did agree to meet for dinner the following week at her apartment where she would invite someone whom she described as remarkably intelligent and personable, her friend, Daniel Ellsberg. I cannot remember whether I had previously heard of Ellsberg, then a rising star at Harvard in the domain of strategic studies, and destined to ride ever higher in that firmament after giving a series of widely heralded public lectures on the logic and utility of nuclear threats. This was a topic dear to the hearts of leading war thinkers of the time who, in my judgment, irresponsibly believed that nuclear threats could serve the strategic purposes of NATO if cleverly used without raising the risks of nuclear warfare above acceptable levels. Nuclear threats gave the United States a supposedly safe way to use nuclear weapons advantageously without 'wasting' their strategic potential. As a social event, the dinner was not memorable had not Dan gone on to do great things. It led to no desire on anybody's part to arrange any future meetings, much less to embark upon friendships. Somewhat embarrassingly, I remember the occasion more for the food than the conversation.

In any event, the dinner was even more awkward than my date with Brenda a week earlier. I felt our conversation that evening seemed strained and polite so long as it managed to stay clear of Dan's passion at that time, which I interpreted, perhaps wrongly, as an infatuation with American militarism and Cold War ideology. The evening made me aware that I had drifted to the left during my three prior years at Ohio State, making me distinctly uncomfortable with someone who seemed so enthralled by warfare, and also championed America's role in the world. I never imagined that Dan was destined to become the most famous political dissenter in the entire Western world upon the release of the Pentagon Papers more than ten years later. His fame has lingered, being reinforced by Dan's frequent anti-nuclear acts of civil disobedience, his powerful talks around the world, and his semi-confessional and deeply troubling books. Dan's legacy resurfaced during the last decade as the antecedent to the spectacular whistleblowing disclosures of Chelsea Manning, Edward Snowden, and Julian Assange. In recognition of his contributions to such displays of public conscience Ellsberg deservedly received the 2018 Olaf Palme prize in Stockholm, awarded for moral courage.

Friendships: The Rhythm of Work and Play

In many ways, my friendships with Georges Abi-Saab and Saul Mendlovitz, were the most enduring part of my year at Harvard, more professionally valuable, although distinct from my formal learning experiences. Georges was the best trained legal mind among the doctoral students at Harvard, a brilliant Egyptian Christian with a gracious manner that won him widespread affection and admiration, and remarkably, even among those with whom he disagreed. We took many long walks along the Charles River, and spoke of women, law, and movies in that order, while the sun set and the college crew teams glided by, practicing for upcoming races. Georges was more inclined toward Harvard-style legal thought than I was. He was politically progressive, economically sophisticated, and jurisprudentially conservative in the European style.

Georges always claimed to be a cross between a womanizer and a pasha, and to dampen any critical response to such self-stereotyping he would disarmingly assert, 'You know, I am an Arab.' He confessed to his fantasy of finding a subservient female partner who would adore and serve him without expecting too much in return except basking in the glories of his intellectual excellence, social grace, personal kindness, and professional eminence. A few years later Georges seemed to find what he was looking for, although definitely not an Arab. Rosemary was a soft spoken, pleasant, and well-educated Swiss bourgeois lady who viewed Georges as a gift from the gods, loyally making his life better in many ways, even acting as his chauffeur, through the decades.

With Saul, friendship became more and less than with Georges. Saul was bright, idealistic, outspokenly proud and assertive about his Jewish identity, then captive of an unhappy rather neurotic gentile wife who insisted that they play at religion by being devoted Unitarians, whatever that meant to them. In the 30 years following our Harvard shared experience, I collaborated with Saul on various world order projects, the most ambitious of which was the World Order Models Project, known as WOMP, and we had a friendship that was truly close, but with some rough edges of disagreement and rivalry.

Saul, Georges, and I hung out together frequently. Rather incredibly, given his in-your-face Jewishness and anti-Trinitarian Unitarianism, Saul Christianized our triangular friendship by dubbing it 'the Trinity,' casting himself as the Father, Georges as the Son, and assigning me the non-corporeal role as Holy Spirit, surely an irreverent and non-descriptive, if not heretical, way of describing the novelty of our unlikely deep friendship. The label stuck over the decades as our private way of acknowledging the special quality of this friendship. Surprisingly, despite being far apart geographically, diverse in personality, and gripped by different life challenges, our bonds of friendship flourished ever since leaving Harvard. We seized opportunities to meet in Geneva and New York whenever our travels converged. I think we each in our different ways wanted to keep alive this last enjoyment of student life at Harvard, despite the many pulls and stresses of our distinct life choices that came later. We remained aware that at Harvard we had, for once, the time needed to nurture enduring friendships that would never be reproduced elsewhere, which turned out to be true.

What Endures

When I finally submitted my thesis in the Fall of 1963, 'The Adequacy of International Law for the Cold War Era,' my examiners were the highest regarded Harvard international law specialists, Milton

Katz, Richard Baxter, Roger Fisher, and Louis Sohn. The exam was somewhat awkwardly scheduled in the midst of my second teaching year at Princeton, and functioned as a sort of post-mortem last chapter of my Harvard student experience, as well as being the last chapter of my formal education.

I can no longer remember whether I feared or welcomed the prospect of being called upon to defend the McDougal approach. I had no idea how to prepare for such a boundaryless examination. I could be asked anything about my academic field, my publications, and the thesis. I took a train from Princeton to Boston feeling vulnerable and apprehensive, not knowing what would be my fate on the following morning.

Almost all of the questions put to me by these four renowned professors throughout the entire examination were based on my first published article in the *Temple Law Quarterly*, which was devoted to the theme of horizontal and vertical conceptions of international law. As soon as I started teaching international law at Ohio State I became preoccupied with the question of how to convince skeptical students that international law was really law, despite lacking enforcement capabilities and governmental institutions that we associated with law and order within the territorial confines of the United States. I focused on the distinctiveness of international law as a horizontal legal system, and never tried to make the implausible case that international law was law in the same sense as law in a well governed domestic society, which I identified as a *vertical* legal order.

I argued that law is effective and reliable in many areas of practical importance in international life even absent enforcement capabilities, provided the logic of reciprocity is applicable or there are perceived common interests present (as with regulating international air travel, establishing maritime safety, regulating diplomatic interaction, respecting sovereign immunity). This order of formally equal sovereign states is what I called a horizontal legal order. I would point out to students that *domestic* law was frequently violated despite its elaborate police and enforcement capabilities. This was obvious in relation to white collar crime, and there were many other instances of lawlessness in our own country, none more shameful than the double standards used by law and government institutions to discriminate against African Americans. Yet few doubt the existence of the national legal order, despite these defects, although there are frequent calls for closing loopholes, making specific reforms, and achieving more robust and equitable enforcement with respect to race and class. The vertical dimension of world order represented the geopolitical override of the juridical equality of states. Such verticality can be illustrated by the right of veto in the UN Security Council, double standards with respect to human rights, and the impunity of geopolitical actors when it comes to accountability for international crimes.

After what was little other than a pleasant conversation with these Harvard luminaries, my feared 'ordeal' of the thesis exam turned out to be a walk in the park. I returned to Princeton that evening with a sense of accomplishment that I had earned a Harvard doctoral degree without great exertion, and with an unacknowledged debt of gratitude to the unreasonableness of Dean Griswold. I had the feeling that my Harvard examiners viewed the event as a ritual duty they were expected to perform rather than, as proclaimed, a genuine test of a candidate's qualifications. They didn't approach the occasion as one involving a serious assessment of whether or not I was a deserving doctoral candidate on the basis of what I had submitted to satisfy the degree requirement. The Harvard brand took a small hit in my mind, although since I was the beneficiary, it never occurred to me to advertise my opinion.

Looking back, I guess these years at Penn, Yale, and Harvard prepared me for the thickest Ivy of them all, Princeton. Because of my inability to identify with institutions, I never attempted to enjoy the satisfactions of any alumni experience nor did I feel any sense of obligation 'to give back' to these institutions what they had certainly given me, an easy entry to a cherished professional career in academic life. My professional life was not what any of these institutions derived pride from producing, but that is beside the point. They served my purposes by providing the cultural and scholarly resources that enabled learning to proceed in near ideal surroundings, and for that, I remain deeply thankful. These Ivy sites of learning and elite social bonding enclaves were subconsciously responsive to the wishes and values of the financial districts of the great world cities, especially New York, and to citadels of political power, particularly Washington, looking with great favor on careers devoted to diplomacy, finance, business, as well as the professions of law and medicine. It was only later that I came to appreciate that Yale, Harvard, and Princeton also served as major recruiting centers for the CIA, and even provided influential advisors on how to use culture effectively as an ideological weapon in the Cold War. I suppose that these great universities that evolved in a rhythm just slightly behind the tides of social change, could be interpreted as privileged centers of learning and elite socialization where the resources of knowledge are put directly, and even more so indirectly, at the service of power, wealth, and prestige.

CHAPTER 7
Returning to Ohio State

Returning to Ohio State after Harvard did not trouble me. I looked forward to resuming my teaching and writing life, as well as reviving friendships, finding a place to live, and regarding Columbus as my permanent residence. I was not at all sure about whether the future would produce any activist engagements additional to my professional identity as teacher/scholar.

What came to bother me personally later on was the Ivy ethos that 'activism' should be limited either to lending advice to the government or working as a highly paid consultant in the private sector. What was frowned upon, yet formally tolerated as academic freedom, was civil society activism, especially if expressive of an anti-establishment slant. I was passive as a student, hardly realizing that there were public protests taking place at the time. My university student years, 1948-1955, in any event, seemed quiet to me, which reveals more about my political detachment than descriptive of reality. The major concerns that activists cared about those days were the avoidance of nuclear war, ending the Korean War, and wondering about how seriously to take Joe McCarthy's opportunism in generating a red scare hysteria. All of these political tremors by and large escaped my notice. I was still kept busy trying to detach myself from my father's anti-Communist outlook without knowing where to go on my own.

In many respects my adult life did not begin until I moved to Columbus, Ohio in the Autumn of 1955. The contours of the life that I have lived over subsequent decades took shape in those six years spent at Ohio State University as a new faculty member of the law school. It was only in this midwestern hinterland that I began to discover who I had been, who I was to become, and most of all, who I wanted to be. When accepting the offer to teach at OSU I snobbishly downgraded the prospect in advance as 'a one-year sentence to the American gulag.' I soon overcame this distasteful East Coast arrogance, convinced by the intellectual, political, and inter-personal vitality that I had experienced at Ohio State from day one.

Now after the Harvard sojourn I believed Ohio State would fill this political vacuum for the rest of my life! What the Ivy League never achieved, the Big Ten managed almost immediately, although not, as might be supposed, by its athletic exploits.

Beyond the routine I anticipated when returning to Ohio State, came the unanticipated in the form of enchantment and romance, which turned out to be as challenging as it was satisfying.

Radiant Love

When Sally Appleton entered my life, it was an entirely different story from my prior romantic attachments. This time I was the needy one, and she in full control of the chaste boundaries of our special form of intimacy. Above all, Sally made me acutely conscious of my religious boundaries. When we met, she was known to me previously only as 'a published poet.' Sally was a PhD student in English who was immensely liked and appreciated by the literature faculty. We were introduced to one another by an acquaintance from the East, Gene Lichtenstein. Gene had married the former girlfriend of my first year Yale Law School roommate. Gene, a notable character in his own right, was working as a freelance journalist when we reconnected in Columbus. He was loosely associated with *Esquire,* then aspiring to be a serious fiction writer, who gave up that ambition years later, becoming a professional therapist. Later still Gene turned up in Santa Barbara to reenter my life married to the museum director at UCSB. Gene was deeply drawn to Sally. Sally conveyed to me an ambivalence about Gene, discomforted by his unabashed secularism and otherwise indistinct character, which ran against the grain of her vibrant being. She was usually very generous toward others, almost never critical, never mean or indulging in gossip, and so this distancing from Gene seemed uncharacteristic, and her willingness to share such feelings, I treated as a gesture of trust in our new friendship.

When I met Sally, she was determined to become a nun, preparing to enter a convent after completing her OSU degree. Encountering someone resolved to live a dedicated religious life was new to me. She definitely possessed the temperament that would made such a commitment credible, yet her playful emotional responsiveness suggested other more worldly possibilities. My enduring impact on Sally's life may have been to awaken enough competing feelings as to lead her to reconsider whether life in a nunnery was the right life choice.

Sally was radiant, enchantingly lyrical, fun to be with, intelligent, nurturing, lovable, without flaw or blemish, and a social delight. Sally set high standards for herself while being somewhat skeptical about the worldliness of my background. I was partly drawn because of her intense religious commitment. I found the hot flames of her belief sensuous, while at the same time moving me closer to the altar of conversion than I could have imagined possible. Perhaps, my motives were mixed, although I did my best inwardly and outwardly to separate my feelings for Sally from a deep personal interest in exploring the possibility of becoming a practicing Catholic. Sally was herself a convert to Catholicism, fleeing an Episcopal upper-class childhood that treated church as a place to meet social peers and important people, but in ways that lacked a spiritual engagement. Destructive alcoholism and promiscuity in her family cast shadows over Sally's East Coast upbringing. It undoubtedly pushed her to seek something radically different.

Sally encouraged my belief that I might be capable of producing poems that were not a humiliation. We exchanged poems every Thursday. I was happy to do this, although I felt the pressure of producing a poem that would not be disappointing. Sally was nurturing in response yet forthright when it came to criticisms and suggestions. She made me feel that I was not wasting my time writing poems. We became otherwise close, sharing friends and cultural life. I bonded with her Catholic intellectual friends. We formed a group committed to weekly readings of Tolkien, the Oxford fabulist greatly in fashion among intellectuals at that time. When we finished reading aloud a Tolkien chapter, we often discussed the challenges of being religiously oriented in secular academic atmospheres. I recall some contact with John Noonan, later well known for his role as a federal judge with strong Catholic views, who had graduated from Harvard dissatisfied with the overall campus experience. John described his ambition to establish a first-rate university with an essential and explicit Catholic identity. Noonan did not regard either Notre Dame or Georgetown as Catholic enough or sufficiently distinguished academically to satisfy his vision.

A member of the Tolkien group, a very smart professor of philosophy, Tony Nemetz, invited me to spend a weekend with him at a Franciscan monastery near Cleveland during a retreat at which we were both asked to speak. I remember making remarks that charted my personal trajectory, and afterwards receiving a standing ovation from this highly appreciative group of men, who also responded to Tony's wit and wisdom with a comparable enthusiasm. I wanted to perform well, not only for my sake, but also because I hoped positive feedback would reach Sally's ears. I sought her affirmation of me as a person almost as much as I wanted her love.

Sally also did her best, without exerting pressure, to share her religious life with me. She had become very devoted to a parish priest in Portsmouth, Ohio. We drove several hours to attend Sunday mass at his church, and more memorably, went to a pre-Easter midnight mass and dawn private breakfast in Father Howard's private apartment. I was deeply moved by partaking in the experience, but whether glad because it brought me closer to Sally or because I was quite enthralled by the ritual occasion I will never know. Both elements were present, as was the resonance of my childhood attendance at the neighborhood church in Manhattan that allowed my Irish nanny to keep her faith alive despite being far from her native Ireland.

At some point I told Sally that I was hoping we could marry in the future. I indicated my willingness to take instruction from a local priest as the necessary preparation for any conversion to Catholicism. She was more receptive than I expected. I remember Sally saying over dinner at a restaurant that she never expected me to seek such a strong commitment, and when I did, she took it as a sign of seriousness that made a great difference to her, almost as if a grant of permission to express stronger feelings and bolder intentions. She was, in other words, more responsive to my declaration of commitment than I hoped or expected. Afterwards, I felt we were 'in love,' yet still chaste, not allowing these warm and tender feelings to be sensually expressed prior to marriage, a position new to me, but one I respected.

Resisting Catholic Temptations

A sensitive and devout young priest, Father James Cooney, in a local Columbus parish took on the task of providing pre-baptismal instruction. We met regularly to discuss Catholic faith and doctrine. I listened attentively, hoping that the process would succeed as I didn't want to disappoint Sally, nor even this priest who seemed to regard me as a sympathetic potential convert, and gave of himself fully. I knew that my relationship with Sally would come to an end if I didn't make the commitment, and yet in my own mind and hers, we didn't want this process to lose its integrity by being reduced to satisfying private and personal wishes.

Finally, in the summer of 1960, I called Father Cooney from Newport, Rhode Island, where I was lecturing as part of a summer school program at the Naval War College, and told him I was ready to be baptized as a Catholic. He seemed elated. On the plane from the East I remember being nervous and apprehensive, acting uncharacteristically distant when I accidentally met a friend on the plane.

Father Cooney was waiting for me at the airport and drove me to his parish residence where he invited me to stay for the weekend. He asked me if I would like to ask my two well-known OSU colleagues and Tolkien reading mates, Tony Nemetz and Bernard O'Kelley, if they would be willing to serve as witnesses at the baptism ceremony. Sally, naturally my preferred witness, was not around, being in residence at a writers' colony. I asked Father Jim for time to think it over. He agreed, and I retired to my room wrestling with the tension between my strong desire not to disappoint and my realization that I could not accept the whole truth of Catholic doctrine, neither its metaphysics, nor its theology. I remembered thinking that people born into such a faith do not have to go through such a commitment process unless they feel compelled to abandon their birthright identity. In the end, my Enlightenment subconscious and anti-institutionalism were more engrained than I had realized. I emerged from my bedroom, declaring that I was not ready for baptism. This gentle priest did not hide his disappointment, yet he remained compassionate and non-judgmental, as was Sally, although it would soon have a negative effect, although not immediately, on what had been the upward trajectory of our relationship.

My departure for Princeton was the definitive and irreversible rupturing event. After I received the invitation in early 1961 Sally made clear her hope that I would not accept. She reasoned that Princeton was a central hub of elite secularism, what she termed a place of 'dry learning' dedicated to preserving the established order. I had forgotten until then that Sally's conversion to Catholicism was bound up with her formative work experience and personal closeness to the Catholic Worker community founded and led by Dorothy Day, a radically progressive, charismatic figure who had exerted powerful influences on such inspirational Catholic luminaries as Thomas Merton and Daniel Berrigan. For Sally Princeton was not only a citadel of wealth and the established order, against which Dorothy Day had struggled on behalf of the poor and vulnerable, but it also likely seemed to her a return to the world of her family that had brought misery to her childhood. I didn't treat her opposition to my Princeton option very sensitively at the time, contending that her concerns were exaggerated. I was undoubtedly seeking to divert attention from my admittedly conventional career ambition to teach at a high prestige university. I also realized that my presence at Princeton would have pleased Dad had he been alive and was my final attempt to show my condescending mother and her even more condescending family that I was not, after all, a lost cause. I suppose I was also influenced by faculty friends, such as Rolly Stanger, who could not believe that I hesitated even an instant before exclaiming a joyful and expectant 'yes' when given such an opportunity.

I may have been further pushed in a Princeton direction by subconscious anxieties. Sally's purity began intimidating me as we grew closer together, especially in relation to my love for her. I felt sure that I would somehow become a disappointment, hurting her terribly, and in doing so, wound myself forever. In the back of my mind, I recognized that I was not yet ready for monogamy in either spirit or substance, and that this reality would in one way or another doom a marriage to someone who lived her ideals as fully as Sally seemed to do. In this sense, Princeton offered me an escape from both Catholicism and Sally, which I did not acknowledge to myself, but which quickly became evident. We wrote letters initially, but Sally did not want to pursue what for her had become a dead end. She soon married someone else, had children, and as far as I know, lived a quiet satisfying life in upstate New York, maintaining her strong ties to Catholic activism along the lines so vividly drawn by Dorothy Day and the Berrigans. We met only once in subsequent years when I was an expert witness at the criminal trial of several Catholic activists who had committed civil disobedience at a military base. Sally was in the audience, came to talk at the break, we exchanged pleasantries without much affect, yet her glow remained, and I have never once regretted the uplifting and lasting effects of our intimate few months.

Despite the absence of a single sensuous kiss, Sally remains my fondest romantic memory until my present wife, Hilal, never tarnished on my side by the slightest taint of disillusionment. She was supremely who she was, and there can be no greater compliment to someone who was so humanly appealing.

The Princeton Invitation

When I unexpectedly received the invitation from Princeton to spend a year at the Center of International Studies, Rolly got the news from his friend, Gardner Patterson, the dean of Princeton's Woodrow Wilson School, before I was formally contacted. Rolly instantly searched for me at the law school, finding me in the midst of teaching a seminar, knocked on the door, beckoning for me to pause the class to receive some urgent news, and come out of the room, which of course I did. I assumed the worst, that someone had died or there was an emergency.

At first, I was more stunned than excited by the invitation. It was at once an occurrence beyond my dreams and a serious threat to the life I had been composing for myself ever since arriving in Columbus. The invitation, which had a somewhat ironic academic story behind it, resulted from the encouragement of my appointment by several prominent establishment figures. These individuals, I am quite sure, later regretted this early support, as they came to regard me as an adversary rather than an ideological ally. Cold War alignments not only exhibited political passions, but also separated friends from enemies. As I write, I wonder about myself, what made these ardent supporters of mainstream thought and action, especially in relation to national security and the Cold War, view me early on as one of them. Their later distancing moves made me aware that the claims of merit-based professionalism in academic life are misleading. The real defining criterion of academic excellence is scholarly and political like-mindedness, often unconsciously exhibited. True, there were a few of us who did our best to apply objective criteria when voting on hiring, promotion, and tenure questions. Yet in retrospect I have no regrets that I was a beneficiary of misperception! It did make me wonder if I had allowed my political persona to stay in the closet too long. I 'outed' myself in the years ahead, or more accurately, the pressure of events, especially the American War in Vietnam outed me.

The OSU Footprint

My experience of Columbus and Ohio State was definitely a formative period, politically and personally. Politically, it freed me from my father's lingering conservative influence, and moved me permanently toward the left, but the independent left without ideological allegiance, doctrinal rigidity, or an organization affiliation. Personally, it gave me confidence in my ability to enchant and attract yet left me confused as to what I was seeking in 'the other,' a confusion that would persist until I met Hilal 35 years later.

When it came time to say farewell to Ohio State and Columbus, I felt speechless. My departure was framed as temporary, a one-year leave to do research and teach a single graduate course at Princeton. I left with an expectation and institutional assurance that I could return, although it was known to me and the OSU faculty that the Princeton invitation included the possibility of a permanent career opportunity and even an indication that at some future time, I would be offered a long vacant endowed chair in international law. I felt both challenged and professionally excited by the idea of being at Princeton, although I was aware that it almost certainly precluded any future with Sally, a loss that would be worsened, however much I tried to rationalize it, if I received a humbling rejection at Princeton.

With these ambivalent feelings, I set off for Princeton, curious about what lay ahead, yet still not free from self-doubt. I felt nervous about the prospect of returning to Columbus under a cloud, found wanting not only by the Princeton gatekeepers that I envisioned as medieval style gargoyles but by the love of my life up to then.

CHAPTER 8

Princeton for 40 Years

Hide and Seek

I arrived at Princeton for my visiting year, feeling a certain disbelief that after experiencing adolescent mediocrity, I was now invited to join this hallowed academic and elite learning community. At the same time, I was intent on guarding myself against a feared disappointment in the event that what felt like a flight of fancy ended in a crash landing, which seemed entirely possible. Despite this anxiety, I told others that it would be fine if I returned to OSU without ever receiving an offer of tenure at Princeton. And in some ways this sentiment, although never tested, made me less apprehensive. It felt enough for me to dip my toe in the Princeton pond without any further expectations, although quite likely being asked, however politely, to go back where I came from would have felt humbling, yet probably not disabling.

As it happened, I was given a regular faculty position at Princeton some months later without much hassle beyond being asked to give one public lecture that would be attended by those on the tenured faculty entitled to cast a vote. I was offered a three-year appointment as an associate professor without tenure, but with the assurance that the chair in international law would be kept vacant in the expectation that I would be offered this special opportunity if I received tenure, which I did three years later. I realized then, and never changed my mind, that I was extremely fortunate to fit the qualifications for this appointment to a well-endowed chair while still relatively young.

With respect to the institution, even before my arrival I was worried by Princeton's reputation for social snobbery and elitism, political conservatism, and its image as a WASP recruiting station for establishment careers, especially in finance and government. I soon realized that most of the snobbery was concentrated among the white all male undergraduates, a few genteel departments in the humanities, and, of course, the alumni, especially big donors, who felt a sense of entitlement and mission. Somewhat sheepishly, I confess that I was utterly unaware of Princeton's racist heritage, although over the years I came to know more and more about the racist skeletons adorning the Princeton closet of a hushed past. The influence of Princeton conservative alumni during my first years at the university was essentially sentimental and nostalgic; they were trying their best to keep the university the way they remembered it.

The undergraduates at Princeton were almost all white males, and mostly blond, when I arrived on campus in the autumn of 1961. Their alleged macho ethos, somewhat exaggerated, was not unfairly conveyed by a self-deprecating quip describing campus life: 'a monastery during the week, a brothel on weekends.' Although this self-description supposedly originated at Princeton, it is now used to depict campus life in many college settings.

Princeton started to change its identity in the mid-60s by taking a series of agonizing baby steps, mollifying 'tiger' loyalists by increasing the female presence one modest move at a time, so small initially as to be invisible to all but insiders. There were objections along the way, angry allegations that the Princeton president, Robert Goheen, was betraying tiger traditions by opening the university to women and minorities, which over time would change its character in fundamental ways. Unfortunately for them, fortunately for the rest of us, the tides of change were too strong, and Goheen had excellent social skills as well as stellar traditional Princeton credentials. First came a female faculty member, Suzanne Keller, a socially adept and sophisticated sociologist with flair. We quickly became friends. Then came a handful of graduate students, who could only qualify for admission if they made the rather absurd claim that *only* at Princeton could they complete their education (e.g. exotic languages offered at Princeton but not available at comparable institutions), then there arrived a sprinkling of graduate students, some of whom were admitted apparently by mistakes of the admissions office, who wrongly assumed some unfamiliar foreign names were male. These developments were trivial enough to get by almost unnoticed by the alumni or the Board of Trustees. The Board was reluctant to tangle with Princeton traditions, yet trying to be cautiously responsive to pressures for change, and adaptation to the modern ethos of racial, ethnic, and gender equality. Truly, a balancing act not pleasing to either modernizers or traditionalists, too slow and ambivalent for the former, too fast and questionable for the latter.

What mattered to the alumni, aside from sports, was the under-graduate college, which was the last part of the university community to undergo a gendered and racial facelift. It was this four-year college experience that was charismatic for many Princeton graduates, bringing them back year after year for reunions featuring intoxicated nostalgia, climaxed by the P-Rade along Princeton's Nassau Street. The marchers were clustered by graduating class in orange and black blazers custom designed for each graduating year covering a span of 75 or so years. It made a silly spectacle for non-Princetonians but for the participating alumni it offered a welcome opportunity to relive happy memories.

When women began to be admitted as undergraduates the dam of alumni opposition broke all at once even though in deference to their earlier ambivalence, the administrative process to admit women to the undergraduate class was deliberately increased at a snail's pace and overlapped with greater receptivity to Jewish and African American applicants. This process of adaptation to the values and educational pref-erences of the late 20th century might not have happened without the deeply traditional, yet enlightened, skillful, and committed leadership of Princeton's president, Robert Goheen (an embodiment of conserva-tive decency whom I came to know and admire despite our political differences). Even Goheen had his hands full for some years, dealing with the most rebelliously belligerent members of the alumni, reportedly responding to their embittered denunciations of his policies with sweet reasonableness. In the end Goheen prevailed and earned the respect and affection of all but a few unreconciled tiger loyalists on and off campus.

During the campus unrest associated with the Vietnam War, Goheen was one of the few presidents of a major university who never called the police onto the campus to quell protests, and was rightly proud of this. He kept up a friendly dialogue with those in the anti-war camp, including myself, and his genuine internationalism (he was born in India, and later served as American ambassador in Delhi after giving up the Princeton presidency), commitment to education, a peaceful world, and human rights endeared him to those few of us thought of as on 'the left,' although he himself belonged to and identified with the WASP elite that has always run the university since its founding, and despite his reform-ist efforts, seemingly trusted and felt most at home with members of the established order.

His own career was itself unorthodox, yet impressive, even glam-orous. Goheen was serving in his mid-30s as an assistant professor in the Classics Department at Princeton when he was denied the single available tenure appointment. He apparently lost out academically in a tenure battle to a young colleague in classics. Instead of having to look elsewhere for a job, in a move that was startling for staid Princeton, he was chosen by the Board of Trustees to be the next president of the university despite his young age. Upon reflection, Goheen was a brilliant choice, fitting perfectly into the wax museum image of how a Princeton president should look and behave, while at the same time turning out to be a capable manager of changing with the times. Whether he would have been selected to be president of Princeton if it had been known that he would transform the institution has never been disclosed. Possibly, he was selected precisely because he was thought to have the qualifications needed to make changes long overdue at Princeton. In any event, it happened, and Goheen was both the principal agent of change and a prince of civility during his time heading the university.

Academic life at Princeton was not very different on the surface from what I had already experienced at OSU except there was less time and inclination for friendship and what might be called 'recreational intellectual and cultural life.' The learning and sports facilities were first-rate, and the relative smallness of the campus put everything within easy reach by walking or biking, including the distance from home to office. I developed tennis and squash friends quicker than I found congenial colleagues. During this initial year I made no waves. I did my work, taught a tiny seminar in a room hidden deep in the stacks of the great Firestone Library, and rented a small house from the person I displaced as the international law teacher. Living alone, initially, with only a few friends in the town (none at the university), I was surprised to find more people on the Princeton faculty from my NYC high school, Fieldston, than from either Penn or Yale Law School, or for that matter, from Exeter or Groton, and maybe even Lawrenceville, although I never conducted a survey.

I became gradually disturbed by the way policy analysts with Washington connections were privileged over engaged citizens, and even more so, in relation to what was almost taboo, faculty civic activism. I was disturbed by these double standards, part of the unwritten code that almost all my colleagues followed whether consciously or not. It was treated as a positive credential, a sign of relevance and status, to be invited to talk or consult with the politically and financially powerful, but suspect, and politically incorrect, to self-identify as a public intellectual talking 'truth to power.' In this regard, it was always cool to be invited to speak at a Washington think tank or even better, to be on loan to any part of the national security establishment, including the CIA, or even to collaborate off camera with policymakers. It was far from cool to be perceived as a dissenter from the bipartisan consensus that set the boundaries on 'responsible' discussion. It was obvious that I was first regarded by the campus gatekeepers as a Cold War team player, perhaps because my most vocal backers when I was first appointed happened to be visibly so entrenched, and only gradually did my identity as a dissenter in the public sphere become known. When it did, I was tolerated, but soon institutionally marginalized.

True, it was the Cold War era, but aside from the ideological closure that prevailed (to call a potential faculty candidate 'a Marxist' was by itself enough to have him struck from a short list of preferred candidates); succumbing to such bias at a departmental faculty meeting on at least one occasion, I defended a candidate for a faculty appointment by saying, 'That's wrong. He isn't a Marxist, or in any way ideological.' In retrospect, I am ashamed that I resorted to this kind of reasoning, which implicitly validates the major premise of the gatekeeping faculty consensus. It now embarrasses me that I was reflecting the conformist scholarly mood that made it an academic equivalent to original sin to lend legitimacy to Marxist or even Gramscian worldviews, which should have been welcomed by an academic institution as self-confident as Princeton.

I believed then, and even more so now, that this kind of academic political correctness deprived students of potentially stimulating pedagogical contact with internationally important diverse strains of progressive thought, as well as to deny the campus community the benefits of intellectual pluralism. Of course, it was acceptable to be a critic of Marxism or Leninism in the spirit of 'know thy enemy.' On the Princeton faculty was one of the best informed and intellectually distinguished critics of Soviet ideology in the person of Robert C. Tucker. Bob became nationally known and highly respected after his multi-volume biography of Stalin was published. Bob was liberally inclined, and somewhat ironically, was closer to being my political soulmate in the 1960s than any other member of the Politics Department. Bob joined with me in publicly opposing the Vietnam War. We also collaborated in two publications advocating the denuclearization of American foreign policy, starting with the adoption of a declared 'no first use' pledge. Our efforts were published in an inhouse paper series, appearing alongside two more mainstream security specialists who opposed our denuclearizing proposals.

Both Tucker and Stephen Cohen, a brilliant lecturer and leading interpreter of contemporary Soviet thought, gave Princeton an informed, enlightened, and highly articulate understanding of Cold War theory and practice, which was unusual in that period. They were not among those who wanted to keep the academic ranks of international relations and political theory free of Marxists. Cohen and Tucker embraced a liberal discourse as if there was no other objective way of discussing political reality. It might surprise many that political philosophers and my international relations colleagues at Princeton were even more hostile to Continental European contributions to our understanding of political reality than they were to Marxism and Leninism. Walter Kaufmann, a distinguished Nietzsche scholar, was the single exception in the entire university. And he was viewed as something of a philosophical curiosity, without relevance to mainstream contemporary philosophy. He enjoyed a big following among general readers and undergraduate students, but was treated at Princeton as a quaint philosophical ornament because his professional concerns didn't coincide with the preoccupations of Wittgenstein, Quine, Rawls, and Dewey, and the accompanying 20th century canon of pragmatism, liberalism, logic, and linguistics.

There were other disquieting aspects of my early years at Princeton, including my problematic attachment to the Center of International Studies, which inconveniently happened to be the institutional sponsor of my original Princeton invitation. The Center was under the direction of Klaus Knorr, rational in intellectual style, conventional in Cold War alignment, and somewhat authoritarian as an administrator. Under his leadership the Center achieved notoriety as a leading think tank for strategic studies although located outside of Washington and not formally linked to the government. Klaus lionized such 'war thinkers' as Herman Kahn, Tom Schelling, Bernard Brodie, Albert Wohlstetter, and Alex George. Klaus was a NATO specialist, vigorously anti-Communist, and a RAND enthusiast, and as such regarded the kind of historically grounded realism of Henry Kissinger as old-fashioned and unprofessional. Klaus was a non-Jewish, anti-Nazi German émigré who wanted others to regard him as socially liberal and intellectually open-minded. He was the former, but not the latter, showing contempt for the views of those who rejected Cold War strategic studies and its ideological assumptions as the proper guides to policy formation with regard to national and international security.

Klaus endorsed the mainstream drift of strategic thought, which employed the language of Pentagon rationality, advocating effective use of nuclear deterrence doctrine and security alliances to advance American foreign policy goals, and above all, supporting the pursuit of military superiority in the Euro-centric arms rivalry with the Soviets. In such an atmosphere, I found myself squeezed between my effort to fit in at Princeton and my growing visceral discomfort with regard to an intellectual environment shaped by Cold War hawks in firm control of the academic discourse on foreign policy and national security in those years, also dominating media approaches. This group of war thinkers were extremely smart, adopting an intimidating, cool and detached analytic approach to diplomacy, strategy, and war-making that I believed could have easily ended up, if given full sway, producing unspeakable ruin for the entire world.

I find myself again apprehensive about catastrophic danger in the Trumpist era of autocrats, chauvinists, and militarists. More than even during the Cold War, the citizenry of American society has seemed politically asleep, distracted, uneducated and easily persuaded by militarists to back belligerent diplomacy. Whether the anti-racist backlash in response to the May 2020 police murder of George Floyd will translate into a less militarist international approach seems highly doubtful as the new focus of the bipartisan foreign policy consensus pushes toward a confrontation with China, which is not only geopolitically irresponsible but distracts attention from the urgencies of domestic and international issues that are pushed into the background.

I have to admit that my own intellectual and political immaturity, as well as somewhat conventional attitudes toward world affairs, led me to be silently alienated during these early years at Princeton. I lacked the confidence to be openly oppositional, and I had some doubts as to whether my discomfort with these prevailing views were well-founded, and perhaps I sometimes thought to myself that I was even wrong. Although I thought of myself as progressive after my period at OSU, to articulate dissenting ideas was a challenge I was still unable to meet. I was not yet equipped for open warfare with the strategic thinkers and political realists who dominated the discourse at Princeton. I confined myself to being a somewhat sullen semi-outsider until the Vietnam War brought my dissenting views into the open where they have remained.

For these reasons it might be expected that I would now be ambivalent about my first published book, *Law, Morality, and War in the Contemporary World* (1963). The text danced around many of the policy debates relating to national security. In the end, it advanced a rather tame, and yet, in the Cold War atmosphere, a somewhat controversial

argument for increasing the relevance of law and morality to the conduct of American foreign policy. I was still partially entrapped by the
hegemonic outlook of political realists, who believed the world operated
according to the beliefs of Henry Kissinger and George Kennan, or their
more social science-oriented brethren at the RAND and Beltway think
tanks. The core realist belief was that world history and national security
reflected hard power capabilities and confrontations, and law and morality in war/peace settings were almost irrelevant except as instruments of
hostile propaganda. This also meant that political agency and geopolitical leverage was concentrated in the war-making capabilities of major
sovereign states—an expert-guided, top-down view of democracy and
security in the late 20th century.

From such a perspective, law and morality were seen as mainly
distractions, sometimes dangerously so. Actually, among the war thinkers and grand strategists with the greatest clout, Kennan's comparative
moderation greatly lowered his influence, despite being recognized as
the most perceptive and humane analyst of global policy issues, and
earlier regarded as the principal architect of Cold War policymaking and
theorizing in its containment phase. As the years passed, Kennan became
increasingly skeptical of American military adventurism, and in turn
received criticism from the reigning war thinkers as being old fashioned
in method and out of touch with present strategic imperatives. Unlike
the Cold War militarists, Kennan refused to regard the use of nuclear
weapons and grand strategy generally in the spirit of business as usual,
really nothing more than a new intellectual puzzle testing the capacities
of the rational mind, not fundamentally different from the mental qualities needed to meet the challenges of Rubik's Cube.

In contrast, Kissinger, while not as analytically sharp or method-
ologically rigorous as the RAND group, or as literate as Kennan, was a
skilled translator of this kind of ballistic realism into a language that the
political class dominating the Council on Foreign Relations, the State
Department, and the upper reaches of the Pentagon and the intelligence
services could understand, adopt, and act upon. The published version
of a Council on Foreign Relations Study Group, *Nuclear Weapons and
Foreign Policy* (1957), written by Kissinger caused a big stir by its unabashed willingness to accept the risks and costs of fighting a limited
nuclear war in Europe rather than show any sign of giving in to Soviet
pressures or seeking something so 'crazy' as proposing the elimination
of nuclear weaponry by way of a verified disarmament treaty.

The Anti-War Moment/Movement

This process of changing Princeton from its male gendered past became intertwined in the 1960s with the temporary and unanticipated rise of student anti-war activism. The political depth of this activism was always suspect because it seemed closely connected to the vulnerability of these students, many from privileged backgrounds, to the military draft then in place, risking their injury and death in an increasingly unpopular and unnecessary war. Such self-interest undoubtedly made their commitment to political radicalism highly conditional, a response to a specific situation, and although sincere, unreliable as a guide to the future. The short-term result was a dilution of Princeton elite branding due to what traditionalists, especially in the alumni ranks, viewed as alarming displays of radicalization. I received much unwarranted and undesired notoriety in this period, mostly of an unfavorable nature as a result of angry alumni feedback abetted by some conservative faculty members who resented the campus becoming 'politicized.' Of course, change at Princeton was always resented by 'the old guard,' and regarded as nothing more worthy than a 'politically correct' challenge to the way things have always been. The Vietnam Era was different, as the anti-war atmosphere at Princeton was not directed at the university but at the government and resented by much of the alumni for that reason. I was an opportune target for the conservative pushback as outside the campus I had become the most visible opponent of the Vietnam War affiliated with the university.

Week after week in the late 1960s, the glossy *Princeton Alumni Weekly* carried letters from outraged alumni, mostly harshly critical of my role at the university, written often by Princetonians who had graduated long before I was on the faculty. They blamed me for corrupting the present generation of students by destroying their attachment to flag, church, and family. As a result of my classroom preaching, it was claimed, previously promising students had supposedly become disillusioned with what these guardians of Princeton traditions thought America should stand for. True, in this period, students did sometimes adopt a kind of romantic revolutionary politics that often did not endure much after their first week at a Wall Street bank or financial institution when they began to appreciate the opportunities awaiting them by returning to the fold, requiring only that they give up their adolescent revolt against the established social, economic, and political order. Of course, there were many variations in motivations and levels of commitment reflecting character and class/race differences and relative intensities of ambition.

Several colleagues at the university, notably Arno Mayer, Steve Slaby, Stanley Stein, and Sheldon Hackney (later President of the University of Pennsylvania, and then director of the Library of Congress) were more concretely engaged in anti-war activism on campus than I was, but less known on the outside. These faculty members acted as informal political chaperones at demonstrations and confrontations with campus security personnel. They supported initiatives of students who opposed the campus presence of the Institute of Defense Analysis, a government think tank doing classified counterinsurgency research that was perceived as organically linked to the Vietnam War. Such faculty took some personal risks by supporting student destruction of draft cards, symbolizing their denunciation of an unjust and unlawful war and their related refusal to serve in the military during the Vietnam years even if it could mean jail time or fleeing the country. While political opinions joined these faculty to students, their involvement also expressed an *in loco parenti* outlook that created feelings of responsibility to protect and support students taking political risks for progressive causes that exposed them to possible punitive retaliations.

As far as I am aware among these faculty supporters of student activism, only Steve Slaby was 'punished' by his department in the School of Engineering. His promotion to full professor was unreasonably blocked and routine leaves of absence and annual salary increases were apparently denied to him in an institutional show of disapproval. Steve was a good guy with deeply felt progressive ideals, hopelessly sincere, an earthy sensibility that created a classist mismatch within the sophisticated faculty milieu that prevailed at Princeton. Steve was plain in speech and dress, and whether accurate or not, exhibited a working-class appearance and manner more than that of a typical Ivy League professor. He was the antithesis of the J Crew tweed jacket stereotype, while Sheldon was its graceful embodiment, a talented athlete, aristocratic and of urbane manner, and blessed with elite gravitas, all of which cut him lots of career slack. It was not surprising to me that, as far as I know, Sheldon never suffered adverse consequences even as a result of standing in solidarity with students who burnt their draft cards, a federal offense, nor did Arno and a couple of others whose scholarly stature and social style lived up to Princeton's high and mighty life style profile.

My 'activism' in this Cold War period was almost totally 'academic,' and emphasized my vocational identity as an international law expert in public venues whenever the opportunity presented itself. My early opposition to the Vietnam War, combined with the respectability of being a member of the Princeton faculty and a graduate of the two top law schools, made me a useful anti-war resource in this period. I chaired the Academic Council of Lawyers Against the Vietnam War, was later prominently associated with a double-page ad in the *Washington Post* urging the impeachment of Richard Nixon for his violations of international law, twice went on peace delegations to North Vietnam (1968, 1972), testified before a series of Congressional committees concerned with aspects of the war, including the powerful Senate Foreign Relations Committee then chaired by Senator William Fulbright, the leading Congressional critic of 'Johnson's war,' spoke often at university teach-ins on and off campus, published many articles in law journals and media outlets, and received a Xeroxed copy of the Pentagon Papers directly from Daniel Ellsberg, shortly before excerpts appeared in national newspapers, including the *NY Times*. I also chaired committees concerned with war and intervention at the American Society of International Law and in this role edited a four-volume series with the title *The Vietnam War and International Law*, published by Princeton University Press between 1968 and 1975.

Perhaps, my most satisfying moment in this early experience of political engagement resulted from a visit to campus by Kenzaburo Ôe, the Japanese writer and anti-Vietnam activist, with whom I had been urged to meet by my dear friend, Yoshikazo Sakamoto, a leader of the Japanese peace movement. It was 1967, campus interest in the Vietnam War had reached a fever pitch. I managed to persuade Kenzaburo to give an extraordinary spontaneous lecture, which gathered a large audience, including from my undergraduate class. The lecture consisted of a brilliant mix of literature, autobiography, and politics, given the title '*Moby Dick, Huckleberry Finn,* and the Vietnam War.' The autobiographical element arose from Kenzaburo's disclosure that he had learned English from these two novels that were given to him by an American GI during the occupation of Japan after 1945. In halting English Ôe wove together the themes of the novels to produce a vivid tapestry, portraying the Vietnam War as American innocence gone astray (*Huckleberry Finn*) by embarking on a haunting and self-destructive ocean journey to destroy an intangible phantom evil (*Moby Dick*). This literary way of 'seeing' the Vietnam experience probed the depths of understanding of the prevalent American mood of anti-Communist obsessiveness without ever touching the hot fires of controversy. It was a stunning performance that resonated deeply with the partisan audience, and when Ôe went on to win the Nobel Prize in Literature I was thrilled on his behalf.

Such activities made me a soft target for ardent pro-war advocates, as well as 'the moral majority,' who were against the anti-war worldview, and especially its counter-culture spillover regarded as encouraging sexual permissiveness, long and dyed hair, gay rights, drugs, and hippies, to a far greater extent than they were supportive of what the United States Government was doing in Indochina. William F. Buckley was the revered godfather of a conservative movement that gathered increased momentum over the years, and owed its early impetus to Buckley, author of *God and Man at Yale* (1951), an influential attack on secular liberalism in American universities, integral to a later right-wing reaction to anti-establishment dimensions of the Vietnam Era. I became a favorite target for Buckley who wrote no fewer than four columns for the *National Review*, which he founded and edited, devoted to contending that my lack of conventional patriotism personified what had gone wrong in academic America. Buckley's attacks accused me of epitomizing those Ivory Tower professors who undermine the supposedly red-blooded nationalist sentiments and the civic conscience of students and the nation during a time of war. His invective was sharp and literate, yet ludicrous in its way, criticizing me for being the kind of elitist that he himself epitomized. Buckley, a practicing Catholic, believed that the secular liberals at universities were using the occasion of an unpopular war to undermine patterns of virtuous behavior in the American republic.

Shortly after skewering me in print on several occasions we met by chance while both waiting our turn in a government office prior to being called to testify before a Congressional committee holding hearings on human rights and the Cold War. I was astonished when Buckley greeted me as if an old friend, which instantly disarmed me. I failed even to remind him of how frequently he had demeaned my politics and character in his published columns. In real life, I guess, Buckley's aristocratic and somewhat effete social persona took precedence over his reactionary politics. He clearly relished intelligent conversation, and in that setting seemed to assume that my Princeton affiliation automatically qualified me as someone who shared enough of his worldly concerns and background to be worth conversing with, at least on such an occasion of accidental meeting. In fact, we talked congenially this once and only time. A decade or so later, I was flying to the U.S. from Sweden, and Buckley and his wife were seated near to me. I thought about re-introducing myself, and then I remembered the nasty columns and his overbearing and condescending treatment accorded most guests on his

TV show *Firing Line*. I chose to enjoy an inflight movie rather than seek his companionship.

Actually, if a distortion of minds occurred in this period of campus radicalism, the alumni concern should have been reversed. It was the radicalized students that 'corrupted' me, as their passions were far stronger and better articulated than were my rather mild and realist anti-war ideas and left liberal beliefs. I did find this turn toward progressive political activism by students at Princeton very encouraging, even as I suppressed my own concern that the campus mood was nothing more than a temporary self-interested deviation from elite norms, and acted as if, and certainly hoped, that this progressive current would only grow stronger with the passage of time.

As a known critic of the Vietnam War I was frequently invited to play a leading role in campus events that involved war and foreign policy, and I rarely refused such invitations. But I was very wrong in supposing that this surge of campus activism expressed an irreversible development that would continue to evolve in desirable directions. I had the mistaken, and in retrospect naïve idea, that the failure of the Vietnam War had enough momentum to promote future progressive alternatives in America. I later realized how out of touch I was then with an American political culture that remained disposed toward endorsing nationalistic, militarist, and capitalist priorities, while being slow to overcome internal discriminatory injustices associated with race, gender, and class. Opinion makers in American society were always eager to forget past injustices and were irritated by those outliers like myself who were seen as intent on reminding the public of wrongs and crimes.

So, despite apprehensions, I underestimated how contingent and temporary was this activist campus political mood, and how dependent on a special set of conditions destined to disappear as soon as the guns fell silent. This mood never returned with comparable intensity during my time at the university, possibly because never after Vietnam was the self-interest of these privileged students subject to a life-threatening challenge. After the Vietnam War societal normalcy was quickly restored in the country, especially after the draft was abolished and replaced by a recruited professional, all-volunteer military. Careerism and elitism were almost immediately reseated at the head table of university propriety, bringing back into fashion the 'bicker' process used at Princeton to channel 'eating club' invitations to favored students. The eating clubs, sanctuaries for the Old Princeton composed of white male, upper class, genteel racism, were Princeton's way of ensuring that those students who qualified would not miss out on the alcoholic and erotic indulgences and social networking of Greek frat houses of 'lesser' universities across the land without being demeaned as mere 'fraternities.' Eating clubs kept Princeton's students organizationally apart from these national social networks while creating its own more exclusivist version, somewhat analogous to 'social registers' that set apart the highborn and especially their children from the rest of us.

Conservatism at Princeton in its teaching and scholarly dimensions, as distinct from the political rightest tilt of its Board of Trustees and older alumni, was mainly expressed epistemologically, by way of an institutional reluctance to alter the traditional curriculum and pedagogic style. These attitudes were accompanied by a stubborn refusal to include innovative learning methods or emergent disciplines as courses or fields, reinforced by hostility to such trendy academic fashions as photography, meditation, film studies, and winemaking. When it came to politics, I soon discovered that there were some genteel departments (English, History) whose Old Princeton ethos endorsed the interplay of social, intellectual, and political conservatism, while on broad social issues like desegregation and foreign policy, the center of gravity on campus was closer to what I would describe as 'Cold War liberalism.'

What did induce rather widespread faculty disapproval, as already suggested, was my partisanship in public arenas, taking the form of activist citizen engagement on controversial issues. Policy advocacy by a faculty member was regarded as an unwelcome departure from the European (or Weberian) conception of the professor as properly politically neutered so far as *public* stance is concerned. Of course, this neutering was historically part of the emancipatory struggle in Europe to achieve autonomy for education in relation to kings and reigning prelates. It reflected the compromise reached in the struggle to separate secular learning and knowledge generally from the hegemonic and stifling encroachment on classroom freedoms by nationally influential churches, especially the Catholic Church, and monarchies.

I was first drawn to European intellectuality as an undergraduate at Penn when I felt a literary/philosophical/emotional kinship with Nietzsche, Jaspers, Sartre, Camus, Teilhard de Chardin, and Derrida far more than with Locke, John Stuart Mill, Hobbes, and Dewey. Because of its social democratic theorizing, I tried my best to like the Frankfurt School of Adorno, Horkheimer, and Habermas but never felt stimulated enough by their work or in their presence, and despite several diligent efforts never managed a serious reading of their main works. Except for

Adorno, with his brilliant turn of mind, the others struck me, perhaps wrongly, as humanist extensions of Enlightenment rationalism rather than the kind of spiritually informed radicalism that I was seeking, although when these likes and dislikes took shape, I was still searching. I continued my quest for a political and cultural identity that I could call my own, tiring of rolling with the punches.

"In the Nation's Service"

Princeton's defining ideal—'Princeton in the nation's service' (a phrase attributed to the recently discredited Woodrow Wilson)—was generally understood to mean that it was fine for the Dean of Students to recruit undergraduates for the CIA or for faculty members to act as regular consultants to RAND or the Pentagon. It was sternly frowned upon for faculty members to show support for draft evaders or to oppose on-campus CIA recruitment. Later on, even involvement in the BDS Campaign,[ii] which was tied to the anti-apartheid movement directed at South Africa, became controversial if lines were crossed between quiet protest marches and token civil disobedience. I later realized that I had become administratively marginalized in university life because of my activism as soon as my stand against the Vietnam War gained wider public attention, while often obtaining selective back channel support at the higher echelons of the university. I was told off the record one time by a sympathetic administrator, in a tone midway between a putdown and a compliment, that my activism was costing Princeton $1 million per year.

Being somewhat of a campus pariah was not altogether a bad thing. It freed me over many years from tedious *university* administrative assignments (although not from departmental level chores), which would have meant boring committee meetings and hours spent drafting reports. I am not sure why such a distinction is drawn, but maybe because departmental activities are not noticed outside their immediate scope, while university-wide visibility is regarded as a kind of vote of confidence by those who run the institution.

Faculty publication escaped informal censorship unless perceived to have a 'Marxist' slant, and even then, occurred only indirectly and

---

ii BDS stands for boycott, divestment, and sanctions. It was a worldwide campaign endorsed by the UN to exert economic pressure on the government of South Africa to abandon the policies and practices of apartheid. A second BDS Campaign was initiated by coalition of 170 Palestinian NGOs in 2005 without UN backing and with the goal of achieving Palestinian rights under international law. This Palestinian BDS Campaign has been attacked in the United States and Western Europe as anti-Semitic, which its organizers and supporters vehemently deny.

at pre-tenure levels, often via self-censorship. If it did occur it would be manifested in subtle forms of academic ostracism. Someone intrepid enough to think against the ideological grain would almost never have gotten past Ivy League gatekeepers in the first place.

If faculty research and published work went beyond the realm of the politically feasible (as measured by Washington standards), it was treated as 'utopian' and swiftly dismissed by the academic mainstream as the stuff of dreams or fuzzy exercises in self-indulgence, not worthy of serious academic notice. Research support and professional praise were reserved for those in the social sciences who built formal models or contributed empirical or quantitative studies that exhibited data-driven diligence along with a reliance upon 'scientific' methodologies. It was also possible to dine with the stars of political and legal thought if perceived as elaborating upon the pragmatism of John Dewey and the liberalism of John Rawls.

My enthusiasm for and insistence upon an American foreign policy shaped by international law and responsive to widely shared ethical principles did not fit the prevailing template used to demarcate the realm of the feasible. Such advocacy crossed two red lines. It was perceived as being at once radical critique and utopian conjecture, making me something of an oddity at an establishment outpost like Princeton where 'reason' was conflated with 'realism,' and realism was implicitly concerned with upholding American global scale interests. My advocacy of legally constrained realism was mostly regarded by policy-minded gurus as an irresponsible example of 'thinking outside the box' of academic 'group think,' especially in relation to the rising sub-field of 'security studies.' I pondered, mostly to myself, 'why not peace studies?' Although I could anticipate the cynical answer, I never stopped asking myself the question, and waited until the brilliantly creative Norwegian peace thinker, Johan Galtung, provided convincing answers by fleshing out the contours of a peace and justice worldview.

Unlike such supposedly loose cannons as Noam Chomsky and Howard Zinn, who could be scorned by 'experts' as amateurs, I had to be more overtly discredited given my professionalism with respect to international law and international relations. It made critics focus on my allegedly utopian or contrarian attitudes toward the world rather than my lack of relevant credentials.

I remember being pulled aside after several years at Princeton by Carl Kaysen, formerly of MIT, then Director of Princeton's Institute for Advanced Studies, which became world renowned after giving wartime sanctuary to Albert Einstein and a cohort of extremely distinguished refugee physicists and mathematicians. Carl was known at Princeton as an overbearing charter member of 'the best and brightest,' that is, JFK's Cambridge brain trust. It was this self-anointed group that dreamed up the Vietnam War, and then apparently unsuccessfully tried to reverse course just prior to Kennedy's assassination.

Carl, with only thinly disguised condescension, told me after a university speakers' dinner that my views on Vietnam would have more impact if I stopped 'preaching to the choir,' (that is, rallies and teach-ins) and instead took a train to Washington on a weekend to talk discreetly with Nick Katzenbach, then Deputy Secretary of State. I listened politely, and went my way without explaining why I would never do that, despite having a fondness for Nick, whom I had originally known as a Mac follower while a student at Yale Law School and then as an imaginative and challenging scholar who explored the law/politics interface in collaboration with Morton Kaplan while teaching at the University of Chicago School of Law.

In the social sciences acclaim for faculty accomplishments was harder to come by—one path not taken by me, but by many colleagues who gained fame, outside offers, and even remunerative consultancies by working on public issues of contemporary interest in a non-judgmental either/or manner. As a practical matter this meant putting one's head neither in the sand nor in the clouds, that is, gaining relevance to the lifeworld by sticking to the feasible, while relying on data sets, formal models, and professing standard policy views, foregoing radical critiques of the status quo or affirming revolutionary expectations about the future.

To some slight extent, I realized that Carl was possibly correct if my only goal was to influence public policy rather than strengthen the democratic will to action of an anti-war crowd. But I had no illusions that even if I adopted insider tactics it would make an iota of difference. I had no constituency and my views were not shared by many of the best-known international law experts. My status as a mere professor was far from sufficient to bend even slightly the views of those policy wonks who make things happen in Washington or officials who had access to classified cable traffic, who were usually, in any event, telling bureaucrats in Washington what they wanted to hear. These officials already knew what I had to say and had little interest in being lectured to by an external adversary. Many top bureaucrats privately realized that things were not going well in Vietnam, but still lacked the political will to steer the ship of state in a different direction and suffer a hawkish backlash for doing so. Contrary to Carl's advice, I believed then and now that policy changes come from pressures from below and not from the rational good sense of those in charge. It is the people that make major changes in policy happen, not those who control the machinery of government, who just keep things moving along.

I recall listening to an off-the-record talk by George Ball, an establishment stalwart, a highly influential champion of an Atlanticist and Euro-Pacific alliance approach to foreign policy during the Cold War period, a week or so after he resigned from a top post at the State Department. He told an elite audience at the Council on Foreign Relations, that 'I only began to understand the Vietnam War after I stopped reading the cables.' This was a rare example of anti-war candor by a prominent member of the ruling political class. It reinforced the right-wing lament at the time that the Vietnam War was 'lost' in American living rooms or due to the simplistic qualms of liberal elites, and not on the battlefields of Indochina. Ball was no defector. He was a dedicated and decorated liberal internationalist and chided me angrily once in public, when I questioned the wisdom of the extensive network of American military bases in the Pacific region, especially those in Japan. For Ball the stability of world order in the Cold War period rested on the shoulders of America's global military presence and security alliances, and raising doubts about this rarely challenged tenet of U.S. foreign policy amounted to intellectual treason on my part, or worse, geopolitical idiocy.

I never knew Carl Kaysen that well (the university and Institute of Advanced Studies didn't have much to do with one another), but I had some understanding of his problems as head of the prestigious center. Carl was a quintessential Cold War liberal and public policy profession-al, neither respected nor liked by the math/science core at the Institute who believed their intellectual community should be purist in the sense of avoiding current events and involvements with transient government policy. They correctly understood that Carl was afflicted with that Cambridge syndrome dubbed 'Potomac Fever.' In effect, he was accused of being more interested in receiving a summons to return to govern-ment service in Washington than in raising funds to facilitate a scholarly breakthrough by an Institute member, or by celebrating receipt of a Nobel Prize by one of its members. Carl was one of those typically artic-ulate policy wonks who sometimes gave the impression of treating the scholarly life as 'passing time' until 'real work' was available on Capitol Hill or at the Pentagon or White House. Those were the places where things got decided, not the blah, blah of long faculty club luncheons or scholarly tomes that were stacked on rarely visited library shelves. Only a working arrangement with U.S. Government could satisfy the Kaysen cohort of ambitious policy intellectuals, or so it seemed.

Kaysenites were also devoted internationalists, especially with respect to neoliberal economic policy. The World Bank and IMF were thus viewed as valued professional venues for those young persons who harbored ambitions to be effective in the public sector. Their real-world influence was endorsed intellectually and politically. By way of contrast the UN was seen by these top-drawer policy intellectuals as a bureaucratic dead end suitable for 'losers' in the power/wealth games that so entranced power elites.

To be sure, the math/science group suffered from their own blind spots and a kind of sectarian absolutism. André Weil, brother of the French philosopher and religiously oriented seer, Simone Weil, surprised me one day with a call suggesting lunch; he wanted to talk about the proposed appointment to the Institute of Robert Bellah as a permanent social science fellow, a prospect strongly backed by Kaysen. Unknown to Weil, it happened that Bellah was a friendly acquaintance of mine. We had spent a lively week together in Portugal as 'resource persons' for a group of religious leaders committed to promoting peace in the Middle East. Weil apparently hoped he could persuade me to join him in opposing Bellah's appointment.

As it happened, on this occasion, unlike his advice on influence-peddling on government policy, I shared Kaysen's enthusiasm for Bellah. As a result, I disappointed Weil as I believed Bellah deserved this affiliation with the Institute. I was also put off by Weil's aggressive style that recalled prior joustings with Norman Podoretz and Irving Kristol, founding editors of *Commentary* magazine. Weil seemed to have a larger goal as he let on that he was engaged in a zero-sum plan to oust Kaysen from his position as the director of the Institute. With respect to Bellah, Weil's petulant vendetta was being carried out at the expense of a fine UC Berkeley scholar who specialized in the sociology of religion, a person of the highest character, with a world reputation whose published work was widely read and admired beyond the confines of his specialty.

I recall Weil's dismissive and entirely unwarranted rejection of Bellah's scholarly merit at the end of our lunch: 'I know that I am not a sociologist, but my sister Simone Weil was, and I surely know how to tell the difference between an "A" an "F" when I see work that addresses her issues.' This was a bold and bitter statement that bordered on the absurd given his insistence that Bellah's exceptional scholarly achievements deserved an F. It was disillusioning for me to witness a famous mathematician such as Weil sink to this level in carrying on his petty struggle against Kaysen. Perhaps, his best days as a mathematician were behind him, and he was now devoting his formidable brain to more attainable ends.

Among those participating with myself and Bellah in the workshop in Portugal, I especially enjoyed the presence of Father Theodore Hesburgh, then President of Notre Dame, always approachable and dedicated to achieving a peaceful and just world order. I subsequently had frequent connection with Father Ted who became interested in and supportive of the WOMP world order project, which had long occupied me. His private passion seemed far more constructive than Weil's effort to block Bellah. Father Ted's highest policy priority was to have Jerusalem declared and accepted as 'an international city' with full and equal access to its sacred sites enjoyed by the three Abrahamic religions. He was at once worldly, decent, and pragmatic, religious without being dogmatic or outwardly spiritual, and someone who seemed to prefer listening intently than to professing his own views. Father Ted had that rare ability to work both sides of the aisle, retaining the respect and affection of all, and not always giving away the cards held in his own hand.

In my experience, I contrast Father Ted with another Catholic stalwart, Father Miguel D'Escoto Brockmann, of Nicaragua. Father Miguel was fiercely partisan, progressive, and spiritual, a leading contributor to liberation theology. He became the Foreign Minister in the original Sandinista government of Nicaragua after it came to power following a long struggle against the Somoza gangster dynasty that had ruled and impoverished the country for decades. I had the opportunity in the early 1980s to work closely with Father Miguel for a few days in NYC during the preparation of the Nicaragua Case prior to its formal presentation to the International Court of Justice in The Hague. Miguel was for me and many others an inspirational figure. He became President of the UN General Assembly between 2008-09, appointing me to his formal panel of advisors. When I was expelled from Israel in December of 2008, Miguel offered to organize a supportive press conference at UN Headquarters to give me the opportunity to give the media my version of the events, which was important, given that Israel's official explanation of my expulsion was misleading, dishonest, and published widely without hearing my side of the story. Unfortunately, I declined the offer, exhausted from the strain of my experience, and eager to return home to

California. I regretted my lack of moral stamina, as a press conference under UN auspices might have been a useful platform from which to tell my side of the story, which was being distorted and misreported by mainstream media.

After his death Fordham University established an annual lectureship honoring Miguel, celebrating the memory of this extraordinary man. It was my honor to be invited to give the inaugural lecture. I chose as my theme 'The Spiritual Sources of Legal Creativity,' which was a sympathetic account of Father Miguel's insight into the progressive potentialities of international law. Such an outlook was not a widely appreciated possibility among UN diplomats who were mostly trained to believe that hard power geopolitics ruled the world.

Miguel and Ted were anti-types, yet each achieved a kind of human perfection in their own special and memorable way. It was my great privilege to have known them both rather well over a period of many years. I never felt comfortable addressing them either as 'Father Ted' or 'Father Miguel' or as 'Ted' and 'Miguel.' Neither form of naming felt right, one too formal, the other not sufficiently respectful. I tried my best to find a middle ground, relying on the more formal mode when in the company of others, especially strangers, and becoming more informal when alone or with those in their inner circle.

Pedagogic Ups and Downs

Most of my experiences with students and colleagues over the years were positive, and a source of satisfaction. Princeton required every undergraduate to write a senior thesis in the field of their major. Usually this went smoothly, but I had one memorably disillusioning experience during my teaching life at Princeton, which reveals what can go terribly wrong, causing a hurtful event for an entirely innocent student.

A few students were either too self-confident to invite feedback on their thesis while doing their research and writing, giving me a final product on a take it or leave it basis, or so insecure they wanted continuous feedback that caused me some frustrating handholding moments. If I had to choose, I preferred working with those students suffering from over-confidence, hoping for the best. Of course, most of my thesis students were situated between these extremes. It was sometimes easier for me to establish an enjoyable student/teacher rapport with women, especially those with charm, composure, and inquiring minds, but quite often my connections with male students turned out to be more lasting and enriching. Although my advising role was generally satisfying, this one terrible experience involving student/faculty/administrative relations seems worth discussing in some detail because it illustrates the fragility of academic due process at even a great and secure university and it involved such an abuse of grading discretion as to seem an exaggeration, if I had not had the experience myself.

This concerned a very gifted undergraduate who happened to be the niece of the celebrated *New Yorker* writer, John McPhee, who was teaching nonfiction writing at Princeton. Jean was a high performing Woodrow Wilson School major who chose me as her thesis advisor, and sadly paid a high price for doing so. Her topic concentrated on explaining and assessing Marxist ideas about alienation. She worked hard, and produced a text I found illuminating, well informed by scholarly sources, as well as clearly written, documented, and organized. I unhesitatingly evaluated her performance as a clear 'A.'

Each faculty member was expected to do a certain number of 'second readings' of theses of which they were not the supervisor. Marion Levy, an abrasive reactionary sociologist who made a point of publicly insulting his adversaries, skilled in acerbic debate, and incensed by even a hint of Marxist influence, chose this thesis from those available for second readings as was his right. The fact that he had been a vindictive and very vocal critic of my anti-war role during the Vietnam period should, of course, have made no difference in his evaluation of the thesis or if he felt unable to be objective, he should not have chosen to evaluate this student's work. He did know that Jean was my student, and I half expected that this would result in a snide remark or two, but I never dreamed that it would result in giving a completely unfair grade to this fine student. I should have known better. The only plausible interpretation is that Marion chose this opportunity to vent anger at me by giving her thesis the demolition grade of 'F.'

The student, Jean McPhee, was understandably devastated by the grade, and I, infuriated. I was at first frustrated by not knowing what to do, fearing my impotence given the grading autonomy normally accorded professors, however arbitrary their assessments of student work might be. Every senior thesis was subject to a second reading and grading by someone other than the supervisor, with the final grade determined by averaging the two grades. I felt that this was a flagrant and altogether unacceptable and cowardly abuse of faculty discretion. And worse, it carried a private intra-faculty battle into the delicate and normally fully insulated process of faculty/student grading practice.

The system generally works because few faculty members have so little control over their emotions and private peeves as to abuse their discretion in such an extreme and obvious manner. Even after many years this incident stands out as a transparently inappropriate effort to embarrass and shame another faculty member by victimizing an entirely innocent student. In most circumstances such inappropriate behavior is more subtle, for instance, giving a thesis of this sort an undeservedly low grade of, say, B+, but a judgment safely within the bounds of bureaucratic discretion, and for this reason impossible to challenge.

Long before this encounter, Marion had assumed the role of being my personal nemesis in campus settings, despite befriending me when I arrived at Princeton, supposedly admiring my professional credentials as law-trained. He was often sadistically overbearing toward others at faculty seminars, humiliating even established scholars by acerbically complaining of the imprecision of their conceptual definitions on which their arguments and analyses hinged or mounting a rather petty attack on the quality of their documentation as not based sufficiently on native language sources. James Rosenau, one of the most influential international relations scholars of his generation, was in those years on the faculty of nearby Rutgers and invited to participate in these weekly faculty seminars at Princeton. Jim, who became my good friend, was a particularly hapless target of Marion in these weekly faculty seminars, vulnerable to such academic gamesmanship because he lacked Ivy polish and verbal fluency to counter such overbearing onslaughts of deliberately destructive word play that deflected conversation from the serious sides of the work being discussed.

Jim was a far more imaginative and consequential international relations scholar than Marion ever became in his then trendy sociology sub-field of 'modernization' studies. In retrospect, I suspect that Marion's low level of scholarly performance helps explain the adoption of his vitriolic style of interaction with colleagues and students, which succeeded in diverting attention from his own shortcomings. Marion was little more than a highly stylized fake, flaunting his Texas background and conservative affectations by pretentious life-style choices. He walked around campus accompanied by massive pedigree dogs and boasted about keeping a pet boa at home, wore tailored Saville suits, expensive ties and even a diamond studded tiepin.

Marion was a loyal protégé of Talcott Parsons, the famed system-building Harvard sociologist whose abstractions and conceptual framework were then fashionable, and influential with many talented future scholars seeking a sophisticated theoretical framework for their research. It also seemed timely as linked to the modernization craze that was being avidly promoted at Harvard, MIT, and Princeton, as capitalism's answer to Marxism in the Cold War struggle to control the ideological orientation of development studies adopted by countries in what was then known as 'The Third World.' Marion fit perfectly into this ideological groove, which was part of the West's effort to win favor with the countries of Asia, Africa, and Latin America. If it ended up losing the ideological struggle, Plan B came to the fore. It was at that point that the CIA was expected to turn things around in the desired direction by regime changing covert interventions as happened in several countries, including Iran, Guatemala, and Chile. Each instance of such covert regime-changing intervention produced massive abuses of human rights and prolonged suffering for the peoples of these countries whose sovereign rights were being trampled upon for the sake of American geopolitical priorities.

After being initially immobilized by the sheer brashness of Marion's action, I realized that my best option in these dismal circumstances was to appeal to the Dean of the Faculty at Princeton, and seek his guidance, and hopefully his intervention. In retrospect, perhaps I might have done better by following the chain of command, first seeking advice and guidance from the Dean of the Woodrow Wilson School, with whom I had a cordial relationship. It puzzles me that I seem never to have even considered this less escalating option. The administrative overlord of the faculty at the time was Aaron Lemonick, brother of an All-American football star at Penn while I was student there. I found Aaron to be a person exuding superficial warmth but possessing a spine of honey.

Marion in those years was a formidable and intimidating figure on campus, rhetorically forceful and often demeaning opponents in shrill debate, indulged and appreciated by the university administration during this period of ferment due to his willingness to affirm a politically incorrect devotion to conservative verities about preserving the purity of higher education in the face of Vietnam-induced disorder. For so be-having, Marion was especially liked by closet reactionaries and anti-left members of the Princeton world, what was then being called 'the old Princeton.' Aaron politely listened to my indignant complaints about Marion's outrageous behavior, responding by doing his best to find some non-confrontational middle ground. I remember being unyielding to the extent of causing him visible discomfort.

In the end Aaron proposed a compromise, an unprecedented 'third reading' of the thesis. Perhaps with no malice intended he proposed another anti-anti-war colleague, Paul Sigmund, an ardent Cold War, anti-Marxist devout Catholic, married to the daughter of a Congressional leader in the Democratic Party from the South, and frequently rumored to have himself CIA connections with regard to his specialty, Latin America. Paul also probably didn't want to offend Marion or the Princeton administrative establishment, but at least he recommended that Jean be given a grade of B+, which became Jean's final grade. In some practical sense this was an acceptable resolution from the institution's point of view, but not emotionally satisfactory for either the student or myself. It was an unjust outcome of an ugly interference with academic protocol. She left Princeton in a mood of understandable bitterness despite being a highly touted and extremely popular honors student who had, up to this instance of acute disillusionment, cherished her Princeton experience. She went on to Harvard Law School, and I was told she finished third in her class. I never forgave Marion for this incident, and its progression, from start to finish, exhibiting the worst side of uncontrolled ideological partisanship and personal hostility.

I sometimes allowed myself to wonder what would have happened if the situation had been reversed, and I was the second reader punishing Marion's favorite advisee with an F on his or her thesis! I had little doubt that I would have been, deservedly, sternly chastised and disciplined, possibly suspended, and the incident treated far more harshly if made public. It would have been red meat for that remnant of Old Princeton on the faculty, administration, and among the alumni who were always seeking evidence of intolerance by the supposedly liberal biases of the faculty. In retrospect, the university as an institution did nothing evil in this instance. Its response to my way of thinking was wishy washy and without principle, adopting the role of crisis manager rather than stepping in to overcome manifest injustice.

It is quite possible that someone other than Lemonick might have handled the situation in a more satisfactory, less bureaucratic, manner that included at least the censure of Marion and the voiding of his grade, sending a constructive message to the faculty about either favoritism, or as here, its reverse.

I mention this incident in such detail because it so clearly illustrates how students can suffer when a faculty member acts from personal resentments or ideological bias in such an irresponsible manner. What happened here with a thesis grade also occurs in other contexts, and often skews the evaluation of junior faculty members or candidates for appointment in ways that were rarely subject to challenge or exposure. I should not leave the impression that this was standard operating procedure at Princeton or elsewhere, but that the modes of assessment in academic setting are often either secret or subjective in ways that allow for undetected and unchallengeable manipulation, and seem exempt from procedures of accountability. This makes relations of trust and adherence to self-imposed standards of integrity so vital. When these qualities are not robust in an academic culture, bad things are bound to happen.

Living and Loving

My living arrangements at Princeton during my second year at the university started off more unevenly than I could have imagined. When I had come for a preliminary round of interviews a year earlier, I had met a woman in her early 60s, a free-lance historian, who had also graduated from Fieldston a generation before me, but quickly sought to take me beneath her wing. Jeannette Mirsky was full of social and political enthusiasm, a childless and partnerless Jewish mother-in-waiting ready to bond with, and almost adopt, fledgling intellectual wayfarers like myself. She was scheduled to leave for a research trip to Asia, to write a book on the Silk Road that was never finished. She solicited me to become her tenant. Jeanette was a classic auto-didact, without advanced degrees, highly intelligent and studious, yet deeply aggrieved by lacking any formal affiliation in such a status-saturated milieu as Princeton.

Jeannette put on stunning displays of bravado directed at persons of intellectual standing in the academic world to demonstrate that she knew more about their specialty than they did. She was short, plump and definitely plucky and somewhat overbearing, a bit humdrum in her 1920s wardrobe and sporting an enthusiastic version of non-committal politics, neither left nor right nor even in between, yet rarely in doubt as to who and what was right and wrong in public life.

When I arrived at Princeton, I was initially glad to be sharing her comfortable apartment below the eaves of a three-story building, and above the offices of a national insurance company, well-situated on Nassau Street, Princeton's only main thoroughfare, an easy walk to the campus. Jeannette welcomed me to her apartment as if I were her favorite nephew, a close relative of hers since birth. Jeannette kept postponing her departure, evidently assuming that her companionship and cooking, expressions of generosity given out of good will without any increase in my monthly rental bill, made her continued presence a gift rather than a burden that was causing me mounting distress. As she was protective, warm, showering compliments and serving home-cooked food, I felt ungracious and socially awkward about showing my displeasure. But when hints began to drop that she was considering postponing her research trip altogether, alarm bells screeched. My anxiety at such a prospect approached panic levels. As I badly wanted and needed privacy, one of us had to leave, and I hoped it wouldn't be me.

This intensifying concern finally induced me to gather just enough courage to remind Jeannette as gently as possible that I had rented her apartment with reasonable assumption that she as landlady would be gone, and I would have the place to myself. Despite my efforts to be diplomatic, she was visibly hurt, but soon moved out and on. I believe that if I had not finally disclosed my feelings, allowing the situation to persist, she might have remained for the entire year, convincing herself along the way that I needed her, and appreciated, maybe even came to depend on her caretaking role and emotional support. Such views were not entirely wrong. In some ways she was a great gift to a lonely and shy comparative newcomer to a town like Princeton, especially someone like myself, who lacked most of the social skills needed to overcome the formalities and pretensions of the place.

Initial Contact

I remember having no friends living in Princeton, except my undergraduate flame from Penn, Renée, by then married to a psychiatrist from Luxembourg, Paul Weber, who was ironic, clever, and almost anti-intellectual in ways that were obviously demeaning and hurtful for Renée. Her marriage struck me as one of those life choices that made no sense, and by the time I came to Princeton, its shortcomings were clearly bothering Renée. Our friendship appeared to others as a sensual flirtation, but she was reluctant and I was diffident, and our friendship remained within the bounds of bourgeois propriety. Renée, as a refugee from Hitler's Germany, escaping with her sister, never outlived that trauma but seldom mentioned it. Her PhD was devoted to Martin Heidegger, who she later unconditionally repudiated from a philosophic angle rather than the usual dismissal based on his distressing political opportunism and human insensitivity that he crudely and cruelly exhibited during and after the rise of Hitler. In her scholarly work, she replaced this Nazi sympathizer with devotion to the thought and practices of Krishnamurti, as well as other Indian mystics. She adopted a spiritualized reading of Plato and became a celebrated teacher for courses in comparative religion and philosophic tradition.

And then Naphtali Afriat came along, also an 'adopted' child of Jeanette's, and sometimes accompanied in his social life by his lovesick youngish landlady, Agnus. They lived apart on the Griggs Canal a few miles north of Princeton, yet rural and remote, and were not exactly a couple, yet often together, and always a sight to see, she with a young body and a sense of surprise, 'Oh, what will you do next, you crazy man?' And he, feeling affirmed by her warmth and attachment, seemingly comfortable having her at his side. An odd bonding to be sure, yet without doubt, a bonding.

Naphtali was socially uninhibited. He would stare unabashedly at any woman with long dark hair or arresting eyes even if seated across the room in a restaurant. He would first utter a comment to me without the slightest scruple, 'Doesn't her face remind you of a Renaissance painting?' I learned that this sort of comment was the prelude. Before the meal was over, Naphtali would approach her table, introduce himself with a smile, totally ignoring the presence of a male companion, likely husband or partner, he would say with startling boldness— 'I would like to meet you for coffee. Could you give me a phone number?' The brashness of Naphtali's approach was so gauche as to be usually disarming, and the couple on such occasions looked at one another, presumably not knowing whether to laugh or call the headwaiter over to get rid of this foolish lout. Yet the woman accosted usually smiled, and more surprisingly, often discreetly imparted her phone number on a scribbled note. What, if anything, happened in these incidents I never found out, but the door was seemed left ajar. Of course, such advances in the 'MeToo' era would be undoubtedly classified as sexual harassment, and someone disposed to act as Naphtali did, would probably be somewhat hesitant before acting on such indiscreet impulses. Actually, it was my impression that Naphtali was 'a womanizing aesthete' lacking a single predatory bone in his entire body but delighting in giving credence to the mysteries of his overheated romantic imagination.

Despite these eccentric ways, Naphtali was a valued friend, brilliant in his skill at combining numbers, ideas, and artistic drawings, making results look appealing to the eye while elegantly conveying his thoughts in a highly condensed form. Naphtali became deeply concerned with various dangers he associated with population growth, convinced that he had something profound to impart, although I could never figure out what it was. While wandering about, relying on endearing forms of 'social incorrectness,' engaged in a perpetual search for female flowers in bloom, he finally found what he was looking for, an apparently compliant Italian countess who gave birth to a son, brought up in Siena and Ottawa as if a child of nobility, probably unaware that such pretensions of nobility were out of fashion. Naphtali was concerned not only with the maladies of the world, but also with how he might live as an aristocrat, not crassly materialistic, but with an unfailing self-amused irony that made all that he did, merge in the rarefied atmosphere of an unforgettable and distinctive friendship.

A Few Concluding Words

To be sure, 40 years at Princeton was much more than is conveyed by this sequence of anecdotes chosen to identify salient features of my generally ambivalent experience. All along, I felt it to be a great privilege to teach at such a truly distinguished center of learning. During the whole four decades, I never entered a lecture hall or seminar room without feeling nervous and apprehensive, and at the same excited by this opportunity to talk to and with gifted and motivated students. It was always challenging, and most often enjoyable. I even came to look forward to the signature three-hour graduate seminars in the Politics Department and the Woodrow Wilson School. A great university is also a cultural milieu, and there were always opportunities to listen to the finest minds, greatest poets, and watch the most memorable films, as well as hear from political leaders and outstanding writers. In this respect, Princeton put on a continuous cultural festival of the highest quality if only I was able to handle demands on my time so that I could take advantage of what was available. I never managed to partake more than a small sample selected in ways that reflected my interests and affections, my pleasure tempered by many tantalizing offerings that were forsaken because of deadlines, fatigue, and social distractions.

This long period at Princeton naturally had its ups and downs, especially with regard to my pro and con relations toward immediate administrative leaders at the departmental level. I was fortunate to have the amenities that only a rich university can provide—June Garson, an extraordinary secretary eased my life on a daily basis for more than 25 years, and did so with grace and humor; research assistants who were helpful in a variety of ways, and even a travel budget that let me do things connected with scholarly projects that made me understand that libraries are the beginning and end of research, but what is often most valuable is what lies in between. I was the beneficiary of a series of fabulous research assistants over the years, some becoming valued friends: especially, Claudia Damon, who cast light where she walked and Janet Lowenthal, whose many skills included editorial prowess that rescued my prose from disrepute while often managing to raise my daytime spirits to dizzying heights.

I hope that I have not left impressions of discontent and disappointment. Overall, I lived a life so satisfying in meaning and enjoyment while at Princeton that I could not have imagined it possible until after it happened. I was set free at early age with all the resources needed for personal and professional fulfillment, and with a status that could not have been any higher within academic faculty confines, the security of tenure, abundant opportunities to see and experience the world, and the security that goes with such a university attachment. These career satisfactions were complemented by a series of intimate relationships and enriching friendships allowing me to reach for the planets, if not the stars. I could not have foreseen such a life bounty if I try to reimagine the horizons I had when younger, given my low expectations throughout childhood and adolescence.

There is one final disquieting observation. I had no faculty comrades at Princeton when it came to stepping out from the academy to address public demonstrations or identify with activists. As mentioned, there were a few faculty members who stood in solidarity with anti-war or anti-racist activist students when local protest activities occurred. When it came to war crimes in Vietnam or the Iranian Revolution or the Palestinian struggle for basic rights I felt alone, at best, confronting walls of silence. At different times I have often asked 'why?' without ever producing a truly satisfactory answer. Some undoubtedly felt, correctly it turns out, that there would be a career price to pay within the institution, including a loss of influence and respect. I experienced such losses, although without regrets. More high-minded and thoughtful rationalizations for timidity of conscience and citizenship had to do with the belief that a faculty member would lose the trust of some students if manifesting partisan positions on controversial questions.

I was mindful of these roads not taken, but even now I keep wondering what led me to go off on my own private trail that was not only frowned-upon activism but involved an identity as a scholar relying on unfashionable normative methodologies to carry out a program of research and writing devoted to the long-run promotion of peace and justice with attention especially given to the struggles of the victimized and subjugated. I do not have any doubts about the road chosen but I still do not fully understand what led me to defy basic scholarly conventions and what many of my colleagues and friends regarded as 'common sense.' Even now I wonder how I developed this contrarian persona, which seems to contrast with my inner and outer accommodating demeanor.

CHAPTER 9

Life: Students, Careers, Service

Maintaining Fuzzy Boundaries

Unlike some of my colleagues at Princeton, and later at UCSB, I never felt comfortable with students who became protégées, and as earlier indicated, assuming the role of mentor seemed to imply authoritative guidance, which did not fit with my sense of either personal identity or professional responsibility. I was too unsure of myself in my early teaching years in Ohio, and too intimidated by the Princeton aura, to be comfortable with exerting influences on students' lives beyond doing my best in the classroom and trying to be helpfully responsive in advisory roles. Also, since my sense of being a teacher or scholar was always interactive and reciprocal, I was instinctively reluctant to suspend my wish to teach and learn from students, an attitude that was for me incompatible with the subtly hierarchical character of mentorship.

There is a special set of issues arising from friendships with students or workplace, spilling over the boundaries of professionalism into domains of erotic or emotional intimacy. For me this led me to keep a prudent distance from female students, research assistants, and office staff members. Long before men were finally being sensitized to the nuances of sexual harassment by feminists and public guidelines, I tried my best not to encroach on the dignity, self-esteem, and private social space of women, whether colleagues, staff, or students, while not foregoing the friendly and playful interactions that enliven social spaces if accompanied by sensitivities involving gender, race, religion, and national background. With daily interaction in the workplace over long periods, such boundaries require vigilance as well as responsiveness to changing social norms.

I had one early lapse. There was an attractive woman law student of about my age at Ohio State who befriended me during the lonely period in my life after separating from my first wife. I responded, and we had a consensual romantic relationship that lasted a year or so, including spending the summer of 1958 together in Europe. She was eager to escape the confines of student life, quickly bonded with several of my closer friends on the faculty and among older graduate students. Our relationship was accepted as normal and natural and might be even in the altered atmosphere of the present. We only became intimate after the course was finished. I was never in a position to grade her performance at any point after our relationship began, and she was smart and studious enough to do well on her own. We remained friends through the decades, although without continuing a romantic connection, and she went on to marry, raising on her own three musically talented daughters after her husband's early death. I never lost my fondness for her lively personality and sensual warmth or my admiration for the loving dedication she displayed while raising three children.

Because personal contact is so dependent on impressions and interpretations its character can be misconstrued, either innocently or opportunistically or even maliciously, especially in relations that are structured in a hierarchical fashion. I had one such experience while at Princeton. I had a superficial, although to me valuable and enriching, contact with George Kennan who, after he left public service, became attached to the Institute for Advanced Studies at Princeton. His former research assistant, a young Irish girl, applied for a similar job with me. I hired her, and we were friendly but only in a detached and professional manner. I was not impressed by her ability as a research assistant and decided at the end of the year not to rehire her. Shortly thereafter she complained to the university administration that I had terminated her job because she had rejected my advances, which included a claim of refusing an intimate relationship with me. This was entirely false, but who could know? We never met outside the office or at times other than the normal 9-5 working day. The Human Resources Office at the university investigated her complaint, and luckily for me, the staff women in our departmental office, who were asked about my behavior by the investigators, supported the view that she was flirtatious with me and it was I who failed to respond. Had the office secretaries been displeased with me for whatever reasons, such an investigation could have caused me lots of pain, and some harm. Surely, women in subordinate professional roles have often been targets of predatory male bosses and need and deserve protection. Hopefully, sensitive men will accept this measure of vulnerability to unfair harassment allegations as a kind of 'reparations' for past patriarchal abuse, but when it hits home, as in this instance, it still feels wrong and abusive.

I am fully aware that for far too long patriarchal ethics dominated the employment scene. During my years at Princeton I heard of several ugly incidents of faculty harassment that went unreported, and a few others that were reported but without reaching appropriate punitive outcomes. The injustices that occurred overwhelmingly involved the double victimization of women, first, the actual abuse, and second, the credibility gap that left the woman often humiliated when even well-documented complaints were ignored or even treated with derision. Despite the determined efforts of women, it still seems to be true in the most public instances that the man gets a reprieve by covering up and lying while the woman gets 'punished' for daring to bear witness and telling the truth.

I feel many of us are caught in a social maelstrom that mixes the dynamics of political correctness with the subtle, and sometimes blatant, remnants of cruel forms of sexism and racism that continue to be extremely hurtful. I am reminded of the searing meditations in Claudia Rankine's *Citizen: An American Lyric* in which this fine poet, a woman of color, recounts how she experienced hurt from time to time when those with white privilege falsely assumed her to be a domestic worker or she found herself called by a white acquaintance by the name of a former servant just because of the color of her skin. As a white person, I felt obliged to address any remnants of racism embedded in my subconscious attitudes towards persons of color just as the society as a whole needs to respond collectively to the abuses and inequities endured by ethnic minorities, producing socio-economic hardships and social hurts. This need is often ignored until some kind of crisis arises as occurred after the police murder of George Floyd in the midst of the COVID pandemic, when suddenly neglected patterns of abuse are exposed, outrage by those victimized is expressed, and the dominant society both gives in and regroups in response to pent-up rage and justifiable grounds for discontent.

If righting such historic wrongs results occasionally in innocent and caring men taking a few hits from angry or hurt feminists along the way, it is unfortunate and may be deeply unfair in specific cases, yet politically and culturally it should be accepted as the price to be paid to overcome past injustices—the inevitable friction of rotating wheels of justice resulting from reversing and correcting some burdens of (mis) interpretation. Adjusting the treatment of women by men, of indigenous persons by settlers, of blacks by whites, of poor by rich, of immigrants by citizens will cause individual injustices in the course of enhancing collective justice, and this cumulative process will rightly still be called moral progress even if the net of justice occasionally punishes wrongfully.

Students as Friends and Colleagues

When thinking back it seems natural, even to be expected, that graduate students would more frequently become friends more than undergraduates. This was true even in the liberal arts atmosphere that existed at Princeton, which was a small town dominated by the university. In some college small towns there are stronger student/faculty connections than I experienced at Princeton. Part of the explanation is that in political science every graduate student enrolled at Princeton was working for a doctoral degree. Masters degrees were given out only if a student failed to gain faculty approval for continuing on the path leading to a PhD. It was a rather questionable kind of consolation prize that could be a quite misleading credential.

Some degree of closeness did develop between undergraduates and their faculty advisors during the process of writing a senior thesis, which was a featured aspect of the final year of the Princeton undergraduate experience, often producing work that would be impressive if done by graduate students and occasionally even achieving publishable quality.

When it came to graduate students, the sense of community was greater as the size of the group at any given time was small. The University decided by some arcane method on the number of graduate students each social science or humanities department would be allowed to admit in a given year. If the admitted student declined an invitation, there could be no fallback resort to a backup list. As a result, the size of the graduate cohort was kept small, far less than one for each faculty member, but those admitted were of extremely high quality. Non-academic considerations, such as being an alumni child or an outstanding high school athlete, were irrelevant at the graduate level, which also meant that the graduate students as a whole were far more talented on average, as well as more diverse with respect to class background and ethnicity than Princeton undergraduates even before admissions policies were revamped in the 1970s to admit more minority students and start accepting women. Princeton retained its distinctive character as a frontline research university that also continued to keep its undergraduate college at the core of its educational undertaking. This contrasted with my Harvard and Yale experiences, especially the former, where under-graduate concerns often seemed subordinated in unfortunate ways to the priorities of graduate programs and whims of celebrity professors.

I became close friends with several students who had earlier been in my seminars or had produced their PhD dissertations under my supervision. There is lots of variation in PhD advising. What I wish to emphasize here is the pleasures of fellowship that eroded the hierarchy that can separate professors from their students, especially when the age differences are considerable. Because a student chooses her or his advisor, there is a tendency for relations to be congenial, but not always. And because the number of faculty in the area of choice is so small, it creates some strange bedfellows.

Over the years I supposed I was most influenced by students who were engaged in real world issues involving social, economic, and political justice. Such students usually had a special background that gave them a particular societal interest that was not necessarily exhibited in their academic work. Occasionally, such students would come from other departments, seeking me out not for my academic concerns but rather because they assumed that I would be receptive to their progressive outlook, and I generally was.

For reasons I no longer recall, I had several students soon after I came to Princeton who were from Puerto Rico. In particular, a history graduate student whose name I don't remember persuaded me to take an interest in the politics of the island I had up to that point only known as a favored tourist destination for those living on the East Coast. In any event, at the urging of this student, I agreed to visit the island of Vieques that was then being used by the U.S. Navy as an artillery testing range. Protests were emerging from the fisherman communities on the island whose traditional livelihood and lifestyle were being adversely affected. The visit exposed me to a classic colonial reality. The people of the island felt angered by the situation but lacked political leverage and tactical ideas about how to mount an effective challenge. My own exposure to the situation, which included contact with so-called *Independistas* gave me an awareness of the political dimensions of Puerto Rico, helping me grasp some of the paradoxes that applied not only to Vieques but also to the main island. The sharpest paradox was epitomized by the Puerto Rican habit of singing songs of independence when at bars and cafes, yet when voting on their political future, these same persons supported statehood or even commonwealth status. They didn't want to lose some material benefits, particularly the waiver of tax obligations—a classic

case of mind over heart, or passions giving way to practical considerations. As Puerto Rico and its people have been demeaned during the
Trump presidency, this paradox may have been replaced by a resurgence
of anti-colonial sentiment, accompanied by a call for implementing a
Puerto Rican right of self-determination.

I especially valued learning that the existential problems of ordinary people should not be ignored by intellectuals in their more rarefied
search for understanding issues of poverty and colonialism. This brief
field experience of Puerto Rico prepared me for other issues involving
the interaction of the North with the Global South that came my way,
and it made me more responsive to the relationships between classroom,
library, and struggles for justice on the ground. What struck me as surprising is that so few of my colleagues ventured forth, confining their
engagement with the world to voting in elections, CNN, careful readings
of the *New York Times*, consultancies, and for some serious scholars concerned with current issues, to various archives bearing on their research
interests. To be engaged on the ground as a concerned citizen or worse,
in overt solidarity with a political movement, was viewed by most of
my colleagues with disdain, being inconsistent with their academically
grounded professional ethos. In my resolve to act as a citizen pilgrim I
deliberately blurred this line between scholarship and activism until it
almost disappeared.

Perhaps, the most important student-inspired initiative of the
past 65 teaching years was a student inspired detailed article entitled
'Nuclear Weapons and International Law,' collaboratively written with
Lee Meyrowitz and Jack Sanderson, and published and distributed in
1981 by Princeton's Center of International Studies. More than most
academic writing I have done, this article had some impact on judges
of the International Court of Justice who gave me favorable feedback a
few years before crafting their landmark 1986 Advisory Opinion on 'The
Legality of Nuclear Weapons.' The abolition of nuclear weapons have
been the most pervasive concern over the course of my scholarly career,
and this may be my most successful treatment of the theme, which would
not have happened but for the enthusiasm and collaborative energy of
these two young scholars. Recently, with the encouragement and editorial guidance of my Swedish friend, Stefan Andersson, I have published
a volume of that brings my writing on this theme together, *On Nuclear
Weapons: Denuclearization, Demilitarization and Disarmament* (2019).
So what these students helped me do over 40 years ago has become a

lifetime preoccupation. Scholarship, as with teaching, works best when it is dialogic, and not just an informed monologue.

Connecting the Political with the Personal at the Edges of Academic Life

Among the most intriguing of my relatively early graduate students was one who came from Ilo-Ilo, an island in the southern part of the Philippines Archipelago, coming to my university class from the Princeton Seminary, an institutionally separate facility that trained its students to serve in the Christian ministry in various roles. Lester Ruiz was quiet, courteous, intellectually gifted, and dedicated to promoting a democratic alternative in his native country. My first experience in the Philippines arose in the 1970s when I was invited to be the keynote speaker at a conference protesting the large U.S. military bases in the country that were claimed by critics to compromise Filipino independence and sovereign rights. My talk in Manila lent support to the anti-bases coalition that had strong popular backing in the country, although opposed by the government. I was a bit unnerved by a headline in the leading national newspaper proclaiming 'Falk urges military bases be moved to Guam.' I had never made such a statement and was concerned about being perceived as meddling in the affairs of another country or advocating the further militarization of Guam. Nothing came of the story, although I was never given the opportunity in the media to correct this false presentation of my remarks, which never even mentioned Guam, much less advocated its further militarization, which I opposed.

When Lester became my student, I had been recently encouraged to show interest in the Philippines by a progressive Princeton doctoral student, Walden Bello, who was a radical critic of American imperial foreign policy. Walden became among the most respected critics of U.S. imperialism in the Pacific Region and remains a cherished friend. He was instrumental in organizing a session of the Permanent Peoples Tribunal in 1980 that was held in Brussels devoted to violations of human rights in the Philippines. The Tribunal was well organized, documenting many of the worst crimes of the Marcos dictatorship, which were victimizing the Filipino people. I served on the Tribunal jury and found the proceedings informative and influential. The proceedings were later published in the Philippines and regarded as helping discredit the Marcos government, which together with the assassination of Benigno Aquino and election rigging, seemed instrumental to the rise of the People Power Movement in the mid-1980s that brought about the downfall of the Marcos regime in 1986.

Lester Ruiz organized, through his activist sister who lived in the Philippines, a very intense fact finding visit for me to the country in the early 1980s. I had many meetings in Manila, ranging from several with three extraordinary opposition political figures in the Senate, Joseph Estrada (later President), Jose Diokno, Lorenzo Tañada, as well as the U.S. Ambassador, Nicholas Platt, who received me graciously but taught me nothing I didn't know before. I traveled around the country somewhat, and found myself so exhausted at one point that I had to cancel a meeting with an indigenous leader who had made a long trip from the remote interior countryside to Manila just to talk with me. I have been often tired, but never so exhausted as to cancel a meeting of this sort before or since, but I felt as though I would collapse or faint if I went ahead. I succumbed partly to the hot humid weather, which has always been a challenge for me. Yet decades later I continue to feel pangs of guilt by disappointing this individual. I mention these happenings in this very summary form. I had several similar factfinding missions (India, South Africa, South Korea, Japan, New Zealand) with the same level of extensive contact as that time in the Philippines. Such intense contact with a foreign country, and some leading national personalities, is a condensed learning experience that can have long lasting effects. It illustrates how students shape the work and worldview of their professors without ever having such an objective in mind.

Paul Wapner represented a quite different orientation when we met while he was doing his PhD at Princeton back in the 1980s. From the outset Paul's personal warmth, moral bearing, and political inclinations that were oriented toward civil society activism and environmental concerns made me appreciate him as an especially sympathetic and ethically engaged student. Paul combined a deep commitment to preserving the wildness of the natural world with an excellent command of international relations. His approach was ideologically diffuse, meaning that he seemed comfortable working with Michael Walzer as well as with me, although well aware of our rather antagonistic identities as Jews who thought very differently about Israel and Palestine. Paul later married Diane Singerman, who was also a Princeton graduate student, specializing in Middle East Studies, and later went on to become a respected scholar in her field.

Paul became an intimate friend, close enough to be an occasional tennis and squash partner, and more tellingly, to become independently friendly with successive women in my life while he was a student at Princeton. We have remained close, while he and Hilal, having bonded, collaborated on an edited book dealing with climate change. I doubt that I exerted much influence on Paul, although he maintains I did, except as exemplifying a university career that stretched the normal meaning of 'academic life' to encompass personal exploration and political engagement. Possibly, Paul blames me for keeping him confined to university campuses when he would much rather be kayaking on remote lakes in northern Alaska or camping on his own in the wilder parts of New Mexico.

A strong experience of being directly influenced by an ex-student occurred in relation to Andy Strauss, who went from Princeton to NYU School of Law, and then on to an academic career, currently serving as Dean at Dayton Law School. Andy was a bright and engaged undergraduate with idealistic impulses constrained by a practical feeling for what was politically attainable under existing conditions. Andy developed a commitment to the establishment of some sort of directly elected global legislative body that operated on a global level, either within the UN or apart, and whose members were directly elected by ordinary people throughout the world. I was persuaded by Andy to join with him in writing a series of articles developing arguments for establishing a Global Peoples Assembly or Global Parliament. Our model was the European Parliament, including its evolution from an almost irrelevant institutional component of the European Union to an important source of opinion and influence parallel to that of the inter-governmental institutions centered in Brussels.

Andy's enthusiasm overcame my general reluctance to put much faith in proposals for institutional reforms. I felt that institutional initiatives even if they overcame resistance to their establishment, would be subject to coopting pressures associated with geopolitical leverage and funding sources. Until very recently, the International Criminal Court has been dramatically confirmatory of my concerns, claiming to be entrusted with extending international criminal accountability to all perpetrators regardless of national affiliation, but in practice focusing almost solely on Sub-Saharan Africa, and avoiding situations in which the West was the target of investigation, and probable indictment. This has started to change, with proposed ICC investigations involving allegations about U.S. crimes in Afghanistan and Israel's criminal behavior with respect to the Palestinians. These initiatives have occasioned belligerent pushbacks by the United States and Israel, both denouncing the ICC as itself criminally irresponsible by challenging the legitimate security policies of sovereign states and even by imposing sanctions on several ICC officials because they did their law job dutifully while straying from the rules of the political game. Of course, the ICC is potentially more threatening to the established order than would be a Global Parliament, unless the latter was endowed with lawmaking authority, which is highly unlikely in the foreseeable future. It remains to be seen whether geopolitics can stifle this long overdue rule of law and global democracy initiative.

I found that being responsive to the concerns of students and ex-students for shortcomings in the public sphere was part of my apprenticeship as a citizen pilgrim who happened also to be a teacher/scholar. I felt that support for such projects as the Global Peoples Assembly or the Permanent Peoples Tribunal were natural outgrowths of the worldview that I advocated, and that my participation was a natural consequence. It involved doing whatever I could to change world order in accord with the imperatives of peace, justice, and ecology.

I have not discussed being drawn deeper into the Palestinian struggle by students, and I think that reflected two realities: there were very few Palestinian students at Princeton and I came to my engagement with the Palestine/Israel agenda largely outside the university setting.

Yet I would mention one Princeton undergraduate student, Mark Bruzonsky, who seemed quite strongly Zionist while at Princeton, taking issue with some of my views during a lecture course held in a large auditorium, and friendly with several Israeli military officers who were enrolled in the Masters Program of the Woodrow Wilson School of Public and International Affairs, who sat in a back row apparently scoffing at my words. Mark later surprisingly emerged as a voice of conscience for Jews increasingly uneasy about Israel's treatment of the Palestinian people, forming a committee that commented critically from an insider's location in Washington on issues affecting Israel and the Middle East, especially those dealing with public policy. Mark gave me some reason to believe that my courses exerted an influence on his development, and clearly our policy views converged over the years.

Another former student who later became a real friend was Tom Plate. Undoubtedly our friendship, with a birth long after Tom left Princeton where he acquired a Masters degree at what was then simply called the Woodrow Wilson School (and now the Princeton School of Public and International Affairs), was facilitated by geography. We lived in Santa Barbara since the start of 2002, and Tom has long been based in LA. Among my former students Tom is at the top of the heap when it comes to talent, but also possesses larger than life traits of bravado and self-irony that set him apart. As might be expected, this twinning perplexes many who meet Tom, at least early on, but underneath Tom is an exceptionally caring human being, maybe somewhat afraid to reveal softer feelings of empathy.

Tom has an acute turn of mind, and developed a writing style as vivid as his personality. He contrived a career with several interfaces: the academy and the media, with a specialization in journalism, especially China in recent years, as well as journalism and scholarship. Tom managed to develop professional 'friendships' with a series of Asian leaders that led to conversational meetings that he turned into regional bestsellers, featuring such notable figures as Lee Kuan Yew, Ban Ki Moon, and Mathahir Mohamed. More than other students Tom comes across as a classless champion of ideas that includes a taste for elegance when it comes to life style, generosity when it comes to hospitality, and a kind of grudging acknowledgement that the main honchos of American foreign policy deserve respect, and maybe even deference. I can never quite forgive him either his admitted admiration for Henry Kissinger, or for that matter Ban Ki Moon, both of whom I regard as core operatives of a problematic world, playing no constructive part in fashioning a solution, although both proved adept at serving their geopolitical master.

As discussed, students while enrolled, and even more afterwards, affected the trajectory of my interests and activities in a variety of ways. The community of learning and engagement shouldn't be confined by the time and place during which students were present on campus. From this perspective one of my most satisfying friendships and intellectual collaborations arose from a graduate seminar on international law that I taught while a faculty visitor to Columbia University in the 1970s. Bob Johansen was the star student in the group, and went on to be a world order collaborator, enjoying a distinguished scholarly career on the faculty of Notre Dame, and author of an important book relevant to my own intellectual evolution, *The National Interest and the Human Interest: An Analysis of United States Foreign Policy* (1980). My only grievance through the decades in this regard was that participating in a conference honoring his retirement at Notre Dame, while gratifying and a stirring tribute to Bob, made me feel even older than I was, celebrating the retirement of someone once a student. Bob's longtime wife, Ruth Ann Johansen, was my research assistant for several years, a position far below her talent level, but which she handled with her customary grace, competence, and sunshine spirits.

Finally, I come to Sherri Burr, among my closest friends stemming from her time at Princeton as a graduate student, which was followed by studying law at Yale, and then joining the law faculty of the University of New Mexico. There were few African American women enrolled at Princeton in the years that Sherri was a student, and she made me more aware of the pains inflicted by systemic racism before I understood what it was. She has had an admirable career, specializing in law and the arts, but also doing original historical research on American racism. Among relevant memories is the extraordinary demand for Sherri's talents by law schools around the country that I experienced by way of phone calls from deans seeking ways to persuade her to join their faculty. Thankfully the calls ceased, and I could stop singing her praise only after she ended up choosing to join the law school of the University of New Mexico, partly to be near her family. Sherri remained there until retiring a year ago.

Public Figures

I also had several students who went on to have significant public careers that either pleased or disturbed me, or left me merely impressed with their achievements without either enough knowledge or interest to pass judgment on what they had chosen to do with their lives. I mention several such persons as suggestive of the varying backgrounds of students at Princeton with its signature priority of attracting and grooming future leaders, or as mentioned earlier, 'Princeton in the nation's service.' I suppose it is a feature of an academic career within a relatively small university that draws its student body from American and overseas elites to have contact with some students who go on to have illustrious careers, and to take note of whether their promise was evident while at Princeton or emerged later on. Perhaps, also, because such students often tended to have international interests, and there were limited offerings at Princeton, I was particularly exposed to such students.

The list is rather long, and I will select rather arbitrarily to indicate the diversity of my experience. It happens that the most prominent of all is someone of whom I have no memory, Robert Mueller, former FBI Director and the famously controversial Special Counsel appointed to inquire into allegations of various crimes surrounding Donald Trump's 2016 presidential campaign. Mueller did his senior thesis under my supervision, and I am the only person he formally acknowledges, which he graciously does by thanking me for help. I reread his thesis after literally stumbling upon my role in his past and found myself impressed by the mature way Mueller handled a difficult set of technical legal issues. He wrote about the contested decision as to whether the International Court of Justice in The Hague should have accepted jurisdiction to decide on a dispute between Ethiopia and Liberia and South Africa. The legal question being investigated was whether Ethiopia and Liberia had the legal standing to complain about South Africa's extension of apartheid to its administration of South West Africa (now the independent state of Namibia, but then a Mandate under South African administrative control). I knew the material well as I had worked the entire prior year in The Hague as a member of the legal team representing the two complaining anti-apartheid governments during 1964-65. I was especially impressed by Mueller's detached style and analytic precision combined with a technical competence and nuanced sensitivity to the wider political and legal implications of how the ICJ handled these inflammatory issues of race and colonial subjugation. I found his assessment of the underlying question subtle and enlightening. Mueller argued that although South Africa had made a somewhat better *legal* argument, the law was ambiguous, and hence the *moral and political* case for accepting jurisdiction is the preferred outcome, which happens to be what the court did.

I intend no rank ordering, but another celebrity student whom, in contrast to Mueller, I remember very clearly was David Petraeus who was at Princeton as a midcareer military officer, but quickly rose to prominence in subsequent years. He became Chairman of the Joint Chiefs of Staff, then Director of the CIA, and was even rumored to be a serious candidate for the 2008 Republican presidential nomination had his libido not interfered. I suspect, although it may be either wishful thinking or harmless daydreaming, that if Petraeus had not been informally charged with giving classified material to a woman doing his biography and having an intimate relationship with her, Trump might never have become even a presidential candidate.

Petraeus took my graduate seminar in international relations, given at the Woodrow Wilson School. He was an active participant expressing his views with lucidity and in a forceful manner. He was friendly, likeable, intelligent, optimistic, and seemingly comfortable with the main tendencies of American foreign policy, exhibiting a can do, fix it mentality that came across as confident about overcoming challenges, solving problems. His meteoric career ascent in the armed forces was often attributed to his work in thoroughly revising the Counterinsurgency Manual used by the U.S. Army, especially by taking account of the failings of American policy in Vietnam.

The Petraeus rewrite emphasized building close collaborative relationships with the civilian populations of the countries where the conflict was situated when the United States was intervening on one side or the other. Petraeus' approach was accorded influence in Afghanistan and Iraq, where he was the military commander, after regime-changing interventions in the post-9/11 context reached decidedly mixed results that were strategic failures if appraised by their supposed goals.

Over the years I had several other military officers who took a year off from their career job to gain a certain edge by a year of quality graduate work. I became friends with the son of the West Point tennis and squash coach, and a good player himself. We played squash regularly while he was taking my IR course. After he returned to West Point, where he was a faculty member, he invited me to be the dinner speaker at a banquet dinner held at the end of a highlighted course on the world situation, featuring talks by top national security figures in Washington. Not only were graduating cadets in the audience, but also student delegates invited to participate in the course, drawn from more than 100 American universities were present. These non-Cadets were not happy being fed throughout the week with justifications for government policy by cabinet members and the National Security Advisor.

I never expected to be invited back to West Point and made sure of this by selecting as my title, 'The Menace of Militarism in American Political Life.' The event took place shortly after the end of the Vietnam War, and I felt strongly about these issues, regarding this as a once in a lifetime opportunity. As I recall, the visitors from other colleges were wildly enthusiastic about my presentation, the cadets were somewhat split, and the West Point faculty was definitely annoyed, and avoided me at the post-lecture reception. I felt sorry for the Superintendent of the Academy, General Andrew Goodpaster, a well-known military figure, who was given the awkward job of introducing me. I do not remember what I said to explain my choice of theme, but I do recall the luxurious presidential suite where I was housed for the night, including the well-stocked bar. I have asked myself, 'Was it immature of me to give such a talk?' It may have caused difficulties for my squash partner and friend who was tasked with organizing the event, and who never again contacted me or even thanked me for the talk. I am still uncertain after the lapse of all these years as to whether I did the right thing. At the time, I thought that not informing him in advance about my theme would insulate him from any responsibility, but I fear he was sharply criticized for having given me such a lofty West Point pulpit, and doubt that such a mistake has been repeated in subsequent years.

Another military officer who entered my orbit, Admiral William Crowe, had taken time off from his naval career to work for a doctorate at Princeton. Years later he liked to tell the story that his pals in the navy told him that choosing to obtain an academic credential was worse than a waste of time, it was a career-ending move. Crowe's post-Princeton selection as Chairman of the Joint Chiefs of Staff, the highest official military position, he enjoyed saying, validated his refusal to take a conventional path to the top of the military pyramid. He was appointed first by Ronald Reagan, and then by George H.W. Bush. I was amused, and I suppose pleased, that Crowe asked me if he could teach my class a few years after he had been a student, when he planned to return for an alumni event. Of course, I accepted what seemed more a compliment than a challenge, although I was never fully sure whether this was a way to thank me for the course or more ominously, a belated means of letting me know how teaching should be done. When the time came, this jovial fellow from the hills of Oklahoma who had made good in the big time, was gracious and humble. He gave the students a lighthearted taste of Washington politics.

Early in my time at Princeton Prince Saud Faisal from Saudi Arabia was a student in my undergraduate introductory course on international law. He happened to be assigned to my discussion section, called a 'precept' since the now discredited Woodrow Wilson introduced the idea to claim distinctiveness for Princeton educational style during the years he served as university president. I have to admit that I never managed to figure out this distinctiveness during my 40 years of trying while on the faculty!

As weekly discussion sections generally do, precepts created a more personal atmosphere than a lecture setting of 50-150 students and allowed for some written assignments. Saud Faisal was a pleasantly modest young man who wrote a very good paper on 'An Islamic Approach to International Law.' I remember his paper as being thoughtful, analytical, and rather descriptive, but far from rigid or inflexible in its interpretations. The paper did not touch ultra-sensitive material bearing on family relations, status of women, and personal law. I had no subsequent direct contact with Saud Faisal after his return to Saudi Arabia, where he soon became Foreign Minister, a post he held for many years (1975-2015). I did hear indirectly about him through occasional contact with his younger, also distinguished diplomat brother, Prince Turki bin Faisal.

Yet not all who achieved fame could claim a lightness of being. During my first years at Princeton, Richard Perle was enrolled as a prospective PhD student, taking my small seminar in advanced international relations. He was conceptually gifted, articulate in a soft spoken yet forceful manner, but did not strike me at the time as particularly ideological.

Later Perle became widely touted as the *eminence gris* of neocon strategic thought in Washington, first on the staff of Senator Henry Jackson (known by his critics as 'the senator from Boeing') who was stridently hawkish when it came to foreign policy despite being a Democrat. Perle was later anointed as the guru of the neoconservative clique of policy advisors that surrounded Reagan and later shaped the foreign policy of George W. Bush. Perle was skeptical of arms limitations, hostile to the UN and international law, favorable to pro-democracy regime-changing interventions, and unconditionally pro-Israel. There were many moderates who found Perle's quiet style of exerting influence over fine dinners accompanied by vintage wines disturbing, even dangerous, christening him 'the prince of darkness.' Perle seemed content to be an influential advisor behind the scenes, which was unusual for Washington where public notoriety was normally an essential aspect of the career ambitions of those exerting influence. He was always calm in tone and measured in reasoning, even when advocating provocative warlike foreign policy positions.

An almost opposite case of ideological prominence is that of Norman Finkelstein. Norman was actually the doctoral advisee of Sheldon Wolin, Princeton's lead political theorist. I was initially the second reader of Norman's dissertation, but when Wolin made a decision to accept a position at the Santa Cruz campus of the University of California, I was suddenly thrust into the position of being Norman's principal advisor. The thesis was devoted to the evolution of Zionist thought as understood through a deep reading of the writings of its leading thinkers. I found Norman's text very clear, illuminating, and persuasive in its analysis and conclusions, but I also had some suggestions for minor revisions. Norman didn't receive my criticism in the spirit it was intended. He reacted in an angry and hostile manner, appealing for sympathy to his friends including Edward Said and Noam Chomsky. I remember Edward calling me, half-jokingly, saying, 'What is this I hear about you trying to destroy Norman Finkelstein? I explained as best I could what had transpired.

Norman was an unusually gifted graduate student who arrived at Princeton with a resume that included widely read publications, a record befitting someone who had been a faculty member for years. He had already earned a significant reputation as a rigorous and confrontational scholar highly critical of Israel's policies and practices. Perhaps he felt that as a published author he deserved a kind of deference as a graduate student, but for me he was a graduate student seeking a PhD degree, and my job was to give him candid feedback to help him improve his dissertation. In any event, we both contained the tensions, and Norman received his degree, went on to be one of the most influential and worldly known scholarly critics of Israeli behavior, as well as other topics. Norman had family connections with harrowing Holocaust experience, as many of his close family members had experienced Hitler's death camps. But he was unfairly excluded from academic life, effectively blacklisted after being denied tenure at DePaul University despite a positive recommendation from his faculty colleagues, apparently being undermined from the outside by back channel unsolicited letters, including one reportedly from Alan Dershowitz. It is a sorry tale, and I am sure a cause of lingering distress for Norman who has managed, nevertheless, to remain productive and respected without compromising the quality or critical character of his wide-ranging scholarship.

There is no doubt in my mind that Finkelstein was an early victim of Zionist McCarthyism that has harmed many decent and dedicated academicians by using defamatory innuendo and back channels to mount utterly irresponsible charges of anti-Semitism. In the Trump Era this campaign against Israeli critics has gained hurricane force, relying on what is being called the 'New anti-Semitism' (relying on the broadened definition of anti-Semitism proposed by the International Holocaust Remembrance Initiative equating harsh criticism of Israel with anti-Semitism) lobbied hard at state and federal level to support punitive, even criminalizing, responses to critics of Israel and activists, especially those associated with BDS. It is a somewhat ironic aside that Finkelstein was long an opponent of BDS but may have changed his mind recently. In such matters, facts make no difference when smears are allowed to fashion the public image of a man or woman.

I fondly remember Nathan Shamuyarira. Nathan was also an unusual student, enrolled in the doctoral program at Princeton after Rhodesia declared on November 11, 1965, what was known at the time as UDI, standing for Unilateral Declaration of Independence. The Rhodesian settler elite did not want to go along with the British readiness to give up colonial control and allow a politically independent African state to emerge. Nathan had been the editor of a pro-independence magazine when UDI happened, and he chose exile over subjugation. In personal relations, Nathan was warm and engaging, while politically he was a radical nationalist who strongly backed the belief that Africa, and its resources, belonged solely to indigenous Africans, and not to white settlers. He was also appalled by his encounters with American racism. Nathan was not a brilliant student, but he was intelligent and worked hard, emphasizing the role of the UN in relation to the anti-colonial movement. After completing his work at Princeton, Nathan returned to Africa, first joining the faculty at the University of Tanzania, soon becoming dean while helping to bring two factions together in working for a unified Tanzanian independence movement.

I involved Nathan in the work of the World Order Models Project, and he attended several meetings, contributing uncompromising anti-colonial and anti-imperial perspectives, and helping organize a stimulating meeting of WOMP in Nigeria. He later returned home to Zimbabwe and became Foreign Minister, and a respected diplomat through sub-Saharan Africa. When Nathan came to the General Assembly to represent Zimbabwe, he asked me to accompany him on a scheduled visit with the Secretary General, who at the time was Boutros Boutros-Ghali, whom I had previously known in Geneva. It was one of those protocol occasions, with the SG expected to make time to meet with the highest ranking governmental representative of more than 190 members of the UN. I sensed the fatigue of Boutros while he did his best to show interest and responsiveness. Nathan put forward a wish list relating to developing country priorities and favoring a leading UN role in the global anti-apartheid campaign.

My friendship with Nathan felt very special. We trusted one another and became personally close. I was also a friend of the equally famous Ali Mazrui, yet Ali although fascinating to be around because of his illuminating verbal pyrotechnics, was always at a remove in social space, never fully trusting the safety of his environment, while Nathan had that gift of warmth that made you feel a brotherly contact. With Africans, I also had a brief but captivating fling with a young animated woman from Botswana, whom I originally met in Moscow during a group visit of several days. My response included a strong attraction, and when we met a year or so later in Harari, we did have a brief romantic connection. She is one of the women who entered and left my life without causing scar tissue to form, leaving behind only fond and sensual memories, and thus feelings of 'what might have been' never entirely died even as they faded into the dark recesses of the distant past. Returning to what had become Zimbabwe in 2019, accompanying Hilal on her UN

Mission as Special Rapporteur for the Right to Food, I asked a variety of people about Nathan who had died a few years earlier. All responded affirmatively, exclaiming that he was so uncorruptible that he died in poverty, which was a rarity for individuals who held ministerial posts in the Mugabe government. It turns out that on political issues, Nathan remained a Mugabe loyalist, defending his controversial confiscation of white-owned farms, and I was told he died before finishing a biography of Mugabe.

Lloyd Axworthy was another Princeton PhD student with a predominant interest in the UN, who devoted his entire academic life to the UN. Lloyd as a student was opinionated and questioned settled wisdom about the world, leaving me with impressions of his independence. I didn't follow his career very closely after he left Princeton until he became Minister of External Affairs in Canada during the premiership of Pierre Trudeau. While in that position Lloyd distinguished himself in my eyes for at least two reasons. He put forward the idea of 'human security' as a more comprehensive, less statist and militarist alternative to the conventional focus on 'national security.' It was an idea that caught on, stimulating much discussion in the pre-9/11 era and even leading Japan to establish a Commission on Human Security to consider ways to promote the concept in policy contexts.

The second initiative that Lloyd deserves credit for establishing was a Canadian commission on Intervention and Sovereignty, which was a response to the Kosovo War, and led to the proposal of the norm of 'Responsibility to Protect,' which was adopted by the UN Security Council in 2004, and has had a continuing albeit somewhat controversial impact in situations that had formerly been addressed as calling for 'humanitarian intervention.' The geopolitical manipulation of the R2P norm in the Libyan humanitarian crisis of 2011 has given the whole idea a rather bad name, and helps explain why the UN found itself virtually sidelined during the protracted horribly destructive struggles that unfolded in Syria and Yemen, causing massive and prolonged suffering and the displacement of the civilian populations. More than most intellectuals who get their hands on the levers of power, Lloyd made creative and constructive use of his comparatively brief opportunity.

One of the most intriguing of those among my students who went on to do big things in 'the real world' was Anne-Marie Slaughter. I first encountered Anne-Marie when she was a senior at Princeton. She asked permission to take my graduate seminar in international law, which I gladly gave. Anne-Marie even then was clearly hard wired for worldly success in an American setting—self-confident, fashionably dressed, well-spoken, smart, informed, friendly, pragmatic, and articulate. Naturally, she did well as a student, and later on, when I encountered her in various professional settings, Anne-Marie always seemed in command of the situation. After attending Harvard Law School she was recruited to its faculty, and became closely associated with the professional activities of Abe Chayes, a skilled Washington operative, who had left the Harvard law faculty for several years to serve as Legal Advisor to the Secretary of State, a post he held during the Cuban Missile Crisis.

When Anne-Marie was on the law faculty, I met with her and Abe in New York in his role as head of a small panel, of which I became a member, appointed to advise the government of Corey Aquino on how to recover some of the real estate and bank deposits that the Marcos regime had unlawfully stolen from the people of the Philippines. Anne-Marie was serving as his assistant in this role, and later produced an important book, *The New World Order*, which examined how global governance was being transformed by various forms of inter-governmental networking. Although Anne-Marie was highly successful as an academician, and visible as a foreign policy commentator and strong presence at the Council on Foreign Relations, it seemed clear that her sights were set on achieving prominence in the public sector, possibly as secretary of state or ambassador to the UN.

So far it has not happened, although Anne-Marie served effectively as the head of Policy Planning in the State Department during the Obama presidency, a position given a lasting visibility because its first director was George Kennan. When it came to substance, I found Anne-Marie to be a prudent liberal hawk, ready to favor the use of American military power, especially if it was accompanied by a humanitarian cover. In specific circumstances I always found it hard to know whether Anne-Marie was being true to herself or was somewhat tailoring her views to serve her ambitions, a puzzle I suspect she has yet to unravel for herself. After leaving the government she wrote a widely discussed article in the *Atlantic*, 'You can't have it all,' in which she writes of the difficult tradeoffs between family and work, with a special emphasis on how to manage the stresses that arise from playing an active role in the public sector while nurturing the healthy development of one's children.

Anne-Marie remains young and visible enough to play an important role in the revival of the Democratic Party prompted by the various excesses of the Trump presidency. Whether she can do more by way of ideas than use her abundant skills to reinvigorate multilateral diplomacy remains to be seen. I always found Anne-Marie likable and engaging despite my feeling that she was overly keen to lead a high-profile Washington life. In turn, on more than one occasion Anne-Marie on a public occasion in my presence credited my seminar with giving rise to her decision to focus on international law while at law school and as a young professor. I still have the wish that despite her notable successes to date, Anne-Marie's career fulfillment lies ahead of her.

Asli Bali was my last PhD student at Princeton, and perhaps the most intellectually talented of the lot, as well as being a warm personal friend. On top of all these qualities, she was pure Turkish although raised and educated on American soil. Not surprisingly, of all those mentioned in this chapter, none bonded more closely with Hilal than Asli. After being undecided whether to highlight her student excellence or her public career, I decide to place her here, partly because she offered such a contrast to Anne-Marie, who by happy circumstance, was a member of Asli's PhD committee at Princeton. Putting the comparison crudely, while Anne-Marie was a policy entrepreneur with her laser gaze directed at the Washington scene, Asli became an academic star with an equally intense gaze focused on world issues, particularly Turkey and Palestine. She became a stellar performer while still junior faculty at the UCLA School of Law, and like Anne-Marie, maybe more so, her most memorable accomplishments may lie ahead of her. Of course, I remember being intimidated by Asli who in seminar discussions seemed more informed and perceptive than I, and sometimes challenged my relative political timidity, but always graciously.

Finally, I come to Moulay Hicham ben Abdullah, prince of Morocco, and a graduate of Princeton in about 1990.[iii] Moulay Hicham never took any courses with me. We came to know one another by way of a series of private dinners at which we discussed Middle East and world issues. After his father died while he was still a child, Moulay Hicham had grown up in the palace under the apparently overly vigilant eye of King Hassan II, a gifted monarch but domineering in personal relations and unforgiving to his enemies.

When I first was in contact with MH he was preoccupied with future of the royal family in Morocco. He had an intense wish to serve

---

iii In recent years, Moulay Hicham (which translates as Prince Hicham) has formally dropped his royal title, preferring to be called 'Hicham Aloui,' but since I knew him for so long with his title I think of him in that way, and write accordingly, although I certainly respect, and even admire, his wish to abandon his princely title as part of his deep commitment to contribute to Morocco's political development as a mature constitutional democracy.

his country effectively. He believed that the monarchy in Morocco had to be modernized along Spanish constitutional lines. After Hassan II designated the older of his two sons to become king, Mohammed VI, there was evident disappointment on MH's part that he was not asked to play a leading role in the government. A meeting to discuss the future of the country with the new monarch produced a permanent rupture between the king and my friend. The rest of MH's family has enjoyed a positive relationship with the palace, attending royal gatherings and exchanging presents. I visited Morocco a couple of occasions at MH's invitation, again combining social closeness between our families with a kind of advising role on some policy issues.

MH was definitely a special person even if situated precariously near the center of power and conjecture in Morocco. He had a restless interest in the world that took him after Princeton first to Stanford for a Masters Degree and then to Oxford where he earned a doctorate in Islamic Studies. His future remains indeterminate, but he is one of those highly qualified and humane personalities who would serve the world and his region as well as his country with great distinction if given the opportunity. It will be sad, indeed, if this capable, highly educated and energetic person is denied his life wish to contribute to a more humane and flourishing Moroccan future, the country of his birth that remains so dear to his heart.

A Concluding Note

Especially with respect to students who became friends or made notable contributions I have made some hard choices to keep this text of manageable length and to treat the concerns that were of greatest interest. Perhaps, given my tendency to opt for candor over discretion, those omitted might welcome being overlooked.

These encounters with outstanding students of varying persuasions produced insights and challenges. Along the way, I learned some cautionary lessons on the difficulties of transforming established structures due to the experience of these gifted persons with varying ideas, interests, and ambitions.

CHAPTER 10
Santa Barbara/UCSB

Taking Stock

As suggested throughout, an academic life fit exceptionally well with my interests, temperament. and abilities. Somehow, despite disillusioning experiences and some tedious administrative diversions, I retired from Princeton with almost the same degree of enthusiasm I felt when arriving at OSU 46 years earlier. Even now looking back on more than 60 years of continuous connection with universities in the United States and Europe, I continue to feel that for those who are so inclined, and find good institutional homes, it is a privileged life that provides almost ideal conditions for self-development. This is not to deny the tears, disappointments, limitations, and annoyances along the way, but almost always at the margins of my activities, most often reflecting the pettiness of human nature, my own mistakes, the vocational timidity of academic bureaucracies, and the unhealthy leverage of large donors. This opportunity to teach, learn, write, think for myself, take action as an engaged citizen, and make my voice heard in the public square has been fulfilling for me from start to finish, at least this was my feeling as I prepared to leave our Princeton home at the end of 2001.

The decision to retire from Princeton was preceded by a four-year transition period, starting in 1997, which involved less teaching and no administrative assignments. Retirement from Princeton expressed a bit of institutional fatigue on my part but was mainly motivated by wanting a new set of life circumstances for Hilal and myself. At 70 I figured this was my last good chance to make a life-changing decision. My parting of the ways with Princeton occurred during a time when I was still committed to a variety of political causes, many scholarly endeavors, academic projects, and continuing to enjoy the pleasures of teaching and writing.

I was confident at the time that retirement from Princeton was not the end of the road with respect to either my academic/activist life or my recreational devotion to racquet sports and poetry. There were added entirely personal considerations that had led me to move away, especially the attractive challenge of making a fresh start in a new environment because so much of my Princeton life had been shared with other partners, which cast shadows from the past. They acted as filters limiting the happiness of being with Hilal. Making this move to California also somewhat redressed the career sacrifice Hilal had made when we married in 1995 and agreed to live together in one place. I knew that she was committed to an academic career of her own and had regrets about giving up her Turkish university affiliation. I realize better now, and regret, that I unconsciously earlier enacted the typical patriarchal pattern in which I took for granted that the woman defers to the man's career.

Without much deliberation, we picked California as our chosen destination. Ever since late childhood, I had had frequent experiences in California. My strongest memory was when I was 16 and living as a guest for the summer in the home of Claudette Colbert, the Hollywood movie star, an Academy Award winner who had many celebrity friends in the film industry. It gave me an insider's exposure to the social dimensions of the film industry. The high and low point of the summer were two sides of the same incident. Claudette was a friend of Elizabeth Taylor's mother, and they arranged a date for me with Elizabeth, who had recently become a bright new Hollywood star after her performance in *National Velvet*. The date was scheduled to happen in a prearranged format without our participation, and maybe on her side, without even knowledge and consent. Planning the date seemed to reflect the concerns of the adults in the room as how to entertain a lonely adolescent from far away from his familiar surroundings.

It was so Hollywood! We were first invited to attend a private screening of the recently released *State Fair* at the home of Daryl Zanuck, a leading film producer, and then it was arranged that we would visit a night club where a reservation had been made. I was at the time intrigued and terrified by the prospect. Lacking self-confidence and social grace, I anticipated an awkward experience from start to finish. Elizabeth Taylor was already invested with a charisma that would only grow through the years. At the last moment, I was forever rescued from the experience by a most unexpected intervention. A few days before this day of social reckoning, I was diagnosed by Claudette's surgeon husband with acute appendicitis requiring immediate surgery, and it was I who needed to cancel the date. Weirdly, it was the only date I ever broke in my entire life, and I doubt that Elizabeth ever again had this happen to her.

Of course, as soon as I realized that the date was not going to happen, I felt keen disappointment, my prior anxieties vanishing. This non-event has remained in my fantasy life ever since, glamorized beyond reality by being magnified in my imagination as some kind of 'lost opportunity.' I rationalized to myself that even if I had proved as inept as I feared, such a tinseled experience would provide a lifelong memory, and maybe, just maybe, we could have become friends. Some years later, Zsa Zsa Gabor told me that I reminded her of Conrad Hilton, Jr., who became Elizabeth Taylor's first husband, and so who knows. This made me regret the malevolent timing of this singular hospitalization event. I am sure if the situation had been reversed, and she had broken the date I would have gone through life assuming Elizabeth used health as a lame excuse.

Deciding that Santa Barbara was the right choice for us was not a complicated decision. We were encouraged in deciding by Mark Juergensmeyer, then the director of Global Studies at UCSB, who offered us both part time teaching positions on a year to year basis but with good prospects of continuity. This gave us a meaningful affiliation with a good university and its facilities. It also provided just enough extra income to make our life free of financial stress. In addition to these practical considerations we had several close friends who had long lived in Santa Barbara and loved the place. I had a long collaborative friendship with David Ray Griffin and his wife, Ann Jaqua, who shared my progressive worldview. They immediately bonded with Hilal, and she with them, and our twenty years in Santa Barbara would not have been nearly as satisfying without their friendship. David, already enjoying a worldwide reputation as a philosopher of religion, became a hero for some, a villain for others, by mounting a sustained critique of the official version of the 9/11 attacks, publishing an astounding 11 books to develop his arguments and meet criticisms. I had the honor to write the foreword to his first 9/11 book bearing the title *The New Pearl Harbor*, and paid dearly as it provided fodder for the Zionist defamation mill, which portrayed me (falsely) as 'a conspiracy theorist' and '9/11 truther' so as to convince people that I was not only hostile to Israel, but a wing nut. Through David and Ann we became very close to their friends, Nora Gallagher and Vincent Stanley, she a novelist and he a poet, both having day jobs with Patagonia, the maker of fine clothes for outdoor living, and a rare instance of a successful global company combining profitability with a deserved reputation as a socially and environmentally responsible corporate citizen. With such friends it could rain every day and we would still love Santa Barbara! Such are the joys of true friendship.

We didn't immediately go 'all in,' although almost. We found a one-year rental. We arrived on the ideal day, January 1st, 2002, for a new beginning. What was still formally an exploratory visit quickly became in our minds a foregone conclusion, pleasing to body, mind, and spirit. Although its fine weather was not a big inducement at the outset, it turned out to be rather addictive, making Santa Barbara even more enticing. We also welcomed the ability to play tennis all year, and a social lifestyle far more casual than Princeton. Of course, we arrived before raging wild fires became annual threats to the town, which would have weakened our resolve to make Santa Barbara our permanent home. As it was, we were well beyond the age of surfing, which required us to accept the reality that we would never be regarded as true Californians.

Global Studies at UCSB with its small yet talented, liberally inclined faculty possessed a far more congenial academic community than what I had experienced for four decades at Princeton. We felt welcomed and appreciated. We made new friends more rapidly than we could handle at the university and in town. It was unlike Princeton where the formalities of the East and the strains of Ivy League ambition made friendship feel as if a luxury, time stolen from the higher priority of finishing 'the next book.' Although I never competed in that way, I was affected by the Princeton atmosphere, feeling constantly under pressure juggling writing, teaching, administration, and activist commitments.

Our academic and town friendships gave our university life a sparkle missing at Princeton. It is not possible to celebrate the full range of friendship, but a few had such a special impact on our lives as to make silence a distortion. I think of Gerry Spence, nationally known as a wildly successful trial lawyer who prevailed in several famous cases, and became better known to us as a diamond in the rough. Somewhat deceptively, he paraded before all his Wyoming country image that hid from immediate view a sophisticated sensibility. Gerry overflows with creative energy and greater than life-size empathy. Over many years he has produced novels, an endearing memoir, searing studies of social issues, paintings and artistic photographs worthy of gallery exhibits, and carefully wrought poems that spoke from the heart. His social style reminds me of Oklahoma tornados, mercilessly challenging friends with hurricane force, including taking acquaintances and strangers by sur-prise, always probing others, aggressively exploring what hurts as well as what inspires. Gerry seemed driven by a deep desire to know what lies at the core of another person's being, refusing to be deterred by canons of social politeness even at a first meeting. I noticed a similar tendency in Joyce Carol Oates, the literary phenomenon, a colleague at Princeton, who also used her social time to 'research' the qualities of character of whomever she encountered. Perhaps, people are the 'books' for novelists that we non-fiction writers find on library shelves or through field trips to combat zones.

Another very special person who became our close friend was Elisabeth Weber, student of European philosophy and a leading interpreter of the seminal French philosopher, Jacques Derrida, with whom she worked with in Paris for more than a decade. Together with Derrida, Elisabeth published a book of interviews with leading European intellectuals with the title, *Questioning Judaism*. I accepted the challenge of contributing an Afterword to her quite extraordinary book on how torture, drone warfare, indefinite detention, and racist counterterrorism became the *plat de jour* in the aftermath of the 9/11 attacks.[iv] Her profound commentaries on leading issues of the day deserves much wider attention than they have so far received, and if I were half my age, I would do my best to remedy the situation. As it is, Elisabeth is a most trusted friend and such an ardent source of truth-seeking as to make even the most cynical Platonist impressed, and the rest of us intimidated. As with Gerry she seeks depths and is not content with surfaces. She proceeds by way of intellectual probing rather than his preferred method of emotional excavation.

A third vivid presence among those we came to love in our Santa Barbara experience was Lisa Hajjar. Her zest for life, overflowing heart, and generosity of spirit allows me to forgive her adoration of lawyers and lawyering. In fairness, the lawyers she most celebrates are those working for social causes on a pro bono basis, yet lawyers, nevertheless. Lisa through her forthrightness, knowledge, and passion was widely heralded as the anti-torture queen in the tortured post-9/11 environment. Always impressive academically when confined to her laptop, while sipping wine Lisa becomes a mistress of bravado that requires decoding and lots of love to sidestep her rhetorical extravagances. As a friend Lisa has been exemplary, and her social energy gathered what we came to call 'the Lisa Group,' consisting of likeminded, equally irreverent university colleagues, who have enlivened many a starlit Santa Barbara evening.

When it came to overall living circumstances, Santa Barbara was sufficiently bigger than Princeton to make it much more satisfying when it came to film, restaurants, and art. It was also physically situated on

---

iv See Kill Boxes: *The Legacy of U.S. Sponsored Torture, Indefinite Detention, and Drone Warfare* (2017).

slopes and a narrow strip of coastline squeezed between mountains and the ocean, picturesquely framed by the Channel Islands, which were a few miles from the shore. The combination of consistently blue skies, no humidity, cool nights, proximity to LA, and ocean views made it rather obvious why Santa Barbara became a favorite hangout for the rich and famous, especially serving as a weekend getaway for Hollywood notables. The fires and mud slides came more than a decade later to burst the bubble of our idyllic early years in Santa Barbara. There had been serious fires and earthquakes in Santa Barbara's past, but until this recent series of natural disasters, few doubts were raised to challenge the hedonistic image of contentment that the town enjoyed in the American imaginary.

Cascading Political Disappointment

My commitment to doing scholarly writing remained undiminished after my Princeton retirement, and subject to fewer distractions. I worked without career incentives beyond staying loosely involved in the academic game. I tried to develop further the perspectives of an aspiring citizen pilgrim, but in the altered political circumstances that seemed to prevail at the start of the new century. Ever since the end of the Vietnam War, from my perspective, there has been a downward spiral of political developments in matters that interested me most, including U.S. foreign policy, global political arrangements, and some specific conflict situations in Israel/Palestine, Iran, and Turkey. My earlier beliefs, hopes, commitments, and expectations seemed increasingly out of touch with the unfolding American political reality at home and in the world. Such a downward drift gathered further negative momentum with the election of George W. Bush in 2000 and accelerated a year later in the ill-considered response to the 9/11 attacks. But far worse was waiting to happen in 2016, and the years that followed.

Experiencing Mild Victimization

For the first twelve or so post-retirement years both Hilal and I taught courses in the Global Studies Program at the Santa Barbara campus of the University of California with our teaching assignments agreed upon annually. From the start it seemed an ideal arrangement, given the sympathetic faculty community, appreciative students, a perfect climate, and the willingness to take ample time for friendship. Yet as we were to find out, all that glitters is not always gold. California was even exceeding our expectations. Our lives seemed blessed, but we were unaware of dark clouds gathering just beyond the horizon.

The satisfying harmonies of this blissful early experience were disrupted by several intrusions, not all of which can be blamed on local circumstances. I felt personally victimized by a Zionist smear campaign in response to my Palestinian sympathies and activities. It took me a long time to realize the degree to which refraining from serious criticisms of Israel, however justifiable, had become politically and socially mandatory in middle class urban America, especially among Jewish liberals. There was little attention given to the substance associated with either supporting Palestinian rights or the accuracy of allegations of Israeli wrongdoing. I gave a few public talks in Santa Barbara and LA, wrote some opinion pieces, and did local media events that expressed my empathy for the ordeal being inflicted upon the Palestinian people. I also set forth ideas on how to achieve an enduring peace that might enable these two embattled peoples to live together in peace, on the basis of equality of rights.

Little criticism was said directly to me, but I noticed closed doors that had been previously wide open and some subtle asides in social conversation, especially among the liberal elite in our social circles in Santa Barbara, widely valued in the community for their readiness to fund liberal causes (except Palestine, of course). Friends would tell me that some influential person in Santa Barbara regards me as anti-Israeli. I was informed that the very assertive wife of the dean of the UCSB Arts and Sciences College was a rabid Zionist who was offended by my views. No one at that point, at least openly, indicated that such views, however objectionable, were those of an anti-Semite. That would come later, and mostly from Zionist NGOs that had political agendas. In these liberal circles, it was acceptable to criticize Netanyahu or Sheldon Adelson and AIPAC, but not to be more fundamentally critical of Israeli policies and practices or of a liberal Zionist outlook with respect to Palestinian rights or the American role as enabler.

It became politically correct in these liberal contexts to insist that both sides were equally to blame for the failure to move toward a peaceful resolution of the Israel/Palestine conflict, a view I rejected as based on 'false symmetry.' I regard putting the dominant and the dominated on an equal footing in addressing a negotiating impasse as deeply misleading, especially in this context. Struggle, not concessions by the oppressed, are the only path to progress. As Frederick Douglass, the African American abolitionist who escaped enslavement in Maryland insisted, '[p]ower concedes nothing without a demand. It never has and never will.'

When I became UN Special Rapporteur for Occupied Palestine in 2008 these issues of informal social exclusion intensified, although almost always taking a muted form. I am not sure why the muting occurred. Perhaps, because people liked Hilal so much that there was some reluctance to criticize me too harshly or openly. Once I had this UN job, however, there were many well publicized attacks on me in mainstream arenas, including by Israeli, American, and Commonwealth diplomats at the UN who called me biased against Israel, treating my appointment as illustrative of what they regarded as Israel-bashing that made the UN increasingly illegitimate in Zionist eyes.

Additional to the difficulties arising from my Palestinian solidarity activities, was a certain political estrangement arising from holding progressive views in the essentially liberal environment that prevailed in Santa Barbara. There were two types of liberals, those at the university who preferred Hillary Clinton over Bernie Sanders in 2016 because she could get elected, and get things done, and were comfortable with Biden in 2020 for similar reasons plus Trump fatigue and fascist fears, which I shared, although not comfortably. And then there were the 'Montecito Democrats'ᵛ who are socially liberal, economically Wall Street oriented, and politically at ease with the pro-militarist 'bipartisan consensus' that took shape during World War II, hardened during the Cold War, and has lingered even in the face of Trump's antics. These portfolio (stocks & bonds)-sensitive Democrats would never vote for Trump, whom they find distasteful and destructive, but many would likely stay at home rather than cast their ballot for Sanders, had he been the nominee.

More anguishing than my troubles were the trials and tribulations that Hilal endured in the course of being denied a permanent appointment on the Global Studies faculty, despite having excellent credentials and being strongly encouraged to apply for the opening that had been framed with her interests in mind. Although the non-transparency of the faculty appointment process makes it impossible to reconstruct what happened, it appears that she was a casualty of petty jealousies and some administrative interference, possibly reflecting Zionist hostility to me. We were told that the Global Studies faculty believed that we would quickly forget the rebuff and resume our limited ad hoc connections with the program. If so, it misjudged our personalities. We both decided to resign from Global Studies, severing our relationship, never looking back, and of course never seeking any future social or professional favors

---

v   Montecito is a separate mini-municipality adjacent to Santa Barbara with super-wealthy and Hollywood celebrity residents.

from Global Studies. Many on campus were movingly supportive, but the experience left a sour taste that affected out overall relationship with the university, and even with the broader experience of Santa Barbara.

The good news is that Hilal recovered her professional self-esteem, and more. She was soon appointed UN Special Rapporteur for the Right to Food in 2014, an important and demanding position that brought her into contact with all the leading people in the world concerned with food policy. Her appointment went forward despite a worldwide Zionist campaign to deny her the position for which she was recommended by the UN Human Rights Council Selection Committee that vetted dozens of qualified candidates from around the world. And why such a campaign? Solely and explicitly because I am her husband, a brazen form of guilt by association that even the U.S. State Department rejected. This Zionist vindictive outreach extended to UCLA School of Law where donors intervened to block her research appointment in a food program despite the absence of any sign, other than her choice of partner, that she was interested in the Israel/Palestine struggle, much less an anti-Israeli partisan.

She has taken a position critical of industrial agriculture, sided with agroecology movement that supports greater reliance on small-scale traditional farming and is alert to the health hazards of widespread use of pesticides, a multi-billion dollar business that is dominated by a few cutthroat companies, including Monsanto and Syngenta. I am proud of Hilal for the role she has played, displaying her exceptional social skills as well as her dedication to fashioning a humane food policy.

The California Idyll Ends

Without doubt, we fell under a spell of enchantment upon arrival in California that endured for our first decade. All facets of our life seemed to be satisfying beyond what we left behind in Princeton. Nine months in Santa Barbara, three in Turkey, with much international travel along the way seemed ideal, too good to be true, and so it was.

We knew about the San Marco fire that swept through the canyon near our rented home a decade earlier during our first year in Santa Barbara. It seemed an historical memory of little relevance. The fire threat seemed remote until the last decade. Our first close encounter with natural disaster occurred in the Conchita Mudslide of 2010 that caused 10 deaths, reminding us that nature could hit back with lethal force even striking blows nearby la-la land.

Our more troubling awakening came several years later when large wildfires spread all around California. I remember driving home at night in 2015, and seeing flames light up the sky not too far in the distance. The wind came to our rescue and diverted the fire. In 2017 the huge Thomas Fire that started in nearby Ventura swept in our direction so menacingly that we were required to evacuate from our Santa Barbara home for ten days to escape not only the fire, but the noxious fumes that made the air unhealthy to breathe even with a mask.

A positive aspect of the experience was that we were able to find a satisfying sanctuary for the duration of the danger. We went to Fog Catcher's Inn in Cambria, a hundred or so miles north on the coast, a lovely small town picturesquely situated, and not then or since threatened. We were with close friends, who made the experience feel like an enforced vacation. It was, however, somewhat agonizing for me. The pain from my recent second knee replacement surgery was quite intense, especially as we had to have our meals at local restaurants, which meant much movement and long periods of discomfort, but compared to breathing the toxic air of Santa Barbara it was 'a no brainer.'

Shortly after returning to Santa Barbara, a lethal mudslide took place less than a mile away from our house following a short torrential rainfall. Warnings had been issued suggesting a voluntary evacuation, but having just returned home, we along with many who would suffer from staying behind, did not heed the advice. While sleeping we were awakened by an onslaught of rain and strong winds accompanied by a rumbling sound that resembled a freight train more than thunder. We went to our window and saw a blood red night sky that we assumed was the reflection of a fire, but we saw no flames. A friend called to tell us that the mudslide had carried debris, including many larger boulders, that hurtled down the slope of the mountains, especially carried by overflowing creeks, and leaving a trail of death and destruction. Later we learned that this mudslide did such heavy damage because of a rare geologic event, a downpour amid ferocious winds that slanted the rain, loosening boulders the size of cars from the steep mountain slope with the ground cover having been ravaged by intense fire just weeks before. This event brought the word 'apocalyptic' to our lips, and we realized that we were spared, not by the safety of the location of our house or our prudence, but by luck, and the added good fortune of not living near one of the creeks that swept the death-bearing debris down the mountains at highway speeds.

Becoming 80

In 2010 I became 80. Hilal organized a party of friends and children at Catalina Island thanks to the hospitality of our friend, Paul Amar. It was an unsentimental and happy occasion with its most lasting legacy being the gift of a blog created for me by Zeynep and Andrei, still then her husband. Although the gift was theirs the idea came from Hilal. More than 800 posts later I realize that it was a rather inspired gift, a digital soap box that allowed me to continue to spout my views on anything and everything. I suppose that my acceptance of the challenge drew upon my amateurish interest in many things and the relative ease with which I could compose a readable essay, although I received some feedback that my posts were too academic to engage the short attention spans of the visually dependent non-readers of the digital age.

Despite this, I received mostly positive feedback, and was astonished how amid the millions of venues, several thousand readers found my blog, and many became loyal followers. During this period I had a rather high-profile UN connection with the Palestinian struggle, I wrote on these themes more than on other topics, and my views were sometimes contested in nasty comments that included personal attacks and malicious innuendo. I wavered between responding and blocking, and found neither very satisfying. To this day I sometimes ignore in silence, sometimes respond calmly, and a few times reciprocate with exasperated hostility. Such experience comes with the territory, and especially so in my case, as I take positions on public issues that bring distress to some, anger to others.

A downside of the blog experience, especially until 2014 when my term as Special Rapporteur expired, was that my posts supplied raw material for those seeking ways to discredit me as a critical observer of Israeli policies and practices in Occupied Palestine. UN Watch composed their letters to the high and mighty serving the UN and Western governments based on blogs addressing a variety of themes, which supplemented their research into my past, especially my meeting in 1979 with Ayatollah Khomeini, as well as my opinion pieces connecting American foreign policy in the Middle East with extremist violence in the United States, and a host of other issues relevant to portraying me as an alienated tool of terrorists.

The upside of writing blogs on a regular basis was to create a global network of friends and followers who were appreciative, and helpfully responsive. Without this feedback I doubt that I would have maintained the discipline to continue composing blogs on diverse topics several times a week, which were substitutions for more academic commentary on the passing scene. I treated the blogosphere as a free form, even posting poems occasionally, as well as writing reviews of films and books that struck me as significant in one way or another. Often my posts were republished with and without my permission on several online independent journalistic sites around the world.

In many ways the blog experience was more satisfying, even when account is taken of its downside, than had been my writing of articles for academic journals and edited books, of which I did several hundred over the years. Although I enjoyed exploring ideas, developing arguments, defending controversial conclusions, and seeing my scribbles in print, I only rarely, and then often only after the passage of years, received useful feedback. My published works were scholarly monologues, while the blog posts had a more dialogic character, especially when the comments section produced stimulating responses and interactive experiences.

Revisiting the California Dream

Despite these encounters with a rougher, tougher California, including our disillusioning experience at UCSB, we never entertained the thought of retreating to Princeton, or for that matter, elsewhere, at least not until Trump and the pandemic came along. We had our Turkish home in Yalikavak on the Bodrum peninsula that has brought us annually months of serenity and a national experience far from the familiar American scene. Turkey, despite its host of problems, remains for me exotic, brimming with promise, natural beauty, deep culture, and a human warmth expressed by way of exceptional hospitality. Actually, the yin and yang of Santa Barbara and Yalikavak makes us feel very fortunate, a variation in atmosphere and social rhythms that enhanced our lives for the past twenty years. Since 2016 it has been a relief to be geographically distant for part of each year from the Trump phenomenon that holds captive the minds and hearts of its enemies as much as its enthusiasts. Turkey, too, has its own black sites that should not be overlooked, but neither should they be exaggerated.

I think we have come to understand California more realistically in the last few years. The rose-colored haze has faded, both as it concerns the university and the natural surroundings. We recognize that we are in a habitat threatened by global warming in particularly ominous ways. More severe and frequent wildfires are a grim reminder that the planet is burning up metaphorically as well as literally, and that the mismatch between the technologies of modernity and the natural surroundings is reaching several critical junctures, which if not addressed with a sense of urgency, incline the future toward species catastrophe. Yet our life experience in Santa Barbara from start to finish has given us love, pleasure, and intimacy in many forms. Sartre may have convinced many people that 'Hell is other people' but our experience has delivered a different message, 'Friends make the blandness of heaven bearable, even enjoyable.'

During the whole of the COVID pandemic we were in Turkey, and mainly confined to Yalikavak. The lockdown experience became challenging as the months passed, our plans adapted, and we found good ways to keep the body healthy, the mind active, and the spirit quivering. More cannot be expected, nor should it be sought.

From Santa Barbara: Links with Rome, London, Delhi, Istanbul

Among the perks of an academic life of a scholarly/activist focus on global concerns are many opportunities for international travel. My interests and curiosity led me to travel extensively ever since I was a student, leaving a heavier carbon footprint than I would wish for others, and falling short of satisfying my own ecological demands as an aspiring citizen pilgrim. The lockdown experience of the COVID pandemic has taught me that one can experience the world, digitally and virtually, without flying from place to place. Maybe because of my age that seems less preoccupied with the existential challenges, opportunities, smells, tastes, and overall excitement of being in foreign settings exchanging thoughts, feelings, laughter, and even tears with those whose civilizational roots are distinct from my own.

Most of my residential life has been lived in the towns of Princeton, Santa Barbara, and Yalikavak, while my adult sensibility was shaped by being born and growing up in New York City. During my professional life I had many recurrent experiences in large, iconic cities including Amsterdam, London, Paris, Rome, Athens, Hanoi, Geneva, Stockholm, Delhi, Beijing, Melbourne/Sydney, and Tokyo, with additional recurrent exposures to Jerusalem, Moscow, Vienna, Cairo, Beirut, Mexico City, Rio de Janeiro, Johannesburg, Berlin, Kyoto, Manila, and Madrid. It is these foreign cities, their people, statues, parks, cafes, and special sites, that have given my life its worldly edge, and even bestowed faith in future pleasures if our better selves somehow prevail.

For some years in the early 1980s I took part in annual conferences in Japan on 'Yokohama and the World,' often as an invited speaker, making me ponder the differences between a world order constituted by sovereign cities rather than sovereign states. These events were sponsored by the governor of the prefecture who had the somewhat subversive belief that the interests of his city of Yokohama were not being represented adequately by the national government of Japan, in particular by its allying so closely with the U.S. and failing to seek positive relations with China or North Korea. I found that some urban sensibilities, despite glorious pasts, are nevertheless more concerned with constructing a brilliant future than are folks in the countryside with their tighter ties to habit, tradition, the exclusivist sides of nationhood, and shortages of exploratory space for imagining new futures.

Observing the electoral alignments in my two homelands of the United States and Turkey, it becomes striking that the rural areas provide the populist base for traditional values while cities search for more emancipatory solutions to the stresses of modernity. Of course, the political configurations vary greatly from city to city and through time, reflecting a host of historical, ethnic, and economic factors, but I rest my hope for a cosmopolitan, pluralist, and progressive future on urban sensibilities, without romanticizing cities which also feature large no-go neighborhoods of extreme poverty, drug use, violent crime, gangs, traffic, and pollution, that is, the best and worst of the human condition are currently exhibited within city limits. True, countertrends of fleeing the city to achieve a purer and healthier life in the country or more comfort for middle class families in suburbs are evident, a tendency given a strong push in reactions to the mental strains arising from the pandemic lockdowns.

Illustratively, a telling image is a 2020 story of Portland, Oregon, a state associated with progressive values that has been a site of anti-racist protests in response to George Floyd'a death, when the protesters were challenged not only by local police and urban adversaries, but by gun-toting Trump supporters trucked in from the surrounding countryside. In the most populous American states that give the biggest margins of victory to progressive political tendencies, California and New York, the encouraging results reflect what happens in their cities. Revealingly, their political profiles would be vastly different if only persons living in communities under 50,000 were given the vote. Looking at a Turkish map after its relatively close national elections of recent years, a similar pattern is revealed. It would seem at a glance that the entire country supports the Erdogan-led AKP except for a few large cities in the West where secularists generally have prevailed and progressive mayors are elected. Of course, these patterns are not uniform. We must remember that Erdogan's ascent to national leadership began with his election as mayor of Istanbul. Nevertheless, the hopes for a benign future for humanity have to do with respecting countryside values while pursuing on a local, regional, and global scale a more urban, pluralist approach to living-in-the-world. My experience has combined the distinctive pleasures of living without daily coping with the complexities of big cities. Yet my orientation as citizen pilgrim suggests that the human species must find ways to forge a new world order resting on creative fusions between the need to live benignly in close proximity with masses of diverse others and moderating the urgencies posed by the stark inequalities among the peoples of the world, while working toward the protection of the global common good. Tribalisms, whether ethnic or national, will not be able to meet the challenges of more than eight billion people living together on the planet in the 21st century. My own life has been profoundly nourished by experiencing a variety of world cities. They have served as my private theaters connecting the personal with the political, offering a limitless curriculum of adult education.

What makes the impersonal charm of cities come alive is contact with vibrant residents, encounters that transcend the complacencies of the habitual, offering receptive visitors innovative forms of rapport. These range from intimate to adversarial, and include professional, touristic, and most of all, what transpires in the spaces reserved for friendships, old and new.

Most of my recurrent travels since 1995 have been with Hilal, especially to world cities that connected with her work, overlapping with friendships, and sometimes linked in mysterious ways to our Santa Barbara life. It began pre-Hilal with Mary Kaldor. My collaborative undertakings with Mary made pleasurable many trips to London and Delhi tied to long-term scholarly projects to encourage a softening of the Cold War in the 1980s by what we called 'détente from below,' that is, by pressures exerted via transnational civil society initiatives. And by a worldwide undertaking supported by the United Nations University in Tokyo, directed by the leading Indian social scientist and our friend, Rajni Kothari, on the theme of 'global transformation,' greatly enlivened by his extraordinary student assistant, Vandana Shiva, herself destined to be a leading visionary who, unforgettable even as a graduate student, combined acute scientific awareness with a vibrant bio-ethical sensibility.

In Mary's Brighton home, I first met Daniele Archibugi, a prince of romantic vivacity, who would later become a special friend who forged new paths in democratic thought, and was that archetypical Italian that

Jungian analysts only fantasize of encountering in real life. Daniele's promotion of democratizing political futures had many affinities with the work of David Held, a leading interpreter of political democracy who connected the internal organization of the state with a world at peace. David, who also became my friend, supported our WOMP efforts, and worked closely with Mary at LSE on global governance, devoting special attention to Europe. David was one of the most articulate, imaginative, and productive scholars I have ever come to know personally. His best work explored the nature of democratic governance from different angles. His unexpected tragic death midlife deprived the world of a most fertile mind as well as prevented the composition of his magnum opus, which likely would have tied together the strands of his prolific scholarship in a single golden knot. As an aging scholar myself, such an undertaking has often crossed my mind, but I have still not found the rope!

I had earlier experiences among the fountains of Rome during the 1970s as part of a small group helping Lelio Basso form the Permanent Peoples Tribunal that tried to fill the gaps created by the geopolitical impunity between major states and international criminal law. This bold civil society initiative followed the lead of the Bertrand Russell Tribunal that purported to pass legal judgment on the United States during the Vietnam War, acknowledging the inability of the UN to extend the coverage of criminal accountability to the five members of the Security Council. That assurance of impunity had been given constitutional status in the form of the right of veto, which was the price paid by the UN to entice the geopolitical winners in World War II to join the Organization, and make its claim to represent the peoples of the world credible. It was a delight to work closely with Lelio Basso, an influential Marxist legislator surrounding himself with devout Catholic women, and a devoted ideological follower, Gianni Tognoni, who became my friend in the course of tribunal collaborations. Lelio taught me that it was all right to love life and yet oppose state crime, that harmony between good living and a just world is natural, even necessary. In those years I came to the belief that Rome demonstrated that society could work even as the state disappointed, even failed, and I still hold this view. The Romans know how to live, but not how to govern.

Since 2014 our semi-annual trips to Italy have arisen from Hilal's work on global food security. Rome was headquarters of the UN Food and Agricultural Organization (FAO). Often we stayed in the student San Lorenzo district in an apartment owned by Daniele, giving us a contemporary glimpse of a rundown neighborhood of the eternal city and lots of exposure via Daniele to the Roman social scene. Rome flourished, re-tained its magic, but there were many frustrations with a corrupt political scene and an economic landscape in which jobs for youth were becoming scarce, and leaving the family homestead on reaching adulthood even scarcer. Rome flourished while Italians were suffering. Coincidentally, our friendship with Daniele had a London connection because part of his teaching life was at Birkbeck College where we would meet when both in either city at the same time.

Part of the reason for being so often in London was due to a chance meeting with Penny Green while she and her husband, Bill Spence, were visiting UCSB. Penny, a criminologist, was at the time running a State Crime Initiative at the Law Faculty of Kings College in London, and invited Hilal and myself to spend a semester as Visiting Fellows with some minor lecture obligations. Oddly, we had met Penny and Bill at a dinner at the home of close friends, Avery Gordon and Chris Newfield, who would later themselves resign UCSB appointments so that they could live and work in London. A few years later Penny became dean of the Law Department of Queen Mary University London, and I was offered a position as Chair of Global Law, which meant two months in London for the contract period of five years. At first, our periods of res-idence have coincided with strikes in the British university system over faculty pensions. Then came the pandemic that has temporarily rendered our presence as 'virtual.' To be academically relevant at 90 seems to slow ageing more enjoyably (and, I hope, effectively) than anti-ageing vitamins.

Although the London experience was ecumenical for us, there were some unpleasant reminders of more provincial identities. London is a central venue of Zionist militancy, which should not be surprising considering that the whole project to create a Jewish homeland in Palestine gained decisive momentum a century earlier when the British Foreign Secretary issued the Balfour Declaration (1917) pledging support for establishing a Jewish homeland in Palestine. Wherever I spoke in London after I had become known as a critic of Israel and a supporter of the Palestinian struggle, there were attack Zionists in the audience, often attending such events simply to cause disruptions. Such encounters recalled my feelings of personal vulnerability in UN settings, but I held my ground, and the programs went forward as scheduled. On one occasion I spoke together with Jeremy Corbyn before he became head of the Labour Party at a Palestinian solidarity meeting. A year or so later a British tabloid published a photo of myself sitting next to Corbyn, the caption claiming that by speaking together with such a notorious anti-Semite as myself, Corbyn displayed his own anti-Jewish bias, supposedly confirming the allegations of his accusers.

In my experience, cities reflect the maladies of the world but also serve as inspirational platforms for a satisfying, safe, creative life experience, and the best shot at a benevolent future for humanity. From art galleries to experimental films and political theater, the cultural life of the city encourages us to give free expression to our moral and political imagination flourish, mostly ignoring the stupidities of state power. I have started to dream of a future global architecture designed by urban dwellers, anarchists, and animal lovers.

PART FOUR

ENGAGING THE WORLD
CITIZENSHIP, WITNESSING, ACTIVISM

I was from the beginning satisfied with the cloistered life of a scholar/teacher. It seemed sufficient for me. Yet I gradually became uncomfortable about not carrying my ideas into public arenas when my students and others were being forced to make momentous life choices that risked their losing life, limb, and serenity via their recruitment in carrying out a Cold War foreign policy that seemed to go increasingly against their and my values. I also opposed this globally militarist approach to pursuing American objectives on realist grounds as unlikely to succeed, given the realities of the world as currently constituted. This reflected my belief that the restraints of international law and UN Charter, properly interpreted, not only served American national interests and should be obeyed for that reason, but were also intrinsically related to humane global governance in the nuclear age, and as such, deserved respect.

As I became more publicly vocal and engaged, I downplayed the practical arguments relating to the success and failure of the American grand strategy and focused more on normative considerations, distinguishing right from wrong, just from unjust, legal from illegal. This switch pulled me somewhat against my wishes away from sanctuaries of privacy and seclusion that usually accompany an academic life, and toward the brighter and sometimes glaring lights of media attention and public controversy. Over time, despite periods of withdrawal, I found myself consistently swimming against the current, and found that struggling to keep moving forward became more difficult, not easier as I had hoped. At the last stages of the Vietnam War, I had become rather confident that the flow of history was on my side. Now I believe that what I interpreted as a flow was not wrong, but rather applied to the collapse of European colonial empires, not to the wider trend of Westernization and American hegemonic globalization, as well to its regressive boomerang effects.

CHAPTER 11

America's Bloody Footprint in Vietnam: Descending from the Ivory Tower

Engaged Citizenship in Wartime

It was never my intention to become a political activist. My first ten years as a teacher made me aware that I had strong opinions, which often made me feel at odds with the prevailing political atmosphere among university faculties, especially on foreign policy. I didn't experience these feelings as a call to action but rather as producing some separation from the mainstream. I never unconditionally endorsed the verities or confrontations of the Cold War, or the managerial consensus that the nuclear age could be adequately addressed as a mere continuation of the past. These sentiments made me restless and apprehensive, but I was still not ready to go into the street with those protesting the policies that were the outcome of these Cold War ways of seeing political reality. When I finally did find myself speaking at noisy demonstrations and teachins and even on the street, I now realize that I was gradually assuming the burdens and satisfactions of what was then beginning to be called a public intellectual. During the process, I was not very conscious of my transformation. This largely hidden process, taking place over a period of years, did give rise to some second guessing my somewhat new self. Because my library and classroom concerns were international, it was natural for me to find myself mostly involved in international issues whenever I did become engaged. On domestic issues—race, gender, women, workers—I had rather standard left liberal views, affirming human equality in all aspects and a wide discretion to live as one wished so long as it was not harmful to others, especially to youth. I was not as alive to systemic elements of these deep socio-economic and cultural challenges as I later became.

Before Vietnam, Cuba

It took a further transformative experience for me to begin regarding myself as a kind of Ibsenian 'enemy of the people,' that is, as such a shrill critic of the established order placing myself outside the sphere of conventional beliefs and values.

It took my visit in June of 1968 to North Vietnam in the midst of the Vietnam War before I would come to publicly affirm the exemplary nationalist leadership of Ho Chi Minh and to feel solidarity with the Vietnamese struggle for national unity and post-colonial independence. This visit was the culmination of a transformative process that Castro's words at Cambridge had begun almost a decade earlier. As with any dramatic political identification, there are always reasons that emerge later on to question such leaps into the near dark, often producing reservations about earlier bursts of enthusiasm. However, for me, these affirmations of that single night of listening to ee cummings read his poems and Castro explain his revolution in Cambridge basically held up. Their complementary ways of understanding the world even now remain compelling despite the passage of six decades and the occurrence of a series of subsequent inconsistent developments. Recent disclosures and some trustworthy commentators endorse revisionist views of Vietnamese wartime leadership, contending that Ho Chi Minh may have been the public face of the struggle, but he was not the ultimate decision maker or chief political/military strategist. While such a correction is important it does not affect my reasons for supporting the heroic Vietnamese effort to safeguard their right of self-determination, an inalienable right sanctified by law, morality, and political consensus.

As background for this fundamental shift in my outlook toward Vietnam, it seems helpful to revisit my earlier sympathy for the Cuban Revolution. I initially became professionally interested in the Cuban political emergence as a young international law specialist searching for research topics to write about during my time as a faculty member of the law school at Ohio State. My professional writing supportive of Castro's socialist policies provided the essential background for my deeper, activist engagement during the final decade of the Vietnam War. My interest in Cuba led in other directions, including giving rise to my warm friendship with Leonard Boudin, without doubt the most gifted progressive lawyer of his generation, whose law firm represented the

Cuban Government. My friendship with Leonard and his wife Jean (the sister of the celebrated left journalist, I.F. Stone) was a source of deep satisfaction. I recall spending many stimulating evenings in their West Village apartment in the company of leading progressive intellectuals and UN diplomats.

Leonard was as charming and gifted socially as he was talented legally, as comfortable playing chess at the Harvard Club or in his midtown Manhattan office as he was defending and smoozing with such anti-war celebrities as Phil Berrigan, Eqbal Ahmad, Tony Russo, and Dan Ellsberg, each of whom became his devoted friends. This talent for mingling professionalism with friendship reminded me of my father, although Dad's intimacies were with leading anti-Communist personalities, Wall Street lawyers, and a few Hollywood notables, while Leonard socialized with prominent progressives, including foreign diplomats ranging from the Cuban ambassador to the Irish winner of the Nobel and Lenin Peace Prizes, Sean MacBride. Neither my father nor Leonard could resist the charms of women, particularly if they were beautiful.

The pride, joy, and anguish of Leonard's life, aside from his love of law, women, and chess, were his two strikingly different children: Michael, the older of the two, did the right things all along in Leonard's eyes. Michael was elected to the editorial board of the *Harvard Law Review* and climaxed his career as a lawyer by being appointed a federal district court judge. Kathy, was a different story. She was the prime object of Leonard's fatherly love despite doing many wrong things from his perspective. She was a dark-eyed, intense, and hard-core feminist, paying little attention to how she dressed or looked. She was animated, intelligent, and fun to be around. Kathy made an abrupt transition from Bryn Mawr to the Weathermen, ending up in the Weather Underground after the notorious Village Town House explosion. It was an event that caused shockwaves of concern, revealing that in the heart of Manhattan a group of young radicals were assembling explosive devices that could be used to advance their revolutionary vision.

After hiding from the law for more than a decade, Kathy became involved in 1981 with an imprudent bank robbery that turned lethal, with a bank guard and two police officers being killed, and others wounded. The robbery was organized and led by African American revolutionaries of the Black Liberation Army with support from several members of the Weather Underground. With life-changing irony, Kathy had planned to end her underground existence prior to the planned robbery by turning herself in to U.S. authorities the following week, but was persuaded at the last minute to play a passive part as driver and decoy in the crime to show her comrades in struggle that she was not abandoning 'revolutionary solidarity.' Her involvement in these events turned out worse than expected. After being apprehended, Kathy was sentenced to a long prison term, which had its own set of complications, including the prison birth of her son. After her release from prison Kathy was appointed as an adjunct faculty member at Columbia University, and later became co-founder and co-director of its Center of Justice. Such a career, post prison, is highly unusual.

A week or ten days *before* this life-changing explosion in the basement of the Greenwich Village town house a few blocks away, Leonard and Jean had gathered some of their leftist friends. These included Alger Hiss, the most establishment connected celebrity among those accused of serving the Soviets while holding important government positions. I was invited along with my third wife, Florence. We made the weekday trip from Princeton to be part of the group assembled to meet with Kathy, and her Weatherman co-revolutionary, Judy Clark. The declared purpose of the evening was to talk these idealistic young women out of engaging in violent forms of civil disobedience and what Leonard's generation believed to be a flirtation with romantic style activism that would lead nowhere politically. These veterans of the American left were conversant with Marx, continued to believe more or less in the virtues of the Soviet experiment, and above all regarded a labor movement guided by Marxist thought as the correct path to revolution in the West. This older generation of political progressives had little patience with what they deemed to be the self-destructive political radicalism of Kathy and Judy.

It was a sad, unforgettable experience for me. Instead of an inter-generational meeting of minds, it produced an angry dialogue that exhibited the absence of common ground between old radicals and new revolutionaries, and above all displayed the political intolerance of this out of touch older generation, who nonetheless regarded themselves as wiser. While Kathy and Judy patiently and calmly explained their outlook the graying radicals in the room aggressively argued with them every step of the way, advocating thought and action in accord with the traditional modes of left politics, clearly not grasping the rationale behind the Weatherman sense of revolutionary urgency. Looking back I am not sure that the views of either side were vindicated, or for that matter altogether repudiated. This same sense of 'right action,' as the Buddhists might put it, underlies the debate between the militancy of the Black Lives Matter movement and those liberals warning of the counterrevolutionary consequence of mob violence and police payback. As now, back then, this non-dialogic 'conversation' produced a mood in the Boudin living room that wavered between frustration, anger, and regret.

Florence and I felt at a loss. We were caught in the middle, and realized that, as the evening progressed, the opposing positions were hardening even further in ways directly opposite to what the Boudins hoped would happen. This refusal by their friends to listen to Kathy and Judy, meant that their conciliatory project had failed. This deeply disturbed and disappointed Leonard and Jean, who came to realize that this encounter that they had arranged with the best intentions of parental love turned out to be an utter disappointment, worse than nothing. As the evening unfolded it became increasingly obvious to Leonard and Jean that the disconnect between generational sensibilities and political orientations was too great, and that they themselves felt helpless to intervene.

The last time I saw Kathy was in a high security prison in New York state. At Leonard's request I went for a visit along with Helena Kennedy, a celebrated English barrister, who had represented some IRA activists accused of terrorism, later becoming a member of the House of Lords. The strangest aspect of Leonard Boudin's career—although his whole professional and social life was dominated by progressive causes and friendships with leading radical personalities of his time—was that he himself was essentially apolitical, having almost no engagement with and not even that much interest in political issues except as they affected the law, his clients, and directly impacted friends and family. It was as if he was born with progressive DNA genes—actually, his uncle, Louis Boudin was a respected Marx scholar—but without any vocation to engage politically. Expert lawyering for anti-state defendants was his destiny.

Debating the Lawfulness of the American Policy in Vietnam

My political and public engagement with Vietnam was an unplanned outgrowth of involvement with informal political discussions of Vietnam policy in the early 1960s and a growing commitment to shape my academic studies and identity as a citizen so that they reflected my worldview and ethical standpoint, responding to present political conditions and future aspirations. I was aware, of course, that this kind of normative orientation went against the quantitative and empirical grain of the main trends in social science research as well as being politically incorrect and at odds with the apolitical temperament of law faculties at that time. These fashionable trends in academia sought to ground political and legal studies in scientific methodology in which values were associated with Cold War verities and empirical data treated as the only way to advance knowledge of a scholarly field of inquiry. For me to embrace what began to be called 'normative studies' (that is, studies focusing on legal, ethical, and diplomatic norms) was thus to adopt a position at odds with the epistemological mainstream, which was trying so hard in this period to ground inquiry on such methodologies as 'rational choice,' 'formal models,' and 'game theory.' This meant that worrying directly about human wellbeing or world peace and justice was out of fashion, putting me at the lonely margins of political and legal studies. Even political theorists were seeking empirical grounding for their inquiries, refraining from advocacy in non-academic settings. The anti-Marxist thrust of the times was *to interpret* the world but not *change it*. American social scientists were not drawn to Marxism except as a matter of intellectual curiosity, which in its dogmatic ways also sought to be 'scientific' to avoid being branded 'utopian.' In contrast, or as some might say, in contrarian defiance, I built my academic identity on the basis of visionary and progressive ethics, beliefs, desires, and solidarity with social movements, liberation and empowerment struggles, and victimized peoples, whether in America or elsewhere. If called upon to define my overall identity I would label it 'visionary humanism,' with spiritual receptivity incorporating the mysteries at the core of being, an alternative to 'secular humanism' with its narrower conception of reality resting on verifiability and rationalism.

Beginning in 1963, I took part in many Princeton and East Coast discussions of the Vietnam War as an international law critic, chaired an academic council of a lawyers' committee opposing the war policies, and wrote several articles contending that the U.S. involvement in the extension of the Vietnam War to North Vietnam violated international law and the UN Charter. Among lawyers on the East Coast I had become somewhat known as a result of public debates arising from the controversial *Sabbatino* litigation arising from Cuba's nationalization of the sugar industry. This made me feel reasonably comfortable situated at this interface between the organized bar of practicing lawyers and the academic world. This interface was becoming highly politicized as the domestic opposition to the Vietnam policies grew in intensity.

In the mainstream, which blended anti-Communism, Cold War foreign policy, and liberalism on issues of race and welfare, the role of law was taken far more seriously as a site of struggle than at present, although its leverage with political leaders was never great when it came to issues of foreign policy or peace and security. International law in war/peace settings was regarded instrumentally and always pragmatically by the national policy community, even in those days when liberalism prevailed in Washington. Despite this, international law was considered to be quite relevant to the policy debate in the 1960s, and functioned as a valued public justification for international uses of force even if interpreted one-sidedly to facilitate aggressive moves in American forieign policy. This would not be so later, when the cynical dismissal of international legal constraints became a characteristic of the nationalist presidencies of George W. Bush and recently, even more stridently, if indirectly, by Donald Trump who seems somewhere between unaware of and opposed to the relevance of international law or the UN, and clearly couldn't care less. The liberal slant of the political leaders during the time of John F. Kennedy and Lyndon B. Johnson witnessed the government doing its best to convince the citizenry and world public opinion that international law properly interpreted was aligned with American national interests in areas of political controversy generated by the Vietnam policies, and with other Cold War issues. In effect, American foreign policy was not significantly restrained by international law in war/peace contexts here either, but political leaders and their chief advisors at least made efforts to reconcile and justify policy by law through partisan modes of its interpretation. I and other opponents responded to this rationalizing approach with the argument that international law should be respected and interpreted from a *regulative* perspective that took account of historical considerations and of the world order values of peace and justice at stake. This was no less partisan than what apologists for American policy claimed, but proceeded from the belief that global interests in peace, justice, and liberation transcended national claims of a discretionary right to use international force on behalf of geopolitical goals such as protecting markets, investments, and ideological allies.

Academic loyalists supportive of American foreign policy, including international law specialists, did their best to provide a helping hand to the government by developing legal rationalizations for prevailing foreign policy positions that were being challenged. In this spirit the Legal Advisor's Office of the Department of State was mobilized to produce a public document purporting to show that the extension of the combat zone to North Vietnam after the contrived Gulf of Tonkin incident in 1964 was legally justified. The strained official legal argument was that it was consistent with international law that the U.S. exercise its right to assist the government of South Vietnam in its exercise of the right of self-defense in response to a pattern of attack by North Vietnam labeled as '*indirect* aggression.' Such a legal argument rested on the manipulated fiction that two Vietnamese sovereign states existed, reinforcing the war propaganda that North Vietnamese aid to the National Liberation Front in the South and material involvement in their struggle satisfied the UN Charter requirement of 'armed attack' as a precondition for a valid U.S. claim of support for the South Vietnamese exercise of its right of self-defense. Twenty years later the World Court repudiated a similar legal argument relied upon by Washington in justifying its support for anti-Sandinista policies in Nicaragua.

In this period, I wrote as often as possible to clarify, elaborate, and extend my central contention that international law, *properly interpreted,* mattered, and was being violated by the United States and South Vietnam at great human cost, and in opposition to the anti-colonial flow of history. Despite these strenuous efforts of mine to establish the unlawfulness of American policy toward Vietnam, my work still fell within the main-stream liberal paradigm of legitimate debate on controversial issues. I received many invitations to speak and write, including from conservative institutions, and even from war colleges that train the officer corps of the various branches of the U.S. armed forces. My legal partisanship did not yet situate me beyond the boundaries of 'responsible' discussion. I had a good chance, given this perception, of having my submissions of opinion pieces accepted by national newspapers, which still were functioning as litmus tests for locating the outer boundaries of acceptable public dissent.

In the mid-1960s I also embarked on a project in collaboration with the very mainstream American Society of International Law to bring together the best academic writing on both sides of the debate about the legality of American policies toward Vietnam, starting with interpreting the relevance of the defeat of French colonialism at Dien Bien Phu in 1954. I was able to persuade Princeton University Press, which operated completely independently of the university, to publish a big fat volume in 1968 under my editorship, titled *The Vietnam War and International Law*. The volume attempted to strike a neutral and pluralist tone, in effect acknowledging the existence of legitimate differences of interpretation when it came to the legal rights and wrongs at stake. The war persisted, and the debate extended itself to questions of constitution-al interpretation, tactics of warfare, diplomatic negotiations, war crimes, and finally, peace diplomacy. Due to the unexpected extended length of the war this editing venture ended up as a four-volume series. It remains a resource for scholars seeking an understanding of the international law dimensions of the Vietnam War, which also helps inform debates on subsequent patterns of intervention by geopolitical actors in internal affairs of sovereign states. I meet people from time to time who tell me that they learned about the Vietnam War by reading from these volumes and it changed their outlook permanently.

I experienced no pushback in reaction to my role as an academic commentator critical of the American role in Vietnam, writing mainly from the perspective of international law. I became a frequent expert anti-war witness before Congressional committees and in judicial settings, a role I played then that later became unthinkable even in the decade before the Clinton presidency, that is, long before such reactionary leaders as George W. Bush and Donald Trump were enthroned by electoral mandate. The war colleges in the country continued to extend invitations, and I spoke at places as varied as West Point, Annapolis, and was invited, although declined, to work for RAND and give talks at the CIA. I was asked by several senators who sought a presidential nomination to lend assistance to their campaigns, including Harold Hughes (Iowa), Gene McCarthy, George McGovern, and Jerry Brown. I received an invitation to join the Council on Foreign Relations as a member, and early on was encouraged by staff members to play an influential role in bringing prominent left liberals into this influential arena. The CFR had become aware that its future role depended on bringing on board some of the critical voices that challenged American foreign policy during the Vietnam years. It was hoped that this would make people believe that the CFR was in touch with a changing American scene. More recently, the opposite tendency is evident, reflective of the dramatic shift rightwards in the political atmosphere. Now the search seems intent on identifying persons of rightist persuasion that could help keep the CFR from appearing tone deaf to the bizarre rhythms of Trumpism.

My own experience is emblematic of the dangerous closure of channels for public debate in the United States since the Vietnam period. This closure blocks the expression of views from left of center, although it is structurally compensated by much greater openness to the alt-right perspective that presently haunts the republic from the centers of governmental authority: the White House, Congress, and Supreme Court. For someone like myself an invitation to testify at a Congressional committee hearing, appear on a mainstream talk show, or assist a presidential candidate is no longer even a remote possibility. But for my rightist counterparts, it is now an everyday occurrence, even in such liberal media settings as CNN, MSNBC, and the *NY Times* where the self-assured views of retired generals and intelligence analysts are presented as authoritative, and opposing outlooks ignored.

More generally, less personally, such experience reflects the narrowing of public debate on foreign policy issues after the 9/11 attacks coupled with the rise of the neoconservative wing of the Republican Party, and intensified by a surging alt-right that provided the policy foundations of the Trump presidency. My experience of being denied access to official and establishment venues was a gradual process that redefined my public sense of self. It represented the transition that continued over the next for 40 years from my being a somewhat dissenting liberal academic critic to becoming a contrarian scholar/activist.

Crossing the Line

My willingness to respect the boundaries of liberal dissent began to change abruptly in the Spring of 1968, and never retreated. I had recently returned home to Princeton after three tense weeks in South Africa as an official observer of a political trial of South West African (Namibia) nationalists held before an Afrikaner judge in Pretoria. It was itself an eye-opening experience of the policy and practice of apartheid South Africa, which was the crudest form of racism I had ever encountered, and deeply offended my still essentially liberal form of humanism. South Africa denied me an entry visa to act as an expert witness on behalf of the defense, probably because I had been part of the legal team that challenged apartheid in South West Africa (now Namibia) two years earlier in a World Court proceeding at The Hague. As a way to enure my presence, the International Commission of Jurists, headed by Sean MacBride, formally invited me to observe the trial, and I agreed to do so. It was a demanding journey in many ways, which happened to follow closely after the Tet Offensive in Vietnam that had shifted the balance of opinion in the United States against its Vietnam policies in early 1968. While in Johannesburg I was asked to give a talk on Vietnam at the South African Institute of International Affairs (modeled after the CFR in the U.S. and Chatham House in the UK). I talked critically about the war before an influential South African audience that had previously been supportive of American policies in Vietnam. I felt that many in the audience were showing visible support for the Vietnam War to establish their own anti-Communist credibility in apartheid South Africa. The idea seemed to be that while these 'liberals' were prudently critical of racist policies in South Africa, they wished it to be known that they shared with the political leadership in Pretoria an anti-Communist outlook that coincided with Washington's policies in conducting the Cold War. This kind of support for the U.S. in Vietnam seemed tactically important at the time for liberals in South Africa as apartheid government ideologues were prosecuting opposition to its racist policies by recourse to Anti-Communist laws that had been enacted to enable the defense of apartheid forms of racism to proceed under the same banner as the criminalization of allegedly Communist views and affiliations.

By far my most memorable moment in South Africa descended from the sky. I was a member of International Commission on the Oceans, headed by the former President of Portugal Mario Soares, and was asked by the South African Vice-Chair of the Commission, my close friend, Kader Asmal (widely credited with overseeing the drafting of the new South African Constitution), to write some welcoming remarks to be delivered by President Nelson Mandela. The Commission was meeting in Cape Town at the invitation of the Government in the late 1990s. I was puzzled about how I might find language suitable for this great South African public figure, and struggled to hit upon the right words even more than usual. I was further unexpectedly challenged when the night before Soares informed me that the Brazilian Vice-Chair had fallen ill, and he expected me to respond to Mandela on behalf of the Commission.

The event was held in the South African Parliament, and when I heard my words coming from Mandela's lips it was the closest I have come to an out-of-body experience. When it came my turn to respond myself, I felt that kind of eerie feeling that accompanies talking to one-self in the presence of an audience. After this opening ceremony ended, Mandela came and thanked me for preparing his text, and we chatted informally, but enough to experience his moral radiance. We then went into a conference room where the 40 or so members of the Commission were waiting. Mandela went around the room telling each person about some connection he had with their country. It was the finest display of diplomatic grace I have ever experienced, made even more special by Mandela's humor and vibrant spirits.

The final phase was a reception, which Mandela did not attend, but was held in a crowded room filled with many notables drawn from all sectors of South African society. It was a hot, muggy day, and for the first and only time I fainted while in conversation with a local tribal leader who spoke at a level that coincided with the background noise. When I regained consciousness, quickly realizing I had startled the guests by my collapse in their midst, I recalled that nervousness had kept me awake the entire prior night, and so my most glorious encounter ever had this strange aftermath.

Upon my return from an intense two weeks in South Africa, I received a visit from a pair of French international law professors associated with the International Association of Democratic Lawyers (IADL), a far-left European professional association of lawyers, reputed to be affiliated with the French Communist Party. IADL had received an invitation from Hanoi to send a delegation of lawyers to view the bombing damage in the North, and this French NGO believed that it would be of more use if American jurists could be persuaded to visit Vietnam and then report back their findings to a society intensely debating whether defeating the 'Viet Cong,' as the NLF was derisively called by pro-war groups, was worth the sacrifice of young American soldiers who were increasingly seen on TV in Midwestern living rooms returning home from Vietnam in flag-draped caskets.

With myopic arrogance, the center of gravity throughout the anti-war debate as carried on by the political center was what the war was doing to *us* in America with hardly even a pretension of any concern about what it was doing to *the people of Vietnam,* which was many times worse with far more enduring effects, such as devastated cities and the lingering menace of Agent Orange, the crop defoliant widely used in the south. Whether in postwar films like *Deerhunter* or the fine Oliver Stone trilogy (*Platoon, Born on the 4th of July, Heaven and Earth*) or McNamara's memoir of apology to the American people, the American portrayal of the war focused on the harm that the war did to us as a nation and a people, and not what it did, which was disastrously worse by way of death and destruction, to the Vietnamese people. The political left accurately conceived of the conflict in historical terms as one of the last great anti-colonial struggles and viewed it as a telling sign of American imperialism in decline, but kept its critique abstractly political, without much show of empathy for the mass suffering endured by the Vietnamese people.

At first, I was reluctant to accept this invitation to visit Hanoi, partly because it seemed a bridge too far politically and partly because I anticipated (on this occasion, wrongly) that Florence would be very furious with me if I even considered such a long trip after having rather recently returned from South Africa. I indicated to my French guests that I could only consider the Vietnam trip if it was scheduled in June after the end of the teaching semester. Since the Vietnamese accepted this condition it meant that I had no academic excuse to decline, and to my surprise, Florence on this occasion strongly urged me to accept, an expression of her own intense opposition to the war. It was a time when McNamara was creating 'fake news' with fraudulent claims that the American bombing campaign was the most 'surgical' in the history of air warfare, and that targeting restrictions allegedly risked many American casualties in order to spare civilians and non-military structures in Vietnam. After some hesitation I accepted the invitation.

Before leaving for Paris en route to Vietnam, I was asked to meet with some senior officials in the Department of Defense. My Princeton colleague and friend, Richard Ullman, had taken a year's leave to work at the Pentagon as part of an expert group assigned to make recommendations relating to defense policy. Dick was an exemplary Ivy League liberal of that era, harboring a realist distaste for the Vietnam War coupled with an unwarranted confidence in those with a first-rate Harvard education whom he regarded, without the irony of David Halberstam and 'the best and the brightest.' These Kennedy-era liberals had turned against the war for purely pragmatic reasons and held the belief that after the withdrawal of Lyndon Johnson from the 1968 presidential campaign, peace in Vietnam was just around the corner. Out of curiosity, and a sense that this was an opportunity to show others that I was still prepared to be a team player, I accepted this invitation, took a train to Washington, and went to the Pentagon for the one and only time ever.

It turned out that this was a meeting with Mort Halperin, a Deputy Assistant Secretary of Defense for International Security Affairs, and his special assistant, Leslie Gelb. Mort and Les were Harvard friends of Dick Ullman, who supported one another after graduating in the manner of Harvard tribalism, believing that their crimson blessing was worth more than the authorship of a dozen books, and indeed it did open many East Coast establishment doors. I had been assured by Dick that we all had a shared purpose in seeking an early end to the war. This was true, yet I came away from the meeting with a strong sense of incompatibility between myself and these temporary Pentagon officials who were unapologetically pleased to be part of the foreign policy establishment.

Our meeting at the Pentagon was what is best described by that worst of anodyne words that hide several levels of negativity—'cordial.' Sort of like the evasive 'nice' as in 'he is a nice person.' The meeting came to nothing in the end, but remains etched in memory because of the Pentagon setting and the gulf separating those who are acting as morally engaged citizens and those who gear their thoughts and attitudes to their role as U.S. officials, who never want to be seen as seriously out of step with bureaucratic 'group think.' When such a gulf exists between two types of academic personality, the gulf is wide, and can easily become toxic, fed by feelings of mutual distrust. Human chemistry is more often,

I found, emotional than intellectual or ideological. It concerns how distinct comfort and discomfort zones interact. Often modernists feel that the game of life should be played within existing boundaries and structures basing policy on instrumental reason as opposed to those who act more in accord with the rhythms of the heart and do not restrict their views to realist constraints of feasibility. I look back on that Pentagon meeting as clarifying for me where and with whom I don't belong or, for that matter, want to belong.

The Pentagon meeting was apparently prompted by Gelb/Halperin's idea that I might be entrusted with a letter to deliver to the leadership in Hanoi. It was to be signed by Clark Clifford, then Secretary of Defense, and Dean Rusk, a hawkish Secretary of State. Les and Mort assured me that the main wheels in the government were now turning against the war, that a massive secret historical study based on government archives was discrediting the war in ways would lead the national security bureaucracy in Washington to seek to end the war quickly. This study, which was never expected to be made public, ended up subversively seeing the light of day in a dramatic fashion, becoming infamous as *The Pentagon Papers*. It was in this context that I was being approached to hand deliver an authoritative message of supposedly peaceful U.S. intentions to North Vietnam, to be manifested by a readiness of the political leadership in Washington to reach a diplomatic compromise. I was not surprised that when their Harvard friend Dan Ellsberg broke ranks by making the *Pentagon Papers* public, Les and Mort denounced the breach of government protocol despite their friendship and shared Harvard bonds.

I was told that carrying such a letter would greatly enhance my stature in Hanoi, and far more significantly, might actually strengthen prospects for an early peace agreement. I was convinced and ready to accept, but then in a deceptively casual tone Les and Mort added a condition—I must agree not to speak publicly against the war in the future. It did not take me a moment's thought to decline. I sometimes wonder how undertaking such a role as designated emissary of the U.S. Government might have affected my experience in Hanoi and possibly more fundamentally altered my political life.

I felt indirectly admonished by such a condition, and also recognized that had I agreed, it would make me duly suspect in relation to the European sponsors of my trip. I had already accepted their invitation to speak at a big public event upon my return to Paris after North Vietnam. To this day I have no idea about the contents of this official letter, and maybe it had not yet been drafted at the time of our meeting. I never had regrets or second thought about refusing to be gagged, although it left me with feelings of enduring dislike for Gelb, the senior person at the meeting. Not too surprisingly, Gelb later became president of the Council on Foreign Relations and a leading centrist civilian voice of the American foreign policy establishment. Halperin subsequently achieved prominence in Washington as consultant, NGO star participant, and respected public commentator on issues of the day bearing on foreign policy, arms control, and the use of international force, while never burning his bridges to the establishment. Mort always struck me as a crafty pragmatist, adept at leaning slightly to one side without losing his balance. He successfully positioned himself as a uniquely qualified insider critic, the sort of Washington civil society representative who is safe enough to be given a seat at many policymaking tables and podiums, and reliably capable of delivering mild dissents at important debating venues to create misleading impressions of dialogue and diversity.

Moving to the Margins

It was only long after this first trip to North Vietnam that I came to realize how much those two weeks altered my prior identity as a re-spected international law critic, with appropriate affiliations and proper background. The trip, highly publicized, made me, if not a pariah, at least situated on the far left, and no longer a promising, and more importantly, reliable young scholar with top echelon public service potential—going to North Vietnam while the war was still going on put me almost in the same disreputable category of suspicious characters as Jane Fonda of 'Hanoi Jane' notoriety and her then guru husband, SDS founder, Tom Hayden, who went on to become a senator in the California state legislature. The second taboo I violated, although more obscurely, was to expand the critical arena of Vietnam scholarship by contending that American policy in Vietnam was not just imprudent policy, doomed to failure, but that it had several 'criminal' dimensions, which automati-cally evoked comparisons to the prosecution of German and Japanese political leaders and military commanders at war crimes trials held with great fanfare at Nuremberg and Tokyo after the end of World War II.

In the late 1960s and early 1970s I spoke at many law schools about the relevance of the Nuremberg precedent both for holding American leaders accountable and for giving citizens reasons to resist the unlawful recourse to war in Vietnam as well as with respect to violations of the laws of war committed in the course of combat and intrinsic to the coun-terinsurgency strategy guiding military operations.

This linkage between Vietnam and Nuremberg was brought to far greater public notice by Telford Taylor, a socially aristocratic and broadly cultured former army general who, as a young military officer, served as a member of the prosecutorial team at Nuremberg. Taylor published a book with the daring title *Vietnam and Nuremberg*. Telford was highly intelligent, humane, and elitist in style. He could please sophisticated NYC audiences with impromptu piano renditions of classical music when not teaching constitutional law at Columbia Law School. Telford, besides being a retired general, never alienated American audiences because he limited criticism to realist-style denunciations of the Vietnam policy as imprudent. Taylor contended rhetorically that what the United States was doing in Vietnam was worse than a crime, it was a huge geopolitical mistake. The implication, so dear to the sensibility of liberals, left unchallenged American purity of motives and its militarist foreign policy, while condemning Vietnam policy as a terrible failure of judgment.

Admittedly, this liberal condemnation of the war had been my own starting point back at Ohio State in 1960 when the issue was still hypothetical, doubting that the U.S. should back with force the Saigon regime's refusal to subject its claim of legitimate rule in South Vietnam to the test of national elections that was understood to be a referendum on reunification of Vietnam and ending the division of the country agreed upon in 1954 after the French were defeated in what was know as The Indochina War. This plan for an electoral test in 1958 of whether the people of South Vietnam wanted a unified country had been solemnly agreed upon in the Geneva Accords signed in Paris after the French defeat in 1954. These elections were not held as promised for narrow political reasons. It was widely believed in Washington, including by then American president, Dwight Eisenhower, that Ho Chi Minh would have been an easy winner, had the people of Vietnam been allowed to vote, and while the reverberations of the 'who lost China' recriminations were fresh, it was thought unacceptable in Washington to suffer another ideological defeat in Asia given the Cold War atmosphere. Would the U.S. be a different country today if it had allowed reunification of Vietnam to occur via elections rather than after a devastating and discrediting war that lasted almost ten years? Only later did it become better understood that, despite ideological affinities, North Vietnam deemed China a far greater menace to Vietnamese political independence than the United States. Much later still, Vietnam, once unified under Hanoi's leadership, became an example of rapid economic growth, poverty alleviation, and handled the COVID-19 challenge as well as any country in the entire world.

It amused me then and even now that Edward Said and Telford Taylor, besides their membership on the Columbia University faculty, shared at least two additional loves in life: the piano and the game of squash. I am not sure whether they knew each other, and am rather sure they never played squash against one another, and so I can at least make the claim that I played both of them on quite different occasions. Edward and Telford were also both, despite their differences in background and foreground, socially elegant, dressed tastefully, cherished high culture and good food, and each possessed the kind of physical stature and emotional composure helpful when consorting with various types of royalty. In very different ways, I admired them both, although Edward was my cherished friend while Telford was only a friendly acquaintance and sparring partner on issues of common concern relating to the Vietnam War and its political fallout. Telford stretched his liberalism to the limit, playing a major role in controversial judicial challenges to Vietnam policies. This included defending Marcus Raskin, a radical thinker and co-founder of the Institute for Policy Studies, in a Boston trial of a number of prominent anti-war figures who were prosecuted by the government because they encouraged unlawful resistance by young Americans to participating in the Vietnam War as draftees.

Subverting the UN Charter and its Prohibitions on Uses of Force

It is against this background of intellectual engagement with Vietnam that my views evolved, leading me first as a scholar, then as a citizen, and finally as an activist to opposing the war from the perspective of international law in tandem with the insistence that U.S. foreign policy would actually benefit from adherence to my understanding of the relevance of international law. Of course, there were American apologists who mounted legal arguments that supported the United States, especially justifying the military extension of the internal war raging in the South to North Vietnam. The most notable argument advanced to support the American role was based on South Vietnam's right of self-defense against an external enemy, an argument embedded in the larger framework of the United States as the guardian of the free world against the expansionist ambitions of totalitarian Communism.

My view was that a coherent *legal* case (although weakened by the *moral* and *political* improprieties of the early phases of the military intervention and by interfering with the dynamics of self-determination)

could be made for giving military assistance to Saigon. Even granting
such legality it did not overcome the unlawfulness of extending the
war to North Vietnam in 1965 by putting forth a spurious claim of
self-defense, given the absence of 'a prior armed attack,' which the UN
Charter set forth as the sole ground of a valid claim of self-defense. The
central objective of the UN Charter, in its effort to prevent future major
international wars, was to make 'aggression' unlawful and to narrow the
circumstances when a state could lawfully resort to force by claiming
self-defense. It seemed to me from an early stage in the war that there
was no valid legal basis for claiming self-defense in Vietnam, and that
it was also highly imprudent and reactionary to put forth such a claim.
It would then become a precedent, useful to any government seeking to
circumvent Charter norms on the use of force. More immediately, the
effect of such a claim was to expand the scope of the combat zone and
the magnitude of the war, and above all, it was an undertaking designed
to undermine the right of self-determination of the Vietnamese people,
and as such, geopolitically regressive and out of touch with Third World
nationalism that was preoccupied with achieving self-determination.

The Vietnam War was seen as a major challenge to whether the UN
Charter would be interpreted 'geopolitically' or 'legally.' A consensus of
expert opinion of jurists around the world shared my legally grounded
interpretation, but the vital legal norms at stake were seriously weakened
because the geopolitical approach prevailed in Vietnam. Geopolitics has
ever since displaced deference to international law in any context involving international uses of force with grave consequences for international
law and the UN. Of course, I am claiming that my understanding of international law as a deliberate constraint on geopolitics is correct, while
others, mostly in the U.S. or UK, insist that the whole of international
society is framed by a recognition of the primacy of geopolitics, which
thus is expected to override international law when these two sources of
authority collide. How else can we explain the veto given to permanent
members of the UN Security Council other than as an acknowledgement,
for better or worse, that geopolitical priorities are the highest source of
effective authority in international relations, including within the UN?
It represents a shocking recognition that neither law nor the UN could
override the political will of those sovereign states who most endanger
the peace and security of the world. It remains true that world order re-
volves around the maneuvers of 'geopolitical Darwinism,' which meant
accountability for the weak and impunity for the strong when it came to
matters of peace and justice.

At least during the Vietnam War, American political leaders made a serious effort to justify their actions by reference to international law, an effort repeated during the Obama years to reconcile drone warfare with international law, given the post-9/11 strains. Such efforts, although far from persuasive, have not even been publicly attempted in comparable situations during the presidencies of George W. Bush and Donald Trump. These leaderships, drawn from Republican ranks, basically invoke sovereign rights and national security interests as a sufficient justification for uses of force in carrying out foreign policy, seeking to minimize accountability to U.S. law even in relation to Constitutional limitations on recourse to war. In this regard, the Charter framework on war making, weakened during the Vietnam War, has been rendered virtually obsolete, except when useful as a means of registering complaints about the behavior of adversaries. (e.g. Russia's moves against Crimea and Ukraine). In effect, international law has been undergoing a declining relevance in the war/peace context ever since the Vietnam War. This decline has spilled over into other crucial policy areas such as human rights, climate change, and international economic relations, and coincides with a decline in the quality of U.S. global leadership.

I remember in the 1960s being accosted on several occasions by Richard Gardner, notable for his writing about international economic issues and his promotion of Cold War hard-line views. Dick did little to hide his personal ambition for success in official Washington after taking leave from the Columbia Law faculty, finally being rewarded for his service and his views by being named ambassador to Italy. When I complained to Gardner about the deficiencies of American foreign policy because of its embodiment of 'international liberalism,' his sarcastic riposte was to ask me in a condescending tone: 'What would you prefer, 'illiberal internationalism?'' At the time in the 1970s I responded as caustically as I could, 'No, progressive internationalism.' Now we are learning the real world difficulties of living with 'illiberal internationalism.' The present posture of opportunistic or transactional nationalism is indeed worse from the perspective of humane values, war prevention, and world economic stability than was the liberal internationalism that the Democratic Party embraced during and after the Cold War period.

A Transformative Journey

Against this background of convoluted preparation and evolving political consciousness I embarked somewhat fearfully on what turned out, unexpectedly, to be a transformative journey to Vietnam, supposedly undertaken for the single purpose of viewing and then reporting back on the devastation wrought by the American air war. Discovering my deepest political and spiritual bearings were not among my aims or expectations when the time came for departure. Yet it was this journey more than any single experience before or since that has had a permanent impact on my moral, legal, and spiritual consciousness. It may be that growing up as a de facto only child, coping with loneliness of a motherless home and a preoccupied father, taught me to depend on my own wits and understanding to plot an independent and contrarian course in life. In the years that followed childhood, I took few cues from collective sources, including family, country, and social milieu, feeling after many years of groping that I was finally standing on something solid, and it was my own.

Traveling to Vietnam was neither simple nor direct. It meant first stopping in Paris for a briefing and to obtain a visa for travel to North Vietnam. Since such travel was then not permissible for U.S. citizens, the visa consisted of a separate paper that was inserted in the passport, while the passport itself was not stamped. I wondered when this happened whether such an evasion of the restriction on travel would lead me to face some kind of legal challenge or penalty on my return, even possibly a criminal prosecution. Arriving in Paris in the late Spring of 1968 was itself memorable. The city was in a state of high tension, the Sorbonne was occupied by a student movement whose militants were continuously demonstrating, shouting radical slogans that proclaimed a revolutionary future that never was to be. My IADL hosts were friendly, helpful, and encouraging, and after a day living in the Latin Quarter, I was on my way to Cambodia for a double transfer of air connections to International Control Commission (ICC) flights—first to Vientiane, Laos after staying overnight in a Phnom Penh hotel and then on to Hanoi. My only recollection from the stopover in Cambodia was that of a young porter who took my luggage to my room, asking me if I wanted him to fetch a girl as my companion for the night. When I said 'no,' he replied, 'Don't worry, she's my sister.' I said no a second time, and he then responded with a smile, 'Oh, so you prefer boys. I can also arrange that, as well.' After I assured him that I wanted to spend the evening by myself we had no further discussion, but he didn't hide his disappointment.

After taking the short flight from Cambodia to Laos I recall little other than an ugly yet revealing incident in the lobby of my overnight hotel. An American, almost certainly part of the U.S. paramilitary presence in the country, was checking out, paying his bill with U.S. dollars. The hotel clerk gave him some change in Lao paper money at which point the American actually threw the paper money back at the hotel clerk, exclaiming in a contemptuous tone, 'I don't want this worthless junk.' Although I didn't label my disgust at such vulgar behavior at the time, it strikes me now as the kind of instance of white supremism that, when so crudely expressed, kindles hatred of U.S. imperialism in foreign countries. It is opposite to the reaction I have experienced due to my spontaneous respect for civilizational diversity, which has made me reluctant to disapprove of what is unfamiliar or seems 'inferior' in non-Western countries. My non-judgmental attitude is part of a refusal to criticize seeming shortcomings in societies exploited by the West. To this day I am appalled by imperial arrogance and Orientalist insensitivity, and even more, by the absence of self-criticism. I wonder sometime whether I have gone too far in the other direction, being hyper judgmental toward what I find in my own world, and overly tolerant toward whatever goes on elsewhere.

The flight from Laos to Hanoi was on an ancient converted B-12 (or B-16) World War II bomber, now handling cargo for the International Control Commission (ICC), an international body set up after the French Indochina War to facilitate the transition to a new political order. The flight felt unsafe. The uncomfortable seating arrangements on the plane were an inevitable part of such a wartime visit as this was then the only way for an outsider from the West to reach Hanoi. I imagine others came from the Soviet Union and China more easily and directly, and likely more safely. As the plane's engines loudly droned, even sputtering, while crossing the Laotian mountains, I feared we might crash before I reached my destination. Even now I think that flight in an overage plane was probably more hazardous than wandering around in North Vietnam under wartime attack.

We arrived at the airport late at night, with lights of the city dimmed or non-existent, creating an eerie atmosphere where persons and vehicles were experienced as mobile shadows. I was met by a government delegation, greeted warmly in a manner that was immediately reassuring, and an official car was waiting to drive us to our hotel from the airport. Going from the airport across the Red River was like entering the outer precincts of Dante's Inferno. We were part of a convoy of military vehicles without headlights moving through a shadowy grid and making our way across a makeshift pontoon bridge constructed after the former 'permanent' bridge was destroyed by American bombs. We arrived after an hour of slow driving at our hotel, which was plain yet adequate. On the following morning we began our carefully arranged strenuous program. The first meeting was with the Minister of Trade, Pham Anh, and his principal assistants. For no plausible reasons, this ministry had been given protocol responsibility for arranging our visit.

After the Minister greeted us in a warm and friendly manner, he went on to say that the Vietnamese government and society wanted peace as soon as possible, and further, that its struggle was waged against the American government, not the American people. He reassured us by saying that once peace was restored the two governments could have friendly relations. He underscored these points with an historical allusion to the several occasions over the centuries on which Chinese invaders were repelled, then, rather than being treated as hated invaders, were given an elaborate farewell party in Hanoi to signal the Vietnamese desire to make an immediate transition from war to peace and commence good relations. We were assured that this could happen in this war despite the widespread devastation and suffering inflicted by American military tactics. Of course, I recognized the familiar Communist propaganda distinction between the government as enemy and people as friend, but this Vietnamese appeal seemed more genuine as it was backed by a lengthy national narrative and by an evident preoccupation about defending future Vietnamese sovereignty especially in relation to their Chinese neighbor.

Minister Anh also stressed the ethics of leadership associated with Ho Chi Minh, and this was again repeated in various ways throughout the ten days. The 'Uncle Ho' image seemed to live in the hearts and minds of the Vietnamese with whom I had contact. There was a special emphasis on Ho's attitude of admiration toward the American Declaration of Independence, and his earlier hopes at the end of World War II that the 4th of July values of the Declaration would prevail over alignments with European colonial powers, in Vietnam's case, France. We were told that in this spirit, despite the American role in supporting the French, including providing most of the French war budget at the end of the Indochina War (paying up to 80% of French military expenses), Vietnamese school children were required to memorize the Declaration of Independence throughout the course of the entire war. These same themes were accentuated in the very impressive Revolutionary Museum, which we visited in the afternoon of our first full day in Hanoi.

Among the offerings at the museum was a hagiographic film depicting the life of Ho Chi Minh. I remember the opening line: 'There are many beautiful flowers in Vietnam, and the most beautiful of all is the lily; there are many beautiful men in Vietnam, and the most beautiful of all is Ho Chi Minh.' Also, at the start of the film evidence was presented of Ho's early resolve to improve the harsh life of the Vietnamese peasant seen toiling with a plow amid terrible heat. In reaction, Ho developed a strong commitment to bring modernity to the country so as to relieve pressures on the poor, especially those in the countryside, which was where the overwhelming majority of the population lived. After finishing his introduction, the Minister turned to us for a response, which was the common give and take ritual throughout our time in Vietnam.

I responded by thanking our Vietnamese hosts for their warm welcome despite the severe difficulties facing the country. I also mentioned that many in the United States were now opposed to the war, and to the whole political rationale relied upon to justify attacking Vietnam in such a vicious way. I expressed my understanding that American policy toward Vietnam had sought to restore Western control after the French had failed to reestablish colonial rule at the end of wartime Japanese occupation. I had little doubt that this American undertaking would be defeated in the end. I also said that we had come to Vietnam to learn and see for ourselves what havoc had been visited on the country and would share our experience with government officials and the public after our return to America.

In the days that followed our time was well spent. We experienced warm hospitality and a respectful sensitivity to our national identity. Our Vietnamese hosts showed their appreciation of the awkwardness of our position as Americans behind enemy lines at a time of war. We were not asked to sit on anti-aircraft gun emplacements or undergo photo ops while in the presence of Vietnamese maimed by American bombing. We did go to a Vietnamese hospital on the outskirts of Hanoi, and visit a ward containing bomb victims. It was difficult to talk with badly wounded individuals, and I remember how hard it was for me to find the right words of empathy and regret at the bedside of badly wounded Vietnamese soldiers and civilians. The main parts of the city of Hanoi had not been bombed, although the outskirts had. Even the Red River Delta dykes were threatened with attacks on several occasions. We also went by military vehicle with some government people to several cities a few hours from Hanoi that had been devastated by repeated bombing, their small urban centers lying in twisted ruins.

I remember a ride in the humid heat on a bumpy road in a fast-moving military vehicle with no springs more vividly than the scenery or the stops we made. I do recall a middle-aged diplomat from the Mekong region in the South telling me that our driver had lost his entire family in an attack on his village, and yet if we were to be attacked on this trip, he would give his life to save ours. It was an ethos of responsibility to visitors repeated in different forms during our time in Vietnam, and often attributed to the teaching and example of Ho Chi Minh, who counseled forgiveness and reconciliation in line with deep Vietnamese traditions, which were themselves intertwined with Confucian and Buddhist influences.

After several days in Vietnam, cut off altogether from everything previously familiar in my life, and beset by some rumors that the American bombing pause might end any day, I had a kind of premonition that I would be trapped in Hanoi for many months, and reside vulnerably in an active war zone. Such musings were worrisome. I adopted a fatalistic attitude, wondering how I might best handle such an eventuality if it did come to pass, which it didn't. As my contact with a variety of Vietnamese increased, including interpreters, officials, and helpers of various kinds, I was struck by their spontaneity and playfulness, as well as their sense of pride about overcoming their weaknesses in the context of their encounters with American air power. I remember one Vietnamese soldier telling me that his regiment had learned that when a bomber dives to make a strike, it becomes rather vulnerable to simple rifle fire at the end of its dive during the fleeting moment in which the plane attempts to regain its normal flying altitude. This was just one example of many that expressed the Vietnamese good-natured readiness and ingenuity to 'make do,' a Vietnamese analogue to the American 'can do' spirit, later given an Obama twist by the phrase, 'yes, we can.' The Vietnamese told many jokes about the heavy handedness of the Americans, contrasting their indulgence of comic relief with the imperious humorlessness of their Chinese neighbors.

Throughout our visit I was captivated by the radiant smiles of the native daughters of the country who spoke what little English they knew with captivating charm. Years later this experience would be greatly deepened and confirmed in 1999 when Hilal and I stayed for a few months at the Hanoi Club while I was teaching an intensive course at the Vietnamese Diplomatic Academy. It was there we met Huyen Giap, who later became our informally adopted daughter, loving and much loved, joyful and affectionate, despite having been born into an impoverished war-torn world, and enduring famine conditions at the end of the war.

During our ten days or so in wartime Vietnam there were formal dinners almost every night. I remember sitting next to an elegantly dressed female Vietnamese diplomat who explained our meal to me as as symbolizing the different terrains of Vietnam—each course reflecting the food of a distinct terrain—from the mountains, valleys, rivers, and sea, and if it was an elaborate meal, then each of the four seasons would be associated with one of the dishes served.

Meeting the Prime Minister

Unquestionably, the climax of our visit, and its public importance, were two meetings with Pham Von Dong, the Prime Minister of Vietnam. Pham came from Hue in the center of the country where the ancient capital was located and French cultural influence was at its height. I remember that he asked if we followed French theater and literature, telling us how much he had enjoyed French culture during his youth. More seriously, he asked about prospects in the U.S. for ending the war, and indicated the Vietnamese readiness at the highest levels to negotiate a political compromise that, to my surprise, included the acceptance of an American military presence in the South and a provisional coalitional government that would organize national elections under international supervision. I had a definite feeling at the time that I was being informed about an authoritative diplomatic initiative. I knew that Pham was not the supreme leader of Vietnam, that Ho was the political top figure but too ill to meet with foreign visitors, and that General Giap was Vietnam's legendary military commander who was credited with defeating the French, but was generally unwilling to meet with outsiders. Finally, there was the ideological chief, Le Duan, a shadowy figure who some believed was the person who wielded decisive power in running the country and shaping its war diplomacy. I did not try to figure out the Vietnamese power structure, feeling confident that Pham Von Dong's authority was sufficient to convey government policy on the war. As this was the first time I had met an active foreign leader (though as a child I had superficially known my father's friend/client, Alexander Kerensky, the post-czar interim Russian leader, who lacked the aura of actual political power, living modestly in New York City as an exiled private citizen). I was impressed by the trappings of high office—a massive office in a beautiful villa. When we arrived at his official residence, Pham greeted us on the steps as if we were important visitors, a status we neither claimed nor deserved.

When it came time to leave Vietnam, I experienced a mysterious sadness that was hard to explain. The time had flown by. We had made many contacts that strengthened feelings of solidarity and planted seeds of friendship. We spoke confidently to our Vietnamese hosts about keeping contact and promised to recollect warmly the laughter and tears that were at the core of this Vietnamese experience, and came to the surface during our sendoff at the airport lounge.

Aftermath in Paris

I can't remember why it happened, but my arrival in Paris was treated as something of a media event. I gave my impressions of the situation in North Vietnam and of the opportunity to end the war. I did an extensive TV interview with CBS's Charles Collingwood and had a long discussion with the well-known *NY Times* correspondent, Hedrick Smith. Both were exceedingly interested in the possible peace initiative outlined to us by Pham Von Dong, showed some willingness to listen to what I said about the bomb damage (mainly, I think, because there was news value in challenging McNamara's misleading claims of precision bombing). However, when I referred to the immorality and unlawfulness of bombing the Vietnamese countryside where the villages had no military targets, and the only notable buildings were churches and hospitals, I ran into a stone wall of passive resistance that blended indifference with cynical derision. We had been told several times in Hanoi that earlier, when there was heavy bombing, many pilots disobeyed their orders not to return to their bases without dropping their payload. Rather than obey, they had dumped their bombs in the Gulf of Tonkin. Media personalities, seeking to uphold their credibility, showed none of the moral scruples shown by some of the combat soldiers, who were differently motivated, seeking to uphold their humanity rather than their mainstream credentials.

What made the strongest impression on me at the time was not the favorable media coverage of my trip (the *National Review* was an exception), but the disinterest by the most liberal and otherwise sympathetic journalists in those parts of my presentation of the war that condemned such a lawless assault by the U.S. high-tech war machine. I wanted above all to share my impressions of the horrors inflicted on this totally vulnerable low-tech Asian country whose people were determined by sheer human willpower and nationalist fervor to defend their homeland, whatever the costs. At the time, I was far from convinced, myself, that this sacrificial resolve of the Vietnamese people, given the millions of casualties and vast destruction, would in the end prevail. As the world discovered, persisting Vietnamese resistance finally politically neutralized and overcame American military dominance and geopolitical resolve.

This reversal of the power balance in Vietnam was for me the salient lesson of the Vietnam experience. It is a lesson that the American political class and the media refuse to learn, and so the mistakes of the 1960s have been repeated over and over again, most notably in Iraq after 2003, and in the blood-soaked distant lands of Afghanistan, Syria, Yemen, and Libya. To understand why this stubborn refusal persists in the face of so much contrary experience is to gain insight into the degree to which the United States has succumbed to an outmoded model of governance and security, with its political imagination locked within a militarist cage with the keys under the elusive control of the American deep state and its private sector infrastructure embedded in the arms industry, think tanks, and corporatized media.

Returning to America

While flying back to the United States I anticipated being publicly criticized, and maybe even prosecuted, for violating the 18th century Logan Act that made it a crime for American citizens to engage in what was described as private diplomacy. Actually, I had no need to worry. The *NY Times* featured my trip on its front page for several days with the suggestion that I may have uncovered a promising path to ending a war that was increasingly unpopular at home, causing deep and dangerous fissures in the American body politic. The media coverage urged the U.S. Government to hear what I had to say, and sure enough I received a friendly call from the State Department asking if I wanted to come to Washington to discuss my trip, or if not, they could send someone to 'debrief' me. I chose this latter option and had a congenial meeting in Princeton with a junior State Department official. Nothing ever came of this opening, although my enduring belief is that the Vietnamese leadership was ready to negotiate an ending to the war that was more tactically and strategically favorable and less diplomatically humbling for the U.S. than what Kissinger ultimately negotiated with much fanfare, even receiving an undeserved Nobel Peace Prize for his efforts, four years later. This unnecessary delay in bringing the war to an end produced in its wake heavy casualties and hardships in Vietnam and a sharpening national divisiveness at home from which the U.S. has never fully recovered—highlighted by its humiliating 1975 departure from Saigon with its Vietnamese collaborators fearing retribution, and begging for sanctuary.

An Ecological Bump in the Road

A few months later in the fall of 1968 Florence and I arrived in Palo Alto to accept a year's invitation to be a Visiting Fellow at the Center for Advanced Study in the Behavioral Sciences located on a hill adjoining the campus of Stanford University. I had indicated in my application to the Center that I wanted to write a book on International Law and the Vietnam War, bringing together my scholarly work of the 1960s in a coherent form. This was my intention upon our arrival, but it was soon abandoned.

It turned out my research and writing plans were early casualties of the Center experience. During one of my first days at the Center I had a casual conversation with Pierre Noyes, a Stanford faculty member while we were both getting a drink at the corridor water cooler. To my continuing astonishment, that conversation radically altered my research agenda, not only for the year, but permanently. No such casual encounter has ever had such a profound impact on my scholarly life. Pierre was someone of great intellectual passion, an utterly convinced neo-Malthusian, quirky and brilliant, working for years as a theoretical physicist on unsolved puzzles in the study of the elemental forces of life and energy throughout the universe. He fervently believed that population growth was exerting unmanageable pressures on food supply and the resource base of civilization, and that these realities were creating an unacknowledged species survival challenge deserving the urgent attention of someone like myself. I didn't realize I was so impressionable, but on this occasion, I allowed myself to be persuaded, and never regretted it.

My reconfigured research was devoted to what I came to think of as 'the ecological problematique.' I gave the inquiry my own touch, heavily influenced by concerns about a future war fought with nuclear weapons and my belief that it was crucial for the future of humanity to strengthen the role of international law and the UN System without losing sight of state-centric realities. By such a realist trope I meant to take account of the degree to which the world would continue to be organized around the capabilities and political will of territorial sovereign states, especially the leading states, for the foreseeable future even in the face of the recommended and necessary adjustments for the sake of ecological sustainability. At that time of Cold War geopolitics, the retention of this statist role was basically referencing the political structure underlying the rivalry between the U.S. and the Soviet Union. For this reason, most sophisticated discussion about world conditions focused on the geopolitics of bipolarity.

As I was trying to work out a conceptual framework for this newly initiated work-in-progress, the Cultural Editor of the *New York Times*, Israel Schenker, came to the Center to do a story on what went on at such a strange educational institution that had no courses, students, library, or projects. I am not sure he ever found out, but he did choose me as one of a half dozen fellows to interview, and seemed rather drawn to the themes and outlook of my proposed book that was still at the pre-writing planning stage. Schenker devoted most of his feature story on the Center to my book project, which when finally written and published, appeared under the title, *This Endangered Planet: Prospects and Proposals for Human Survival* (1972).

Schenker's article, testifying to the strong impact of publicity in the *NYT*, produced a flurry of sight unseen offers from prominent publishers, an experience I had never had before, nor since. In fact, the TV celebrity head of Random House, Bennett Cerf, flew to Palo Alto just for us to have breakfast together and convince me on the advantages of publishing with his firm, which I ultimately decided to do, probably mistakenly. There was a personal twist that may have tweaked my unconscious. My father had been the lawyer for Random House when it was founded and knew Bennett quite well, although he had lost this client some years earlier. The account was shifted to Cerf's brother in law when he remarried. Bennett was more than a bit surprised when he discovered that I was Ed Falk's son, but that didn't alter his salesman's zeal or style. In retrospect, Bennet was something of a Trump avatar, being a leading personality on a popular TV show called *What's My Line?* that involved a mix of personalities, and for its time, bearing comparisons with *The Apprentice.*

Cerf's offer of a 10k advance seemed a lot to me at the time, although matched by several other leading publishers after the Schenker article. Bennett Cerf also offered me the editorial services of Carl Erskine, a courtly southerner who was William Faulkner's editor, and Faulkner was then my favorite writer. As my editor, Carl brought me little useful guidance and some tension as he believed strongly that the only thing that mattered for the human future was limiting population growth. He didn't agree with my emphasis on the ills of militarism, environmental pollution, and impending resource scarcity, and especially disliked my criticisms of the U.S. global role. I held my ground despite being decades junior to this somewhat fabled giant of the publishing world. The book did appear under the Random House imprint but without any marketing enthusiasm. In retrospect, I realized it was my mistake to publish with Random House. I was disappointed by the visible absence of encouragement shown by Erskine, but it seemed too late to do anything about it. This low level of support contrasted with the promotional energy devoted to the *Limits to Growth* study of the Club of Rome. *Limits* argued a similar thesis to mine but without the war/peace dimension, and managed to suck most of the oxygen out of my ecological trial balloon. At the time, I always believed that my approach was more nuanced and exhibited a clearer understanding of the global situation. Yet the combination of the well-funded promotional campaign mounted by the Club and the fact that its assessments of the global situation relied upon the findings of computer-generated data overwhelmed the marketing, findings, and recommendations of my book. Such a data-crunching methodology was much more in line with the intellectual fashion of the time than was my qualitative approach based on values, historical analysis, political interpretation, empirical evidence, and the potential benefits of a global rule of law. Unlike *Limits to Growth*, which has long since disappeared, my book, although making little stir when published, seems to have had a longer and more active shelf life, and is often cited in recent ecological literature devoted to global issues.

In the last ten or so years I have thought about doing a revised version of *This Endangered Planet*, often encouraged by others, but never mobilized the energy to take on such a mammoth undertaking. I continue to believe in framing the ecological argument to encompass the war system. Yet the overall analysis would need to be modified to take adequate account of climate change, biodiversity, industrial agriculture, global migration, the leveling of population growth, as well as the perverse democratic popularity of autocratic forms of governance that tend to be dismissive of ecological prudence. Above all, a reframing would focus on the human condition as facing an extinction threat that can only be successfully addressed by the affirmation of global solidarity, the superseding of geopolitics by ecological and ethical consciousness, supplanting war by law and nonviolent mechanisms of conflict resolution. Only by fashioning of a robust global rule of law, sustained by the existential reality of a sense of global community, a commitment to global justice, and a far more autonomous and effective United Nations could the deepening challenges of the present be humanely addressed.

Although taking on the ecological problematique seemed a fork in the road, it did not end my concerns with the Vietnam War and its spillover effects at home and in the world. While at the Center the dean of the Stanford School of Law, Bayless Manning, implored me to teach a course on law and war. To do so required a special exception as the Center enforced a strict rule that its fellows devote their residence exclusively to research. The Stanford campus, although not the virtual war zone that Berkeley briefly became, was in some ferment. It was partly inflamed by an inept and indecisive president and the provocative campus presence of a private sector think tank, the Stanford Research Institute or SRI, doing war-related research. Stanford law students were demanding of their dean an elective course dealing with Vietnam issues, and I was the only one around with those interests and credentials. I enjoyed going down the hill once a week for the semester, encountering in the course several students more radical than I, several of whom preferred jail to compliance with selective service demands. I testified in court on behalf of one of the students in my Stanford course, who was also drawn to the cultural side of 'the war at home,' which meant recreational drugs and hanging out communally with flower children as the 'families' of the future. Such a futurist vision of America was never meant to be and retreated rather quickly from the cultural scene frontiers in the aftermath of the shocking Manson murders and the pushback engineered by Nixon's awakening of the 'moral majority.'

By 1969, the 'war' at home became the epicenter of the anti-war movement, and Vietnam concerns had become the tip of an iceberg. This meant that the movement had come to have more to do with rock music and LSD, and a rising feminism, than it did with condemning the Vietnam War, although these disparate preoccupations were bound together in the minds of many young people. I was old enough to feel the strength of being a participant in the anti-war movement while feeling a mere sympathetic spectator, looking in from without, when it came to the culture war being fought with such weapons as long hair, flower girls, music, and Bob Dylan's lyrics.

The Center provided other targets of opportunity, as well as a galaxy of academic superstars and personalities who sometimes managed to obtain societal roles that exceeded their talents. George Shultz was undoubtedly in retrospect the most famous fellow of our year, and due to our shared Princeton experience (he as an undergraduate and varsity football stalwart) and rough equality on the tennis court, we became shipboard friends, that is, a friendship that flourished only so long as the journey lasted. We played tennis at least once a week, and as George's Washington star began to rise, it was obvious that he was headed for government. I was struck by George's modesty, verging on humility, that I experienced during our routine of a post-tennis drink where we talked, and he showed himself to be a better listener than I a talker. Listening is not a trait associated with Washington insiders. He knew of my opposition to the Vietnam War and sought from me a better understanding of why his children should be so opposed to the war. I gave my reasons for opposing the war, and he nodded without arguing, yet carefully refraining from showing any sign of being persuaded. I suspect that these qualities paid off in his rise to prominence in Washington where he moved from one cabinet post to another, occupying in the end cabinet appointments of greatest prestige and influence (State and Treasury, after starting off as Labor Secretary).

I never fully comprehended George's success, including his later celebrity as a high-profile business executive and venerable elder statesman. This extraordinary record of achievement in the public and private sectors seems to rest on being a nice guy of moderate intelligence who held conservative views that embodied the Cold War consensus, and seemed reproduced in his lifestyle and modest demeanor. While he was receptive to views that reflected the preferences of the right, he was not dismissive of liberals, or even progressives of my stripe. I never heard George express an original idea or adopt a distinctive position on an important policy issue. His amazing career confirmed for me that the path to success *near* the top of the governmental pyramid has generally more to do with *emotional IQ*, elite connections, and ideological affinities than it does with brainpower. At the very top, the characteristics that made Shultz so successful seem not to work for most bureaucratic high fliers. Modesty and passive virtues such as listening intently do not seem personality attributes that lead to success in public arenas, and so George's experience at the pinnacles of government remain something of an unexplained mystery.

Actually, with Irving Howe, then editor of *Dissent Magazine*, a social democratic venue, co-edited with Loui Coser, both also fellows that same year, I had a far more tense relationship than with Shultz. Irving, and even more so his wife, Arien Mack, were strong supporters of Israel. They believed that Israel's security was dependent on maintaining a close positive relationship between diaspora Jews and the U.S. Government. They were thus wary of the anti-war movement, elements of which veered toward sympathetic solidarity with the Palestinian struggle. At Irving's invitation during the year, I contributed a piece to *Dissent* expressing my views on the Vietnam War, but we were far apart with respect to Cold War geopolitics and the Israel/Palestine relationship. Irving, in the spirit of former leftists, was a hardline anti-Soviet 'socialist' and an unapologetic advocate of a Zionist approach to the politics of the Middle East.

Undoubtedly, the kindest, gentlest, and likely most creative of the fellows that year was Albert Hirschman, an economist who swam swiftly against the tide of formal modeling and mathematical analysis, yet managed to be highly respected among most of his professional peers. Albert was normally a fellow at the Institute for Advanced Studies at Princeton where he developed his theoretical ideas about how power is exercised in economic settings in several short, provocative books that were widely read and discussed, especially, *Exit and Voice* and *Passions and Interests*, including by mainstream economists, despite never relying on graphs or models.

Albert and his Russian wife became our friends, sharing dinners, and a fondness for ping-pong. Albert was a European Jew who during the Nazi period managed to stay safe. He was timid, soft spoken, and quietly ironic in social settings. He became professionally known and appreciated by offering aid and comfort, and often institutional refuge to a series of Latin American progressive intellectuals at Princeton, including Fernando Henrique Cardoso and Jose Serra who, after a period of military dictatorship in Brazil, became prominent political figures whose political orientation shifted from the social democratic left to the neoliberal center, which functioned as the center-right in a Latin American context.

More dramatic than the politics of the period was my homelife at Stanford. Florence decided to study for a Master of Arts Degree in theater criticism, abandoning forever her earlier successes as an off-Broadway actress. Her graduate work was preparatory to becoming a doctoral student at Rutgers in the English Department. She seemed to enjoy this turn toward academic work, and became a knowledgeable and insightful interpreter of current theater trends. More consequential for our life was the birth of Dimitri on April 13, 1969 after a long and hard labor. I was allowed to be present in the delivery room at the Stanford Hospital, and had a long conversation with the lead doctor, an opponent of the Vietnam War, who was eager to discuss its legal and political dimensions. We talked through the night for many hours, and when Dimitri finally emerged, I experienced the full thrill of a human birth for the first and only time in my life. Florence, while weakened and very tired, joyfully greeted this happy ending. It turned out that Dimitri was from birth and ever since something special! I never lost this feeling despite the strains of a collapsing marriage and a life of my own that had more than the usual share of pressures, preoccupations, and diversions.

Among those at the Center was Leon Lipson, an intellectually formidable and ideologically driven Soviet law specialist on the faculty of the Yale Law School, who thinly veiled his contempt for my anti-war activism. More than anyone else in my experience, Leon resembled in many ways my Princeton nemesis, Marion Levy, previously described. Like Marion, Leon managed a stellar academic career at a leading university despite his failure to produce any notable scholarship. He was also similarly aggressive, acerbic, and a reliably potent defender of conventional lawyering and prevailing political orthodoxies. McDougal once confided in me, 'I don't know what's wrong with Leon, but he seems to be blocking my effort to have you invited to join the law faculty.' I was hardly surprised by this disclosure, and tried not to view Leon with resentment. I knew that I was not anti-Soviet enough to suit him, and maybe published too much, or maybe I was just not the kind of person he wanted to have as a colleague. Actually, I neither wanted to leave Princeton for Yale at the end of the 1960s, nor would I have wanted to turn down a Yale offer had it been forthcoming due to the efforts of the professor I most revered. Fortunately, I never faced the dilemma as the invitation never came! At times of frustration at Princeton, I had a few scattered Yale fantasies, but they were fleeting. I knew from my prior Ohio State and Yale days that I didn't want to teach vocationally minded students, grade final exams, or live in New Haven. Princeton was nearer New York, offering by then friendships and an undemanding teaching schedule, and allowing me the pleasures of a daily sports life with a network of tennis and squash friends that might be difficult to reproduce elsewhere.

Those Vietnam years did involve venturing forth from the academic cloister, experiencing the wider canvas of life. Returning to Princeton after my year at Stanford, I felt glad to resume its quiet, familiar rhythms. These rhythms turned out to be less quiet than what they were previously as the Vietnam War persisted and my engagement as advocate and activist continued. An ugly endgame ensued in Vietnam: the Christmas Bombing around Hanoi. The Kissinger/Nixon effort to keep faith with pro-war constituencies in Saigon and Washington resulted in tens of thousands of unnecessary deaths and ruined many lives in both countries. The last stage of the war left a legacy of bitterness among returning American soldiers and a deep sense of loss in Vietnam, which was shielded from collective despair by the extraordinary victory of this small peasant society against the American military juggernaut. The United States was not a gracious loser in Vietnam. It did nothing to relieve the hardships experienced by the civilian population during the ending of this long war. These hardships in Vietnam included severe hunger verging on the danger of famine, a reality ignored by Washington at a time when it could have erased many of the bad memories of the war by a show of empathy and generosity. At best, we can say that the U.S. Government suffered from its inexperience of dealing with the challenges of lost wars. Unfortunately, several lost wars later, there are no signs of its learning from defeat.

I discovered that I was changed by Vietnam in several respects—a clearer political profile, a willingness to go beyond liberal conceptions of responsible dissent, and above all, an existential identification with those who struggle in America and distant lands to achieve elemental rights, whether in Da Nang or Selma, whether for gay and trans rights or for the rights of migrants and asylum seekers. In the end, I opted for an inclusive and non-judgmental affirmation of humanity in all its diversity as the supreme moral criterion of identity, community, and solidarity. Despite resuming my American life, I never lost my love for Vietnam and its people, which was given vibrant concreteness through our continuing contact with Huyen, as well as her son and American husband. Vietnam may not have been as heroic in times of peace as it was in times of war, but the Vietnamese people sustained my fondest memories of that first visit to this great country when revisiting for a couple of weeks in 2016.

Without the American intervention there would have been no war in Vietnam. The Saigon government would have collapsed on its own without putting up much of a struggle, and Vietnam would have been quickly reunified as a single country. The real struggle in Vietnam was between the U.S. intervening military and the Vietnamese people who were predominantly responsive to the patriotic call to fight for political independence in a struggle that commenced against their French colonial masters, and continued against the American interlopers who may have been motivated by Cold War geopolitics but were objectively seeking to uphold the colonialist subjugation of a proud and venerable Asian nation. It was the clearest possible case of a geopolitically motivated military intervention by the West to defeat the exercise of the right of self-determination by a non-Western country.

CHAPTER 12

Repatriating Three American Pilots

There were some developments of a more activist character in the early 1970s. The Cambodian extension of the combat zone in Vietnam, as a result of Nixon/Kissinger efforts to impair Hanoi's capacity to supply its forces in the South, meant humanitarian and political disaster for Cambodia and caused a strong anti-war backlash in the United States. American leaders looked upon demonstrating angry protesters from their office windows and wondered what to do. The Cambodian operation was treated by the American media as a major reescalation of the war. The Nixon leadership presented this operation as necessary to create a favorable bargaining atmosphere for reaching an agreement with Hanoi that would flip reality by making it look as though U.S. was the winner despite withdrawing its troops and failing politically to sustain the Saigon regime and an anti-Communist South Vietnam. This reescalation challenged the previously growing public belief that the American War in Vietnam was finally coming to an end. When this suddenly seemed not so, it caused a revival of anti-war protest activity at a heightened level of anger.

It was in this context that Paris peace negotiations between the parties made their slow start, with arguments about the shape of the table where the negotiators sat taking months to resolve. Against this background I was approached to be part of a four-person delegation that would go to Hanoi to receive three American pilots, who were being held as POWs but were scheduled for release and return to the U.S. under the control of a peace group escort. I hesitated at first to accept this invitation, not immediately appreciating the importance of demonstrating that the peace movement could do what the U.S. Government was unable to do. In this period my son, Noah, was born, and I was reluctant to be gone for such a long trip, although I knew that the pilots being held as POWs by North Vietnam remained the priority issue for Washington since abandoning any idea of prevailing in the political struggle. In this sense, it was a potentially triumphant moment for the anti-war movement to show by dramatic deed that its actions freed several POWs without firing a shot while the U.S. Government's intensified military assaults had come up empty.

After some gentle persuasion, including being chided for my failure to leap at the chance to participate in such a blue-ribbon peace mission, I accepted the invitation. The other three members of the delegation were leading anti-war figures: David Dellinger, the oldest defendant in the most important national trial following the Chicago protests at the 1968 Democratic Convention and someone with a long and widely respected anti-war activist experience that included a prison term during World War II resulting from his unwavering pacifist commitment to nonviolence; Cora Weiss, a dynamic organizer and philanthropist who was a founder of Women Strike for Peace and the leader of an organization that kept contact with the families of American POWs in the prisons of North Vietnam, as well as being a prominent activist in relation to a series of left liberal causes, including a leading role in opposing apartheid in South Africa. David and Cora were the informal heads of our delegation as they had received the invitation in their role as co-chairs of the Committee of Liaison with Servicemen Detained in Vietnam, which for years handled mail back and forth between U.S. POWs and their families in the U.S., a humanitarian service that complemented its anti-war agenda.

The third member of the delegation was Rev. William Sloan Coffin, Yale Chaplain and later senior minister at the Riverside Memorial Church, who combined a socially elite background with an adventurous role as a paratrooper in World War II. He had parachuted behind enemy lines in Europe, spoke Russian fluently, and was one of the finest public speakers I have ever heard, combining a charismatic presence with a penetrating wit and sharp policy criticism underpinned by a totally credible invocation of American ideals. Bill Coffin was someone who changed many persons' outlook by his inspirational talks that brilliantly combined humor with idealism, imploring Americans to live up to what he passionately believed was the true American way.

I had some trouble holding my own in such a group of anti-war celebrities, which was augmented by two prominent media personalities—Peter Arnett, a New Zealand born veteran journalist who had covered many wars and was then working for Associated Press, and John Hart, a senior reporter with NBC TV. These were the first major media persons from the U.S. that were permitted entry to North Vietnam.

As we were to be strangers to the released POWs, who had been away from their normal social interactions and families for long periods, and might be anxious about whether to place trust in us, relatives of each American pilot scheduled to be released were invited to accompany the delegation. The anti-war mother of one of the pilots joined us as did the wife of another; but the third pilot, a career officer, did not respond to this offer, and we never found out much about his relatives. This bright idea of softening the encounter with the outside world after confinement in a remote Vietnamese prison was basically that of Cora Weiss, who had developed through years of contact a maternal attitude toward the POWs and their families, creating nurturing relations while at the same time maintaining her overriding commitment to an anti-war agenda.

The Release and its Vietnamese Aftermath

It is not clear whether the Vietnamese timed the prisoner release to have an effect on the presidential elections scheduled in the U.S. for November of 1972, but this political dimension of the events was paramount in the treatment of our mission by the Western media. In the American political setting, the safe return of the imprisoned pilots was seen as a crucial challenge to the Vietnam policies of the Nixon presidency. It was pursuing a contradictory belligerent course—escalation to reassure Saigon and retain credibility as an alliance Big Brother while claiming at the same time to seek a diplomatic negotiated end to the war. It seemed that Washington's 'peace diplomacy' aimed to bring what had become an extremely unpopular war in the United States to an end in a manner that disguised to the extent possible a humiliating political defeat. And defeat it was, as there was a general expectation that South Vietnam would soon be absorbed by North Vietnam into a single, sovereign Vietnam to be governed by the Communist government in Hanoi. It was precisely to prevent this anticipated outcome that the war had been undertaken a decade earlier.

When the three American pilots were released in Hanoi, the occasion was treated as a major public event in North Vietnam, with a large press conference, which included direct Western coverage by the journalists Arnett and Hart. There was a double drama involved. Nixon's resumption and even expansion of the American bombing campaign coincided with the Vietnamese release of prisoners of war via representatives of the American peace movement—not, as would have been more conventional, as an inter-governmental gesture of good will. The pilots were obviously stunned to various degrees by their release, glad to be free yet worried about being accused of being collaborators when they returned home. Each of the pilots had signed a statement of remorse about their role in the war prior to their release that expressed opposition to the war.

We soon realized that with the upcoming elections in the U.S. and a political concern in Washington that these pilots would likely denounce the Nixon approach to ending the war by escalating it, our mission attracted an increased attention that inevitably mixed humanitarian and political elements. Our preoccupation with perceptions back in the U.S. intersected with the Vietnamese letting us know that any future prisoner releases would depend on our returning these three individuals to the United States under our escort. This inserted a challenge that underlay the whole post-release experience. It was evident to us that the American Government would almost certainly make a major effort to gain control over these men at the earliest possible stage to prevent their contact with the world media. And then there was our related responsibility toward the pilots to figure out the best way to avoid this happening. We were also somewhat fearful of being manipulated by activists back home, who were eager to use the testimony of the pilots to intensify anti-war propaganda without any concern about what this might do to their lives. On a lesser scale, we were ourselves somewhat concerned about being disciplined or at least chastised for supposed expressions of disloyalty toward an American war that was still ongoing while we were in the enemy heartland.

I was fascinated by this interplay of perspectives: the media wanting good stories; activists wanting to get credit for a peace movement breakthrough; pilots wanting a low profile, and their relatives wanting a humanly comfortable reentry experience. Cora, Dave and Bill were all admirably sensitive to the pastoral priorities of the situation and made it very clear that none of us wanted to be manipulative toward the released pilots. We accepted a primary responsibility for the wellbeing of these pilots placed in our custody. We wanted to do everything possible to make future releases of remaining American POWs happen as quickly as possible. We also did our best to expose the cynical moves by the U.S. Government to avoid hostile media coverage at almost all costs without seeming to be indifferent to the humanitarian aspects of such a prisoner release, but rather showing concern about the psychological stress being experienced by these men just released from the presumed anguish of their captivity in Vietnam.

Before leaving Vietnam, we followed an itinerary prepared by our Vietnamese hosts that included visits to several sites of major bombing. At the same time, we decided that returning, as we came, by way of Laos, was not a good idea if we were to uphold our part of the release bargain. We felt that we would likely lose our control over the pilots as soon as we landed in Vientiane, given the extent of American political influence in the city. We believed that the only way to achieve a successful escort under our auspices was to proceed by way of Beijing, Moscow, and Copenhagen before landing in NYC. Even such a planned travel route presented problems beyond what we anticipated. We were not aware of the secret imminent moves by Washington to normalize relations with China. Such a long overdue step was soon to be given global attention in the form of a dramatic Nixon/Kissinger visit to Beijing.

This diplomatic prospect was of the greatest significance to Chinese government but unknown to us. This made our transit plans more complex and delicate than we could have imagined. The Chinese above all wanted to avoid antagonizing the leadership in Washington on the eve of the American elections and seemed worried that facilitating such a journey through their country would seem hostile and unfriendly. And then there was a further difficulty that we didn't fully appreciate until we encountered it.

Arranging for China and the Soviet Union to cooperate even on something as simple as coordinating our travel plans was no simple matter. The tensions between these two Communist titans was at a crisis level, perhaps partly reflecting Moscow's concerns about the damage that U.S./China normalization would do to their own global role and ambitions. This tangle of issues was further stressed by the Soviet interest in working more cooperatively with the U.S. so as to sustain the atmosphere of *détente*. And even our planned change of planes in Copenhagen was more problematic than we realized. Denmark was a NATO member, and their allowing our transit could be seen as an indirect challenge to the Cold War policies of the United States, and thus a blow to alliance solidarity.

While doing our best to deal with the logistical side of these travel arrangements we spent a week in the Vietnamese countryside. Because of the media coverage of the release in Vietnam, the pilots were recognized by the Vietnamese people wherever we went. Somewhat to our surprise they were met mostly with curiosity, and only rarely with hostility. These pilots represented contrary realities to the Vietnamese and the Americans. For the Vietnamese, the pilots were the human embodiment of a high technology enemy invader that had devastated their country, destroyed many of their villages, and killed their children and other relatives. For Americans, the pilots were highly skilled and valued military officers, heroic victims of what was portrayed as a cruel and abusive enemy; they had become in the United States objects of almost universal sympathy, having done their best for their country albeit in a stupid and failed war effort, who were paying a high price by being captured and held captive in Vietnamese prisons.

The three pilots each exhibited distinct responses to the war and their situation. Actually, all POWs in Hanoi were inaccurately called 'pilots,' although some had other roles on the planes that were shot down. Only one of the three released men was actually a pilot: Mark Gartley, originally from Maine but residing in Florida. Mark had been in a Hanoi prison the longest, four years, had developed a strong anti-war outlook in tandem with his spirited mother who traveled with us on the mission, and was an activist against the war. Mark expressed genuine remorse about bombing a peasant society from high altitudes and was generally the best educated and informed of the three. Norris Alphonso Charles, an African American accompanied by his shy and devoted wife, Olga, was a Navy radar officer on a fighter plane when shot down. He had opposed the war long before being captured four months earlier after he parachuted from his plane. After his released in Hanoi, Norris worried that he might be treated as a collaborator with the Vietnamese enemy upon his return, and felt out of touch with what was going on, making him uncomfortable about the prospect of facing the media. It was clear to us that Norris' main aim was 'private peace,' and we fully respected and sympathized with his concerns.

The third person released, Major Edward Elias, was a career officer assigned to photo reconnaissance on an unarmed plane, who was given the job of assessing the bomb damage. He was aloof and somewhat sullen, and probably signed the anti-war statement solely to obtain better chances for an early release without actually subscribing to its contents. Even while we were still in Vietnam, he seemed ready to disown the act, perhaps to keep his military career on track for the few years left before he became eligible for retirement. Unlike the other two, whom I believe entered the military as part of arrangements that paid for their college education, Elias had chosen the military as a profession. He also made clear that our anti-war auspices were not congenial. He was also seemingly not at peace with himself, appearing unhappy and alienated, despite having just been freed from a Hanoi prison. He hardly interacted with any of us. This was entirely different from the other two who were friendly and put their trust in our good faith.

Before leaving Vietnam the delegation, without the three released pilots, had a session with six or seven other POWs still in captivity. The group looked healthy and spoke in a positive vein about their treatment. Undoubtedly their words were being monitored, and they probably hid the darker sides of their prison experience. To this day, I am unsure what to believe at this stage of the war. Some supporters of the war and several prominent released prisoners contended that every pilot endured frequent torture, while others including myself came to think that the worst mistreatment would have occurred in the first years of the war, and especially at the point of capture when a pilot was seized by Vietnamese villagers after parachuting to the ground when their plane that had been hit by anti-aircraft fire.

I had two subsequent conversations about prison conditions in Hanoi worth recalling. The first was shortly after my return with Jane Fonda and Tom Hayden in their Santa Monica home. They entreated me to join with them in reassuring the American public that the POWs in North Vietnam were not being tortured. I disappointed them by declining to make a public declaration for which I had no evidence. In contrast was a conversation years later with the first American ambassador in Hanoi, Pete Peterson, a former POW (for 6.5 years from 1966), who was outspoken in his insistence that torture was a pervasive feature of prison life, a view also expressed by the most illustrious of these prisoners, the late Senator John McCain. Of course, torture is never acceptable, nor lawful, and especially not when there is no pretext of obtaining information of impending attacks, but at the same time it is rather common in such situations of asymmetrical warfare where the weaker side has few chances to express its outrage and fury against the attacking side, or to seek to impose prohibitive costs for continuing its attacks.

As far as I could tell, the Vietnamese leadership, following the lead of Ho Chi Minh, basically endorsed the view that the American government, not the American people, were their enemy, and that once a soldier was captured, he should be treated humanely as mandated by international law. I seriously doubt whether this soft line was followed in all situations, but even its articulation produced a far better collective mentality than the tendency of Western propaganda to view a foreign people as a whole as the enemy, holding them individually and collectively responsible for the behavior of their governing authorities even if a dictatorial regime allowed them no voice in shaping policy.

Under American Bombs

Unlike my visit in 1968 when there was a bombing pause, the proximity of the combat reality of the war was present in 1972. The resumed bombing of North Vietnam was generally interpreted as being connected with an effort to improve the U.S. position in the Paris negotiations and as a public display that the U.S. commitment to the Saigon regime was alive and well, even as the political undertaking was being undermined and soon to be abandoned. In this regard, it was completely in violation of the most basic principle of customary international law of war, namely, the requirement that uses of military force be proportionate and justified by considerations of *military* necessity. Here the objectives were distinctly *diplomatic* and *psychological* as the political and military goals of the war had been renounced. Those Vietnamese lives lost in this period, whether civilians or military personnel, were thus the consequence of unlawful continuations of combat operations and should be considered war crimes.

This dynamic reached its ugly climax in the so-called 'Christmas Bombing' of the North (mainly the outskirts of Hanoi, Haiphong Harbor, and surrounding villages and towns) in December 1972. This militarist gesture led the Vietnamese negotiator at Paris, Le Duc Tho, to turn down the 1973 Nobel Peace Prize when offered jointly to him and Henry Kissinger, presumably for finally reaching an agreement to end the Vietnam War. Shamelessly, as might be expected, Kissinger accepted the award, although he was complicit in and unapologetic about the Christmas bombing's criminal complement to what were supposedly peace negotiations. His war-mongering career shamed the Nobel Peace Prize Committee for conveying the impression to the world that Kissinger was a man of peace in harmony with Nobel's vision when he established the prize, a mistake repeated in 2009 when the prize was awarded to Obama, who unlike Kissinger, had early in his presidency made a couple of dramatic peace pleas, later abandoned, with respect to Israel-Palestine and the endorsement of a world without nuclear weaponry. The Norwegian author and peace activist, Fredrik Heffermehl, has led an international campaign for more than a decade to build pressure on the Nobel Prize Committee to honor Alfred Nobel's vision of peace and warlessnesss.

The flimsy pretext for the bombing was the refusal of Vietnam to agree to the official release of American prisoners, numbering just over a hundred, who were being held captive in Hanoi prior to a withdrawal commitment. In anger Nixon launched the largest air campaign of the entire Vietnam War, with 129 B-52 bombers dropping on Hanoi over 20,000 tons of explosives in 729 sorties over the course of several days on either side of Christmas Day. Kissinger contended that the bombing was so effective that it brought the Vietnamese to their knees, but the evidence suggests quite the opposite. The text of the final agreement as signed by the governments was virtually the same as the language in the agreement before the bombing began. Not only did the bombing lack any credible military vindication, it also had no political effect, leaving behind a dominant impression that the United States was behaving like the wounded bully it was, strengthening the impression of being a bad loser.

Our experience in the countryside close to Hanoi confirmed this general pattern of heavy bombardment that had ended the 'pause' declared by Lyndon Johnson when he unexpectedly withdrew from the presidential race in 1968. Our group left a Vietnamese village only ten minutes before it was bombed. Seeing the smoke from fires caused by the bombs made us realize our jeopardy. The released pilots absorbed this experience of viewing air warfare from the ground without much comment, although telling us what we had previously heard, that many pilots dumped their bombs in the Gulf of Tonkin, finding no appropriate targets, yet not disobeying orders to return with empty bomb bays. It was evident to us that these villages were not legitimate military targets, having very few structures, usually only churches or temples, and sometimes a health clinic or school. This unlawful use of air power was subject to no accountability, reminding the world that geopolitical actors enjoy impunity in war/peace situations even if they suffer political defeat. In other words, there was no 'victors' justice' for the Vietnamese as there had been for the victors in World War II, who sanctimoniously prosecuted the surviving defeated leaders while holding themselves non-accountable, just as they would more recently, in the aftermath of the 2003 Iraq War in which only the leaders of the country victimized by the war of aggression were prosecuted and punished as war criminals.

In World War II the Allies avoided accountability at the subsequent-war crimes trials by way of 'victors' justice.' In Vietnam, U.S. criminal accountability was avoided by what might be described as 'geopolitical impunity,' that is, although the U.S. lost the war, its power and leverage as a geopolitical actor shielded it from accountability under international criminal law. The Christmas Bombing, which caused at least 1,000 Vietnamese deaths, was widely condemned at the time. I have described such behavior that is beyond the reach of international law yet violates fundamental legal norms as a 'Geopolitical Crime.'[i] Although geopolitical crimes are not part of international criminal law in a formal sense, their condemnation is one way of acknowledging moral and political wrongdoing. I would hope that at some point geopolitical crimes would be recognized as crimes under international law. Indeed, if world order is ever to be grounded in universal morality and cosmopolitan values, geopolitical crimes must be incorporated in prevailing notions of governance and legality. So long as geopolitical impunity persists, it is a sad delusion to think of establishing a global rule of law or displacing the unregulated *global law of power.*

Our most dangerous moment occurred on a moonlit night as we were being driven from a village to a guest house in the countryside where we would spend the night. While we waited in a long convoy to cross a river on a seemingly fragile pontoon bridge, an air raid warning came, and the sound of bombers filled the night air. I was convinced that soon we would be doing our best to avoid falling bombs. The convoy offered the planes a high value military target consisting of a long line of army trucks filled with soldiers and supplies. My most vivid memory of this scary occasion was provided by Bill Coffin, at once a man of God and a fearless adventurer, who seized on this danger as giving us an existential understanding of the way this war disrupted the lives of the Vietnamese people. While Bill was absorbed by this 'teaching moment,' I trembled in silence, assuming my life was about to end, spontaneously calculating the gains and losses of my life at age 41. For reasons forever unknown, the attack never came, we crossed the river, and came safely to our lodging for the night. As it turned out we shared our bedrooms with gigantic mosquitos that managed to penetrate the netting that hung over our beds, posing a threat that proved more sanguinary than our earlier experience that night of bombs that never fell. I remember when light came in the morning I was not surprised to see that the walls were stained with fresh blood and the remains of the dead insects that had brought us misery through the night.

---

i For some elaboration see my article, https://transnational.live/2019/08/16/geopolitical-crimes-a-revolutionary-proposal/, which I intend to further develop in a book in progress.

Comradery

Given the tensions arising from the interaction of strong personalities in tense situations where political judgment was required at every
turn, the attention of the world media acted as both a magnet and a trap.
It was a magnet as there was always the temptation to try to demonstrate
that this effort by peace activists was having a positive impact on public
opinion and awareness, which was also a way of vindicating ourselves as
acting humanely and constructively—insofar as critics were contending
that what we were doing was politically helpful to the enemies of the
United States, the leadership in Hanoi. It was also a trap on the personal
level, as it created competitive impulses to seize the nearest microphone
and make a personal splash. Bill Coffin and I gave way to Cora Weiss
and David Dellinger, as long-term, seasoned and more senior peace
movement leaders when it came to media relations.

At the same time within our group were two experienced media
practitioners. Full of zest and the impartiality of a professional observer
of wars, Peter Arnett would go anywhere on the planet for a good story,
regardless of the danger, without seeming to possess any inclination to
favor one side or the other. He was energetic, playful, and fun to be
around. Peter was physically on the short side, puckish, sporting the
sensibility of a leprechaun. I ran into Peter in 2017 at a social gathering
in Ho Chi Minh City, and found him undiminished, not even much per-
turbed by the fact that his daughter was married to John Yoo, notorious
author of the Torture Memos rationalizing torture for detainees. When
I asked him about that, he smiled puckishly, limiting his reply to a few
words: 'He treats her well.' Such are the benefits of being apolitical.
In 2003 Peter gained global notoriety by interviewing Saddam Hussein
in Baghdad at the start of the Iraq War. The dramatic backdrop of this
interview was greatly heightened by the fact that the war was initiated by
a nighttime 'shock and awe' air and missile attack, which also solidified
Peter's deserved reputation as a fearless journalist situated at whatever
ground zero was at the top of the news at that moment.

The Long Journey Home

Even before leaving Hanoi we realized that planning the trip home
was about politics much more than it was about the logistics of travel. We found ourselves torn between the pros and cons of the media's
consuming hunger to cover these events, our strongly held anti-war
sentiments, and our primary sense of responsibility to protect the dignity and privacy of these former POWs entrusted to our custody. These

three men had been cut off from world news for varying lengths of time, were concerned about how their words and release would be received in the U.S., and were at the outset of our contact with them, unsure of how much to trust us, their temporary minders, given our activism and presumed peace movement motivations. Were we not in their eyes a new hazard replacing the old?

In planning our secure return to the U.S., we were partially rescued by the good offices of the Swedish ambassador in Hanoi, Jean-Christophe Öberg, helped by Cora's strong contact with the Palme leadership in Stockholm. This physically imposing and humanly engaging man had already earned international notoriety and the gratitude of the Hanoi leadership by bringing international journalists to view evidence that Nixon had indeed initiated systematic bombing of the dikes in the Red River Delta. If such bombing had continued, it would have caused disastrous flooding, harming vital sources of food, and resulting in massive civilian casualties. We heard estimates that as many as two million Vietnamese civilians might have died from flooding and starvation. We were also told by the Vietnamese Prime Minister, Pham Von Dong, that the national struggle would have continued even if the dikes had been destroyed. He told us that Vietnam had a 50-year plan of resistance that included, if necessary, a retreat to mountain caves. A journalist with *Le Monde,* Jacques Decornoy, who was close to the Vietnamese leadership, told me a year or so later in Paris that he had actually seen the text of this detailed plan for carrying on the struggle for Vietnamese independence far into the future.

Our alternative travel plan called for us to go through China to Beijing, and from there to Moscow, and then on to Copenhagen before boarding a flight for the return to the U.S. The Swedish ambassador allowed us to send cables from the embassy to receive assurances from the Danish government. My assignment was to inform officials in the State Department that we were engaged in a humanitarian mission, seeking to repatriate three American POWs released to our custody for travel back to the United States, and that non-interference with the mission would hasten future prisoner releases. Although there was never a formal response, I was told privately that such a communication was welcomed in Washington, and while not entirely respected, did have the effect of inhibiting official criticisms of our trip.

After a stopover of several days in the Western city of Wuhan, long before the city became notorious as the origin of the COVID pandemic, we arrived in Beijing, and were confined to our hotel. As some sort of

weird compensation for this confinement, we were fed almost continuously and in gourmet fashion. The Chinese government obviously did
not want us to be seen or identified in public, and sought, successfully,
to have us avoid media contact. Nevertheless, they were cooperative,
friendly, and ensured our security.

Our stop in Moscow told a totally different story. At the airport,
there was no Soviet security provided, and American embassy officials
showed up carrying military uniforms for the pilots to put on once they
decided to accept the offer of a return to the U.S. under government
auspices. Bill Coffin almost got into a physical fight with a top embassy
official, insisting that we had agreed to escort these men back to the
U.S., and their removal from our custody would preclude future releases. Although Major Elias seemed to waver, all three pilots resisted the
embassy pressure and stayed with us. Undoubtedly, they were wrestling
with the dilemma of facing discipline back home or breaking faith with
fellow prisoners still in captivity who may have felt responsible to the
POWs left behind in Hanoi if their transfer had not proceeded as their
Vietnamese captors had desired. After a scene of some disorder in the
airport, the American officials backed off, and we proceeded to board
our connecting flight to Copenhagen. Once in Copenhagen, the media
was present at the airport in full force, filling a large press room with
dozens of TV cameras. Our delegation explained the mission, and the
pilots refrained from taking questions or making statements. We wanted
this mission to be portrayed as being of a purely humanitarian character,
despite its political overtones.

Someone in the Copenhagen Airport had given me a copy of the
NY Times, and on the flight back I was shocked and saddened to read
that my close friend, an informal mentor, Wolfgang Friedman, had been
killed in a street mugging while walking from his office at Columbia
Law School to the train station at 125th Street where he daily caught
a commuter train to bring him to his Westchester home. As I read this
tragic story, I recalled a conversation with Wolfgang a few years earlier
where we had discussed an earlier similar incident near his Columbia
office in which he had successfully fought off several muggers who
demanded his wallet. I commended Wolfgang's courage but drawing on
my experience of growing up in Manhattan, I strongly urged him not to
repeat such resistance if he was unlucky enough to have something of
the same kind happen again. I remember pleading with him to simply
surrender whatever was asked. At the time Wolfgang replied movingly,
yet as it turns out, tragically, that he had experienced Nazism as a Jew

growing up in Germany and vowed never to allow himself to be physically harassed by anyone in the future. In retrospect, given our separate experiences of life, we were both right!

I also remember, when reading of Wolfgang's death on a trip back from an area of heavy combat in Vietnam, that I asked myself the question, 'Where is the war zone?' Although the author of influential books on international law, especially its economic aspects, Wolfgang somehow was outside the circle of insiders at the top of the academic ladder in the United States, never receiving the recognition his humane and innovative scholarship deserved. Yet his violent death was a reminder that all our lives are contingent, and that much of our fate in life, whether good or bad, is determined by forces beyond our control.

As soon as we landed at JFK pandemonium broke out. The sound system informed us that 'regular' passengers were requested to leave the plane, and the others instructed to remain seated. After this happened, a group of Pentagon officials in civilian dress boarded the plane as if performing arrests, seized the three pilots in the presence of their disbelieving and shocked relatives, claiming that these individuals for their own sake were being taken to military facilities for 'medical debriefings' that might last for several weeks. Of course, we assumed that this traumatic reception was mainly a government ruse to avoid contact with the media at this delicate political time. The lead Pentagon official, Frank Sieverts, was a former Princeton midcareer student who happened to be an acquaintance. After the pilots were removed and driven away in three separate cars waiting by the runway, our delegation was still seated, somewhat stunned by the way our arrival had been handled. Frank apologized to me for how the incident had unfolded. He explained that he was following Pentagon protocol on how these released POW pilots were to be treated after arriving in the U.S. landing.

The drama ended as soon as we left the airport, parting ways. The prisoner release was a world story, with Mark Gartley appearing on the weekly cover of *Time*. Cora kept up with the families of the pilots. I exchanged Christmas cards for a few years with Gartley, with whom I had several good conversations while we were together. He ran for Congress, but I have lost track of him and the other two.

A Personal Reflection

There is no doubt that returning to North Vietnam a second time deepened my experience of the society and affection for its people. This second departure from Hanoi amid laughter and playfulness recalled what I had so much enjoyed four years earlier while our reception in the Chinese airport across the border was by contrast orderly, austere, and formal. In my mind I contrasted Vietnam as a survivor society and compared it to China as an imperial society, although in an Asian mode that in recent centuries was itself victimized by Western imperialism. I never lost my admiration for the Vietnamese cultural temperament and its people, especially their ability to enjoy the comic sides of the most tragic circumstances, while coping in a good-natured way with the disorder and suffering of a devastating war, and for their creative and innovative gift of problem-solving, which was always an occasion for smiles signifying resignation combined with imaginative, yet strong-willed resistance. Despite facing the greatest difficulties, the Vietnamese generally rarely complained, accepting their sorrowful destiny as if it had been decreed by God, although theirs was a Confucian/Buddhist society without any visible inclination to sustain lived reality with metaphysical explanations (as in the monotheistic religions).

I enjoyed the fellowship of the escort mission, and the adventure of retaining the pilots under our custody on the way home. Later I wrote an academic article about POW repatriation by private citizens as deserving of protection in international humanitarian law. I was attacked personally by conservative zealots, including by William F. Buckley for daring to put forward my dissident views on the proper treatment of American POWs, a domain he believed belongs exclusively to the government. I remain more unconvinced than ever about the propriety of deference to governmental claims of authority in matters affecting peace and justice, especially when humanitarian issues are at stake. A democratic society under present world conditions is increasingly dependent on citizens of conscience and brave whistleblowers to counteract a militarized security state emboldened by surveillance technology. What we did then for these three POWs was right then and would be right now.

Unlike my initial trip to Vietnam, this second one reinforced my public identity as an anti-war activist but did not have the transformative impacts on my own political development as did the trip in 1968. The POW repatriation in 1972 did generate worldwide media attention, even excitement, more danger, and it was certainly more enjoyable because of sharing this experience of high drama with congenial comrades who were also warm and caring friends. Yet this time I returned to Princeton unchanged, although perhaps the earlier transformative experienced was refreshed and reinforced.

Revisiting Vietnam After the War

I followed events in Vietnam rather closely, and was disappointed by the U.S.'s vindictive finishing touches that in the end hurt the U.S. more than they punished Vietnam for daring to prevail. The American public understood the outcome better than did the political class in Washington that made no secret of rejecting the anti-interventionist public mood. I regarded the societal anti-intervention reflex as politically welcome and an enlightened collective response to a colossally imprudent and wrongful turn in American foreign policy. Foreign policy elites dubbed what they regarded as a negative public mood as 'the Vietnam Syndrome.' This label was intended as a critique of the American people's reluctance to use American hard power in distant military undertakings as a result of the Vietnam experience. It was not until the Gulf War in 1991 that an American leader was finally able to proclaim, as George H.W. Bush did, '[w]e have finally kicked the Vietnam Syndrome in the sands of Arabia.' This post-Vietnam militarist exclamation by Bush, Sr. echoed a prevailing Washington belief that the American military machine, if properly used, could still win wars at acceptable costs. These periodic wars were regarded as needed to reinforce submission to the globalist vision that guided American international leadership, as well as to safeguard the globalizing neoliberal economic order established after 1945. Bush, Sr.'s claim that military capabilities could determine a *political* outcome was at best mistaken, as his son was to discover after attacking Iraq in 2003. If the stakes of war are to prevent territorial aggression, as in relation to Kuwait in 1991, there is greater relevance for traditional realist calculations than if the stakes involve military intervention undertaken with the intent of imposing by force a political future that disregards sovereign rights. Bush, Jr.'s presidency would have fared better had he ignored his father's claim, and instead accorded the Vietnam Syndrome the prudential and moral/legal respect it deserved.

By the 1990s the U.S. Government was ready to normalize relations with Vietnam, but in measured steps. Vietnam remained receptive, having experienced a costly border skirmish with China, and believing that their security was more threatened by their Communist neighbor that had been their enemy for almost two decades after the French left the country than by the distant American center of capitalist power. In reality, a unified, independent Vietnam would be a stable presence in the region, an outcome probably more consistent with American strategic objectives in Asia than had the American War in Vietnam ended with a Saigon/American victory. This is the geopolitical irony that has never been properly understood, much less acknowledged by Washington war planners, who sought to restore an image of American infallibility if U.S. ideological warmongering policies overseas are to be supported by public opinion and Congressional appropriations.

My next opportunity to return to Vietnam came as a result of an invitation to serve as a lecturer on a Princeton Alumni tour of South Asia in 1993. The tour by cruise ship started in Singapore before visiting Saigon, by then renamed Ho Chi Minh City, and Phnom Penh, featuring a visit to 'the killing fields' associated with the genocidal events in Cambodia during the years of Khmer Rouge rule in the early 1970s as well as a sunrise trip to the magnificent ruins at Angkor Wat. The stop at Ho Chi Minh City was brief but of interest. The city seemed vibrant and seemingly enjoying a return to political normalcy. I suspect it would have looked exactly the same if the war had never taken place or had turned out differently.

This wider exposure to South Asia was personally very satisfying, but the more memorable experience was shipboard, which enabled interaction with wealthy conservative Princeton alumni and their friends and relatives, especially at meals, which were more elegant in presentation than their culinary quality warranted. We were no more than 80, not counting the crew. My role as a lecturer on the political aspects of the cruise seemed, at first, a challenge, given the right-wing leanings of the more articulate passengers. I was told by one of the Tiger alum passengers in the spirit of full disclosure that some of those on board had considered canceling their reservations when they discovered that I would be the lecturer. My reputation with Princeton alumni was that of a rabid anti-war, anti-American troublemaker who had been a baleful force on campus in weakening, if not overturning, hallowed Princeton traditions. One passenger, who later became friendly, told me cheerily that he had expected me to appear with horns on my head. In turn, I had my own reservations about this assemblage of rich pleasure seekers who had paid $18,000 per head for a bit over two weeks on the water. Among the passengers were several executives from the disgraced Wall Street investment firm of Drexel Burnham, notorious for its junk bond escapades in the 1980s, and a couple of NYC real estate moguls, who gave me a pre-Trump mouthful of Trumpism, which even in such a small dose I found indigestible.

Glimpsing Vietnam At Peace

In 1999 I again went to Hanoi, this time with Hilal, to teach in a Ford Foundation program that was supposed to bring young Vietnamese diplomats up to speed on international developments. It was a three-month program with course meetings of four hours per day throughout the week. Such a teaching schedule was demanding, and more so because the language abilities of the students was uneven. I co-taught a course on international institutions with Peggy Karns, a dutiful, somewhat girl-scoutish International Relations professor from the University of Dayton who super-conscientiously prepared her daily presentations. She was determined to teach our students more than they were capable of learning within our allotted time, given their limited language skills and weak substantive background. Our presentations in English were summarized by an interpreter. How well, we can only imagine, and if we knew, we would likely weep.

We found that the students were friendly and many were eager to learn as much as they could. Three surprises awaited me as I came to know them better. First, they seemed far more interested in Buddhism than in Marxism/Leninism, even as it was channeled to them through the life and thought of the still vibrant memory of their national hero, Ho Chi Minh. We were invited for meals at Buddhist temples and given Buddhist literature to read.

Secondly, after the last class these young diplomats arranged a karoke evening, which turned out to be a wildly successful way to remove student/teacher barriers, and even gave me the courage to exhibit my pathetic singing voice. In all my teaching experience in the 'free' West I never experienced any comparably joyful course finale!

Thirdly, I was surprised that some of the older diplomats taking the course, shared their happy memories of earlier academic experiences in Moscow, which included various types of romantic bonding. They exhibited nostalgic attitudes of gratitude toward the Soviet Union for their studies there. They also tended to be appreciative of Soviet support for Vietnam's national struggle throughout the long war with the Americans.

This preference for the Soviet Union over China was reinforced by a meeting we had during the prisoner repatriation trip with a former close associate of Ho Chi Minh during his period of exile in China. This individual, a sage diplomat, later became Vietnam's foreign minister. He said that Mao himself treated Ho unkindly and with disrespect, as a cultural inferior. He felt that such a judgmental putdown of the Vietnamese revered leader was expressive of China's historical treatment of Vietnam as a tributary state, owing fealty to China. One expression of this tension was the widespread feeling among the Vietnamese of anger that the Chinese had prolonged their suffering during the Vietnam War by discouraging Hanoi from pursuing a diplomatic solution. This angered the Vietnamese leaders who interpreted Chinese pressure as desiring the Vietnamese to carry on the revolutionary struggle against the U.S. at a huge cost to Vietnam while preoccupying Washington and leaving China alone.

In response, I recalled that the early sections of *The Pentagon Papers* completely extinguished Vietnamese identity, participation, and agency, calling the North Vietnamese military forces, 'Chicoms.' This geopolitical interpretation meant that in the American view, the enemy in the Vietnam War was China rather than the Vietnamese national movement, which was misleading in the extreme. This ideological misreading of reality helps us understand why the American military superiority brought to the battlefields of Vietnam had almost no impact on the political outcome of the struggle, which was always a matter of Vietnamese self-determination, with a rather minor and uncertain impact on China. The fact that China and Vietnam engaged in a short bloody war with each other with complicated and highly contested issues at stake shortly after the American withdrawal shows how far off the mark was the sinophobic original American geopolitical rationale for its intervention in Vietnam.

A further observation of the Sino-Vietnamese relationship occurred a few years later when I was in Beijing as the guest of the government seeking to grasp how the Chinese viewed their experience in the Vietnam War. My Chinese hosts had gathered for my benefit over 50 Vietnam experts in a large room, inviting me to pose questions. I introduced the discussion by describing my anti-war activism, and then asked the assembled specialists for their interpretation of the Vietnam War. Several of these 'Vietnam experts' described at length their view that Vietnam was an ungrateful ally, emphasizing that China had delivered large quantities of supplies during the entire course of the war, including military equipment, without ever receiving any show of appreciation from the leadership in Vietnam. It was also said that China lent this assistance in a period when its peoples were enduring severe economic hardships. Further, that such assistance was being delivered at great risk to the Chinese due to repeated American air bombardment of the sole rail link between the two countries.

Hilal and I enjoyed our time in Hanoi in 1999. We lived at the Hanoi Club, an expatriate hangout with several excellent restaurants, bought simple bicycles to get around the city, and learned to navigate by foot or bike the special hazards of intersecting rivers of bikes and scooters that then constituted the traffic of the city. We had an engaging language tutor who tried a couple of times a week to teach us elementary Vietnamese, which turned out, despite his best efforts, to be a futile undertaking. I found it difficult even to distinguish the tonal variations for words spelled in the same way but having vastly different meanings. Our tutor was so patient, staying with us long beyond our lesson period, expressing his determination to do everything possible to make us learn Vietnamese. At the end of our time in Hanoi, we invited him to join us at one of our favorite nearby restaurants. We discovered that despite his being a college graduate he had never before had a meal in a restaurant, affording us a small window on the income gaps and poverty of the country.

After three months or so of teaching and living in Hanoi we were scheduled to do some lectures in Ho Chi Minh City. It was my first real exposure to the South, as the Princeton cruise visit was too short to count. We arrived stricken with food poisoning on a hot and humid day, Hilal severely and I more mildly, although still hampered by fever and nausea. I foolishly kept an appointment for tennis with some students who had gone to the trouble of making arrangements for a court. It was not a prudent move on my part, but I survived. Despite being ill, we managed to get a sense of the contrasting atmospheres of Hanoi and Ho Chi Minh City, which still managed to hold on somewhat to its Saigon and French colonial past and was as commercially minded as Hanoi was governmentally oriented. It's ironic that the center of post-French colonialism's last stand should be named after the legendary leader of the Vietnamese Communist Party while the northern city where Ho resided retained its traditional name. Although Ho Chi Minh City could hardly any longer uphold the colonial claim of being 'the Paris of Asia,' it was still resplendent; its wide tree-lined boulevards allowed those so inclined to retain imperial memories of past French glories.

Leaving Vietnam for the Last Time

I was conscious as I entered the departure lounge that I was unlikely at my age ever to return to Vietnam. It provided me with the occasion to realize how much I had gained over this half century of contact with Vietnam. It had provided a learning experience for me, especially with respect to the misguided American attempt to prevent the national liberation of the country, doing immeasurable harm and yet, fortunately for all sides, failing to reverse the flow of history. It helped me became politically what I was meant to be, thanks mainly to the people of Vietnam, their struggle, their friendship and inspiration, and even their victory in a long cruel war that also inflicted lasting damage on American wellbeing.

The United States, significantly, has never taken responsibility for the persisting damages caused by the war. These include continuing birth deformities associated with the widespread use of Agent Orange to counteract Vietnamese ambushes from tall vegetation and the toxic areas where this dangerous pesticide, stored and left behind in large quantities, continues to pollute ground water and soil.

On a more personal level, my long embrace of the Vietnamese experience, expressed my more private resolve not to be corrupted by the lure of power and wealth, and yet not to become alienated from my own social milieu in the process. I am still trying to find the point of equilibrium in the public sphere that as a child I had searched for, and never found, in relating to my mother's rich and snobbishly materialistic family. Because this search involves the combining of contradictory goals, the points of equilibrium when attained are unstable and temporary, leading to cycles of disillusionment and a reconfigured and resumed quest that reflects the altered horizons of fear and hope. After the American War in Vietnam I was hopeful about the future of both countriess, yet now in the throes of Trump and Trumpism I am fearful for my native country and more generally about the prospects for human survival.

My public stature fell after the end of the Vietnam War during which it had risen more than I then appreciated. Perhaps the end point of this momentary notoriety was the mid-1970s when *Time* magazine did a feature consisting of profiles of the fifty most important persons in America. *The Village Voice* ran a story on those who were cut at the final stage, mentioning me as among those who had deserved to be selected. If such a survey was to be undertaken by a leading national magazine in 2020, it is inconceivable that I would even be considered worth an interview, much less survive the vetting process until the last cut. The political compass began moving to the right, and Zionist smears took their toll on my reputation.

CHAPTER 13
Iran Erupts

Why Iran?

From my earliest outreach as a fledgling member of the academic community, I developed an interest in issues of U.S. intervention in foreign societies as part of my ongoing quest for a scholarly/citizen activist identity. This interest goes back to a student research paper I had written under the guidance of Myres McDougal while a student at Yale Law School. It may be that the theme of intervention appealed to me as it became clearly a way of challenging the global reach of U.S. foreign policy and bolstered my long struggle to substantiate it in scholarly terms. It also reflected my youthful moral rejection of my father's traditional nationalistic and patriotic orientation, reflected in my early affinity with the weaker side in any rivalry, whether in sports or politics or even social relations. This personality trait has been especially evident in my relations with Dimitri and Noah. Perhaps, too fearful of intervening in their lives I shielded them from exposure to values and commitments that I believe in and might have had positive effects on how they chose to live their lives.

As with Gandhi's resolve to stand with 'the last man' I instinctively opt for the underdog, not dogmatically but in the spirit of a Rawlsian emphasis on fairness or in an effort to understand how someone 'other' conceives and experiences reality, as well as instinctive reactions to cruelty and avoidable suffering, including with respect to animals (excepting stinging insects) and sometimes plants.

The elected Mossadegh government was overthrown by a coup that restored the dynastic Pahlavi regime to power in 1953. Even back in the 1950s it was widely assumed that the CIA had played a major role in arranging for the Shah to recover the peacock throne, but only after some decades was this nefarious American involvement in the overthrow of a democratically elected leader fully documented, graphically recounted in *All the Shah's Men: An American Coup and the Roots of*

Middle Eastern Terror by the respected journalist, Stephen Kinzer. This form of coercive and covert diplomacy of intervention came wrapped in Cold War rationalizations. Less frequently acknowledged were the strong capitalist motivations that were as much a defining feature of American foreign policy as was the rivalry with the Soviet Union or the dislike of leftist nationalism. The official rationale of U.S. intervention was to prevent, or if necessary, to reverse moves toward the adoption of a nationalist, let alone a Marxist, approach to economic development or toward embracing Moscow as an alternate source of support for public policy in either the economic or security spheres.

A year following the coup engineered in Tehran, the Arbenz Government in Guatemala was covertly overthrown by U.S. intervention. In the same period, the Soviets were carrying out brutal interventions of their own, harshly suppressing the Hungarian uprising in 1956, followed by hegemonic initiatives in East Germany, Poland, and elsewhere in Eastern Europe. Insofar as I strongly opposed the symmetrical pattern of interventions being carried out by both these rival superpowers, my American identity did not color these critical assessments of international behavior, and rather reflected my law-oriented political consciousness. I remain convinced that powerful states would be pragmatically benefitted by adhering to the discipline of international law and the UN Charter when it comes to uses of international force. In war/peace contexts, I favor a kind of humanistic legalism that strikes me as responsive to the lurking dangers of a third world war fought with nuclear weapons, as well as a sense that smaller and weaker states and their populations are as entitled to self-determination, democratization, and sovereign rights as stronger ones. The norm of self-determination expresses the fundamental rights of people to determine their own future, provided it adopts a governance form that is inclusive of ethnic and religious differences and sensitive to human rights. Self-determination has been interpreted over the past 75 years as entailing rejection of colonialism, and its sequel, hegemonic geopolitics, and represents the flow of history. Israel, aided by special historical circumstances, managed to defy the flow, succeeding in establishing a colonialist state in the middle of the 20th century based on exclusionary ethnic principles that dispossessed and permanently displace the resident majority Arab population.

The overthrow of the Mossadegh government along with the Soviet intervention in Hungary had produced a pre-Vietnam rupture in my thinking about world order and the conduct of foreign policy. These interventions illustrated the imposition of external constraints on democratic choice placed on countries deemed of strategic importance to either side in the Cold War.

Around this time at Princeton I was invited to comment on a public talk by the much-celebrated liberal historian, Arthur Schlesinger, Jr., which elaborated and defended the exclusion of Castro's Cuba from the Organization of American States on grounds of ideological incompatibility. The rather specious U.S. argument contended that the values of Marxism/Leninism were so incompatible with the ideals of the Western Hemisphere that the international norm of non-intervention should not apply. My comment objected to such an ideological justification for interference with the sovereign rights and self-determination of a small neighboring state. I pointed out that the U.S. Government had previously lived comfortably with what might have been more appropriately regarded as an ideologically incompatible government, the Cuban gangster regime, which was deeply entangled with organized crime. No one in Washington ever objected to the predatory and corrupt Batista dictatorship that had ruled Cuba before Castro, Guevara, and their comrades successfully staged the Cuban Revolution. I mention this evening at Princeton because it epitomized for me the uncongenial worldview of a leading Cold War liberal intellectual. I based my objections to Schlesinger on abstract principles of sovereign rights. I still lacked the self-confidence to express support for the kind of socialist development that the Cuban Revolution was implementing so impressively, considering the sanctions and hostility to its internal development by the giant to Cuba's north. In other words, I debated Schlesinger within *his* liberal framework rather than relying on more progressive argumentation. I remained hesitant to stand too far apart from the crowd, and maybe on some occasions I still do. As it is, I am provocative enough to annoy liberal heavyweights without being openly progressive enough to seem radical, and therefore, sometimes stranding myself politically in a no-go zone

In effect, as is characteristic of international relations in general, the strategic interests and ideological alignments of the United States took precedence over deference to the sovereign rights of other countries and respect for the right of self-determination. Iran was of special interest to the West, not only for Cold War reasons but because it was a major source of oil. The unquenchable thirst for oil fed capitalist ambitions as well underscored strategic priorities. It seemed that the Cold War hostility to Mossadegh crossed the threshold of geopolitical tolerance more because of his economic nationalism than the main cover story justifying the coup that focused on his alleged moves toward accommodating Moscow. Mossadegh's worst offense was nationalizing the Anglo-Iranian Oil conglomerate. After the Shah was restored to power in 1953, the oil industry was immediately returned to private ownership and administration, but there was also a dramatic shift in the national pattern of corporate ownership that paralleled the changing geopolitical landscape. The Iranian oil industry after the coup was placed mostly under the ownership and administration of major American oil producers, while the British acquiesced in this loss.

By predestined coincidence I was invited in 1958, out of the blue, to contribute a paper on just such a theme of intervention by geopolitical actors in the internal affairs of sovereign states at a conference on International & Comparative Law held in Brussels and linked to the Belgian Expo. I accepted without a second thought and produced a paper that tried to substantiate the hypothesis of symmetrical patterns of intervention by the United States and the Soviet Union, which were both in violation of international law and seriously eroding the sovereign rights of weaker countries to the detriment of their respective populations and in violation of the most basic normative premise of world order based on the centrality and equality of sovereign states and their constituent nations' vital national interests.

Iranian Student Leftism in America

Before the revolutionary movement erupted in Iran, there was widespread evidence of strong anti-Shah sentiments among Iranian students on many American college campuses, which I understood as an amalgam of Mossadegh-style democratic nationalism and a more left anti-authoritarian radicalism heavily influenced by Marxist traditions of thought. I became gradually involved as a supporter of this activism from a human rights and democracy perspective. Again, as with Vietnam, it was the imperial interventions of American foreign policy that led me by stages toward making this political commitment. The Shah, with his so-called 'White Revolution' designed to make Iran modern in a hurry, subsidized large numbers of students in Iran to study abroad at American universities with the idea of providing the skilled labor needed to manage the envisioned technocratic infrastructure for the country. High quality overseas education was conceived by the Shah's government as a way to accelerate Iran's transition to modernity. Large groups of Iranian students were concentrated in several American universities notable for their programs in engineering and agriculture. At first, these student activists seemed almost all to be of a left secular persuasion with very little indication of religious affinities. One of their most passionate and prominent voices was that of Reza Baraheni, a self-dramatizing poet and controversial left ideologue with a Trotskyist orientation.

These students were understandably fearful of SAVAK, the savage Iranian intelligence service that was assumed to be observing any anti-Shah political activities during their study period abroad with an eye toward punitive action upon their return home. Despite this, many were defiantly and intensely critical of the Shah's leadership at campus public events. These young Iranians were mostly from urban middle class backgrounds, and generally not outwardly religious.

A pivotal event in Iran was the exiling to Iraq of a then rather obscure clerical figure, Ayatollah Ruhollah Khomeini, explicitly in response to his leading role in supporting increasingly aggressive protests against the violent anti-clerical actions of the Shah as well as against the privileged treaty presence of American military forces in 1962. Khomeini was widely quoted at the time as saying that if an Iranian ran over a dog he would likely be treated more harshly under Iranian law than would an American soldier who wantonly killed an Iranian citizen by reckless driving. Such a taunt, while provocative, was accurate. The Status of Forces Treaty between the two countries under which 45,000 U.S. forces were present in Iran exempted these soldiers from accountability under Iran's criminal law. At one point in this protest period during which Khomeini played a prominent role, the Shah gathered all the leading Muslim clerics together, demanding a pledge of fealty to be shown by kissing the hand of the Shah's ring finger. All the assembled religious leaders submitted to the Shah's demand except Khomeini. In response, Khomeini was exiled, first to Turkey for a year, and then to Najaf, a religious city in Iraq, in 1965 where it was expected he would fade to obscurity, and never be heard from again. As we in the West came to know, this treatment of Khomeini was one of the Shah's most significant tactical misjudgments when it came to dealing with the religious sentiments of the Iranian people, as well as animating the intense opposition of Iran's religious leaders to his rule. It is not widely appreciated that the movement against the Shah had deep roots in opposition to his secularizing and Westernizing father, Reza Shah (1925-41), and in the earlier Iranian democracy movement that achieved control of the country briefly in 1904-05. The growing anti-Shah resentment within the powerful clerical establishment over the years was the setting for Khomeini's dramatic emergence from religious obscurity to political ascendancy.

The extraordinary Khomeini phenomenon, still largely misunderstood in the West, is brilliantly depicted by Baqer Moin in *Khomeini: The Biography of the Ayatollah.*

In the mid-1960s, I also came across the fascinating writings of Ali Shariati, then hailed as the philosopher of the future revolution in Iran. In various ways, Shariati's ideas were exhibiting his commitment to socialist values while strongly affirming Iran's Islamic cultural background. What made Shariati so prophetically influential was his recognition of the powerful mobilizing potential of Islam as compared to the ideologies of the secular left that were worrying Washington. This Cold War mentality prevailing in the U.S. helps explain why the government was blindsided by the revolutionary movement as it emerged. In fact, because of the anti-Communist animus of Islamic radicals due to its atheism and anti-Soviet outlook, the U.S. mistakenly assumed the Muslim religion was a natural ally in its overriding effort to defeat political moves from the left, and used various inducements to recruit followers from the ranks of religiously devout Iranians active outside of Iran. Undoubtedly, the wily tactical skill of Khomeini exhibited a willingness to ally with alien secular, even left, political constituencies to achieve the overriding goal of liberating Iran from the Pahlavi dynasty. But Khomeini was not about to jump from the American skillet to the Soviet frying pan. When the Soviet ambassador sought to express Moscow's readiness to bond with Iran, Khomeini rebuffed this decisively, even in the face of anxieties about a second pro-Shah intervention by the U.S.

Hence, it is hardly surprising that American worries with respect to Iran were focused on the supposed threat to the Shah's rule posed by the Tudeh Party. Tudeh was categorized in American policymaking circles as a dangerous Moscow-oriented Communist Party, viewed as a Soviet Trojan horse. Its potency as a political force was enhanced by the fact that it drew part of its membership from workers in the Iranian oil fields. It was certainly true that the Tudeh Party reflected political tendencies definitely opposed to U.S. influence and the Shah's imperial form of governance. But what was not true is that religious dislike of the secular left in Iran would ensure Islamic alignment with the West and the United States. This false inference led to serious mistakes that contributed to a major strategic defeat for the U.S. in Iran.

I became good friends in these years with Mansour Farhang, an articulate and politically engaged professor of international relations at the University of California college campus in Sacramento. Mansour, an ethnic Iranian, held strongly pro-democracy views that were extremely anti-Shah, although neither Marxist nor Islamist. Mansour both shared and was influenced by the Shariati outlook, and early looked upon the anti-Shah movement among students with approval, justifying intellectual solidarity with religious opposition groups, although himself favoring liberal secular modernization for a post-Shah democratizing Iran. Despite many years of residence and a successful academic career in America, Mansour never lost his primary attachment to Iran, and soon demonstrated his willingness to turn his back on his American experience, including giving up U.S. citizenship and his university affiliation with the State University of California, Sacramento. When the upheaval in Iran unexpectedly and suddenly emerged, Mansour's once implausible dreams seemed to be coming true. His revolutionary vision was emancipatory, a pluralistic democratic society with human rights for all, including a willing affirmation of the religious leadership in the popular movement against the Shah, which he regarded as the most promising vehicle for transformative change, given societal attitudes in Iran.

After his strong support for the Iranian Revolution, including a tactical acceptance of its religious character, Mansour was among the first of the prominent Western exiles from the Shah's Iran who then became disillusioned with the repressive direction taken by the new leadership. He rather quickly converted this disappointment into action, but in the months before this disillusionment happened, Mansour would play a significant role in the first phase of post-Shah Iran. Because of our friendship I stayed closely in touch with him, and through him with the turbulent developments of 1978-1980. I will return to Mansour's deepening disillusionment with developments in Iran later in the context of a broader secular disenchantment with the Iranian Revolution. As far as I could discern Mansour, and other secular liberals from Iran who had lent ardent support to the revolution, never desired a reversal of the political movement that drove the Shah into exile and led to the downfall of the Pahlavi dynasty. There was no interest in fomenting a counterrevolution of the sort that produced the regressive Egyptian coup of 2013 that brought the oppressive Sisi military regime to power in place of Mohamed Morsi, the elected leader who had been the presidential candidate of the Muslim Brotherhood. In contrast, this liberal opposition to Iranian theocratic governance wanted drastic reforms, including freedom and respect for secular lifestyles in the country, though these secularists were mostly anti-monarchist, and unlike imperial exile groups they were not hoping for another coup that would restore the Shah to the throne for a second time.

In the years just prior to revolution I also came to know Abdolhassan Banisadr who was living a seemingly lonely life in a small walkup Paris apartment. He was accessible, exhibiting a visionary belief in the future of an Islamized Iran, freed from dynastic rule and from international capitalism. Banisadr struck me as at once humble and ambitious, not hiding his hope to be the first president of the post-Shah Iran. He had been working on an elaborate plan to restructure the Iranian economy to reflect Islamic values. When we first met, I found him a dreamer, gentle in manner, and strangely apolitical in his way of being-in-the-world while unwillingly living in exile. To my surprise Banisadr was soon to realize his grandiose dream, becoming the first president of the Islamic Republic of Iran, yet this extraordinary ascent quickly became a nightmare for him. He was forced to flee the country to avoid imprisonment at the hands of the radicalized Revolutionary Guards in the aftermath of the seizure of the American Embassy by Iranian students in November 1979.

Banisadr's story is central to understanding the competing ideas and personalities seeking to exert control over the Iranian Revolution. This story tells how Ayatollah Khomeini was unexpectedly able to gain the upper hand in defining and shaping the Iranian Revolution, removing secular liberals from positions of influence and fulfilling his deeply held theocratic vision of establishing an Islamic Republic guided by the most eminent religious leader. As in Egypt, Iranian liberals did not know their own country, and so underestimated, and were generally taken aback by the frenzied popular appeal and deep roots of the Khomeini leadership. And unlike in Egypt, in Iran the religious institutional establishment was effective in organizing a governing process efficient in their pursuit of political goals. This was done under more challenging circumstances than existed in Egypt after the Arab Spring. While the Egyptian counter-revolutionary coup was welcomed by most major regional state actors in the Middle East and by the United States, similarly but conversely, in Iran the revolutionary process was ineffectually opposed by these same political forces, bringing hardship and anxiety to the Iranian people.

What I learned from these Iranian political activists and players explains how my interest in the events in Iran developed. The Iranian ferment also offered me a new opportunity to express opposition to American intervention in a distant country. This opposition was reinforced by my rising awareness of the Shah's severe repression. It was a controversial involvement from the outset, even more so than with Vietnam, despite the absence of any American combat role in Iran.

From Theory to Practice: How the Impossible Happened

Sometime fairly early in 1978, a protest movement started in Iran. In a manner somewhat similar to the beginning of Palestine's First Intifada in 1987 or the Jasmine Revolution in Tunisia late in 2010, it began with a spark that set off an entirely unexpected bonfire. The spark that ignited the Iranian Revolution was an incident in a remote part of the country that epitomized the violence of the Shah's regime when encountering any sign of popular opposition, and mysteriously, was a tipping point stimulating expanding ripples of opposition. Why such incidents occasionally produce political earthquakes is one of the deepest mysteries of collective human behavior, catalyzing upheavals that come as almost total surprises and can only be rationally interpreted and explained after the fact by experts who 'show' that what happened unleashed latent revolutionary unrest which, although not anticipated, could be explained as all but inevitable. Overlooked were the deep roots among secularists and clerics of opposition to the Westernizing Pahlavi monarchy with its embrace of Western modernity, especially international capitalism at the expense, and resulting alienation, of its own national private sector.

At first, the opposition incident in Iran seemed like an inconsequential ripple on the surface of a stable, if authoritarian, governing process. When criticized for his denials of human rights, the Shah responded curtly with words of derision: 'when the people of Iran behave like the people of Sweden, they will have earned the right to enjoy comparable freedoms.' But when the demonstrations grew ever larger, repeated at 40-day intervals, the religious edge of the anti-Shah movement began to become unmistakable. It was becoming increasingly evident that the Iranian monarchy was facing a serious and mounting nationwide challenge to its authority in 1978 as the months passed. Cassettes containing messages of inspirational guidance from Ayatollah Khomeini were being played in mosques and demonstrations all over Iran, rallying opposition, counseling nonviolence and unity while insisting on uncompromising struggle and total victory. In tandem, state violence was being deployed more freely to demoralize, if not crush, the opposition.

Two tendencies could be observed in this innovative politics of resistance. Some demonstrators placed flowers in the barrels of guns pleading with the soldiers to join their nonviolent struggle, while others chanted 'leaders, leaders give us guns.' In other words, there were tensions evident on the level of tactics. It seemed that it was only Khomeini's insistence on nonviolence that kept the movement unified and willing to endure casualties without striking back. Later events in Iran would make clear that Khomeini was not a follower of Gandhi's path. Khomeini's commitment to nonviolence was purely pragmatic, yet intelligently mindful of the tactical advantages in Iran of avoiding violent engagements with the superior firepower of the Iranian state, and by doing so, retaining its moral high ground.

A turning point in the struggle came in September 1978 when Iranian military forces responded to demonstrators massed in Tehran's Jaleh Square by closing off the exits, and firing machine guns at helpless, unarmed and trapped demonstrators, killing and wounding several dozen. The American response, while chilling, was not altogether out of character, yet when publicized, it became extremely provocative to Iranians. Jimmy Carter declared a recess in the Camp David negotiations between Israel and Egypt that were taking place and were widely applauded for achieving a temporary breakthrough for peace in relations between the two previously antagonistic countries. The recess was specifically declared to allow President Carter to make a congratulatory and highly publicized phone call to the Shah, commending his lethal response to the hostile demonstrations. It was reported, in particular, that National Security Advisor Zbigniew Brzezinski praised the violence of the Shah's security forces as finally displaying the necessary toughness needed to deal effectively with growing popular opposition. This message from Washington in response to what was being experienced by those sympathetic with the anti-Shah movement in Iran as an atrocity removed any doubts in the ranks of the Iranian movement that the United States Government was once again opposing democratizing political change in Iran. It vividly recalled the widely resented American role in 1953 that assisted the pro-Shah coup that overthrew a dedicated and popular nationalist elected government.

After this Iranian activists in Iran and internationally with pointed irony referred to Carter's infamous 1977 New Year's toast to the Shah when he and his wife were guests at the Niavaran Palace: 'Iran, because of great leadership of the Shah, is an island of stability in one of the more troubled regions of the world...a great tribute to you, Your Majesty... and to the respect and the admiration and love which your people give to you.'

In fact, developments in Iran contributed to the weakening and later downfall of the Carter presidency. His alleged blunders were blamed by conservatives in America for the collapse of the Shah's government in Iran. It is fair to say that both leaderships were hurt by their betrayal of human rights. In the American case the support of the Shah's repressions grossly contradicted Carter's claim to put human rights on the top of the post-Vietnam U.S. policy agenda. Even more damaging to Carter's credibility at home was the ineptitude of Washington's feeble efforts to save a strategic ally in its hour of need. It was another one of those instances in which the upper echelons of the U.S. Government, despite extensive CIA presence in Iran, badly misinterpeted the emerging balance of forces in Iran, and to some extent refused to heed what the intelligence briefings were apparently conveying as events unfolded. At a very late stage, Washington dispatched a leading NATO general to Tehran with the mission of rallying the Iranian military to do what was necessary to defend the monarchy, but the general found no receptivity among those he consulted with in the armed forces. The Iranian military had become itself alienated from the palace due to the Shah's distrust of his own armed forces.

In Princeton, as these developments unfolded in Iran, we did our best, with the strong encouragement of several progressive students, to grasp the reality of what was happening. By listening to a variety of Iranian voices we may have developed a better sense of Iranian realities than did either the Washington policy community or the mainstream media. We organized a series of public meetings and teach-ins at which Iranian speakers depicted the wrongs of the Shah and the special character of the struggle being mounted by the Iranian people. I moderated or spoke at several of these events. Our outlook was shaped by an overt commitment to human rights and democracy, and a critical stance against Cold War interventionism and global capitalist geopolitics. Although Princeton did not have a big contingent of Iranian students as did several nearby universities in Philadelphia and New York, there seemed to be sufficient interest in the community to produce large and vigorous audiences for these events.

I was greatly helped in these campus activities by two graduate students in the Princeton School of Public and International Affairs,[i] Robin Broad and John Cavanaugh. Robin and John happened to be delightful human beings who added much enjoyment to our underlying effort to make creative use of academic freedom to get a better understanding of confusing international developments. For me personally, having

---

i Until the protests of 2020 following the police murders of George Floyd, this academic institution was named The Woodrow Wilson School of Public and International Affairs. The name was officially changed by university authorities in acknowledgement of Wilson's racism. Woodrow Wilson had been president of Princeton prior to becoming president of the United States.

students like Robin and John through the decades is what has made me feel that teaching for a living was the most rewarding life I could have imagined for myself. Robin and John happened to be the first students ever at the School from the state of New Hampshire. They had never met before Princeton, later married and each went on to achieve great things separately and together, never losing their deep commitment to making the world a better place for every person on the planet. With such a New Hampshire success story, who dares say American-style federalism has failed.

Visiting Revolutionary Iran

The invitation to visit Iran came to me as Chair of the Committee Against Intervention in Iran to lead a delegation of three to obtain an understanding of the unfolding Iranian revolutionary experience that I believed was being misinterpreted in the West. I was not sure how to make the visit worthwhile, but thought it presented another invaluable opportunity to visit the site of a previous notorious U.S. intervention against the forces of democratic nationalism.

Both of my first choices for traveling companions and delegation members accepted. I asked Ramsey Clark, with whom I had remained in contact since Vietnam days. Ramsey had, in the meantime, become publicly associated with the political left. Nevertheless, he remained one of the most influential and respected voices of civic conscience in America. He was remembered as the Attorney General who had turned against the Vietnam War, possibly foregoing career prospects that could have resulted in a presidential nomination. With his Texas roots, he was rumored to be Lyndon Johnson's choice of a successor. Ramsey was talented, austere in dress, familiar with the classics of philosophy and political thought, and outwardly humble yet accustomed to deference and exercising leadership, which turned out to be a strain at various points during the trip.

Philip Luce was the second person invited to join the mission. He was a well-known religious anti-war activist. Philip first gained global prominence by defying protocol at a critical stage in the Vietnam War to show a delegation of visiting U.S. Congressmen the infamous 'tiger cages' in a South Vietnamese prison where Saigon's political prisoners were being confined in small cages meant for animals. Philip took various other actions to call attention to the abuses of American foreign policy in Vietnam and elsewhere in relation to conflicts arising in 'the Third World.' Despite these brash public displays, Philip was exceptionally shy in normal social settings, yet when moved by moral outrage he could roar like a lion, indifferent to what others might think, unintimidated by security pushbacks in the face of disruptions, oblivious to social etiquette. In other words, when called for, he was ready and willing to cause trouble, although always non-violently. I admired his temperament and style, as well as his politics of moral outrage.

We were a harmonious group, with only the routine frictions that inevitably arose from being constantly together for two weeks in situations of tension and uncertainty. Ramsey had some remarkable gifts that I came to appreciate. He never took notes but could recall the details of specific conversations during the trip although we had separate long meetings with dozens of people. When protocol called for an exchange of greetings, Ramsey rose to the occasion, with artfully crafted sentences and quotations from the Western philosophical canon, including Aristotle and Rousseau as well as Jefferson and Madison.

I sometimes felt uncomfortable when Ramsey delivered longish 'lectures' to Iranian religious leaders on the virtues of American liberalism and the rule of law, recommending without qualification the applicability of this American constitutional approach to the Iranian political future. Partly my discomfort was with such displays of what I term, in the spirit of Edward Said, 'political Orientalism'—this eminent, upright, and good-natured American was telling Iranians what they must do in their own country to set things right. Our Iranian hosts were aware of Ramsey's prominence, treating him as the distinguished leader and spokesperson of our delegation, which at times tended to sideline the somewhat divergent views of Philip and myself. I, in particular, was more interested in posing questions and listening, than in proffering political advice that struck me as somewhat inappropriate, at least if not solicited. I thought, given the purpose of our visit, that it would be more helpful to hear what these individuals felt to be important in the near future with respect to their hopes, expectations, and fears about the Iranian revolutionary process that was daily unfolding.

At this point, the revolutionary fervor in Iran created a strong impression of overriding unity, with religious and secular activists joining arms. We walked in solidarity in the largest demonstration I have ever seen, several million peaceful marchers with no police presence, a massive gathering walking the streets of Tehran with quiet dignity, and seeming to delight in the bliss of this public celebration of revolutionary victory. Obviously buoyed by the departure of the Shah from the country a few days earlier, many of those with whom we spoke still couldn't believe that this unplanned revolution had actually succeeded. There were no divisive slogans during the march, and no hints that only a few days later, deep fissures in the anti-Shah movement would emerge, producing the first glimmers of the political violence *within* the ranks that would overcome the exceptional degree of solidarity that had persisted as a matter of expediency as long as the Shah remained in the country and in control. The serene political atmosphere of the demonstration drastically changed quickly after the religiously led elements moved coercively to consolidate their control over the anti-Shah movement in ways that excluded those who were suspected of seeking a secular and liberal future for post-Shah Iran.

We made good contact in this period with Ayatollah Mahmoud Talaghani, the leading Muslim cleric in Tehran, who had a reputation for being a social liberal, an Islamic leader supposedly promoting socialist values. At first, Talaghani was apparently reluctant even to meet with us as he opposed the presence of Americans in the country at the time. However, as soon it was made clear and credible by our hosts that our sympathies were with the revolutionary developments, he totally changed his demeanor, extending our first meeting well beyond what was scheduled and seeking additional meetings, which were arranged. As with other religious leaders with whom we met, we sat in a circle on the floor, not such a comfortable position for me, but there were offsetting compensations. I was impressed by the non-hierarchical sense of community that took over once we were sitting in such a circle; anyone's voice was as good as anyone else's, which seemed characteristic of the democratic ethos evident at most Shi'ite gatherings. I found this Islamic atmosphere congenial, giving me a false confidence that despite the emergent turmoil, all would be worked out as the Islamic Republic of Iran stabilized a new constitutional order for the country, provided, of course, that outside forces didn't try to interfere—a pious hope.

This gentle and physically frail cleric, with a waiting room overflowing with ordinary Iranian petitioners seeking guidance or help, was strongly supportive of the revolutionary process. He endorsed the belief that going forward the new Iranian leadership would be respectful of human rights and dedicated to lifting the mass of Iranians from the depths of poverty. Talaghani was highly critical of the Shah's reliance on economic policies in accord with the priorities of *international* capital markets that, he insisted, intensified inequality and corruption in the country on a massive scale, and did little, if anything, to alleviate poverty.

Talaghani was clearly a theological moderate, although the significance of his pluralistic approach only became evident after the revolutionary momentum had carried the country far in a fundamentalist and theocratic direction. We were told that his far less dogmatic pproach to Islam was greatly encouraged by his children, who apparently held Western progressive social and economic views of a socialist character. He fully acknowledged the crucial role played by Ayatollah Khomeini in ridding the country of the Shah, while refraining from affirming what seemed to be Khomeini's increasingly articulated hard line on religious practice and political arrangements for governance. Talaghani soon afterwards came to be regarded with suspicion, if not hostility, by the leading members of Khomeini's entourage. We were told that Talaghani's popular following was deemed a threat to Khomeini's image of Iran's preferred future. Talaghani died unexpectedly rather shortly after our visit, with rumors circulated that he was poisoned. As far as I know these rumors were never confirmed nor refuted, and so a certain mystery hangs over the memory of this humanly impressive cleric.

While we were in Tehran we became friendly with a professor of mathematics who had been active in the national movement as a secular opponent of the Shah's rule. In the course of our visit, he became extremely worried by the fundamentalist religious overtones of the revolutionary leadership and by disclosures of its non-pluralist approach to the future governing process being established in Iran. These realizations alarmed the non-religious liberals who had been active in the revolution but were now seemingly being pushed aside. Our friend told us one morning that he had stayed up through the night reading Khomeini's *Lectures on Islamic Government*; 'it scared the shit out of me.' He interpreted Khomeini's political vision as based on theological ascendancy and the strict application of *sharia* principles, which contradicted the looser pluralistic ideas that had earlier guided and framed the unified opposition to the Shah. I have often wondered what happened to this very likable and intelligent secularist as he witnessed with each passing month his worst fears being realized. Looking back, it seems clear that the liberal secularists, who played important roles in the revolutionary movement, were so preoccupied with getting rid of the Shah that they didn't think ahead to the future, and when they finally awakened, it was too late. In contrast, the more ardent religionists took advantage of their long view of change as well as enjoying the backing of the Iranian masses who seemed fervently religious in that historical moment where their movement achieved a remarkable victory for traditional values in the country, and who had been harmed and enraged by the Shah's neoliberal embrace of globalization, including deference to Washington, and even more so, by the repudiation of Iran's deepest cultural and religious traditions.

Next on our schedule was Qom, the small religious city of mosques and madrassas, to meet with Ayatollah Mohammed Kazan Shariatmadari, a learned cleric, and someone who in religious circles enjoyed the reputation of being a leading, if not the leading, Islamic scholar whose theological knowledge and precision was deeply respected. Our meeting was quite revealing in the sense that Shariatmadari, while welcoming the revolution, refrained from mentioning Khomeini by name, prefiguring later tensions, and accusations by Islamic radicals that this revered man of religion, who was reputed to be from a wealthy landowning family in Tabriz, had compromised himself by real estate dealings with the Pahlavi palace. Yet this effort to discredit Shariatmadari might be better explained by reference to ideological issues. He opposed clerical participation in government, adhering to his understanding of traditional Shi'ia precepts, and thus was correctly perceived as being skeptical of Khomeini's theocratic ideas and practices advocating the clerical domination of the constitutional foundations of the Islamic Republic.

More notable for us at the time than the valuable meeting itself was its unexpected stormy aftermath. After leaving Shariatmaderi we found a small restaurant on a large square at the city center of Qom dominated by several mosques. We were accompanied by a couple of young people from Tehran who were part of the hospitality group that handled our logistics, members of Bazargan's staff. After a pleasant lunch we walked for a few minutes around the picturesque square, soon realizing that we were being surrounded by a quickly gathering crowd shouting angry slogans directed at us and carrying Khomeini posters. Although the slogans were in Farsi, we learned from our Tehran companions that we were targets of an angry chant: 'Death to the Shah, Death to Americans.' I am not sure of the exact date, but these anti-Shah demonstrations were reaching their climax, and were likely more intense in Qom than elsewhere. Our presence in this religious city occurred a few days before the Shah left the country, never to return, and tensions were at their height as the outcome of the ferment was as yet unresolved and seemed precarious.

As the mob atmosphere intensified, whipped to a fury by two young mullahs who led the chants of these several hundred agitated Iranians, I became more and more frightened, contrasting myself unfavorably to the Texas cool of Ramsey, who seemed unfazed, at least outwardly. Our Iranian friends tried to say that we were not working for Bell Helicopter and were much too old to be off duty soldiers. It was explained to the leaders of the agitated crowd that we came to Iran at the invitation of the revolutionary movement. At first, these pleas on our behalf were dismissed, but when documents from Bazargan's office were produced, the mood changed instantly from menacing to fraternal. We were invited to share a meal and offered posters. We thanked these militants in Qom for their offers, but begged off, indicating commitments back in Tehran, which actually existed. We were, in fact, over-scheduled day after day. As we drove off, I was still shaken by what I felt was an agitated gathering on the verge of turning into a lynch mob. It has remained for me one of those near-death experiences that will remain vivid as long as I live, or at least as long as the past has not slipped away to become an enveloping mist. In any event returning to Tehran indeed felt like returning to Carter's 'island of stability'! Thinking back, at that time the outcome of the revolution hung in the balance. The Shah was still in the country, rumors abounded of an imminent intervention from without, and there were fears of another bloody crackdown by the beleaguered Pahlavi palace, which never happened. The Shah did abdicate a few days later, and the worst fears of the opposition never materialized, although new quite different fears soon emerged.

The Shah Abdicates, but Does He Really Leave?

A few days later our program called for another trip outside Tehran, this time to Gazvin, a mid-sized city, a couple of hours away. We had been invited for lunch at the home of a local doctor who was one of a group of doctors who dealt with injured movement demonstrators at the Gazvin hospital. A widely reported incident had occurred a few days earlier when the Shah's soldiers and police had entered the hospital, seizing some of the wounded, causing havoc, and threatening doctors and nurses. When we arrived at Gazvin, lunch was being prepared by several women, while the two dozen men present were encouraged to continue talking in the living room. We were told of the atrocities committed against medical workers and demonstrators, including doctors, several of whom were among those gathered in the room. The lunch was elaborate in keeping with Iranian traditions of home cooking excellence, and the gender segregation was patriarchal even in this seemingly liberal atmosphere. We often heard while in Iran that it was the men who mostly engaged in emotional flights of fancy, while the women shone the light of reason on life's happenings whether in the home or in politics. Yet when it came to social gatherings or political discussion with foreigners, it was the Iranian men who took over, with women relegated to the background as providers rather than participants.

What made the day memorable for all of us gathered was the announcement while we were drinking coffee at the end of the standup meal that the Shah had just left the country, turning over governance of Iran to Shahpour Bakhtiar, as a caretaker prime minister appointed to preside over a kind of royal regency council at a time when the revolutionary movement was closing in on complete victory. Early radio reports disclosed widespread skepticism among Iranians as to whether the Shah had actually abdicated or rather was setting a trap for his high-level opponents who would be certain to reveal themselves at such a transformative moment. As we drove back to Tehran to keep a prior appointment to meet with Bakhtiar in late afternoon, it became apparent that the news of the Shah's departure had by then been widely accepted as accurate. Horns were blowing, hastily prepared bumper posters proclaiming victory were attached to the increasingly dense traffic streaming toward Tehran. Iranian flags suddenly appeared everywhere, denoting a celebratory occasion of extraordinary significance as cars were coming in greater and greater numbers from all directions, heading for Tehran to display and share their happiness at this dramatic turn of events. As never before, I felt I was touching the live tissue of revolution, having the sense of history being made before my eyes. There was no doubt about it. On that night at least, January 16, 1979, beneath a cloudless sky, with streets vibrant with revolutionary joy, a new Iran was born. Only a few days later that same Iranian sky would be filled with ominous clouds of many shapes portending a more troubled future.

It was not easy to reach the government building where Bakhtiar's office was located. There were crowds everywhere, and the streets were clogged with traffic. We finally made it, and the prime minister was gracious, vacuous, and told us nothing we didn't previously know. He seemed to live up, although in a subdued manner, to his reputation as a Francophile, implying both unmistakably secularist affinities and a European social style. It was political theater of a sort.

During our meeting there were other officials and security people in the room, some of them presumed to work for SAVAK. The atmosphere suggested that we were meeting with a nominal leader who was being told what he could and couldn't do by the real holders of whatever power remained in the now crumbling established order of the country. In other words, Bakhtiar, even in the absence of the Shah, was not running the show, and was never meant to be more than a pawn in a chess game where the major pieces were moved by others. This became unmistakable to us after we asked if he could arrange visits to the political prisoners in Evin Prison and to the ordinary criminals in that same prison facility. Bakhtiar turned to one of the large men in city clothes for guidance before responding to our request. He then told us it would be fine to visit the political prisoners, but it was not possible on such short notice to make a visit to the part of the prison complex that housed ordinary criminals.

All in all, the meeting with Bakhtiar was notable for its insignif- icance, perhaps reflecting uncertainty at that point as to whether the old power games were altogether over, as all were perhaps focusing on whether or not the Shah might yet resume his rulership, quite possibly as in 1953 returning on the wings of a coup engineered by the CIA. There was no clarity as yet as to whether we were witnessing a phase in an unfinished struggle to remake Iran or participating in the collapse of dynastic Iran. The future seemed to hang in the balance on that night, symbolized by the crowd noise from the streets of Tehran and the solemn ambiguities of the political situation, exhibited by the tone and substance of this meeting with Bakhtiar, the acting head of state.

In Evin Prison

We arrived at Evin Prison at the appointed time late the following morning of January 17, 1979, and were told to sit in the waiting room until called for our meeting with the prisoners. It turned out to be a long wait, but hardly a waste of time. To my astonishment, the only other person in the waiting room was the colorful maverick from Texas, Ross Perot, the CEO of Electronic Data Systems, who would later run for president in the U.S. on an independent, economically conservative platform, challenging America's typically unfriendly reception to third party candidates. [Perot managed to obtain 18.6% of the popular vote on his first and only try in 1992]. True to Texan reputation for fearlessness, Perot had come to Iran despite the perilous conditions in the country to gain the release of two of his employees, held in prison on charges of spying. Perot, quite surprisingly given the circumstances in Iran, suc- ceeded in arranging their release, and his endeavor typified that quality of radical individualism that makes Texans proud.

It was entertaining to watch these two overachieving, differently celebrated Texans, Ramsey Clark and Ross Perot, verbally jousting with each other: one tall, lanky, still the darling of the liberal/left establish- ment, the other short, fiscally conservative, a somewhat pugnacious and know-it-all business phenom. Perot seemed to have simplistic, yet pungent, answers for all the big questions roiling American politics in the late 1970s. While in this prison waiting room, Perot produced a string of clever one-liners in response to Ramsey's more artfully phrased observations about what was going wrong in America. Indeed, both men felt that Washington was to some extent their adversary. Ramsey had come to this position more recently, and primarily as an insider, with particular concerns about America's role in the world. Ramsey's ideas were along the same line as mine, although more legalistically phrased by reference to respect for the rights of others, and less concerned with geopolitical and economistic implications. We shared opposition to the kind of interventions and militarism that had become staple features of American Cold War policies and postures.

Perot had a different agenda. He wanted to organize the world according to his free enterprise precepts, starting with the U.S. Government, which, he felt, should be run by capitalist winners like himself, rugged individualists who reached the top by brawn and brain. Perot opposed deficit spending and welfare handouts, favoring a lean and mean government that repudiated what he believed was the unsound economic legacy of the New Deal. Of course, such a vivid encounter of opposing worldviews didn't alter a single iota of the way either of these stubborn Long Horns viewed the world, but it did make the lengthy waiting time go by almost too quickly. Looking back perhaps unfairly, Perot prefigured a more humane and intelligent version of the Trump presidency, including the similarity of their displays of extreme narcissism without the slightest sign of embarrassment, not realizing that the word 'humility' was part of the English language.

Perot got to see his employees before we were taken to the section of the prison housing political prisoners, which was far cleaner and more pleasant than the areas reserved for common criminals, whom we could at least observe while walking by their overcrowded and dilapidated cells. I wondered about this discrimination in treatment, which perhaps reflected class differences, but also may have been based on the idea that today's prisoners could possibly be tomorrow's leaders. Ramsey, Philip, and I were separated when invited to enter, and I was directed to meet with maybe one hundred religiously oriented prisoners, including some who were soon to be released, some becoming immediately influential in the new scheme of things. At first, I was led into a poorly lit large meeting room in which it was hard to get a good look at the hundred or so waiting prisoners. After I was introduced by a prison guard, several prisoners spoke up. They were initially and understandably suspicious of what I was doing in Evin Prison at this revolutionary moment, and didn't hesitate to show their displeasure with my visit. Why was an 'innocent' American even in Iran at this time, what were my affiliations? With some anxiety and doing my best to explain the reason for my presence, I managed to persuade the assembled prisoners that I was in their country to observe, learn, and do my best to inform the American public. I also mentioned that I had been heading a committee back in the States that opposed the Shah's repressive policies. During these comments I was holding in check my own anxieties that it would have been an easy matter for the prisoners to seize me as a hostage, demanding their own freedom in exchange for mine. Such a tactic struck me at the time as not only plausible, but quite sensible, all things considered, yet thankfully it never happened.

After these mutual explorations, the spokesperson for the prisoners relented, asking me to give my impressions of what was going on in Iran. It made me realize that these prisoners had been cut off from the world, although they did know—how could they not—the startling yet welcome news that the Shah had apparently abdicated on the previous day. I spoke of my impressions of the revolutionary ferment, and the seemingly irreversible developments, but indicated my sense that the revolution still lacked a clearly defined trajectory. I observed that the interim reins of government seemed to be held by moderate, secular intellectuals and technocrats who were appreciative of religious outlooks but didn't then conceive of Ayatollah Khomeini as the future political leader of the country. I felt that most Iranians I had encountered regarded Khomeini as the enormously influential public face of the revolutionary movement, but not a person who aspired after or was equipped to take over governance of the country. This impression was confirmed by Khomeini himself a few days later when we met with him in Paris. Whether there was a subtext to this outward show of disinterest in being the new leader remains locked in a black box.

After I finished my unrehearsed remarks to the assembled prisoners, there were many questions, and even the secret service people present seemed interested in what I was saying, especially when it concerned what to expect from Washington. As with Khomeini, there were widespread apprehensions among the prisoners that before long there would be a counterrevolutionary coup attempt orchestrated by the U.S. Government. The return of the Shah to reclaim his throne was seen by these political prisoners as a definite threat and live possibility. Others thought that maybe the scale of the revolutionary movement would discourage a scenario similar to 1953, but rather that in a new coup Washington would seek either to install a military leader or possibly find a secular figure who would promise to bring prosperity and democracy to the country as a whole without changing its Western alignment. Even in this prison atmosphere, the air was filled with conjectures about the future of Iran, given the internal and international uncertainties present in the prevailing situation and the diversity of expectations and goals of those with whom I was meeting.

Following an exchange of views, those who had been imprisoned at Evin for more than five years were given the 'privilege' of preparing my lunch on a primitive jail stove. The food, as I remember, was good, although simple. What stood out, then and now, was that one of my 'hosts' at this Genet-style prison lunch was Massoud Rajavi. Rajavi was the head of the militant anti-Shah socialist inclined organization, Mujahadeen-e-Khalq (MEK), that later on became an increasingly controversial and militant anti-regime organization, widely discredited in international circles as a terrorist organization, yet gaining support from Western counterrevolutionary sources, which it has enjoyed up until the present time.

At the time I was impressed by Rajavi. I found him to be engaging, bright, young, energetic, and eager to discuss serious political issues, and even to listen to what I had to say in response to his questions. In that highly artificial prison atmosphere Rajavi was friendly and hospitable, making me feel at home, which I experienced as intensely ironic, given our respective situations.

During the next two years, I twice visited Rajavi in Paris, and on the first occasion did an interview that was published in *Alternatives,* a journal devoted to global issues. When we talked in Evin he was intent on recounting the story of his organization, how many young 'martyrs' in his circle had been created by the Shah's bloodthristy security forces. He asserted that every member of the central committee of the Mujhadeen except himself had been killed. I was disturbed at the time by this grim narrative, but also by what seemed to me Rajavi's unhealthy fixation on martyrdom and severe repression and resistance, and what this might mean for the future of politics in Iran. It also became clear that despite Rajavi's recognition of the contributions of Shariati, he was much more a secularist than an Islamist. He made his opinions clear. He did not endorse the views of Ayatollah Khomeini about how to shape the future of Iran. I listened sensing that trouble ahead was likely, which manifested itself a few days later. Shortly after being released from prison, as were all political prisoners, Rajavi almost immediately chose exile, moving to Paris where his brother, a doctor, lived. There is a strange irony in the fact that Rajavi arrived in France only weeks after the man who would soon become his archenemy returned to Iran to be greeted by millions of cheering Iranians as the charismatic and authentic leader of the revolution, a revolution which was still seen by the new leadership in Iran as 'Iranian' rather than 'Islamic,' though this would change in the months ahead. It never became clear to me what kind of role Rajavi wished for himself and what sort of future for Iran.

What came to alienate conclusively many critics of the Islamic Republic who had been previously sympathetic with Rajavi and the MEK was MEK's responsibility for political assassinations of adversaries and for lending support to Iraq's attack on Iran in 1980, with active, although covert, encouragement from the Pentagon.

Visiting the American Embassy

It took my best persuasive effort to get Ramsey Clark to agree to a meeting with the American ambassador in Iran, William Sullivan. I cannot remember the details, but Ramsey had had an earlier unpleasant encounter with Sullivan during the Vietnam period. I argued, correctly I think, that for our presentation of the Iranian revolutionary realities to be credible upon our return to the U.S., it was necessary for us to have heard how the American embassy viewed the situation. After all, our basic mission, at least as I and the third member of our group, Philip Luce, perceived it, was to learn what we could and offer informed commentary on what was happening in this unique revolutionary situation. For Ramsey it was less about learning or listening, and more about instructing and advising.

When we were ushered into Ambassador Sullivan's elegant office, I was surprised to be the first of our group greeted, not warmly, but confrontationally. Sullivan's (un)welcoming greeting: 'I know Professor Falk thinks I am a war criminal.' I was not entirely displeased by being greeted this way. It meant that my testimony before what I think had by then become the (Senator Frank) Church Committee on Foreign Relations in the U.S. Senate, had had some impact even on Sullivan himself. Indeed, I did testify to the effect that this ambassadorial appointment of Mr. Sullivan was an inappropriate move to make in post-Vietnam America. Sullivan had become widely known for his unusual counterinsurgency activism in Laos while he was serving as ambassador, so much so that

General Westmoreland, no shrinking violet, referred disapprovingly in his memoir to Sullivan as more a military officer than a diplomat, commenting 'he should have been a field marshal!' Sullivan was particularly notorious for his operational command of 'the secret war' in Laos during the 1970s that involved heavy bombing of the countryside, causing many casualties with the objective of disrupting Vietnam supply lines from the North and making sure that the Pathet Lao, the Communist movement in Laos, didn't prevail. None of Sullivan's background entered our discussion, which never departed from developments in Iran.

Sullivan conveyed to us two major interpretations of relevance. The first was that the embassy, including himself, had been 'blindsided' by this massive popular mobilization achieved beneath the banner of political Islam, which managed to shake loose the foundations of what was assumed to be the most stable and secure U.S. ally in the region. Iran had been regarded as a formidable military power with a governing structure believed to be in complete control of the internal political scene. Sullivan had come over time to appreciate the strength and religious character of the movement, telling us that he had urged Washington to accept the outcome of the revolution rather than continue a futile opposition. Sullivan reached the conclusion that pro-Shah opposition was a lost cause, a conclusion that the Carter White House rejected.

His second disclosure was his unexpected tension with Zbigniew Brzezinski, Carter's National Security Advisor, who evidently heeded the diehard guidance of the Iranian ambassador in Washington, Ardeshir Zahedi, and thus refused to authorize the embassy in Tehran to make any accommodating or reassuring gestures to post-Shah Iran. No one will ever know what might have happened with respect to U.S./Iran relations if Carter had followed Sullivan's advice instead of that of his National Security Advisor.

It was clear that Sullivan had expressed himself *on the record* during our meeting, doing little to hide his exasperation with the approach taken by Washington that seemed to presage a dismal future for U.S./Iran relations, one that is again moving toward new intensities of confrontation more than 40 years later. How different might have been the whole history of the region had the United States decided to live with this expression of the Iranian people's right of self-determination? It was the same type of fundamental and costly geopolitical mistake that the U.S. made in Vietnam, and elsewhere.

There are two principal explanations why the national security establishment continually makes such gross errors. First, there is a failure to recognize the emergence of new limits on the effective role of military power in the last half of the 20th century in the face of a rising tide of nationalist and anti-colonial resistance, resolve and capabilities. In effect, non-Western nationalism was in the end stronger than Western militarist interventionism. An appreciation of these new realities of power would help us to understand the collapse of European colonialism despite the military *inferiority* of anti-colonial forces. Secondly, and less easy to explain, there has been a stubborn refusal by most policy makers and think tank strategists to formulate a foreign policy on an understanding of these military limits, resulting in recurrent demonstrations of military failure in a variety of political circumstances yet producing no appropriate course corrections. Undoubtedly, sustaining a war industry-based domestic economy partly explains this inexplicable refusal to learn from repeated overseas military failures. What apparently has defied general understanding is the realization that, in recent historical circumstances, major political changes are most often produced by popular mobilizations of domestic populations in reaction to the intrusion of external economic and military forces that seek to impose their political will in defiance of sovereign rights. At the same time, the rise of demagogic leaders shows that peoples, while resisting foreign interventions, seem increasingly willing to submit to governmental subjugation, in some instances deemed necessary to effectively rid themselves of foreign domination, perceived as the greater evil.

After we left Iran, Carter's Secretary of State, Warren Christopher, who had served under Ramsey when he was Attorney General, made contact to confirm that Sullivan had really made those provocative statements critical of Washington at our meeting, and that he had made no effort to declare the exchange of views off the record. After Ramsey confirmed, it seems that Sullivan's career suffered a major hit, which we neither anticipated, nor intended. Until then Sullivan was considered highly successful by bureaucratic measures, but afterwards his career seemed to nosedive. As is so often the case, Sullivan seemed to have been rewarded for his record of war crimes in Laos, and then punished for his accurate and conscientious assessment of the unfolding situation in Iran and his constructive encouragement of a pragmatic response to the collapse of the Shah's regime. Sullivan definitely understood that the absence of domestic forces in Iran ready to fight for and sustain the restoration of dynastic rule that had governed Iran, almost without interruption, for the prior 2,500 years, meant that there was really no political alternative for the United State other than to accept the new reality and hope for the best.

It is tragic that this advice was not followed, and it left me with a somewhat sympathetic feeling toward William Sullivan that I had never expected in view of his earlier role in Laos during the Vietnam War. I had not wanted harm to come to him as a result of his forthrightness in our meeting, which I suspect took that form because he felt so frustrated by Brzezinski's refusal to address the new Iran situation in a realistic fashion.

A Conversation with Ayatollah Ruhollah Khomeini

Shortly before leaving Iran we were told that we were to be given a rare opportunity to meet with Ayatollah Khomeini during a Paris stop-over on our return to the United States. The meeting was presented to us as an expression of gratitude for coming to Iran at this time of turmoil and having useful talks with a wide range of personalities. We arrived in Paris with a variety of intense impressions arising from our meetings of the prior two weeks. Among the most salient were the views of a leading human rights lawyer who insightfully complained that 'the revolution happened too quickly; we are not ready to shape the future.' Women were not shy about saying that they had swallowed their resentments about patriarchal hegemony in Iran so as to maintain unity during the struggle to get rid of the Shah and its imperial trappings, but that this was a calculated and temporary move. The rallying cry of women with whom we met was, without exception, 'we're next!,' but four decades later, their moment has never quite come, as far as I can tell. At least one 'modern' woman told me that she was at first fearful of this rise of Islam, but then became glad to save time and money previously wasted by her cosmetic rituals and Western dress. She said that since wearing a chador, she had more time to concentrate her energies on activities she really cared about. This may not have been a typical reaction among the secular women of Tehran, and did not take account of the coercive enforcement of Islamic dress and the prohibition of alcohol that underlay the impression that the Islamic Republic imposed these Islamic cultural features as steps towards consolidating a fundamentalist regime in Iran, a country whose people were often described to us, I now think inaccurately, as socially conservative but not particularly religious.

We met the Iranian religious leader in his by then famous tent at Neufle-le-Chateau, a Paris suburb, where Khomeini met visitors and spoke with the media. Since coming to Paris Khomeini had become far more visible on the global stage, giving interviews, making statements to hundreds of assembled journalists, sending cassettes to his followers in Iran, and taking an active role in guiding the daily resistance that was advancing its campaign to drive the Shah from power to unexpected heights. Khomeini's seemingly urbane interpreter was the American-educated Sadegh Ghotbzadeh, whose personal story of rise and fall epitomized the experience of many initial non-clerical supporters of the Khomeini leadership. Ghotbzadeh became Foreign Minister in the first elected government, subsequently ran for president but did poorly, was accused of betraying the government he served, and was later executed as the revolution began to consume its own earlier loyalists, a pattern mirroring the anti-religious French and Russian revolutions, but in the Iranian case it was an ideology with a core religious animus that motivated this purge of its own ranks.

When I spoke at the French Club as the luncheon speaker at the World Trade Center a few weeks later, I was seated next to the French ambassador to the UN who told me an intriguing story bearing on Khomeini's rise from international obscurity and the misperceptions of power in the secular West. In 1978 Saddam Hussein no longer wanted Khomeini to remain in exile in Najaf where he was fanning the flames of a potentially provocative anti-Shah movement in Iran that could produce an unwelcome crisis in Iran/Iraq relations. In response, Khomeini applied for a French visa. This diplomat, then the French ambassador in Tehran, sought advice from the Shah. 'Shall we issue him a French visa?' The Shah, implicitly acknowledging Khomeini as a formidable opponent, responded affirmatively, 'I want him as far from Iran as possible. Please grant the visa.' The French Government extended Khomeini a visa, but only for three months. When it came time for renewal, the diplomat returned to the palace to determine whether the Shah had changed his mind, given Khomeini's increasing impact on world opinion after assuming his Paris residence. But no, the Shah again urged France to extend the visa of Khomeini saying once more that he wanted him to be geographically far away from Iran. This seems bizarre, so wrongly presupposing that power and influence in the modern world remain a function of geography rather than reflecting access to global communications. Such a spatial mindset ignored the non-territorial reach of media and world opinion in the late twentieth century.

This conversation preceding my talk took place in the Windows on the World Restaurant at the top of the World Trade Center, the only time I had ever been present in this iconic structure, the scene of convulsive events that changed world history after it was targeted by the 9/11 attacks in 2001. Of course, nothing of this sort occurred to me then, but often looking back I was reminded that what seems almost permanent can vanish from the earth in an instant.

Our conversation with Khomeini started with a few pleasantries, but quickly turned serious, with the already world famous ayatollah directing several questions at us, while we sat quietly, entranced by his shining black eyes. He asked whether we thought the U.S. Government would accept the outcome of the revolutionary developments in Iran and seemed to suggest that if there was such an acceptance, normal relations between the two countries would be possible and desirable. Unquestionably, his main preoccupation, in common with what we heard repeatedly throughout our trip, was whether we thought that the U.S. Government would attempt to repeat the experience of 1953, and intervene to restore the Shah to the throne. This was far from an unreasonable or paranoid concern, given the history of the U.S. relationship with Iran since the 1953 coup and considering the strategic importance of Iran as a Cold War ally, unconditionally supportive of U.S. interests in the region.

Khomeini also, somewhat surprisingly, asked us whether earlier contracts for large-scale arms purchases by Iran would be respected by the U.S. Government in the new post-Shah environment. He was definitely curious about whether the Shah, who had not yet settled on where he would reside after leaving, would end up in the United States, and if he did, whether this would influence American policy toward Iran. Mansour Farhang, months later, told me that when the Shah did end up entering the United States, apparently to receive medical treatment, he, Mansour, was asked by Khomeini whether he thought that the health claim was genuine. Mansour said he told Khomeini that he believed health was the real reason as the Shah was suffering from cancer. Khomeini responded, 'Then, it's acceptable.' Khomeini changed his mind after the student seizure of the American Embassy a short time later, taking its American occupants hostage, and successfully demanding from the government a more radical implementation of Iran's revolutionary future. It seems that events on the ground changed, Khomeini shifted his priorities from guarding against a pro-Shah coup to realizing his revolutionary vision of an Islamic governing structure for post-dynastic Iran.

When it came our turn to pose questions, we asked for his views on the movement that he now appeared to lead, and that had succeeded in deposing the once seemingly mighty and invulnerable Pahlavi dynasty. Iran was a key oil producer, a strategic centerpiece in containment geopolitics that controlled American grand strategy in the Cold War period, and a country from which the CIA mounted surveillance projects and intelligence operations aimed at the Soviet Union while doing whatever it pleased in Iran. Khomeini responded without evasion, succinctly, and with the clarity of an informed person of comprehensive understanding. As might be expected, he insisted that if the United States wanted to have good relations with Iran in the future it must not continue to use Iranian territory for these purposes, at least not without the explicit consent of the Iranian Government.

We asked how he viewed the Iranian Revolution, and what it meant for the future. Before responding further, he corrected our formulation. 'What happened in Iran was an *Islamic* Revolution, not a revolution with nationalism at its core, but rather its character was shaped by Islam as a religion and a civilization.' This answer is more important than it seems as it was his indirect way of saying that the most relevant community for the people of Iran was not their nation, but rather their participation in the non-territorial Islamic *umma*, and that the revolution that started in Iran had much unfinished business throughout the Islamic world. Significantly, Khomeini made no reference to sectarian strains associated with the Shi'ia/Sunni split that was to haunt the region in the early 21st century, especially after the United States launched its attack on Iraq in 2003.

Turning to our question about his own future role, Khomeini first indicated that he entered politics reluctantly and only because in Iran, 'there was a river of blood separating the people from the government.' With apparent sincerity and a certain solemnity, he declared to us that upon returning to Iran after more than 15 years of exile he looked forward to resuming a quiet religious life in Qom. Everything about his demeanor and body language lent credibility to this assertion as a sincere expression of his desire, at least at that moment. It is important to remember that he had been outside of Iran for this long period and must have wondered about the reception he would receive upon his return from the Iranian people and from the religious community in the country.

I remember asking about the fate of Jews and Bahais in post-revolutionary Iran, knowing of Khomeini's hostility to Israel and the Bahai religion. These two minorities were rumored to be in big trouble because of their high-profile collaboration with the Shah's reign. In the background was my awareness of the fact that the distrustful and insecure Shah had relied upon these vulnerable and rather small minorities to fill key and sensitive governance positions. Their utility was directly related to their vulnerability. Apparently, they were assumed to be too weak and isolated to mount any kind of oppositional movement that might be tempted to challenge the imperial order.

The Shah didn't even trust the leadership of the Iranian armed forces or the elites of the more influential ethnic groups that formed the backbone of Iranian society. What Khomeini said interested me at the time, seemed thoughtful, and appeared to be an accurate portrayal of his views. Khomeini said, in effect, 'the Jews have a great historic tradition and are a genuine religion.' He added, 'That is, provided they don't get themselves entangled with Israel, they have a secure future in the country, and it would be a tragedy for us if they left Iran.'

For Bahais his response was dramatically different: 'The Bahais are a sect, not a genuine religion, and have no place in the new Iran.' The Bahais are viewed by many Muslims as heretical, not an authentic religion but rather Islamically derivative yet heretical in recognizing Bahá'u'lláh or The Bab, who lived *after* Muhammad, as a prophet, contrary to the Islamic belief that Prophet Muhammad is the final prophet sent by God. Beyond this, the Bahai reliance on reason rather than revelation made their faith suspect for many devout Muslims. As it turned out, Khomeini was credited shortly thereafter with actually moderating aggressively punitive moves against the Bahais. This intervention by Khomeini has been believed by some close observers of the Iranian scene to have avoided what could have turned into genocide. The danger was real as drastic retribution against the Bahais was being demanded by several radical and emotional young Shiite mullahs.

During the interview Khomeini disclosed three other aspects of his worldview that seem worthy of notice from the perspective of the present. First of all, Khomeini spoke openly of the potential for the spread of political Islam throughout the Middle East and North Africa. In his speaking, and his writing, although steeped in the Shi'ia tradition, Khomeini never invoked or endorsed the kind of sectarian cleavages that became so evident in relations between Iran and several Arab countries in the twenty-first century, especially with Saudi Arabia. Fostering sectarianism was one of the worst legacies of the U.S. occupation of Iraq after 2003. The American diplomat, Paul Bremer, in charge of administering the occupation of Iraq, made it a policy priority to displace the Sunni leadership relied upon by Saddam Hussein to rule over the Shi'ia majority population. These purges of Sunnis, especially in the upper ranks of the Iraqi armed forces, contributed to the rise of extremism in Iraq, and apparently to their staffing of the upper military echelon of

ISIS. Bremer seemed wrongly to have believed that Iraqi nationalism and internal Balkanization would prevail over transnational religious and civilizational ties, while weakening the state of Iraq, long the highest regional priority of Israel with respect to its Arab neighbors. What followed as a result of elevating the Shi'ia on sectarian grounds was not the expected affirmation of a West-leaning Iraqi nationalism but rather the forging of a far stronger linkage to the Iranian Shiite theocracy, the very opposite outcome to the geopolitical goals sought by the American attack and occupation.

This is a central point that Western thought consistently misses or confuses: the Westphalian template of territorial sovereign states that emerged in Europe since the seventeenth century just doesn't have the same political potency and ethical legitimacy in the less territorial modes of thought that have resonance in Islamic domains, especially in Arab countries, Turkey, and Iran, though probably less so in Indonesia, Malaysia, Pakistan, and India. Khomeini's primary imaginary was Islamic and non-territorial, and this suffused his outlook at least until Iraq launched its attack on Iran in 1980, and Tehran's nationalist reflexes responded, displaying surprisingly robust defensive capabilities as reinforced by an outpouring of patriotic unity.

A second related viewpoint articulated by Khomeini, again expressed without the slightest hint of sectarian sentiment, was an attitude of intense hostility toward the Saudi dynasty. He viewed the House of Saud as corrupt and oppressive, no less so than the Pahlavi dynasty had been in Iran. He associated Saudi corruption with the adoption of Western lifestyles and values by the royal elite, which he viewed as more of an identifier than the rigid Wahhabist version of Islam imposed on the Saudi populace and being subsidized elsewhere by the Saudi government, especially in Asia. Undoubtedly, this hostility toward the Saudi monarchy was also aggravated by the fact that the most sacred Islamic sites, Mecca and Medina, were under corrupt Saudi control. Khomeini was clearly offended by what he believed to be Saudi exploitation of their nationalist supervisory control over the most sacred places of Islamic worship that rightfully belonged not to a sovereign state but to the Islamic community as a totality.

The third response of interest related to our question about the fate likely to befall those in Iran who had performed dirty deeds on behalf of the Shah's regime. Khomeini indicated his expectation that Nuremberg-type trials would be held in which charges of criminality would be prepared and considered in an atmosphere of a judicial proceeding administered in accordance with due process and the rule of law. Such trials never took place. Instead political figures accused of playing leading roles in implementing the Shah's repressive policies were summarily executed, and never given any meaningful right to mount a defense of their behavior. The explanation given by critics of these summary executions is that if public trials were held, the testimony of these prominent defendants would implicate several close associates of Khomeini who had worked with or for the American government when Islamic identities were favored in American intelligence circles as a counter to Marxist tendencies.

It was actually our group that brought the meeting with Khomeini to an end, seemingly surprising Khomeini, as he abruptly stood up, bade us farewell with few words, and hastily departed from the tent. As we rushed to catch our flight, I realized that we had just experienced something very valuable, an open and revealing conversation with a figure destined to make history for his country and the Islamic world. I was struck by the seeming severity of Khomeini's sensibility as it came across to us. Throughout the interview I had wanted to ask this venerable religious figure about the place of joy and pleasure in life but never got the chance. I was admittedly hesitant to raise issues likely to be rebuffed or declared irrelevant, and thus possibly interfere with Khomeini's willingness to be cooperative and responsive.

I am reminded of my conversation at a UN lunch eight or nine months later with Mike Wallace, the famed CBS TV journalist who had then just returned from Tehran where he tried to have an interview with Khomeini in the midst of the U.S. embassy hostage crisis. Wallace realized that he had messed up his assignment and, rather disarmingly, asked me what he could have done differently to get better results. The problem with Wallace's approach, as I saw it, was partly his aggressive effort to pin the ayatollah down as if questioning an American political leader at a press conference. The inappropriateness of this style was accentuated by Wallace's phrasings of his questions in the language of the bazaar. Wallace acted as if the release of the American hostages seized from the embassy in the fall of 1979, the most salient issue at the time, was a matter of striking a bargain, getting the price right to obtain benefits for Iran that would be sufficient to induce an end to the crisis through the release of the Americans being held captive. This approach badly missed the point. For Khomeini the hostage crisis raised issues of principle that related to the past uses of the embassy as a base for intervention in the internal affairs of Iran and to worries about future interventions, as well as undisclosed issues about internal Iranian politics. Wallace knew about my meeting with Khomeini, which prompted him to seek my opinion. He seemed after the fact to understand that his approach was ill-suited to elicit useful responses from a religious leader who probably had never visited a bazaar in his entire life and undoubtedly felt insulted by the implication that the hostage crisis could be reduced to resemble a routine transaction with a Tehran shopkeeper.

Khomeini did return to Iran less than two weeks after our visit and was greeted by massive delirious crowds viewing him as an Imam, a very sacred identity in a variant of Shi'ia thought that contained an expectation of a triumphal return of the Mahdi, an imam who had disappeared centuries ago, whose return would signal the beginning of the end of history. In fact, we found that in Iran a clue to someone's political outlook was conveyed by the term of respect used—ayatollah, grand ayatollah, and reserved for those most devoted and sacred, in fact reserved exclusively for Khomeini, imam. Khomeini appeared to keep faith with what he told us in Paris by immediately taking up residence in Qom and living in accord with his religious daily routine. Yet the tumult in Iran made his life anything but serene. His daily schedule included a continuous trail of visitors and journalists from Tehran seeking his opinions, and often his guidance. He was also surrounded by a large number of clerical leaders who pushed their belief that only Khomeini could keep the revolution from going off the rails by adopting a secular form of governance. There was a credible worry in these religious circles that the revolution was being hijacked by secularists and currently led by leaders too weak to protect Iran from its internal and external enemies who were exerting a variety of pressures and posing counterrevolutionary threats.

What has remained enigmatic in my mind, and for a time I tried to persuade knowledgeable friends and others to interpret this for me, was the differences between what Khomeini said in Paris and what he did in Iran. Mansour Farhang, who had considerable early contact with Khomeini and possessed the analytical tools to present the relevant issues, could have done an illuminating political biography of the transformation of Khomeini from primarily a religious leader who always had a keen interest political concerns and the need to challenge Western modernism and secularism in Iran into a theocratic figure who became a post-revolutionary political leader endowed with supreme authority. In a deep sense, Khomeini, even while leading what appeared to be a quiet religious life in Iraq was intensely 'political,' and so regarded by many religiously oriented activists, including many of his former theology students. There are several obvious lines of explanation for this transformation from a religious figure engaged in politics to a political leader who was intensely religious. Perhaps, more than one explanation is relevant: Khomeini, out of the country for so long, didn't realize the hold he had on the popular sensibility that emerged from the revolution; despite his intentions in Paris, the secularists and liberal Islamists immediately in charge of the country seemed too ambivalent in outlook and too indecisive in method to withstand the mounting perceived counterrevolutionary threats. Khomeini is likely to have come to feel something more radical was needed to save the revolution from inside enemies as well as outside threats of intervention. It also may be relevant that the Khomeini closest advisors were theologically oriented Muslims, who believed that only this charismatic religious leader could lead the country through a transition process able to secure the establishment of the Islamic Republic of Iran, avoiding the Western and modern traps of liberal secularism and materialist socialism. This central uncertainty surrounding the last stages of Khomeini's life journey remains.

On arrival in the U.S., there was a large press conference at which Ramsey did most of the talking. I felt he spoke rather blandly without conveying my impression of this extraordinary individual who seemed more suited to the fifteenth century than the twentieth, yet was emerging in Iran, throughout the Islamic world, and on the world stage as a leading political player.

Almost immediately on reaching home I received a phone call from an Opinion Editor of the *NY Times* inviting me to submit a profile of Khomeini, asking that my text be submitted in 24 hours. He told me that the American people knew nothing of this 'medieval figure' who seemed to embody the spirit of the Iranian Revolution. I thought it was a good opportunity to express a more sympathetic view of what was happening in Iran, but would have welcomed more time to prepare something vetted by others and more reflective of my own complex sense of Khomeini and what his role would be in Iran once he returned to country. As it was, I was trying to write about Iran's future without the dark forebodings then being disseminated by the media, which accorded undue respect to the failed policies of the Carter/Brzezinski pro-Shah approach. I wanted to convey my belief and hope that the path to normalization with Iran would be explored before Washington rushed to adopt a confrontational approach. I realized that this risked rebuff and failure, but I thought then and still think now, that it was a foreign policy risk worth taking.

My opinion piece was published on February 16, 1979 with a provocative and irresponsible headline, which I was never shown prior to publication. This was a typical display of the arrogant *Times* style. The headline, 'Trusting Khomeini' was not at all the impression I wanted to convey. I never would have chosen such a headline, nor if consulted, would I have agreed. For years that headline, far more than the nuanced article, generated an array of insults, including death threats, and allegations that I had been coopted and brainwashed by the new Iranian leadership.

Some Princeton alumni were angered by such a presentation of my views in the mainstream media, and maybe even more so, by my camaraderie with Ramsey Clark. Ramsey had come to be considered the most outspoken and influential apostate from the American establishment and its postulates of national security. Not since Dan Ellsberg released the Pentagon Papers in the early 1970s had a member of the political elite so defied the bipartisan consensus that set narrow limits on acceptable political behavior for the United States political establishment.

More than my stance on the Vietnam War, including the trips to Hanoi, this visit to Iran generated a backlash that had many ripples, leaving me somewhat stunned as I had mainly gone to Iran to observe and learn without any advance political agenda. My prior involvement with Iran concerned the protection of human rights, not with choosing a political future for the country, yet I was sharply criticized for alleged meddling in political matters. In the ensuing months, the influential liberal *NY Times* columnist, Anthony Lewis, was a guest speaker at Princeton. At a reception afterwards we had a conversation about events in Iran. Tony knew of my visit and opinion piece and took the occasion to launch a rather nasty personal attack. He criticized me for my support of the Iranian Revolution and for my opposition to the Shah. I was particularly surprised by how supportive Lewis seemed of the Shah, given his credentials as the superstar liberal journalist of the era.

Lewis upset me even more by following up on our conversation by writing a scathing column on March 12, 1979 that condemned my views on Iran as dangerously naïve. I was further depicted by him as typical of someone from the clueless left. The attack by Lewis was followed some weeks later by an unsigned editorial in the *Times* that mentioned only me by name as guilty of double standards, as having complained loudly about the Shah's violations of human rights while remaining silent when it came to the repressive behavior by the new anti-American Iranian leadership. Actually, the *Times* published this unsigned editorial without ever giving me a chance to explain my views of post-Shah Iran. The editorial ignored the fact that I had formed a committee, which I chaired, that was indeed focused on exposing the serious human rights abuses in the *post-Shah* period.

A Second Eruption: The Hostage Crisis

Political developments in Iran were not smooth or easier to interpret. My main continuing line of connection was by way of Mansour Farhang, who was appointed to be Iran's first post-revolutionary ambassador at the UN, with a Fifth Avenue official residence put at his disposal. Elections had put the moderate Islamists such as Banisadr and apolitical secularists and technocrats in charge of constituting a new state in Iran. Khomeini initially remained in Qom, but as it became evident that despite the elected leadership, on important issues of policy he was the de facto authoritative leader, with officials holding high positions in government deferring to him. The naming of Iran as the 'Islamic Republic of Iran' correctly conveyed the reality of a constitutionally based theocracy emerging in the country. Whether cause or effect, strong countercurrents of opposition and repression created continuous tension in the country, abetted by pro-Shah exile communities in the West, by Israel, Saudi Arabia, and the U.S.

Hostility to the United States was a signature issue for the new leadership in Tehran and its most radical support groups, including religious Iranian students. Early on the American Embassy was briefly occupied as an expression of continuing revolution. The 1953 events were kept relevant as fears persisted that it was only a matter of time before the U.S. would encourage some kind of counterrevolutionary event although the coup option seemed unavailable due to the collapse of the Shah's armed forces and the rise of the Revolutionary Guards to positions of primacy in safeguarding the security of the government. Yet this did not entirely dissuade those favoring a counterrevolutionary scenario from seeking other options to destabilize and reverse the outcome.

Two developments expressed both the radicalization of the revolutionary process in Iran and the credible reality of the counterrevolutionary backlash. First, there was the increasing emphasis by Khomeini on the Islamic character of the revolution, leading to violent encounters with former allies in the struggle against the Shah, most notably with the MEK. This standoff was highlighted when a bomb assassinated an individual whom many in Iran regarded as the most influential ayatollah other than Khomeini, Mohammed Beheshti. MEK was accused by the government, although the facts remain shrouded in controversy. Also indicative of this trend was a steady stream of anti-American commentary, featuring references by Khomeini to the U.S. as 'the great Satan.'

Secondly, there was a buildup of a variety of counterrevolutionary pressures. Although a coup did not seem viable, the tension on the Iraq/Iran border was seen as threatening a possible effort by Washington to achieve regime change in Iran by overt military intervention. It was thought that with Iran's military forces in disarray almost any military attack would bring about the rapid collapse of the new political order, either followed by an invitation from Iranian notables for the Shah to resume his rule or by an attempt, supported by the U.S., for members of the Iranian secular elite to cobble together a government that was neither monarchist nor Islamist.

The sequence of actual events was different. The Shah was admitted to the United States, after visiting several other countries, raising the anxiety level in Tehran, although it remains obscure whether the Shah's presence would have eventually produced a heightened effort by the U.S. to reverse the outcome of the revolution.

It was in this context that I was again invited to visit Tehran, this time by the office of Banisadr, now President, with the idea of helping in some unspecified way to hasten a non-provocative ending of the hostage situation at the embassy. Each day that the hostage crisis continued was bad news for Jimmy Carter's presidency, making his leadership appear weak and ineffectual, unable to protect America's vital strategic interests or even its public servants when in jeopardy.

Days before receiving this personal invitation from Iran, I had been asked whether I would be willing to accompany Andrew Young on a forthcoming trip to Tehran for the purpose of negotiating the freeing of hostages. We thought, given the pressure on Carter with a presidential campaign months away, that this signal from Iran would be welcomed by the White House. I met with Young and Ramsey at the home of Ramsey's mother in Washington to discuss this possible venture. Young seemed ready to go and was well qualified by political credentials, personal composure, and experience as a diplomat, having served in both the U.S. Congress and as U.S. representative at the UN. An additional political asset was that Young was from Georgia, the same state as Carter. It seemed promising. Further encouragement for this initiative arose from the fact that Khomeini had made a public statement that Iran would look favorably on an African American emissary sent by the U.S. Government to negotiate an end to the seizure and occupation of the embassy by revolutionary Iranian students. Under these circumstances Andrew Young seemed the ideal emissary for such a mission.

There was, however, one condition set by Young that was never fulfilled, which brought this initiative to a halt before it began. Andrew Young insisted that he receive a green light from the White House before agreeing to participate in the mission, and this not was given. Later the head of the Iran Desk at the State Department, a friendly apolitical civil servant, told me 'that Brzezinski would rather see the hostages remain forever in Tehran than see Andrew Young get credit for their release.' Such are the bureaucratic rivalries and political imaginaries of ambitious men that often undermine crucial implementations of foreign policy.

At the time, I was disappointed by Young's insistence on prior approval, but in retrospect I think he was right. Without an official endorsement Young could not give Khomeini any credible assurances about non-interference or moves toward normalization, and without this quid pro quo the mission would almost certainly have failed, and produced media criticism directed at Young for private meddling in the affairs of state.

The hostage crisis worsened as the November 1980 election neared, and rumors filled the air with reports of a daring rescue operation to do by force what had not been achieved by either diplomatic pressure or appeals to international law. There were also suggestions, later validated, that the leadership in Iran was prepared to reach an agreement with Carter's opponent in the presidential race, Ronald Reagan, and would hold off with releasing the hostage until there was a new president in the White House—that came to be known as 'the October surprise.'

It was against this background that I decided to make this second trip within the year to Iran, accompanied by my friend and the foremost peace activist in the U.S. from the Global South, Eqbal Ahmad. Born in Pakistan, Eqbal was a brilliant speaker, combining insight, judgment, passion, and humor, and became well known subsequently as the closest friend and political mentor of Edward Said. Eqbal was of rock star quality, featuring exceptional speaking ability, progressive politics, and a strong, warm personality. He was often adored by young women as if a political matinee idol. Eqbal enjoyed this adulation, and on occasion further magnified his greater-than-normal exploits by exaggerating his life experiences, and by his enjoyment of the limelight. At the same time, Eqbal was extremely generous with friends whether notable or obscure, a fine cook of Pakistani food, and frequently frustrated by his own failure to write major scholarly books and articles, goals he coveted and was clearly capable of achieving.

We arrived in Iran at the poorest of times. Iraq was escalating the border clashes, and the war that would consume the energies of both countries for almost a decade was just getting underway. These preoccupations meant that we were never able even to meet with Banisadr, although he had personally extended the invitation. He was desperately eager to resolve the hostage crisis, being fully aware that he was rapidly losing his grip on power and as a result, losing Khomeini's respect and support. As with all aspects of Iranian governance, Banisadr's authority totally depended on the continued backing of Khomeini, and he was losing out as Khomeini was shifting his allegiance to the students occupying the embassy and insisting on a more revolutionary agenda.

We did have a long useless meeting, including lunch, with Sadegh Ghotbzadeh, formerly Khomeini's interpreter in Paris and now Foreign Minister. Ghotbzadeh was aggressive and egotistical, yelling at his staff and showing not the slightest sign of political intelligence or religious sensibility. While we talked, he was cleaning his fingernails with a glittering gold plated nail clipper the likes of which I had never seen. He lamented the persistence of the hostage crisis, indicating that it was shifting power ever further away from the elected government. As earlier mentioned, Ghotbzadeh himself became a casualty of the revolution, executed for alleged anti-regime activity, an accusation that may or may not have been accurate.

We also met with Ibrahim Yazdi who would be another early casualty of the high-level purges of the new political order, but a much more admirable and likable political figure. After a brief tenure as Foreign Minister, Yazdi had become the chief editor of the *Kayan* newpaper, the most influential source of news and opinion in Iran, read by many educated Iranians. Yazdi too was worried both about the theocratic severity of the government, and by American manipulative designs carried out in secret. In that setting, but not subsequently, Yazdi endorsed the conspiratorial view that the U.S. was itself run by a rightwing cabal headed by the Rockefeller family, with the Council of Foreign Relations operating as its nerve center. Such a conspiracy outlook struck me as a harmful and essentially misleading interpretation of the American political scene, less convincing than attributing policies to the 'deep state.'

Eqbal and I were glad to leave Iran after a few more frustrating days. We fully realized that our mission was not feasible, especially when the government was doubly distracted by purging the opposition, sometimes harshly, and by consolidating control of the government by radical Islamic forces through the control of the bureaucracy and by institution building, with a mandate to promote Islam in every nook and cranny of Iranian culture. I also feared that we could get trapped in Iran either as a result of the onset of war with Iraq or through some side effect of an American attempt to liberate the hostages being held at the embassy. When we finally lifted off from the tarmac in Tehran I felt greatly relieved. Unlike Vietnam, where I had ambivalent feelings of possible entrapment during my visit in 1968, I definitely feared being stuck in Iran. Somehow ten years earlier, I had the feeling that if necessary, I could have made a life in Vietnam if unable to leave. I didn't feel that this would be possible in Iran. I felt that in post-revolutionary Iran I would be a lost and lonely soul, if I survived at all.

Looking Back

As far as personal development was concerned, Iran was almost as important as Vietnam but not at all transformational. It did give me an appreciation of the potency of Islamic values, and the potential of mobilization from below by and for the masses in the Middle East. I was to witness the same pattern, with less explosive results, in Turkey twenty years later, and in the Arab world ten years after that. I came to understand that these societies were deeply religious, and the secularization and Europeanization that had been so enthusiastically embraced by urban elites, had never been accepted by most of the population, especially those living in villages scattered throughout these countries. Urbanization, although extensive, had also not altered the deeply entrenched cultural affinities, conservative social traditions, and religious sensibilities of those migrating from villages to the cities, a dynamic mainly spurred by the search for employment opportunities.

I came to understand better why religiously anointed leaders were by and large hostile to the West and to the cultural values that accompanied modernization in the West, while affirming the role of science and technology in improving the lives of their peoples. Each national situation was different, and the policy effects reflected national and individual styles of leadership as well as the reception accorded by the West. Iran suffered a serious backlash as a result of its challenge to U.S. strategic interests and from an Iranian diaspora, partly monarchist and partly secularist that achieved leverage in the internal political life of the United States and Europe due to its orientation, and which continues to seek confrontation if not counterrevolution. Such belligerent attitudes have more recently been reinforced by the governments of Israel and Saudi Arabia, enjoying unconditional support in the Trump White House, and raising serious risks of war in a region already beset by multiple political tragedies.

At the same time, my basic response now as then is noninterventionist. I did not subscribe to the view that Khomeini's Iran was worse for the Iranian people than the Shah's Iran, or that externally manipulated regime change to improve the human rights situation would make life better for the Iranian people. I was impressed that the consensus among CNN experts that Iran would be unable to resist the Iraq invasion in 1980 had proved wrong and out of touch—yet even so it was not discredited. Although the Islamic Republic turned repressive and cruel toward its adversaries, it proved able to construct a governing system along Islamic lines that was surprisingly stable and durable despite continuous provocation, international sanctions, and military threats. Compared to other regimes in the region Iran was governed in accord with relatively free elections that sometimes disappointed the clerical elites. On several occasions it brought leaders to presidential power who were generally more flexible than the dogmatic Islamic outlook of Khomeini and the hardliners among followers, including his chosen successor, Ayatollah Ali Khamenei.

I was in Iran, mainly Isfahan, for a conference just prior to the presidential election in 1997 that was won by the moderate clerical figure, Mohammed Khatemi, against all expectations. I remember being told by several Iranians unhappy with the theocratic government that the religious overseers of the political process would not allow Khatemi to run, and if they did, he would never be allowed to win, and if he should somehow win, he would not be permitted to appoint his own cabinet, and certainly not be allowed to include any women in the cabinet. On all counts, these all-knowing critics were wrong. Khatemi took over the governing process without any political friction, was active internationally, including taking the initiative to establish a Dialogue of Civilizations under UN auspices at a session in New York City in which I was invited to participate. I was impressed by the very philosophical tone of Khatemi's keynote address on that occasion, making learned references to many thinkers from various civilizational backgrounds in keeping with the spirit of his proposal.

Of course, Khatemi encountered increasing resistance from Islamic hardliners at home, and the next and sixth president of Iran (2005-2013) was a populist and inflammatory leader, Mahmoud Ahmadinejad, who agitated the West by his rhetoric, and was portrayed as sponsoring a jihadist approach to Israel. There is no doubt that Ahmadinejad relied on irresponsibly provocative language, touching raw nerves in the West, but his views were delibeerately given an even sharper edge than their actuality by the inflammatory way they were translated and presented, especially by those with Zionist alignments.

Ever since Ahmadinejad the Western hard line has prevailed in the Western imaginary, and although Obama briefly, at a political cost, broke away from the confrontational consensus by negotiating the 2015 agreement dealing with Iran's nuclear program, the trajectory of U.S. relations with Iran became dangerously confrontational, called 'maximum pressure' by Trump's minions. With Israel and Saudi Arabia both seeking regime change in Iran as the highest priority of their foreign policy, the U.S. under Trump has escalated its confrontational diplomacy, repudiating the nuclear agreement, creating maritime incidents while intensifying sanctions, and even, incredibly, assassinating Iranian general Soleimani while he was in Iraq to pursue peace talks—all of which have been increasingly raising the risks of a devastating regional war.

Following the ebb and flow of internal developments in Iran and the variety of external provocations, it is something of a political miracle that the Islamic Republic of Iran has so far withstood covert operations from the West including assassinations of its scientists, cyberattacks, incitement of internal unrest, and a range of crippling sanctions led by the United States. It seems instructive to compare the longevity of the Islamic Republic of Iran with the very short life span of the Muslim Brotherhood's ascendancy in Egypt where the elected leader was deposed after a year in office by a well-orchestrated and bloody coup that brought back autocratic governance to Egypt under the guidance of a brutal general. Iran's durability is partially explained, I believe, by the acceptance of the Leninist view that if a revolution is to succeed it must remake the state in its own image, and not try to create the new order by compromising with and relying upon embedded and antagonistic bureaucratic elites, earlier institutional arrangements, or entrenched social and business elites.

In the end, Iran led me to appreciate the empowering and sometimes emancipatory role of religiously inspired political movements, perhaps in some situations offering the only alternative to submission and collective misery. Such a generalization currently applies especially in the Islamic world where the political process has so often been deformed by Western interference, including the corruption and manipulation of elites, especially with oil uppermost in mind. At the same time, I came to understand more concretely that religion could also become a source of repressive government and abusive societal intolerance, and act in extreme ways in the course of giving religious doctrines and beliefs operational relevance, victimizing especially women and secular opponents. Political communities in the Middle East have become extremely polarized on the subject of religion, being either for or against.

I situate myself in the middle, which is often a lonely place, being unacceptable to both sides. I continue to believe, unlike many of my secular friends, that if the world is to find a way to meet the intensifying global political and ecological challenges it will have to work in tandem with the inclusive potentialities of the great world religions, as complemented by the spiritual awakening of those with secular identities who have wrongly placed their trust and confidence in instrumental reason to address the planetary policy agenda.

More than my other experiences with controversial issues, my early anti-Shah partisanship gave way to detachment with respect to Iranian internal developments in ensuing decades. What did continue was my opposition to neocon and purported human rights pressures favoring intervention, subversion, and confrontation. I continue to believe that Iran and the United States would be better off in this century by respecting the dynamics of self-determination under almost all conditions. Of course, there are costs arising from such a course, but in the post-colonial world this remains the best option in a world order that lacks reliable and effective mechanisms for protecting the *human* interest or promoting *global* wellbeing. I would rather put my trust in the uncertainties of self-determination than in the militarist machinations of geopolitics, which so often has meant military intervention.

CHAPTER 14

Establishing a Jewish State in Palestine

When the Personal Becomes Too Political (or the Political Too Personal)

On no issue has the personal and political been more intertwined in my life experience, especially since the turn of the 21st century, than with respect to the long struggle involving Palestine and Israel. The roots of my engagement are earlier. They deepened during the last twenty years of the 20th century. As explained earlier, my childhood sense of being Jewish was weak despite those early years of my life coinciding with the Holocaust in Europe, and reinforced by contact with several celebrity Jewish refugees who were in the circle of my father's friends in New York City. The Jewish refugees whom we knew seemed to be doing really well in their new surroundings and did little to evoke the kind of empathy that we now bestow on those fleeing from persecution, combat zones, and impoverishment. Our family had no family connections with anyone who lost relatives or friends in the death camps of Europe. I never in this period connected the horrors I read about in newspapers or heard on radio broadcasts with my own reality. In some dim way I realized that as a Jew I would have been shipped to a death camp solely on the basis of my racial identity if I had been exposed to these ugly realities being experienced by Jewish kids similar to myself growing up in Hitler's Europe. I came to appreciate that the happenstance of my birthplace in 1930 could have been a matter of life and death, but it never led me to adopt a tribalist, or even a nationalist, sense of fractured identity.

I remember uncritically accepting the early glamorization of Israel as having become an exemplary state by heroically prevailing against much larger neighboring Arab countries despite being outnumbered and outgunned, by making the desert bloom, creating vibrant and innovative kibbutz communities, and mostly populated by happy young people who seemed to be continuously singing and dancing. Israel managed to make the West believe and affirm this national narrative, which then included the erasure of the Palestinian people or their presentation as backward, dirty Arabs, who were racist and inclined toward terrorism. There was a widespread belief that Israel was creating an emerging utopia along the lines portrayed by the movie, *Exodus,* that would bring modernity to the region, while overcoming every obstacle placed in its path.

This national narrative ignored the catastrophic reality that in the process of establishing Israel, the incoming Jews had cruelly displaced, dispersed, and oppressed the indigenous Palestinian people. Part of this Israeli narrative portrayed the majority native population as denationalized and backward 'Arabs,' who were unwilling to allow Jews to create a sanctuary for themselves on a fragment of barren territory, which was tiny if compared to the fictive pan-Arab nation that encompassed the whole of the Middle East and North Africa. The Zionist posture included literalizing, publicizing, and internalizing the slogan attributed to the Arabs of 'throwing the Jews into the sea.' Such an image created an existential fear of a second holocaust that led many Jews to be genuinely fearful. It also led public opinion in the West to feel protective toward the infant state, especially in view of the West's deferred guilt arising from its failures to react more effectively against the extreme racist anti-Semitism of Hitler's Germany.

I was not exposed to compelling versions of the countervailing Palestinian narrative of indigeneity, ethnic cleansing, Europeanization, settler colonialism, and geopolitical manipulation—to say nothing of the onset of targeted assassinations, torture, collective punishment and apartheid—until much later. I had no relatives who migrated to Israel, or who thought of themselves as Zionists, and I had no strong emotional ties to the fate of Israel or Palestine. My rather simplistic view then and now was to favor approaches that would allow both peoples to live together in peace, equality, and mutual respect. I was opposed then and now to either the disregard of Palestinian grievances and rights or to turning the clock back by somehow undoing and reversing the Zionist project of creating a Jewish homeland in Palestine.

I favor binational coexistence based on equality, mutual respect, and human rights.

This sense of personal detachment changed briefly during my first visit to Israel, which took place shortly after the 1973 War. Israel came close to losing that war, and this sense of national vulnerability overcame for several years the triumphalist mood that resulted from the Israeli victory in the 1967 War, which had greatly enlarged Israeli territory, showcased its formidable warmaking capabilities, and greatly strengthened its strategic alignment with the U.S. The 1973 experience had a temporary chastening effect on the sort of Israeli and Zionist *hubris* that had emerged after 1967, and has again reemerged in a cruder form during Netanyahu's long belligerent right-wing leadership, especially as abetted by the Trump presidency.

When I visited Israel in 1973 to take part in a conference and other academic activities, I was viewed with some suspicion by my Israeli liberal nationalist hosts in these university circles but was not treated as altogether lost to the Zionist cause. I seemed to be regarded as an American secular and assimilated Jew who might yet be reeducated, if not recruited, which seemed to explain the attention my visit received. I was favorably impressed by the vibrant intellectual atmosphere of excitement with ideas and ideals that I encountered in Israel, and a vision of peace then espoused by many of the Israelis I met that I found congenial. For the first time in my life I valued and experienced positively my Jewish identity and even felt at this moment of temporary enchantment that I might have had a challenging and satisfying life if I had chosen to live in Israel, even shamefully forgetting during this interlude about the Palestinian plight. On reflection, I realized that with a different upbringing in the U.S., I might have evolved somewhat in the manner of Jeff Halper, a leading peace activist in Israel seeking to uphold Palestinian rights and yet an unrepentant Zionist.

Jeff's Israeli life is worth reflecting upon. He had become an anthropologist in the United States before emigrating to Israel and building what struck me as a satisfying life for himself in Israel as a progressive, confrontational Zionist activist. He lectured around the world and became known and admired, especially for leading the effort to oppose the demolition of Palestinian homes that stood in the way of Israeli expansionist and Judaizing plans in Jerusalem, or were carried out as collective punishment of the families of alleged Palestinian terrorists. Despite his oppositional stance and the rightward drift in Israel Jeff has never indicated any defection from his Zionist identity or any intention to become an Israeli expatriate. He still believes that a humane accommodation of Jews and Palestinians is possible, and in the end necessary. Recently he has shifted his hopes for peace away from a decent version of a two-state solution to that of a single binational state, a major modification of the Zionist Project that remains a nightmare scenario for most Israelis and nearly all Zionists, and is viewed as a mission impossible by diplomats and policy experts, although less so than in the past, at least in private.

Back in 1973, at first, I didn't know what to make of these unexpected sentiments of identification with Israel. This mood of attachment didn't persist very long after my return to America, quietly fading away, although never entirely forgotten. Even during this experience of affirming my Jewishness, there were several dark spots. I felt uncomfortable about what seemed a general atmosphere of unconcern about Palestinian wellbeing and aspirations even among these enlightened Israelis. I also reacted somewhat against the accompanying sense of Jewish superiority, taking the form of secularizing the idea of being 'the chosen people,' over-achievers in the world, whether by overcoming constraints on their lives or resulting from a biblically grounded racism that claimed a disproportionate greatness for Jews as measured by achievements in the arts, science, finance, and business, as well as by having created Israel itself, a modernizing powerhouse that stood as a testimony to Jewish talent and resolve. Even if such claims could be validated empirically, their articulation always bothered me, and seemed crassly insensitive to the dangers of linking race and genes to human worth, which Jews more than others should avoid. As the Israeli historian, Shlomo Sand, has demonstrated, these claims of racial superiority rest on false and manipulated claims of genetic linkages between Ashkenazi Jews and biblical era Israelites.

In these still early stages of involvement, my views and outlook were fluid, and probably impressionable because emotionally and intellectually superficial. Although gradually separating myself from the Israeli worldview, I was aware that in the late 1950s, more so than in 2020, that Zionist outlooks had close to a monopoly over the moral space pertaining to the Israel/Palestine struggle. Encroaching on that space with contrary ideas and interpretations seemed certain to engender a furious and discrediting response. In the last few years, attitudes have begun to change due to Trump's one-sided support for Israeli territorial ambitions, Israel's undisguised expansionism and shift from a diplomatic to an apartheid approach to managing Palestinian grievances, and the degree to which Black Lives Matter and Palestinian activists seem now aligned in a common struggle.

Firing an Academic Bullet at the Israel Ship of State

In my early years at Princeton I probably identified myself, at least professionally, as someone who was not a Zionist loyalist by writing

a long article for the *American Journal of International Law* on a raid
by Israel that destroyed 14 civilian planes on the ground at the Beirut
Airport. Israel justified the attack on December 28, 1968 as a lawful
reprisal to a terrorist incident that had occurred two days earlier in Beirut
when an El Al plane was attacked, which was blamed on the Palestinian
Front for the Liberation of Palestine. I argued somewhat legalistically
that since Israel was not acting in self-defense such a reprisal was an unlawful use of force in direct violation of Article 2(4) of the UN Charter.
The Israeli Legal Advisor, later Israel's Permanent Representative at
the UN, Yehuda Blum, wrote a lengthy response in the same journal
challenging my analysis point by point, basically contending that Israel
enjoyed an 'inherent' right of self-defense by virtue of its sovereignty,
and that its attack directed at unoccupied planes was a proportionate response. Of course, legal issues of this nature never get resolved by back
and forth legal debate, and contrasting positions often reveal more about
the political sympathies of the author than the legalities at stake. In my
defense, I would contend that I have consistently opposed *international*
recourses to force that expanded the legalistic interpretations of Charter
guidelines drafted to constrain the discretion of sovereign states to use
force internationally without Security Council authorization.

I acknowledge that such a posture of strict interpretations departs
from my overall view of interpretative flexibility when it comes to international legal obligations, but I think this kind of legalistic exception
is indispensable in the nuclear age, given the mass horrors arising from
modern warfare, as well as the abuses of small states by way of geopolitically motivated interventions. I would support creating exceptions if
in a given context a use of force was convincingly based on a reasonable
claim of necessity by the government of a sovereign state to avoid an imminent or ongoing serious threat to its security. Illustrative instances of
such an exception to strict canons of interpreting Charter norms on claims
to use force would include lending lawfulness to an armed intervention
to prevent or mitigate genocide, or possibly, to address serious instances
of ecocide. But geopolitical manipulations of humanitarian arguments
make it questionable to endorse exceptions to Charter prohibitions on the
use of force. The aggressive attack on Iraq in 2003, which lacked a UN
mandate, was a gross example of a geopolitical undertaking that should
never have happened if the UN Charter had been followed. A subtler manipulation occurred in 2011 when the Security Council was persuaded by
an appeal to the R2P norm by NATO governments to authorize a No Fly
Zone in Libya for the protection of the civilian population of Benghazi,

while the operation carried out was a regime-changing intervention that climaxed with the execution of the Libyan head of state, producing chaos throughout the country that has continued for the ensuing decade.

Meeting Golda Meir

In this period, I was surprised to receive an invitation from Martin Peretz, a prominent intellectual Zionist supporter and publisher of a somewhat liberal magazine, *The New Republic,* to meet with Golda Meir in her hotel suite at the Waldorf Astoria Hotel in NYC. Golda Meir, the only American born Israeli prime minister, was visiting New York to attend the annual UN General Assembly meeting for the political leaders of the world. Golda, as she was called in the pre-'Me-Too' days then prevailing, was engagingly personal and informal in style while being analytically incisive, and uncompromisingly nationalistic in substance, dismissing with a flick of her wrist the fatuousness, in her view, of Palestinian claims to statehood. She articulated for those present a stark contrast between the deeply ethical Israelis and the amoral Palestinians who in her view did not even care for their own children. She echoed for us the spirit of her notoriously nasty and racist remark that, 'peace would come when the Palestinians care more for the lives of their children than the killing of ours.' Even without thought out views at that time, I was offended by her moral arrogance even as I was impressed by her self-confidence, lucidity, and poise. Golda may have looked, as was frequently being said, like the typical Jewish grandmother, but she had a mind and will of steel, which was immediately evident as soon as she started to talk with those of us crowded into her spacious hotel suite, presumably a cheerleading audience. I was an outlier who listened, feeling alienated from the tone and content of what she was saying.

Serving the United Nations

My UN experience led me to an opposite kind of consciousness of what it meant to be Jewish to what I experienced when visiting Israel in 1973. On the one side, I was accused of being biased against Israel, and guilty of what was coming to be known as the New Anti-Semitism, which alleged critics of Israel were hiding hatred of Jews behind a façade of harsh legal, political, and moral criticisms of Israel, a self-proclaimed Jewish state. Critics of Israel, by supposedly holding the country to higher standards than applicable to other states, were guilty of 'Jew hatred.' I found this Zionist pushback entirely disingenuous. For one thing, Israel, more than other states, was brought into being as a legitimate state by favorable action at the UN, which gave the UN a special responsibility to see the process through by rendering justice to the Palestinians. This responsibility remains unfulfilled, and has turned into a ghastly horror for Palestine and Palestinians. By allowing Israel to become a UN member without treating the Palestinian claims equally made the UN complicit in all ensuing developments, including the displacement of the UN by the highly partisan United States. The minimum expectation, given the Arab identity of Palestine in 1947 was to treat the two peoples equally and especially with respect for applicable rights of self-determination. True, Jewish survivors of the Holocaust deserved and needed a secure sanctuary, but that did not justify, after the British Mandate ended, displacing and subjugating the resident, majority population of Palestine that bore no responsibility for the crimes committed against Jews by the Europeans. And the Holocaust could not justify overlooking how the Zionist movement in the 1940s relied on terror tactics to induce the British to give up its mandatory role and entrust the infant UN with working out an equitable accommodation between these two peoples. Unfortunately, the UN, subject to a Western colonialist outlook, gave only scant deference to the idea of self-determination, which was becoming the uber-norm of an emergent new world order that was on the verge of treating colonialist forms of governance as illegitimate.

Another reason for those in the West to single out Israel for criticism was the extent of Western, and especially American, diplomatic and financial support it received, indicators of the extent of its leverage in the West and pointing to its responsibility for much of the turmoil in the region that has devastated the major proximate states of Iraq and Syria and promoted the sanctioning and isolation of Iran. And finally, the Israel/Palestine struggle had already assumed a high-profile international status due to its imposition of apartheid conditions on Palestinians, giving rise to an anti-apartheid opposition not unlike the earlier preoccupation with South African apartheid, which apologists for apartheid similarly argued singled out South Africa for criticism despite the fact that Africans elsewhere on the continent were allegedly worse off. It is relevant to observe that two most globally admired opponents of apartheid, Nelson Mandela and Desmond Tutu, both saw the Israeli treatment of the Palestinian people as a crime in many ways comparable, if not worse, than the Afrikaner treatment of black South Africans.

For me the New Anti-Semitism is a vicious polemical ploy, nothing more, nothing less, which has the unfortunate side-effect of deliberately blurring the boundary between Zionist pro-Israeli propaganda and real anti-Semitism. This way of smearing Israeli critics compounds the long record of Zionist opportunistic relations with anti-Semitism, whether with Nazis to prompt Jews to emigrate to Israel or with evangelical Christians or dictatorial and rightist governments around the world. While smearing critics of Israel's patterns of criminality in abusing the Palestinian people, Zionism has been willing to make opportunistic common cause with those who do in fact espouse hatred of Jews.

A Liberal Stab in the Back: Human Rights Watch

After my appointment by the UN Human Rights Council as Special Rapporteur for Occupied Palestine, I became more visible as a critic of Israel and hence found myself on the radar screen of activist Zionists. As myself a Jew who was so accused, I was also demeaned in Zionist circles as 'a self-hating Jew.' These labels were designed not just to discredit, but also to be hurtful, and were coupled with mean spirited efforts to present my views on other controversial issues out of context so as to make plausible the argument that, besides being an unsavory anti-Semite, I was also a feckless and misguided political leftist. It was the apparent intention of these critics to spin some of my undeniably harsh criticisms of American foreign policy to make them appear as either outlandish or as lending support to terrorism. Although I somewhat expected such allegations to be associated with any effort at the UN to hold Israel accountable for violations of human rights and international law, I was taken aback by the extent to which even such blatant character assassination was accepted as valid by those whom I believed knew better. It disappointed me that U.S. and British Commonwealth diplomats from white settler societies with liberal profiles at the UN, and even NGOs that prided themselves on their apolitical objectivity when it came to human rights, sought to discredit by false allegations those with the temerity to call attention to Israeli abuses of the Palestinian people or violations of human rights.

In some ways my most disillusioning experience was with Human Rights Watch (HRW) and its director, Ken Roth. It was so bad because I expected better, suggesting I had not yet escaped altogether from my illusion that those who base their reputation on the embrace of liberal values would act in an ethical manner in concrete situations. The whole incident is too long to recount in detail, but sufficiently disillusioning that it became a defining part of my late life learning experience about the hypocritical core of liberalism as a stance toward the world. I found this disconcerting because HRW did engage in criticism of Israeli policies and practices, and itself suffered some pushback because of this, perhaps explaining why they would want to create distance between their approach and mine, which was interpreted as one of solidarity with the Palestinian struggle.

Unlike HRW, UN Watch (UNW) did not hide its Zionist dedication to Israel behind a liberal pretension of objectivity. In brief, UNW, the bulldog ultra-Zionist NGO stationed in Geneva that had never missed an opportunity to taunt and defame me, wrote a letter to HRW indicating it was shocked that someone with my anti-Semitic views would be allowed to become a committee member of an HRW entity. In fact, I was only a nominal member of an inconsequential Santa Barbara Committee of HRW, which I joined mainly because of friendship with its chair. For similar reasons, I had encouraged a former celebrity student to support HRW. He became a donor, a board member, and enjoyed exceptional credibility as a leading member of the royal family of an Arab country. After HRW received the UNW message the chair of the local committee was immediately instructed by NY headquarters to remove me from the committee, and advised to invoke a technical rule about a conflict of interest resulting from my current role as UN Special Rapporteur on Palestine, then in its fourth year. When informed, I said okay, and thought no more about it until the next day when UN Watch issued a self-congratulatory press release claiming a victory, saying that due to their initiative I was stripped of my position because my anti-Semitic views were even too much for a liberal organization like to HRW to abide. I felt betrayed by HRW giving credence to UN Watch's initiative and by the local HRW branch's failure to inform me honestly about what led HRW to act as it did when it requested my resignation.

I was also stunned that my Santa Barbara friend had not been straight with me in her communication, although when confronted, she apologized. Disappointed but still not completely disillusioned, I made what I thought was a routine request, asking that HRW should clarify its action by publicly indicating that my removal from the committee was based on their rule governing conflict of interests. I was outraged when told that Ken Roth refused to issue a clarifying statement, thus being content to leave the impression in the public domain that the interpretation of the incident by UNW was indeed accurate. I was told that several senior staff members at HRW urged Ken to change his view, but he refused. I happened to be on a panel with Roth dealing with Syria at the University of Denver a month or so later, and I repeated my request, which he brushed aside with the comment, 'no one pays any attention to what they say,' which was a perverse form of reassurance considering that HRW had itself paid attention at my expense. Roth refused to listen further to my reasons for wishing the public record to be cleaned up.

In retrospect, I realized that HRW, or at least its Executive Director, actually agreed with the complaint of UNW or feared funding consequences if he failed to act, given the strong Zionist presence on the HRW Board. Roth was undoubtedly relieved to have a technical justification for doing what they likely wished to do for substantive or ideological reasons. My concern, which turned out to be justified, was that my reputation would be somewhat further harmed by the way the incident was handled. UNW, as should have been fully anticipated, continued to publicize their spin on the incident widely, without the slightest pushback by HRW. This did in fact give objectors to my talks and participation in conferences a line of attack that lent a certain quality of reasonableness to their objections—if I was too extremist even for the supposedly most liberal of human rights NGOs, HRW, then innocent audiences should be protected against my hateful views and it was reasonable to deny me a platform.

Damage to my reputation is not a momentous issue in the larger scheme of things, but its unfolding did reveal the way critics of Israel more vulnerable than I were being blacklisted and punished in various ways, usually covertly in the course of a calm, private discussion without requiring explanation or justification. After this experience, I never wanted anything further to do with HRW, and will not change my mind so long as the HRW leadership remains the same, despite applauding much of their work.

The Closing Circle of Engagement

There was no clear path that led me to become so centrally involved with *activist*, as distinct from *academic*, support for the Palestinian struggle. It was one thing to write scholarly articles noticed by only a few colleagues with similar concerns, and quite another to declare myself in essential solidarity with the Palestinian national struggle in settings that attracted public attention. From my interpretative standpoint Israel's policies and practices warranted a posture of relentless criticism due to the reactionary manner in which the Zionist Project was evolving at the expense of Palestinian expectations grounded in law and morality, as well as many agreements that called for respect of Palestine rights, which Israel had itself accepted. Such behavior on my part implied a willingness to touch the third rail of American politics. I had long been

alive to these inhibiting realities, and had kept a safe distance from political engagements that were transparent shows of direct support for the
Palestinian national movement until the 1980s, when in my late 50s. I had
already been scorched to some extent by my earlier engagements with
Vietnam, and especially Iran, and didn't relish the idea of being burned
alive at the stake of Zionist versions of 'political correctness.' And yet,
without being pushed, I ended up doing what I had long avoided.

I have often asked myself, 'Why?' Friendship was a factor, above
all with Edward Said. With Edward, it was the combined strength of his
arguments and the force of his personality. After the 1967 War when he
initially became himself publicly engaged with the Palestinian national
movement, and was soon identified as the lead Palestinian intellectual
in American and European settings to challenge the pro-Israeli consensus through a series of well-argued books, especially *The Question of
Palestine (1978)*. This book contained a devastating critique of Zionism's
impact upon Palestine, a harrowing account of Palestinian victimization,
and a humanely crafted view of how these two peoples might be led to
live decently together in peaceful coexistence. For this to happen Said
insisted that a spirit of equality would have to pervade any political arrangements to be agreed upon. Said coupled his depiction of the injustices
of Palestinian dispossession with a recognition that the Jewish presence
in the country had to be accepted and no longer challenged. At the same
time Said believed that a sustainable peace could only be achieved if
Palestinian victimization was fully and formally acknowledged by Israel
in a format that was open and public. Although Said did not put forward
a proposal, his approach, if acted upon, might have led to establishing
the kind of truth and reconciliation commission that many felt smoothed
the transition in South Africa after the collapse of apartheid. From the
perspective of the present, it is obvious that Said's vision failed to take
full account of the expansionist priorities and geopolitical complicity of
the United States, as well as the failures of Palestinian tactics and leadership, especially the failure to put forward their own version of a peace
proposal. This combination of factors, abetted by regional developments
that made Arab governments, already wary of their own citizens, also
wary of the Palestinian struggle and open to reconciliation with Israel,
worrying that Palestinian success would lead to democratizing pressures
in their own countries. The result was a new, if fragile, balance of forces
favorable to the pursuit of maximalist Zionist goals as put into practice
by right-wing leadership in Israel, and since 2017 greatly facilitated

by Washington's endorsement of the Netanyahu agenda regardless of international law or the UN consensus.

Said's position in American intellectual life was complex as he gained prominence as the leading Palestinian spokesperson in the West without losing his status as one of the most influential and admired interpreters of culture and literature active in American academic life. His early work illuminated the writings and relevance of Joseph Conrad. Such a focus on this particular writer, who illuminated the dark corners of the colonialist mentality, could be viewed as anticipatory of his more widely read later political writing. Said's primary point of departure was always culture, broadly conceived as reflecting the postmodern academic turn that became highly attentive to social and political readings of primary literary texts. His breakthrough book was, of course, *Orientalism*, which, as he delighted telling friends, had been rejected by 22 publishers before being taken on by Pantheon Books, and then becoming one of the most discussed and broadly influential books of the last century. Edward, although born a Christian, was an unabashed secular humanist by the time I knew him. He had a long and deep engagement with European literature and classical music and was himself a first-class performing pianist who also enjoyed writing sensitive critical reviews of classical musical performances, especially opera.

Although he served for some years as a member of the Palestinian National Council, and put up with 'the Old Man' as he and others affectionately referred to Arafat, he came to have increasingly strong principled and tactical disagreements with Palestine's approach to ending the conflict as carried into practice by the umbrella organization, the Palestine Liberation Organization or PLO. He felt, correctly in my view, that Arafat's deference to and trust in the good will of Washington was a huge mistake and detrimental to Palestinian prospects for a sustainable peace. The accuracy of this perception was later confirmed by the carefully researched scholarship of Rashid Khalidi and Jeremy Hammond, which demonstrate the covert obstructionist role consistently played by U.S. diplomacy at all stages of the conflict. Such behavior served Zionist priorities that sought time and delay, enabling Israel to pursue its expansionist territorial goals with respect to 'the promised land' to the point that a truly sovereign Palestinian state became impractical. Although Said initially endorsed the 1988 PLO decision to normalize relations with Israel if it ended the occupation by withdrawing to 1967 borders, allowing a Palestinian state to be established, he soon repudiated such an approach. Said began to insist that a single secular bi-national state with full protection and equality of human rights for all its inhabitants was the only path to a true peace as distinct from a ceasefire misrepresented by diplomats and media as 'peace.' Edward came to believe that a two-state approach, which Israel made increasingly clear it would not accept, would perpetuate inequality and keep the struggle alive, intending merely to obtain a ceasefire rather than a mutually acceptable and sustainable solution to the long Palestinian ordeal.

Edward was passionate about his commitments, as well as his likes and dislikes among public intellectuals. He was harshly critical of liberal Zionists who claimed a moral outlook but were ready in practice to accommodate Israeli expansionism and its accompanying abuse of Palestinians. In this vein, he regarded Michael Walzer as the poster child of moral hypocrisy, one who hid his Zionist biases behind a smokescreen of ethical abstractions that minimized the injustices inflicted on the Palestinian people. Walzer also welcomed teaming up with leading Zionist intellectual figures, none more than with Bernard Lewis, a mean-spirited polemicist who relied on scholarly arrogance to heap scorn on those with whom he disagreed, including myself.

I am reminded of a similar kind of social failure involving the talented Lebanese Middle East scholar, Fouad Ajami. Fouad originally became a visiting faculty member at Princeton due to my enthusiastic endorsement. Some years later he changed his outlook on Middle East issues and American foreign policy in a manner that aligned with Washington geopolitics as shaped by the neoconservative movement. In a twist, he soon became the darling of the Near East Studies faculty, and shortly after Fouad became the most trusted Arab voice on CNN, as well as a frequent guest on other widely watched TV shows. He became 'America's leading Arab voice,' trusted and invoked by the political right.

I cannot remember how I came to know Fouad Ajami and become his patron and good friend in the early 1970s. He was a gifted academic interpreter of the Arab political consciousness despite having lived his entire life in America. My former wife, Florence, and I became such close friends with Fouad that when we went on short trips to do lectures or attend conferences, Fouad stayed at our house, caring for our children, Dimitri and Noah, one of the few people we would trust with such a precious challenge. I mention this personal detail because it indicates how close we were prior to Fouad's 'conversion.'

In this period of close friendship, at Fouad's request, I arranged a social meeting with Edward and Eqbal Ahmad, fostering relationships which went well until they didn't. The break came when Fouad some months later indicated his unwillingness to criticize Israel on controversial issues, which then involved Israeli attacks on Lebanon and U.S. military assistance to Tel Aviv. I remember Eqbal, always a peacemaker, suggesting that even if there was disagreement on political issues, friendship should not be sacrificed. Fouad was unmoved, declaring that he no longer wanted contact. Fouad's family came from a Shiite village in southern Lebanon with relatives raising tobacco and owning some land in Palestine that they were accused of selling to the Jewish Agency in charge of acquiring land for Jewish immigrant settlers. Fouad, along with many Lebanese, blamed the Palestinians, and specifically the Palestinian Liberation Organization (PLO) for overriding Lebanese sovereignty and undermining its national security by provoking Israel, a dynamic that he believed justified the 1982 Israeli attack and occupation. These events were accompanied by the expulsion of the PLO leadership and fighters from Lebanon as well as leading to the horrifying Sabra and Shatila refugee camp massacres in the aftermath of Israel's occupation and days after the related assassination of the Maronite leader, Geymayel.

It was never entirely clear what motivated Fouad's turn to the right, although it was linked in various ways to his disillusionment with the Palestinian national movement and likely the effect of the Palestinian presence in southern Lebanon. Whatever the explanation, our friendship waned, although without any clear break. Fouad became an outspoken ally of Zionist members of the Princeton Community, including the main figures in the Near East Studies Center, with the backing of the influential anthropologist, Clifford Geertz, a social scientist with a permanent appointment at the Institute for Advanced Studies and Fouad's friend. Geertz was rumored to be on the MacArthur Foundation selection committee that awarded the coveted 'genius award,' and Fouad was a surprise recipient. This spectacular recognition of scholarly excellence completely subsidized five years of non-teaching academic activity. It was in effect an extended sabbatical leave writ large in neon letters. There is no doubt that Fouad was intellectually gifted, but that his work at that stage warranted this level of recognition was doubtful, and made skeptics assume that his swerve to the right politically, and especially with respect to Israel, was an untold part of the genius award story.

After 9/11 Fouad even became a White House consultant, including an advisor apparently valued by Dick Cheney, giving his opinions weight on such questions of policy as to how to respond to the Arab World and how to counter the rise of political Islam. He offered informed commentary that reinforced the worldview and responses of the presidency of George W. Bush, lending his support to the global war on terror, including the attack on Iraq in 2003. Edward was angered by Fouad's role in legitimating hostility to Islam, affirmation of Israel, and his seemingly fawning submission to the political whims of the militarist wing of the American political establishment. He sharply criticized his role in public, implying that Fouad had become 'an Uncle Abu,' a demeaning illusion to Uncle Tom, insinuating Fouad's complicity in the Palestinian tragedy and the general suppression of Arab aspirations.

A few years after Fouad resigned his position at Princeton, long after our friendship had lapsed, I accidentally ran into Fouad while walking on a Washington street. We greeted one another as if still friends, and stopped for coffee with a shared intention to avoid our political differences, but intentions rarely carry the day if such differences touch our lives. Fouad broke the political ice by dramatically declaring that Edward was trying to get him killed. I expressed doubt, saying that I could not believe this. Fouad elaborated that Edward was giving talks in Egypt and elsewhere in the Middle East, including Lebanon, in which he criticized Fouad by name. Edward inflamed Arab audiences by insisting that Fouad was a liability in the struggle to realize legitimate Arab objectives, centering on self-determination for the Palestinian people. It was this kind of 'loose talk' in the region, Fouad insisted, that could get one assassinated. We parted without any pretension of renewing our once intimate friendship. My earlier quasi-mentor role in Fouad's pre-conversion social and professional life had become a distant and fading memory.

Fouad's death made visible the polarized impressions that he left behind. For his high-profile admirers, Fouad was the most trustworthy Arab voice of his generation, informed, incisive, moderate, sympathetic with Israel, and even favorable to regime-changing U.S. interventions, Westernized, yet rooted in Arab culture. Fouad became consistently supportive of the American foreign policy agenda, whatever it involved, whether it was celebrating Israel as the only democracy in the Middle East or acting as a Third World cheerleader for George W. Bush's disastrous 2003 regime-changing war of aggression against Iraq. For his critics, Fouad was indeed an Uncle Abu sellout, seeking fame and fortune from the imperial elites of the West and turning his back on the suffering inflicted on Arabs, even by Arabs on Arabs as in Saudi Arabia. In one prominent instance seemingly counter to his new orientation, Fouad refused to condemn the stoning to death of a woman in Saudi

Arabia for alleged adultery, claiming an unwillingness to pass judgment on non-Western civilizational practices. Personally, I never wanted to accept the loss of this close and once enjoyable friendship although realizing it couldn't continue. Parenthetically, it made me appreciate that genuine friendship, as distinct from collegial and professional connections, was not easy to achieve at Princeton, and should be valued when it was. The loss of this true friend on the altar of political differences was for me always bittersweet, an occasion of personal regret.

It was this patchwork of friendships and antagonisms that formed the background of my public political engagement with Zionism on one side and the Palestinian national movement on the other. In some ways Edward and Fouad represented anti-types whose respective brilliance of exposition and opposed commitments helped frame my own groping for a legally and morally sound position. As time passed, I followed Edward's lead and felt Fouad had crossed the battle lines to lend his services without reservation to the pursuit of a reactionary foreign policy in the Middle East, including the invasion of Iraq and support for Israel, a disquieting realization.

I have no way of gauging the career and personal effects of my dual posture of hostility to the Zionist agenda and sympathy for the Palestinian struggle, but I have enough evidence to convince me that there were adverse consequences in academia, the media, and the public sector. I received sufficient confirming feedback for these perceptions of pushback, not only in North America, but throughout the West, to make me feel that this assessment is essentially accurate, and not fueled by paranoia.

Although she privately shared my views, Hilal felt strongly that I should be more guarded in my criticism of Israel and Zionism for prudential reasons. On several occasions I respected these feelings, and refrained, or at least softened, my anti-Zionist responses to unfolding events. As I have contrasted Ajami and Said as regards mainstream standards of inclusion and exclusion, I would cast myself as Alan Dershowitz's polar opposite. Dershowitz, despite his alignments with the most aggressive forms of settler Zionism, somewhat disguised his extremist views behind self-validating claims of domestic liberalism, remaining a welcome visitor at the White House and regular commentator on CNN. He has retained this 'credibility,' maybe even enhancing it, by emerging as one of the most prominent and credible supporters of the Trump presidency among self-proclaimed Democrats. My own experience before and after encounters with these American Zionist 'first defenders' indicates I enjoyed mainstream access before and virtual exclusion since. What makes this experience of wider interest than personal pique is that it didn't happen after my controversial opposition to U.S. policies in Vietnam and even Iran, but only after I entered that fiery zone where even angels fear to tread!

Anyone who claims there are no double standards when it comes to dissenting from the mainstream views on Israel/Palestine should consider this contrast between myself and Dershowitz, or for that matter any pro and con pairing when it comes it comes to issues Israel cares about, including members of Congress who can be blacklisted in American politics forever just for making moderate criticisms of Israeli lobbying tactics or complaining about the level of American military assistance, while their polar opposites, extreme advocates of Zionist goals and Israeli solidarity are elevated to the highest levels of political credibility and influence. Nikki Haley, the former UN ambassador in the first years of the Trump presidency is an excellent example of the latter, even emerging as a future possible Republican presidential candidate partly on the basis of her UN-bashing and slash-and-burn defense of Israel's wrongdoing.

Actually, I have not minded my exclusion from the corridors of power. I never liked dealing with the mainstream media, which consistently pressured me to tone down my opinions or wasted hours of my time for the sake of including a single out-of-context, discrediting sentence or phrase in a feature story. Since becoming a media pariah in the U.S., I now am only approached either by those associated with the alternative online media in the West or by media outlets from other parts of the world, often in countries whose governments are at odds with Washington or Tel Aviv. This experience seems worthy of notice to illustrate the systematic rightward trajectory of the mainstream media, which reflects the broader trends in American politics but also shows the accentuation of this slant if Zionist toes are stepped upon.

By Way of Experience

My more direct experience of the Palestinian ordeal came in stages. Just as I discovered that I had unknown affinities when in direct contact with the reality of a Jewish state, I found out that I was moved to tears by experiencing indirectly the suffering inflicted on the Palestinian people by the occupiers of their land. I went to the West Bank in the early 1970s as part of a Ford Foundation project investigating life under Israeli occupation. I was expected to consider the occupation from the perspective of international humanitarian law, and ended up writing two articles that appeared in the *Harvard Journal of International Law*, one of several collaborations with Burns Weston, a friend and fellow McDougal acolyte who had a notable career as a scholar and had developed a widely respected human rights center at the University of Iowa School of Law. Our first article produced an acidic response by a political science professor at Rutgers, Michael Curtis, who turned out to be a protégé of Bernard Lewis, and wrote critically in a condescending tone that emulated Lewis's style. While visiting towns in the West Bank we met with mayors who had been shot with live ammunition by Israeli security forces. We actually witnessed an incident in which IDF soldiers were chasing Palestinian youths, firing weapons, although we were never able to confirm whether live ammunition was being used.

I came away feeling that Palestinian life under Israeli occupation was brutal in this pre-Oslo period, when the West Bank as a whole was directly under unified Israeli military rule, justified by the claim by its legal experts that, since the sovereignty of the West Bank was 'disputed,' Israel was not obliged to comply with the Fourth Geneva Convention, devoted to specifying the obligations of international humanitarian law as it related to belligerent occupation. By relying on sophistic reasoning Israel claimed the discretion to ignore the international insistence that the West Bank, along with Gaza and East Jerusalem, were 'occupied territories' according to international law, and that this required Israel, as occupier, to uphold international humanitarian law—including an obligation not to alter in any way the nature of the civilian society being temporarily occupied. As should be understood, international law is often defied by governments if there is no sufficient political will available to ensure its implementation, but the prolonged occupation combined with the covert and insidious settlements policies that violated the letter of Article 49(6) of the Fourth Geneva Convention made the Israeli abuse of its occupation role particularly flagrant. This reality epitomizes the Palestinian tragedy. International law sides with the Palestinians, but sufficient political will needed to implement its rules is absent, being effectively neutralized by Israel and the United States.

In the background of this debate was the contested meaning of Security Council Resolution 242, which seemed on its face to call for an Israeli withdrawal from all territories occupied in the 1967 War, but which Israel claimed depended on prior negotiations to fix permanent borders and resolve the refugee issue. I would come to the view that only high paid or ideologically inclined lawyers could so misinterpret the obvious intention of 242, which was to deny Israel any lasting benefit of acquiring Palestinian territory by force. Not only has Israel refused to withdraw after the passage of more than 50 years, it has made a meaningful withdrawal a practical impossibility by constructing more than 200 unlawful settlements, some heavily inhabited, all over the West Bank, expanding their size, population, and township properties continuously with some announced future goals projecting a Jewish population in these territories as high as two million. Settlement expansion is reinforced by additional territorial encroachments including a separation wall and an elaborate network of 'Jews Only' roads. Additionally, the settler movement and annexationists have steadily gained leverage within Israeli domestic politics and make no secret of their unalterable opposition to the establishment of *any* Palestinian state. During the last years the endorsement of these provocative developments by the Trump presidency, together with strong moves toward Israeli accommodation with the major Arab countries including the recent normalization agreements with Israel by the UAE and Bahrain, has made Israel feel so secure that Palestine is no longer a divisive issue among Israel's main political parties except in rare circumstances. One such circumstance was the 2020 annexation debate about claiming de jure sovereignty over those portions of the occupied West Bank where the settlements are located.

My next important direct experience of Israel/Palestine was a visit to Gaza in the mid-1990s to attend the first (and maybe the last!) international human rights conference ever held in this long tormented, crowded, and impoverished territory. I came with Eqbal Ahmad and we stayed in Marna House, a guest house humanized for me in Gloria Emerson's fine account of her year spent in Gaza published in a book titled simply, *Gaza*. Eqbal was substituting for Edward Said who had been invited to be the keynote speaker but was unable to obtain a visa due to objections not by Israel, but in this instance from the Palestinian Authority. Eqbal gave a stirring speech that doubled as a lecture on the failure of Palestinian diplomacy at Oslo, and was generally critical of the Palestinian approach to their struggle, both with respect to diplomacy and resistance. He contrasted the professionalism of Israeli diplomats with the emotional flights of fancy of their Palestinian counterparts, which ended up producing agreements that were good for Israel and bad for Palestine. Although not quite repudiating the Oslo framework as Edward certainly would have done, Eqbal criticized the text that guided the diplomacy. He took especial note of its failure to affirm Palestine's right of self-determination, and the horrible effects of dividing the

West Bank into three administrative zones to reconcile Israeli security arrangements with direct control over its unlawful settlements. Such Balkanization was further aggravated by numerous checkpoints throughout the West Bank greatly inhibiting Palestinian freedom of movement and subjecting Palestinians to long daily waits that were humiliating and often physically abusive. Eqbal also criticized Palestinian recourse to armed struggle, arguing that suicide bombing and terrorism were counterproductive gestures of resistance for the Palestinians. Instead, he counseled the Palestinians to engage in popular mobilization and have recourse to large-scale nonviolent tactics, ignoring the fact that when the Palestinians resorted to nonviolent resistance they had to face violent repression rather than reciprocal Israel gestures pointing toward a possible accommodation. Eqbal, as a certified Third World progressive activist, could get away with a presentation that talked down to his Palestinian audience in a manner that progressive Westerners would not dare do. In fairness, his humor and rhetorical flair distracted the attention of most from the arrogance of his argument.

The conference in Gaza City also gave us a taste of Palestinian factionalism. Arafat had reportedly felt insulted because he had not been invited to open the proceedings. He would not agree to meet with us, two of the principal speakers, despite the fact that we had previously been welcomed by him in a long, informal meeting in Beirut. Among the prominent features of the event, aside from Israel allowing it to happen despite Gaza being then subject to a harsh direct form of military occupation, was the participation of several Israeli academics and NGO human rights experts. I was apalled by the unanticipated sight of Israeli armored vehicles slowly patrolling the streets of Gaza City with manned machine guns seemingly ready to mow down civilian protesters. It gave me an eerie feeling of what this kind of occupation meant day by day for Gazans, both psychologically and physically. It differed dramatically from the less intrusive occupation imposed on the West Bank.

Another impression that stayed with me was the runway near the border set up only for Palestinians seeking permission to cross into Israel for work or medical treatment. The access corridor that must be passed by Palestinians to reach the Israel border personnel was completely hemmed in by wire meshing with a ceiling so low that anyone approaching the window where their IDs and work permits were cleared was forced to walk in a humiliating deeply stooped position. Israelis, when asked about the corridor responded defensively. They claimed the wire meshing was a reasonable security precaution, supposedly making it almost impossible for a Palestinian to draw a gun and shoot. It seemed to me, then and now, that this setup was not for security, but to drive home to Palestinians a stark message of subjugation. An armed Palestinian could have kneeled in the passageway, and fired shots without difficulty, but to approach the Israeli monitoring window in this stooped posture of a supplicant was an unmistakable way of inscribing inferiority.

Fact Finding and Faultfinding

My next opportunity to be engaged directly with the Palestinian ordeal was in 2000 in the form of an invitation from Mary Robinson, former President of Ireland and then UN High Commissioner for Human Rights, to join John Dugard and Kamal Hossein as members of a three-person fact finding inquiry into a variety of allegations associated with Israel's administration of Gaza. The focus of our inquiry mission was to investigate charges that Israel, in exercising its administrative control over Gaza, relied on excessive force, collective punishment, and oppressive tactics in violation of the Fourth Geneva Convention governing Belligerent Occupation. Prior to embarking on the mission, we were asked to come to Geneva to be presented to the Human Rights Council. John Dugard was a well-regarded South African jurist admired for his defense of human rights and the rule of law during the apartheid era in his country. Kamal Hossein was a lawyer who had been Foreign Minister of Bangladesh shortly after its political independence and was well-known and respected in UN circles, especially as a result of his recent role as UN Special Envoy to Afghanistan. As these individuals were introduced by the High Commissioner at a plenary session of the Human Rights Council, there was only praise voiced, but when my name was mentioned, the Israeli representative asked the chair to be recognized, despite Israel not being a member of the Council and its most embittered critic.

The Israeli diplomat indicated opposition to the launching of an inquiry as a gratuitous insult to Israel. He complained that Israel was being singled out for scrutiny despite the neglect by the UN of far worse situations in the world. In addition, he argued that my inclusion in the mission was particularly unacceptable. To make his point he criticized a recent article of mine, alleging bias, published in MERIP that criticized Israel's handling of recent Palestinian resistance activities from the perspective of international law. In the article I was especially critical of Israel's reliance on lethal force in suppressing protests surrounding Ariel Sharon's provocative visit to the Al Aqsa Mosque in 2000, a dynamic that led directly and predictably to the outbreak of the Second Intifada. Mary Robinson responded to the criticism by pointing out that my academic credentials were more than sufficient qualification for this assignment.

It turned out to be a very taxing yet worthwhile undertaking. I had known John Dugard since he showed me around in Johannesburg, including the Soweto Township, back in 1968 during my first visit to South Africa. I was in South Africa on an earlier international mission, although not connected to the UN. I had been appointed by the International Commission of Jurists to be an Official Observer of a political trial devoted to the resistance activities of 35 South West African (Namibia after independence) leaders who were charged with a variety of crimes. John was someone I respected for his integrity, decency, intelligence, and public commitment to the protection of human rights. I also liked his friendly, open manner tinged with a gentle ironic touch. From my law perspective, John was somewhat too legalistic, making overly careful efforts to separate political preferences and moral convictions from his legal analysis, fostering the illusion that this is possible and desirable. Hence, at that stage I regarded John as a legal positivist with a soul, although his close contact over the years with the abusive Israeli regime of control gradually led him to become forthright in condemning Israeli behavior without hiding his political and moral judgments behind a curtain of legal technicalities.

Kamal Hossein became an instant friend and spontaneous soul mate. Kamal worked skillfully and effectively to shape a consensus among the three of us. The whole experience was greatly enhanced, logistically and substantively, by the enthusiasm, informed intelligence, and efficiency of the UN Staff person, Darka Topali, who lifted our confidence higher than heaven by christening us 'the dream team.' Over the years I have grown accustomed to being on the receiving end of both undeserved insults and excessive compliments, being defamed by some, while overly praised for courage and accomplishment by others. Actually, I conceived of my contribution as nothing more than an honest and conscientious bearing of witness to what I observed and believed to be true and right, somewhat enhanced by my professional background and interest in conceptual and normative clarity. It was this sense of my work in this and other controversial issues centering on a blending of professional confidence and engaged citizenship that allowed me to fend off even the most demeaning insults without losing sleep. It also avoided pretexts for vanity as I fended off the praise of others as nothing more than an expression of gratitude for truth-telling and witnessing in settings where many qualified experts shied away because of the controversial effects of being seen as a critic of Israel's behavior.

The three of us on the mission got along extremely well in our joint effort to seek the best possible understanding of the situation in Gaza, as well as holding a series of meetings in our hotel, The American Colony, situated in East Jerusalem. We met with a variety of relevant Israeli personalities in our genuine attempt to understand both sides. These meetings included such leading Israeli academicians as Ruth Gavison and David Kretchmar. They were both liberal critics of Israeli occupation policies, yet supported the Zionist Project and shared what they told us was the near universal Israeli view that the return of any large number of Palestinian refugees to their pre-1967 places of residence in Israel was a dealbreaker when it came to finding a peaceful solution. We talked together during our visit as if was still possible in 2000 to believe that a Palestinian sovereign state could be established via Oslo diplomacy and political compromise reached on issues separating the two sides.

Even then I was not comfortable with presupposing that the Israeli leadership really was willing to agree to arrangements that would establish a sustainable peace. My own belief, which I shared privately with Kamal, was that Israel would insist on an unreasonable level of security for itself, which would by its nature entail permanently unacceptable levels of insecurity for and antagonism toward the Palestinians. I regarded Israel's true intentions were conveyed by the practice in Israeli internal discourse of referring to the West Bank as 'Judea and Samaria,' that is, as integral to Israel's purported biblical entitlement, and dooming the stubbornly held international conviction that the only solution was based on a territorial partition.

When it came to the preparation of our report to the UN Human Rights Council, we had no trouble reaching a consensus on the major allegations. We found the evidence of Israel's deliberate reliance on excessive force and collective punishment in Gaza so overwhelming and manifest as to not require much discussion, calling only for an effective presentation of the evidence that led us to reach these conclusions.

Our report was completed, submitted, and accepted, and our mission was viewed by the Office of the High Commissioner as a success, undoubtedly enhanced by Darka's unfailing enthusiasm and promotional efforts. John was made Chair of the inquiry, undoubtedly a stepping-stone to his being selected the following year as Special Rapporteur for Occupied Palestine.

Our worst moments during the mission, from the perspective of personal safety, occurred in the large Khan Younis refugee camp in southern Gaza. We visited the main hospital where there were new patients present who had been seriously wounded during the prior 24 hours. Near the end of our visit a shooting incident occurred involving an Israeli military outpost that was close enough to be in range of a strong stone thrower. Several of the injured Palestinians at the hospital were in serious condition and seemed sedated. We were told by the attending doctors that Israel had used some kind of new ammunition that inflicted wounds never seen before and which were very difficult to treat by conventional medicine. As we left, walking around the camp and talking to some of the older residents, we noticed that several children, none over 12, were throwing small stones in the direct of the outpost. The stones posed no risk of injury whatsoever to the Israeli soldiers, but it was treated by the outpost as a provocation. This mild act of symbolic resistance by children was met by the soft clicking sound of bullets fired by Israeli soldiers. The quietness of the bullets made the threat seem unreal to us. Our UN companions knew otherwise, and quickly herded us behind a barrier to safety. We had to leave Khan Younis before finding out whether any of the children that had provoked the Israeli response were killed or wounded. It left a vivid impression of the pervasive asymmetric interplay of symbolic resistance by Palestinian civilians and lethal violence by Israeli military personnel that informed the daily life of occupiers and occupied alike.

After our mission we went our separate ways, though my path has crossed John Dugard's quite often. John has gone onto to hold important positions in high prestige institutional settings, and Kamal too has been active within his own country and internationally. Actually, it has been Darka, John's assistant during his six years as Special Rapporteur, who provided the social glue that kept each of us aware of what we were all doing. Although we had encountered a terrible human ordeal in Gaza, it was subsequently to get worse as I discovered during the next decade when I took over from John in 2008 as UN Special Rapporteur on Human Rights in Occupied Palestine.

Special Rapporteur (2008-2014)

John Dugard served as Special Rapporteur for the UN Human Rights Council in the period of 2001-2008. John's reports were always well crafted, and toward the end of his second term, put forward well-reasoned arguments that reached important conclusions. His reports portrayed the occupation of the West Bank and Gaza as characteristic of European colonial structures and as dependent on apartheid structures for control of the Palestinian territory it was administering. It requires little knowledge and less imagination to anticipate that Israel would react with anger. As Dugard's second term as Special Rapporteur was drawing to a close, I became aware that Israel was lobbying hard to find a compliant successor to Dugard who would diligently overlook Israel's flagrant, daily violations of international law. Yet, this campaign was not at all assured of success due to the political atmosphere of the Human Rights Council, one of the few political arenas in the UN System where it was hard for the West to exert sufficient influence to control politically sensitive appointments.

It was against this background that I received the first of several phone calls from the Office of the High Commissioner in Geneva inquiring whether I would accept an appointment as Special Rapporteur for Occupied Palestine, if the Human Rights Council agreed to the recommendation of the Selection Committee and it received necessary support from the President of the Council. At that time, SR applications by candidates themselves were not a requirement for an appointment, and the selection process seemed less transparent and merit-based than it has become in the course of the last decade. Candidates now must complete comprehensive applications forms. These are then vetted by a committee of UN ambassadors representing member governments of the HRC. If a candidate makes the short list, she or he is then interviewed by the whole committee. On this basis, a rank ordering of the top candidates is given to the President of the HRC who has the authority to make the final decision, which was also the procedure in my case. Because the President's decision is discretionary, it can be influenced by mounting significant pressures on the government to which the President owes allegiance, especially if that government is internationally indebted or needs loans.

Hilal, of course, knew about the calls coming from Geneva, but I told her not to worry, that the opposition from Israel and the U.S. would destroy whatever chances I might have had. I believed this. Yet the calls kept coming, and soon I was informed that I had indeed been selected with no dissenting votes by the Council meeting as a whole. Only Canada abstained after having spoken unfavorably about my qualifications for the position. I am almost sure that if the U.S. had not withdrawn a few years earlier from membership in the HRC, my candidacy would have been blocked by this single negative vote. It felt somewhat awkward to be selected in view of my early assurances that it would never happen. Despite some ambivalence, I was convinced that I had to accept the challenge posed by this unpaid and demanding position, which I expected would subject me to vitriolic criticism, not only of my reports, but directed at my character and scholarly Integrity. At the same time, I was pleased that I had overcome the obstacles to my selection. I only learned later on that an intense Israeli lobbying campaign against me was thwarted by a coalition of non-Western governments, responsive to the wishes of the Palestinian Authority, which strongly backed my appointment.

I encountered hostility from the moment my appointment became known. I expected sharp criticism from American and Israeli sources. John Bolton, then George W. Bush's ambassador at the UN, obviously regarded my appointment as a suitable occasion on which to vent his rage. Bolton described me as 'a fruit cake,' not with any intention of praising me as a holiday delicacy but to convey the impression that my views were so bizarre as to be nutty as well as fruity, although he did not specify exactly what led him to such a conclusion. He went on to say that my appointment exhibited exactly the kind of action that made sane and reasonable people view the UN as a rotten organization.

After my appointment was formally announced, I received a variety of private non-congratulatory messages, directed at my blog or email servers, which contained crude allegations along with threats. Typically, I was called 'a Jew hater,' sometimes reinforced by hate language and death threats. I downplayed these unpleasant side effects of the UN appointment without attempting any response or seeking the advice of friends. Above all, I didn't want to worry Hilal who intensely disliked this kind of public calumny and was hoping, in my early years as Special Rapporteur, that I would react to the frustrations of the position, which included inefficient help from the Geneva support staff, by resigning in protest.

Strangely, my initial troubles quickly multiplied, and were as much, or more so, related to my Palestinian backers, whom I deeply angered in my very first appearance at a meeting of the HRC in Geneva in the Fall of 2008. For political reasons motivated by my desire to get away from the limited mandate that only considered Israeli violations of human rights law and international humanitarian law, I proposed widening the mandate to include Palestinian violations. I erroneously thought it would be welcomed and fair to enlarge my mandate in this manner.

To my surprise this proposal, seeming so reasonable to me and likely to strengthen the influence and effectiveness of my reports, received
only lukewarm support from the West and was strongly rejected by the
Palestinian Authority and a variety of diplomatic representatives of Arab
and Islamic members of the Council. They argued that the mandate on
Occupied Palestine as drafted had an appropriate scope, and any effort
to alter its focus, would risk further adverse modifications and even its
cancellation. Privately, I was told by several speakers at the Council's
open session that in the context of discussing Israeli violations, I would
be entirely free to depict the wider context, including the relevance of
Palestinian violations of applicable international law, and I took advantage of this opening to be as evenhanded as possible in my assessments.
Yet in fact because the realities of Israel's abusive and unlawful behavior
were so one-sided due to Israel's overall dominance and oppressive
tactics, my reports necessarily devoted most of their attention to Israeli
behavior. I wanted to avoid the false symmetry so popular in Western
liberal discourse that acted as if responsibility for the failure to find
peace, or even stability, lay equally on both sides, which was only a
shade more reflective of the realities than was the United States tendency
to condemn Palestinian terrorism and castigate Hamas, while turning its
blind eye to the most flagrant Israeli violations of international law.

My troubles with the Palestinian Authority were just beginning.
They were even more infuriated by my initial reports, using their right
to delay indefinitely public posting, because I dared to mention the
governance role of Hamas in Gaza and the acute hostility of Palestinian
Authority toward Hamas. At one point, the second ranked person in
the Palestinian Authority delegation called me in California, urging
me to resign. He thanked me for my services to the Palestinian people.
I also learned that the PA was spreading rumors in Geneva that I had
serious health issues that prevented my proper discharge of the duties
of a mandate-holder. When these efforts failed to dislodge me, the
Palestinian Authority gradually made peace with me. After the stormy
early period, I came to have friendly and productive relationships with
the subsequent PA representative in Geneva, Ibrahim Khraishi, and his
New York counterpart, Riyad Mansour. Both were informed, intelligent,
and tactically skillful diplomats, while being faithful interpreters of the
overly cautious Ramallah approach to relations within the UN. The PA
pressed the Palestinian case, but in ways that ruffled as few European
feathers as possible, exhibiting their priority of gaining the upper hand
in their bitter rivalry with Hamas.

The most troublesome impact of this defamatory campaign that portrayed me as an anti-Semite and extremist on a variety of hot button current issues was the willingness of senior UN officials and diplomats from respected governments, including my own, to accept at face value the allegations made by UN Watch, and sometimes by their brother ultra-Zionist NGO operating out of New York, NGO Monitor. UN Watch would draft well-formulated elaborate letters of denunciation, sending them to important diplomats and high civil servants at the UN, who would then themselves often issue public statements that relied on the defamatory material without attempting to get my side of the story or investigate the accuracy of the allegations.

After Ban Ki Moon, then UN Secretary General, launched one of these attacks on me based on information provided by UNW, I made phone contact with his chief assistant at UN Headquarters, explaining that what was asserted did not correspond to my views and was harmful to my work in this unpaid UN position. The Indian UN official politely responded to my complaint by admitting that the Office of Secretary General did not do what he called 'due diligence,' which undoubtedly meant that they didn't bother to check the sources of the defamatory material. He promised to clear up misimpressions after talking to the Secretary General, but it never happened. I complained in a respectful letter to Susan Rice, then Obama's ambassador at the UN, after she also repeated similar distortions but received no answer. Similarly, Samantha Power, a human rights specialist who had been affiliated with Harvard before being appointed to the UN, and was previously a friendly acquaintance, also attacked my supposed bias. She never bothered to contest the substance of my reports, which were always fact and law based, and often relied on information that Israel itself had collected and distributed. As I said publicly at the time, a person needed only to be 10% objective to arrive at the same conclusions that I had reached!

I mention these issues at this length because I think there should be more effort to protect those who accept these essentially voluntary positions from irresponsible attacks on their competence and views, especially by UN personnel. I was to some extent insulated from interference by the independence that was accorded special rapporteurs, who benefit from being outside the discipline of the UN civil service. At one point, Ban Ki Moon explained to the media that even as Secretary General his hands were tied, and he was unable to dismiss me unless I exceeded the terms of my mandate. Such a finding was extremely unlikely, as almost all member states of the HRC approved of my work, and so declared. Nevertheless, my scholarly reputation in the West was damaged, and even my personal security put at some risk, especially due to the repeated insinuations and accusations of my supposedly Jew-hating anti-Semitism, which was considered more damaging than the polemical Israeli-hating variant being pushed hard in the West by Zionist militants.

I concluded myself that the intensity of these attacks on me, which actually almost immediately lessened after my position at the UN ended, suggested that the position of special rapporteur, especially with respect to sensitive issues of this kind, is more important than I had previously realized. In my case the position was certainly taken seriously by Israel and its supporters. The messenger may be wounded in the line of duty, but most of the message still manages to get across, and the attacks sometimes increase the impact of SR reports that are quite often otherwise ignored. I know from talking to foreign ministers and other officials in several important countries that their own policies toward Israel and Palestine took account of my reports, which included policy recommendations. These periodic reports on conditions in Occupied Palestine were also relied upon by a wide range of civil society actors, including important church groups. Although a special rapporteur may be attacked as biased and unreliable, the reports, if useful, survive such abuse, especially if presenting evidence and analysis that is relevant and helpful to those seeking to comprehend specific features of the Palestinian ordeal, and how it is unfolding. If the person holding the position of special rapporteur has good credentials, they are increasingly more likely to be believed than are pro-Israeli flamethrowers. I felt that I was so regarded, including by the upper echelons of the HRC bureaucracy.

I also had some unlikely good fortune that aided my efforts and raised the profile of the Palestinian mandate. My friend, Father Miguel d'Escoto Brockman, the former Sandinista Foreign Minister of Nicaragua who was described earlier, was elected President of the General Assembly for the 2008-09 session. Father Miguel had been a friend since we had worked together in the mid-1980s on the Nicaragua initiative to have its legal objections to U.S. support for the Contra insurgency, including the mining of its harbors, assessed by the World Court in The Hague. Father Miguel not only hosted a reception at UN Headquarters in support of the mandate in my first year, which the SG attended, but also formally invited me to be listed as a member of his small advisory group while he served his one-year term as president of the General Assembly. Although short-lived, it was more than an honorific designation, and Father Miguel made the most of it. I did assist Father

Miguel in relation to several sensitive issues besides Palestine during his presidential term at the UN. Seasoned UN diplomats told me during the year that no one of Father Miguel's spiritual nature had ever held such a prominent position at the UN, and this seemed true enough, although some admirers of Dag Hammarskjold might object. Father Miguel was guided by what he believed to be the right action to take regardless of what the most important members of the UN were demanding. Such a show of independence was not common at the UN, occasioning both praise for his vision and complaints about his not understanding how the UN works. Perhaps, both kinds of reactions evoked by Father Miguel's style were justified, although I place myself in the front rank of his most ardent admirers.

Lending support to the Palestinian national movement for self-determination was among Father Miguel's most pronounced and contested priorities. He also was dedicated to developing a longer-term vision of UN reform, emphasizing adherence to international law and freeing the Organization from the framework of geopolitical constraints. One year was too short a time span to pose such profound challenges to the UN auto-immune system. Despite a valiant effort, Miguel's intense dedication to the empowerment and spiritualization of the UN produced neither the reformist momentum he hoped for nor any lasting changes. A skeptic might be forgiven for saying that what Miguel d'Escoto fervently wanted caused nothing more than a few barely visible ripples in the oceanic expanse of geopolitics that had long ago engulfed the UN. In this setting where even incremental reformers often swallow the bitter fruit of futility, visionaries can be likened to unwelcome aliens from a distant planet, who will as soon as possible be quietly removed from the premises as disturbers of the peace. Reform, world peace, social justice, and global security is not what the UN is about in its political behavior, but you would never find this out by listening to the speeches incessantly delivered in its halls or reading the language used in its official documents. The good works of the UN are done at the sidelines of world politics in the specialized agencies dealing with health, environment, culture, human rights, economic development, and education.

Wounding the Messenger

My entire effort of six years as Special Rapporteur on Human Rights in Occupied Palestine can be summed up as: to tell the truth, and to draw appropriate conclusions relating to international law and human rights from the realities disclosed by the evidence drawn from my inquiries into Israel's occupation of Palestinian territories. My experience confirmed what I had suspected at the outset, that Israel's policies and practices would be so pronounced, systematic, and flagrantly in violation of applicable legal norms, as to make the truth manifest without much interpretation required—a devastating indictment of the Israeli approach to the occupation of the Palestinian territories acquired in the 1967 War and of what was still in those years and even now being misleadingly referred to as 'the peace process.' I found the evidence of denial of human rights and lawlessness so overwhelmingly in support of this assessment that I naively believed that all but Zionist ideologues and the most ardent pro-Israeli militants would be convinced by such well-evidenced conclusions. I wrongly supposed that rationality and objectivity would prevail over sentiment, crude political calculations and geopolitical alignments at least in UN venues supposedly dedicated to promoting human rights and adherence to international law.

Israeli leaders whether consciously or not, seemed to share my understanding of the factual level of reality with respect to the relevance of human rights and law. In this spirit, they quietly abandoned efforts to defend Israel's actions and substantive policies except by way of the very abstract language of 'security, 'self-defense,' or less legally, by reference to biblical or ethnic entitlement ('our promised land'). This translated, in my experience at both the HRC and the UN General Assembly, into an Israeli and U.S. failure to advance any substantive arguments supporting Israeli claims as to the legality of their contested practices or in refutation of Palestinian grievances. The Israel effort was indirect, and ad hominem, shifting as much of the conversation as possible from substantive issues (settlements, use of force, collective punishment, torture, Jerusalem, and others) to the alleged procedural inability of Israel to get a fair hearing at the UN because of the biased nature of the institutions, its procedures and personnel. In actuality, I found the UN reality to be almost the exact opposite. UN bureaucrats at all levels were incredibly careful to be deferential to Israel's sovereign rights in the Organization despite Israeli persistent efforts to discredit the UN, and even most governments acted with caution when addressing moves to censure or take punitive action against Israel. Of course, Israel's attacks on the UN and its defiance of international law created anger and frustration in some quarters, and in private I often heard views of UN staff and governmental representatives that were highly critical of Israel and its geopolitical guardian in Washington, which were rarely uttered in debates.

During my tenure as special rapporteur I became one of the prime targets of this campaign based on what I came to call 'the politics of diversion.' It may seem odd, but my experience at the UN, over the course of six years, was almost totally the reverse of this Israeli orchestrated critique. At every turn, I encountered senior UN officials leaning over backwards to avoid stepping on Israeli toes. At the end of 2008 when I was detained in an Israeli prison cell and then expelled at the start of my first UN mission, I was deeply disappointed by the tepid response of the UN machinery, from the office of the SG on down the bureaucratic ladder to the staff members assigned to assist me during the mission. Despite UN Member states being obliged by treaty to facilitate the performance of UN undertakings, not a finger was lifted, and no words of public protest were uttered. By way of contrast, Israeli diplomats and concerns were treated with utmost respect, and given access to whatever venues within the UN Israel chose to express their views, which were often inflammatory. I think a truly dispassionate view of the relation between Israel, the UN, and Palestinian grievances would exhibit, contrary to most public perceptions, a pro-Israel bias partly reflecting a systemic privileging of member state interests and partly succumbing to the leverage exerted by the United States. It had not always been this way. In the decades following the establishment of Israel, the UN was strongly critical of the failure of Israel to respect Palestinian rights, rising to a climax with the Zionism is Racism resolution of 1975 (later quietly repudiated), and then subsiding thereafter.

Such a contrarian view of the UN is reinforced by the timidity and ambivalence of the Palestinian Authority that has apparently instructed its representatives to be respectful and accommodating with regard to Israel. Israeli diplomats, in contrast, exhibit no reluctance to attack the UN or Palestinian initiatives rudely and aggressively. To be sure, Israeli assaults on legality and defiance of the international consensus as to Palestinian rights leads to diplomatic frustration, which gives rise to pro-Palestinian resolutions in the General Assembly and occasionally even in the Security Council that criticize Israel, but to little effect, and with no adverse tangible consequences for Israel. There are adverse consequences but not for Israel. The impact of ignoring such resolutions has contributed to an overall weakening of international law and the authority of the UN. When important norms are seriously violated, and then, despite being revealed and confirmed, nothing happens, it casts doubt on whether what purports to be law is really law. Whether the unprecedented sharpness of the pre-annexation debate in mid-2020 will change this pattern remains to be seen in both aspects—whether Israel backs down for more than a decent interval, and if it doesn't whether there will be any serious Palestinian, regional, civil society, or global pushback, including the adoption of international sanctions.

The pattern has become a recurrent kind of discrediting ritual: Israel flaunts, the UN objects, Israel complains and persists, until the cycle is repeated in a different substantive setting. In the interim, Israel denounces the UN, sometimes withholding funds, and does so with the backing of the Organization's principal funder and most important member. Other leading governments ignore or downplay the UN's responsibility toward the Palestinian people that stretches back to the end of the British Mandate over Palestine to find a solution that is fair to both peoples. This goal proved impossible to attain once the Zionist major premise of establishing by force a Jewish state in an essentially non-Jewish society was legitimated as an unchallengeable element of any diplomatic framework for resolving the conflict over the national identity of the territory. If this reality is taken into account, Palestinians have over decades been consistently victimized by this UN approach, including the UN partition proposal of 1947, while Israel has been able to flourish economically and politically, and continuously expand, and at the same time pretend that it is the victim of global anti-Semitism as epitomized by the supposed Israel-bashing UN. Such diversionary propaganda reminds the world that the Holocaust should not be forgotten while at the same time Israel is doing its best to deny ethical and political visibility, much less accountability, for the Palestinian *Nakba*, and its rights and many resultant grievances, including especially those associated with Israeli racism and apartheid.

Diverting the Message

This memoir cannot accommodate the space required to address the substantive issues pursued in my twelve SR reports submitted over a six-year period. The highlights of what I tried to convey to the UN community and its civil society periphery were the evolving nature of the oppressive Israeli regime of occupation, annexation, settlements, and systemic apartheid as indicated by an examination of the distinct operational policies and practices as applied by Israel to the three occupied Palestinian territories: West Bank, Gaza, and East Jerusalem. What I learned while holding the position of SR, daily interacting with both the UN and a variety of civil society actors, journalists, and activists involved with the UN either as partisans or critics, and sometimes with the two roles combined, has had a lasting impact on my political identity, yet without altering my ethical and political commitments.

About the UN

Being part of the UN makes one aware of its scale and scope, as well as its dual ambitions of keeping the governments of member states content and carrying out its mission of making the world a better place from the perspective of peace, justice, development, and ecological sustainability. At the Human Rights Council, my primary venue, the priority was placed on addressing a range of deprivations and crisis situations, with an emphasis on civil and political rights, reflecting the Western approach of stressing individualism and protection against governmental abuse. This initially surprised me as the HRC is treated by the West as a bastion of non-Western and post-colonial hostility to Western values. All is not as it appears! Actually, folk wisdom is more instructive than the controlled media of the West: 'He who pays the piper calls the tune.' Or heeding the insightful cynical admonition: 'follow the money.'

When it comes to effectiveness throughout the UN System, but especially at the HRC, the first level of understanding is that the UN can act robustly when the geopolitical actors favor such initiatives and can induce enough other member states to go along or abstain. The UN will be stymied whenever these same actors are using their leverage to block action. Israel/Palestine offers an ideal optic for sensing what the UN can and cannot do in various concrete circumstances.

In short, the UN is able to investigate and document allegations of Israeli wrongdoing in an objective manner and even able to overcome geopolitical resistance to do so but finds itself unable thereafter to change or punish lawless Israeli behavior on the ground. Whenever the UN tries to follow policy recommendations critical of Israel it inflames diplomacy directed at the Organization, which will be generally spearheaded by the United States, and often backed by the European Union. Since Israel is able to shape the treatment of Western media on these issues, while the Palestinians and their supporters lack countervailing influence, freedom of expression with respect to the UN suffers. The Western public is awash with hostile propaganda rather than truthful and objective journalism that exposes the actuality of Palestinian grievances.

The Goldstone Report on the allegations against Israel and Hamas arising out of the 2008-09 massive Israeli Cast Lead attack launched against Hamas in Gaza is illustrative of this UN pattern. Israel tried its best to oppose the factfinding mission from ever being undertaken but was unable to prevent the initiative from being launched or the report from being issued. Yet very typically, Israel refused to cooperate with the factfinding effort, and after the report was issued, succeeded in blocking every effort to implement the rather cautious recommendations that followed directly from the well-evidenced findings contained in the Goldstone Report. Such blockage was not enough for Israel and Zionist lobbies in the United States and elsewhere. Without the report having been read or commented upon, the U.S. Congress and Executive Branch denounced the report, although if considered fairly it would be apparent to most readers that its interpretations and findings leaned over backwards to exaggerate the significance of Hamas' rockets and to give Israel the huge legal benefit of the doubt by avoiding any consideration of whether Israel was justified under the UN Charter in launching a military operation of this magnitude in a territory considered 'Occupied' by the UN and thus especially protected, according to international humanitarian law. The report exempted issues surrounding the initiation of the cross-border attack from legal scrutiny, limiting its inquiry to objections to the combat behavior of Israel and Hamas during the attack.

Even forcing the shelving of the recommendations of the Goldstone Report was not enough. Zionist forces, including the top Israeli leaders, castigated the distinguished commission chair, Richard Goldstone, in the most venomous language. Under mounting pressures, Goldstone, a well-known international figure, sadly and unconvincingly retracted support for the report bearing his name in a widely publicized opinion piece published in the *Washington Post*. The international reputation of Goldstone took a big hit as his retraction was opposed by the other three members of the commission, each a respected expert. Goldstone had not been spared the anger of Israel and its Zionist supporters despite being a lifelong Zionist and having close relatives living in Israel, nor even by his stature as a South African jurist of national and international distinction. Nothing insulated Goldstone from this vicious campaign of defamatory pushback. Such a chain of developments illustrates how sovereign states can nullify the work of the UN when sufficiently mobilized and geopolitical supported.

In this feverish atmosphere, the UN was content to lie low while the Goldstone drama unfolded, not even offering support for its own emissary as his character was being pulled through the mud and his reputation was irreparably damaged. Goldstone unintentionally gave a lesson to the UN: never appoint a situationally vulnerable person to delicate and controversial roles as they are likely to be more susceptible to personal attacks if they carry out their assignment in an honest way. If they then cave in, it not only undermines the mission but inflicts a heavy blow against UN credibility.

On a more personal note, I was disappointed by this Goldstone Affair that drew attention away from the indictment of Israel's behavior that formed the core of the report. I had worked with Goldstone in the past, both on a Millennium UNESCO project to prepare a Universal Declaration of the Human Responsibilities and as a member of the Independent International Commission on Kosovo, which he chaired. In the course of these undertakings I worked for months at close range with Goldstone, respected him as an administrative leader and regarded him as a friend. At the same time I disliked his approach whenever political considerations arose that were geopolitically sensitive. Such issues emerged several times during the process of evaluating NATO's behavior in the Kosovo War of 1999 when Goldstone disappointed me by deferring to Washington's partisan views of sensitive issues.

As far as the UN staff is concerned, with special attention to the Office of the High Commissioner of Human Rights, my experience suggested great unevenness with respect to competence and outlook. The best of the staff, several of whom I was privileged to work with, were outstanding civil servants, capable, diligent, and ready to go the extra mile to get the job done. Then there were time servers and bureaucratic climbers who did as little as possible and above all did not want to make any organizational waves that might disturb their superiors or agitate important governments. It was also the case, with some exceptions, that the best of the HRC staff members were either near the bottom or top of the ladder, with the weakest in the middle, perhaps a reflection of a wider bureaucratic operational logic that gives rise to dominant forms of careerist competition—a race to the bottom and a climb to the top.

My experience of the UN leadership was also mixed. Over the years I had known and respected several SGs prior to Ban Ki Moon, including U Thant, Boutros Boutros-Ghali, and Kofi Annan, but only with BKM did I have some interactions, mostly related to his efforts to distance himself from my views on Israel/Palestine. He showed the extent to which he was subject to pressure by endorsing public distortions of my views on several occasions. My experience with UN High Commissioners was more favorable. I dealt with Mary Robinson, Louise Arbour, and mostly with Navi Pillay, and found them each to be personally friendly and professionally supportive. Early in my period as special rapporteur, Navi expressed her sympathy for the harsh treatment

I was receiving, and told me that if I wanted to get off the hot seat, there would be no difficulty finding me another position at the UN. All along, despite various temptations to resign, I never was prepared to give my tormenters the satisfaction of claiming a victory by such tactics, having UN Watch primarily in mind because they were so relentless in their efforts to discredit and defame.

It Was Worth It

During these six years I often asked myself 'was it worth it?' and my answer was 'yes, but…' I was less interested in the personal costs associated with career and some friendships, than with whether I was actually making any sort of contribution to the Palestinian struggle for their rights under international law, and more existentially, to the empowerment and emancipation of Palestine from a long period of collective victimization. On this question my conclusion was mixed. I felt that over the course of my mandate, the Palestinian reality on the ground had worsened and the chances for a negotiated, fair, and sustainable peace had almost disappeared. In this regard, my efforts as special rapporteur seem to have done nothing to reverse these Israeli behavioral trends adverse to Palestinian prospects.

Yet on the level of public discourse, which helps shape world opinion, I think my efforts had some effect in clarifying the real nature of what was at stake in these highly contested sets of circumstances where geopolitics was cruelly thwarting elemental justice. Public discourse is a vital site of struggle in this kind of situation, with ideas, images, and language exerting influence, and often eventually altering the balance of forces in ways that are hard to measure and discern but often seem decisive in shaping political outcomes. I suppose as a teacher and scholar I was predisposed to view ideas and perceptions as agents of change, and this gave me the feeling that my work was worthwhile, and the more so, insofar as they had produced such concerted efforts to undermine my role and credibility. I felt I must be doing a good job when the Weizmann Institute in Los Angeles listed me in 2012 as the third most dangerous anti-Semite in the world on their list of ten. I trailed only the Supreme Guide of Iran and the Turkish Prime Minister, Erdogan. The others on the list were mostly also public intellectuals critical of Israel, who were writers and identified in public as supportive of the Palestinian struggle.

In particular, there were several shifts in discourse during my two terms as special rapporteur that had an impact on the way Palestinian grievances and aspirations are perceived and presented. I repeatedly called attention to the length of the Israeli occupation of the West Bank, East Jerusalem, and Gaza, and what this meant for the lives of the civilian Palestinian population. It was my view, which I think came to exert some influence on governments and civil society actors, that prolonged occupation, which I defined as more than five years, involved an unacceptable regime of rightlessness for an occupied population. My admirable successor, Michael Lynk, has carried this line of criticism to the point of concluding that the occupation itself should be declared unlawful, and terminated by the UN as a matter of law.

Israel, for its part, took advantage of its diplomatic strength and a legalistic view of Security Council Resolution 242 to undermine the international consensus on withdrawal and non-acquisition of territory by force that existed in 1967, a principle that then enjoyed the support of the United States and leading European states. This international consensus embodied in 242 was predicated on creating a Palestinian state on the territories under occupation. Not only did Israel refuse to withdraw, it penetrated the territory in a variety of ways including putting forward demands in the name of its security and disputed sovereignty that made withdrawal as contemplated in 1967 practically difficult if not politically impossible. It achieved this result by establishing a constantly expanding archipelago of unlawful settlements, building a separation wall on occupied Palestinian territory, expanding the borders of Jerusalem and then unilaterally incorporating the city into the state of Israel, and insisting on exercising unimpeded control of all border-crossing activities that would ensure its continuing dominance over any Palestinian entity that might have emerged from diplomatic negotiations, as prefigured by its post-disengagement behavior toward Gaza.

Not only Israel, but the Palestinians and the international community made the mistake of territorializing the conflict as one of 'land for peace' whereas the real foundation for peace was 'equality and people,' that is, conceiving of security and sovereignty as equal for Jews and Palestinians and considering the Palestinians as not only those living under occupation but also the refugees in neighboring countries, exiles throughout the world, and the discriminated minority living in that territory recognized as Israel proper. This focus on the Palestinian people *as a whole* remains critical for genuine peace efforts, and the absence of this focus has always been a fatal flaw in the two-state mantra if peace was conceived by reference to people rather than territory. I chafed against the constraints of the artificial territoriality that defined my mandate as restricted to Palestinians living under occupation, reflecting also a fundamental weakness of the partition approach adopted by the UN, which always placed refugee and exile rights at the outer margin of any required responses to Palestinian grievances, and as a result, missed vital concerns, which if neglected, would put in jeopardy any arrangement put forth as a peaceful solution to the conflict, leaving a regional refugee diaspora whose plight remained unresolved. It should be remembered as well that the Palestinian refugee families are the unjust consequence of ethnic cleansing in the 1948 War and subsequently, insofar as that has been coupled with the denial of any right of return or repatriation.

I also did my best to avoid the misimpression of the existence of a static situation by supplementing the idea of 'occupation' with the more dynamic and unrelenting process-oriented de facto reality of 'annexation,' settler colonialism, and political fragmentation. Ever since the *Nakba* the steady dispossession of the Palestinian people has been an ongoing process integral to Israeli state-building and should not be viewed only as an event fixed in time as of 1948. It is the continuation of this process that has eroded, deliberately in my view, the viability of a two-state approach and has worsened the Palestinian situation on the ground while increasing Israeli demands and expectations. Although recognizing that the shape of an agreed solution was a matter solely for the parties, peace-minded Israelis increasingly believe that only a bi-national state can produce a sustainable peace, given all that has happened since 1947. Israel, by making the two-state solution unattainable, has ironically made a one-state solution, whose ultimate features may either contradict (by loss of Jewish dominance) or further discredit (by maintaining Jewish dominance via systemic apartheid) their Zionist orientation, seem almost inevitable.

Indeed, with regard to the latter possibility, I situated the central idea of occupation in its encompassing structure of apartheid as what was required in order to implement the Zionist project of establishing a Jewish state in what was earlier a distinctly Palestinian majority state. In effect, the Palestinians became largely disenfranchised outsiders in their own homeland. The reality of this apartheid construction remained controversial during my UN period, but that determination has subsequently become much more accepted as a key to understanding the structures producing Palestinian victimization and perceiving dismantling apartheid as the one path that could lead to sustainable peace and benign coexistence for the two peoples.

The apartheid solution for Israel was a direct and almost inevitable consequence of the Zionist vision of a specifically Jewish state in a majority non-Jewish state. Israel made clear its racist aspects only very recently in the 2018 Basic Law of Israel as the Nation-State of the Jewish People. There had never been a humane way to achieve this vision of a Jewish State in the historical twilight of European colonialism except by using all available means to overcome the inevitable resistance and even presence of the majority residential population. The Israeli leadership hid for many years this security imperative behind a façade of democracy that was a genuine feature of the project as it concerned its own original social democratic Jewish leadership. This democratic identity was even more crucial for achieving widespread international support, as well as furthering the highest Zionist priority of attracting and persuading Jews to emigrate to Israel from around the world. For Israel to earn the legitimacy that comes from being dubbed 'the only democracy in the Middle East' it needed to annul the perception of a Jewish minority forcibly subduing, while ethnically cleansing, the Arab majority.

A Volcanic Sequel

Not too long after my term as special rapporteur ended, I was approached by a rather peripheral entity in the UN System, the Economic and Social Council for West Asia (Arab World) (ESCWA) to do a research project on a contract basis investigating the allegations that Israel was guilty of the crime of apartheid under international law.

I persuaded Virginia Tilley, an outstanding political scientist, to join me. Virginia had a distinguished record of scholarship devoted to South African apartheid, which included an interpretation of what led to the unexpected downfall of the racist regime. She had also worked in South Africa for several years on a collaborative academic study of a one-state solution for Israel/Palestine. We shaped the UN investigation of the apartheid allegations as one of examining the policies and practices of Israel with reference to *the Palestinian people as a whole*. This departed from prior instances of inquiry, such as contained in Dugard's UN Reports, which limited its examination of apartheid charges to the administration of the West Bank, especially focusing on the discriminatory dual legal regimes applicable to Jewish settlers and Palestinian inhabitants co-existing in the same territory. Without discussing the argument and analysis of the ESCWA study, its central conclusion was that the allegations of apartheid were justified, and accordingly, entailed responsibilities of governments, international institutions, corporations, and individuals to act within their respective spheres of competence to bring Israeli apartheid to an end.

As soon as the report was released on March 15, 2017 it produced a firestorm of reaction at the UN led by Israel and the United States. It was claimed that the allegation of apartheid was tantamount to anti-Semitism in its worst form. This reflex contention was made without any examination of the evidence and analysis in our report, and with no effort to set forth counterarguments. The extent of international outrage was both hysterical and hypocritical. Israeli leaders themselves, going back as far as Ben Gurion and forward to Rabin and Olmert, had warned the Israeli public *in Hebrew* that the failure to find a solution for the Palestinian problem would eventuate in an apartheid structure of control imposed on Palestinians. To be sure the Israeli arrangement would be very different from South African apartheid but containing the same defining element of a dominant race or ethnicity subjugating another race or ethnicity forced to live collectively in bantustans so that it could maintain the exploitative advantages of secure control by victimizing the subjugated race.

The U.S. diplomatic representative at the UN, Nikki Haley, demanded that the UN repudiate the ESCWA report. She attacked me personally along the way and threatened adverse funding implications for the UN if her demand was not immediately acted upon. Alas, the new Secretary General, António Guterres, wasted little time before capitulating, demanding that ESCWA remove the report from its website. The director of ESCWA, Rima Khalaf, resigned rather than comply with such an order. She was replaced by a bureaucrat who dutifully removed the report from the website, but its contents were never formally repudiated.

Again, the dual face of the UN was revealed: its willingness to look at a serious cause for moral concern through the prism of a legally oriented academic study on one side and its inability to withstand a determined pushback by a geopolitical heavyweight of its results, on the other. The inappropriateness of the UN response would seem evident as the study on its opening page contained a clear disclaimer informing readers that the report reflected only the opinion of its authors and did not necessarily express the views of ESCWA or the UN. There are hundreds of UN reports that reach conclusions that are in some way controversial, but they are virtually never challenged and repudiated in such an open political forum.

Actually, the high-profile attack on the report caused its far wider dissemination and influence. The attack by Israel and the U.S. generated much greater interest in the apartheid argument than if it had been ignored or discreetly criticized on substantive grounds. Before the

Secretary General issued his website removal order ESCWA had already disseminated the report by way of its main UN portals. The report can still be found online at many websites and French, Spanish, Arabic, and Italian translations have been prepared and disseminated by civil society groups. Nikki Haley turned out to be an invaluable unpaid publicity agent for our study.

Nevertheless, the incident caused a media stir that directly affected me. I was scheduled to give some university lectures in England and Scotland to launch the publication of my book *Palestinian Horizon: Toward a Just Peace.* I encountered no trouble in Scottish universities, but a disruption occurred at the London School of Economics, and lectures scheduled for the following week at East London University and Westminster University were cancelled, not because of my book, which did not address the apartheid issue, but because the book was overshadowed by the ESCWA report that became a lightning rod for Zionist organizing in London after the much publicized attack at the UN.

As a Citizen Pilgrim

It has been my deep conviction that a citizen pilgrim, true to his or her calling, participates in the here and now as well as envisions and embarks on a life journey to a desirable future. No issue of our time is more ethically compelling for me, given my social location as Jew, American, and progressive humanist, than the plight of the Palestinian people, and the responsibility of my country and its government for indefinitely prolonging this ordeal. If I were an Indian, maybe my attention would be devoted to the liberation of Kashmiris or if Puerto Rican maybe to political independence for the island, although these struggles have not caused the regional havoc brought about by the forcible implant of a Jewish state in the Middle East. I highlight the moral salience of the Palestinian struggle while being mindful that in the aftermath of the Holocaust, when Israel was established, strong sentiments in the West favored the establishment of a secure Jewish national sanctuary, giving the anti-genocide pledge of 'never again' a territorial safety valve. Yet such an argument cannot be properly used as a justification for forcibly displacing another people from their land and homes, and then establishing in their place and without their consent an exclusivist ethnic state.

In working through my experiences with respect to the Palestinian struggle I have tried to show the interplay of my thinking as an academician concerned with international conflicts and my commitments as an engaged citizen who is both an activist with an agenda and a pilgrim on a journey. I suppose the originality of my life experience is to take these academic concerns into the field of public action rather than limiting their relevance to classrooms, libraries, scholarly publications, and reflective vacations in sunny places. To some revealing extent I waited to be asked before immersing myself in these controversial issues of the day, especially Israel/Palestine. I did not go searching for controversy, and generally disliked public exposure. At the same time, I was afraid to be afraid, and so when asked or invited, I almost invariably responded affirmatively. In this regard, my deceptive passivity seems to be the strange source of the strength I possess, befuddling critics and admirers alike. In my view, considered as objectively as I can manage, I am neither as alienated and traitorous as my critics contend nor as brave and formidable as my admirers insist.

CHAPTER 15
The Turkish Enigma

Unlike the political engagements described in the prior four chapters, my engagement with Turkey was from its outset more personal than political, although over time the political became intertwined with the personal. Due to this intertwining, it was different in its essential qualities from my other experiences of foreign societies, and also it has lasted from my early twenties until the end of my life. In India, especially, and to some extent, Japan I also had strong experiences over a period of many years, but never with such intensity at the personal level. My studies of Indian law and collaborations over the course of many years, combined with a deep interest in Gandhi's thought and life, plus more than one romantic infatuation made my experience of India personal and somewhat political, yet mostly academic and intellectual. With Japan, also, I had close connections over many years, including the odd fact that my mother was born in Yokohama and coincidentally the mayor once gave me the key to the city. Still it was my anti-nuclear and anti-war activism combined with warm friendships and collaborative work with university colleagues, that was the driver.

Yet it is Turkey that represents the paramount engagement of my last 25 years, as devoted husband, observer of the political scene, part-time expatriate and resident, including during the COVID pandemic, and as a friend and acquaintance of several leading players in the Turkish political game.

A first encounter

I first came to Turkey almost by chance while still a law student in the summer of 1954. It was in the course of a low budget trip to 'see' Europe, which is what lots of middle-class students were doing in those years when near the end of their studies, just prior to being tested in 'the real world.' I found an inexpensive passage to Britain on what was back then called 'a student ship,' one class without frills.

While on board the ship, I reached the finals of a chess tournament, but lost when I made a blunder late in the match that my German-speaking opponent would not allow me to correct, although I had permitted him to take back a similar grossly mistaken move earlier. Worse than this minor disconcerting moment, I discovered shortly before landing in Liverpool that my passport and cash had been stolen; fortunately, back in those ancient pre-ATM days, touristic travelers kept most of their money in the form of AmEx Travelers Checks. For this reason, the monetary loss didn't distress me nearly as much as that of the passport. This seemed a most unpromising beginning for my first overseas adventure. Happily, my worries were unnecessary. Despite the Cold War tensions, we were then living in a more humane and calmer era, the pre-9/11, pre-pandemic world. I was courteously escorted off the ship before the other passengers, taken immediately to the American Consulate, and after answering a few questions, I was issued a new passport in a matter of minutes, accompanied by words of sympathy. If this happened now, it would undoubtedly, at best, require an extensive interrogation and a long wait before a temporary, so-called 'emergency' passport was issued, and that assumes what is unlikely these days, that the British immigration authorities would allow me to get to the Consulate without a passport.

In any event, a few days later in London I joined by prearrangement my travel partner for the trip and New Haven apartment mate, Jack Ayers, a graduate student in the Yale Drama School and a child actor who grew up playing successive roles as the ageing son in the long lasting Broadway play, *Life with Father*. Jack was openly gay and was my second real experience of the precarious existence of gay people, given the homophobia that then existed even in the most cosmopolitan milieus, such as Manhattan. I found Jack a lively and enjoyable travel companion, although he was hampered by an even tighter budget than mine. We stayed together through Britain, Germany, Austria, and then by train as far as Alexandropolis in northern Greece where we split. I took the continuation of this version of the Orient Express on to Istanbul, while Jack headed for Athens.

A few days before this parting, we had taken a ship along the Dalmatian Coast of what was then Yugoslavia, starting at Rijeka, stopping at Split, and ending at Dubrovnik. It was an exciting voyage, made more satisfying because the dollar was strong, allowing us to eat at the best restaurants and sleep in top hotels on our meager budgets, but more enduring than these enticements, was a stray shipboard comment by Jack with lifelong consequences. He had been wandering on another part of the deck while I was reading, returning with an unlikely exclamation, 'I have just seen the most beautiful girl in the world!' Of course, I was curious, if skeptical. Quite likely our quite different sexual orientations made me assume that his enthusiasms would produce divergent opinions as to female beauty. After I met Jack's version of Dante's 'Beatrice,' I shared his opinion, which changed lots of things for me, immediately and over time. Above all else, that beautiful girl from Canada would later become my first wife, Irene Piggott, and the mother of my first child.

By what felt like a calculated arrangement, but was just an accident, although some would call it 'destiny,' I found myself on the same train, actually in the same compartment with her heading from Skopje to Istanbul. Irene, who preferred to be called 'Rene,' was traveling with two female friends, also from Canada, all three of whom were slightly older than I was. They were friendly and lovely, and I soon became attached to their group, although my eyes and desires were focused on Rene. We were also befriended, as in the then recent films about the region, by a shady German middle-aged character, an adventurer, who turned out to be a drug dealer or more likely just 'a mule.' We later believed that Hans wanted to use us as a cover while conducting his shady business, which apparently involved paying or not paying a debt to a dealer in Istanbul. I found out about this rather risky situation when I returned to my hotel room in Istanbul and found the contents of our luggage dumped on the floor, suggesting that an intrusion had taken place. Actually, Hans, was fun to be with, and knew Istanbul intimately. This made my first experience of this fantastic city the start of a precious lifelong series of encounters.

After several days together in Istanbul, I persuaded Rene to leave her two friends, and continue her travels with me, first to Italy, then North Africa, and finally Spain. As might be expected under such circumstances, we became intimate, undoubtedly without much forethought, as we went from city to city, museum to museum, church to church, hotel to hotel. Europe for me was a kind of ongoing cultural field trip, benefitting from my study of art history during my last two years at Penn. It was thrilling to find so often before me the great masterpieces that I had earlier known by slides further illuminated by the learned commentary of several stimulating lecturers. It made me realize that aside from love of women, I derive great joy from the appreciation of the visual beauty of painting, and occasionally sculpture. I never managed a similar level of appreciation for classical music although I could superficially enjoy the symphonies and chamber music of the great composers and came to like the staccato rhythms of Stravinsky and later innovators of European and Latino musical traditions.

Getting back to first impressions of Turkey, I was enchanted by the beauty of the Golden Horn and the Bosporus, and remember swimming briefly in that spectacular waterway, although intimidated by its swift current. I was awed by the picturesque mosques situated on both sides of the Bosporus and in the Sultan Ahmed neighborhood. I had no idea what sort of country Turkey was at that time, although I had a dim awareness of Kemal Ataturk's role in founding modern Turkey and seeking its Europeanization as a break from its past Ottoman glories. As it turned out, my initial visit to Turkey was far more significant for how my life went forward than as a touristic experience or a first acquaintance with the Turkish political narrative.

When it came time to return to Yale for my third and final year Rene and I, who had become lovers, parted. Rene had previously committed to studying social work in London for the academic year. We shared the expectation that this was not the end of our romantic friendship, although the idea of marriage was not even discussed.

In the weeks ahead this would change. Rene soon learned she was pregnant and, wanting to give birth, proposed joining me. In New Haven. I was perplexed by the situation, at first, not knowing what to do, and even thought briefly about an abortion but I was never comfortable about contemplating such an option. And looking back, I am so glad that I never seriously considered depriving my son, Chris, of a life, which he has so richly endowed with love, decency, and wonderful children of his own, as along with Judy, his devoted life partner and wonderful mother of my grandchildren, Sarah and Matthew. Rene and I were soon married in Hamilton, Ontario where Rene had close relatives. Rene made a strong positive impression among my friends because of her beauty and forthright Canadian personality, and Dad loved her at least as much as I did, which gave me an initial confidence that calmed my anxieties about taking on the responsibilities of husband and father long before I was ready.

At this stage, while drawn to Rene, I remained somewhat wary as I felt we didn't share sufficiently deeply either my somewhat ironic sense of life and social convention or the kind of cultural and philosophic interests that were then foremost in my mind. I was mildly 'counter cultural' before those words were used. Without any design, I distrusted and quietly subverted bourgeois social conventions, while Rene seemed fully socialized into their acceptance. This everyday difference in outlook highlighted gaps of sensibility, for instance, about the ethics of paying bills on time and other matters that seem trivial, yet soon weaken bonds of intimacy, eroding rapport, and building tension. While law was my vocational engagement, lawfulness was never my cup of tea. I was by temperament part anarchist, part pacifist, without considering whether such a disposition would work in the public realms of community and governance. Despite my social science education, the humanities had become my intellectual and spiritual home, helping me find my way in the world, the sanctuary for my closeted passions and a bold counterpoint to my timid personality.

These gaps in sensibility doomed my relationship with Rene after a year or so, although it never destroyed our friendship. In the meantime, our son Chris was born in New Haven. Rene was a wonderfully devoted mother and daughter-in-law, and we went together to live in Columbus, Ohio in the Fall of 1955 so that I could begin my teaching career as a one-year visitor at the law school of Ohio State University. In the ensuing months, my academic life, although initially intimidating, went much more smoothly than my personal life. Rene ruled out divorce so long as my father was alive, sharing fully and reciprocating his love of her. Dad died unexpectedly in November of 1956 from a series of strokes induced by high blood pressure, and so this pledge of hers to defer divorce as long as he was alive did not extend our marriage much beyond its cycle of natural longevity.

Rene soon returned to Vancouver with Chris and resumed her social work career in Canada, while we concluded a no-frills divorce arrangement without incident, and happily without the 'help' of lawyers. I remained responsible for child support until Chris was an adult and made periodic visits to Vancouver to maintain a parental presence, and to the extent possible, to be a conscientious father. My relationship with Chris developed occasional tensions over the years, and overall seemed more cordial than intimate. His development, including his own family experience and his skill in racquet sports, were deep sources of satisfaction and pleasure for both of us that softened the impact of what must otherwise have been experienced by Chris as de facto abandonment.

Revisiting Turkey in 1992

In 1992, almost 40 years later, I returned to Turkey, this time as a member of a European civil society delegation at the invitation of the Turkish chapter of a vibrant NGO, Helsinki Citizens, a societal initiative undertaken in reaction to the geopolitical rivalry at the core of the Cold

War. Our mission to Turkey concerned the protection of human rights in the country, especially as bearing on prison abuse and the internal conflict producing strife between the Turkish state and the large Kurdish minority. Our Turkish hosts were committed activists, as well as impressive intellectuals, and we spent most of the visit under the guidance of Murat Belge, who was a leading public intellectual in Turkey. Murat combined a deep sense of attachment to Turkish culture, history, and politics with strong democratic socialist sentiments.

Our trip started by going to the heartland of Kurdish Turkey, the eastern city of Diyarbakir, crowded, colorful, and poor as compared to Istanbul. We were met at the airport by local Helsinki Citizens committee members, and then driven to our hotel by a Kurdish medical doctor. The roads were covered with ice, it was late winter. While we were stopped at a traffic light shortly after entering the city, a bus skidded into the side of our stationary car. It was an unsettling beginning of our visit, and even more so for our host, whose car was badly damaged.

While in Diyarbakir we met with several local Kurdish leaders and political figures, listened to their grievances, and became convinced that the Turkish Government was guilty of serious violations of basic human rights. The Kurds with whom we met wanted to be treated as a nation *within* the Turkish state, but with autonomy arrangements that would acknowledge their ethnic and cultural identity without severing formal ties with Turkey. The Turkish government was battling the Peoples Workers Party (PKK), an armed struggle movement that was alleged to be seeking an independent Kurdish sovereign state in eastern Turkey. The PKK was a left secular political movement led by Abudllah Ocalan, a Marxist intellectual. Ocalan was captured by Turkish security forces in 1999 and has since been kept in Imrali Prison (on an island close to Istanbul), having been charged with the capital crime of treason, but as yet never prosecuted. Although accused of secessionist goals, Ocalan's later published views advocated a confederated Turkey without any fracturing of the unity of the Turkish state. Even some of the apparently moderate activists among the persons with whom we met had been or were being charged with crimes, allegedly for lending support to the PKK. They were sent to prison on the basis of scant charges, where they were routinely tortured.

When we departed from Turkey, I was unsure of two important things: first, was the government of Turkey trying to discredit Kurdish grievances by lumping Kurdish claims for cultural rights and political autonomy beneath the banner of the PKK armed struggle movement?

Or were the Kurdish claims of moderate political objectives a façade behind which existed solidarity with a continuing PKK struggle to achieve a separate Kurdistan? Secondly, was it plausible for the Turkish Government to treat religious Kurds as supportive of the PKK, given its Marxist and secular identity? This latter question is significant considering that the great majority of the Kurds are devout Muslims who uphold pre-modern cultural traditions and are not drawn to support a radical secular movement unless they are driven to desperation by being suppressed. What seemed obvious after our visit was the persisting distortion of foreign and Turkish commentary by assuming the existence of a unified and extremist Kurdish separatist movement.

Even decades later I have not been able to determine whether there exists a consensus among the various Kurdish communities and political groupings as to the nature of an acceptable solution or as to the coherence of the Kurdish resistance as a unified movement

After Diyarbakir we returned to Ankara for visits with various persons concerned with Kurdish issues and were charmed and impressed by Leyla Zaina, a Kurd recently elected to the Turkish Parliament. Leyla told us her story of reluctantly entering politics after the arrest and imprisonment of her husband for pro-Kurdish activism. She was also alleged to have PKK sympathies, which she denied, and was controversial within the Turkish mainstream who then unreservedly opposed Kurdish moves not only for secession but for autonomy. Either interpretation of the Kurdish national movement was then widely believed by non-Kurdish Turks to erode the Ataturk belief in a strong centralized, unitary, and secular Turkish state that rejected the legitimacy of sub-national identity claims of minority peoples and religious groups. Leyla invited us to lunch in the Parliament dining room. I shall never forget the hostile stare our group received as we walked with Leyla to our table. The women in our Helsinki Citizens delegation regarded Leyla as a feminist role model and arranged to meet her separately for further discussions. I was asked to meet with an NGO formed by psychologists to help torture victims reenter Turkish society after the trauma of abuses in Turkish prisons. I found this to be an indirect, yet utterly convincing confirmation of international reports that torture was being widely practiced in Turkish jails.

Our experience was not wholly given over to the serious work of fact finding. Murat, who happily was extremely knowledgeable about Turkish restaurants, cafes, and cultural life, enlivened our experience during the visit. He also had an aunt in Ankara who had some extraordinary photos of Murat's father that included pictures with Ataturk and his entourage. Murat's father had been a cabinet minister in the early days of the Republic, who had married Zsa Zsa Gabor when she was 18, shortly after she had been selected as Miss Hungary. Although Murat was the biological child of an earlier Turkish wife of the minister, he was deeply interested in restoring this lost connection with his celebrity stepmother. Murat was surprised to the point of being startled when he learned that I had known Zsa Zsa since I was a child due to my father being her lawyer during a drawn out divorce from Conrad Hilton and later her friend.

Murat had no way on his own of being in touch with Zsa Zsa, yet for reasons that we never spoke about, badly wanted to be in contact, investing strong emotions in the fact that she was his stepmother. I have the impression that not much happened after Murat did establish contact, but I did my part by finding out her Belle Aire address, and writing a message of introduction, which turned out to be my last contact with this enticingly unforgettable personality.

The culmination of the formal reason for being in Turkey was a large press conference at which I was asked to present on behalf of our delegation its central, provocative, and agreed recommendations for handling the Kurdish challenge—supporting its claim of Kurdish *internal* self-determination, which both corresponded with our sense of the situation and reflected the wishes of those with whom we met. I was most of all struck at the press conference by the partisan and nationalist behavior of the Turkish journalists who presented themselves not as independent investigators, but as unofficial representatives of the government, openly advocating military opposition to the Kurdish national movement without seeming to feel the inappropriateness of being openly partisan. I recall one journalist proudly telling me afterwards that he regularly attended meetings of the National Security Council and knew there would soon be an offensive by Turkish forces coinciding with the approaching Nevruz holiday celebrating the coming of Spring that would inflict heavy losses on what he called 'the Kurdish insurgency.' It is notable that what we felt would bring peace to Turkey, ending the killing by giving equal rights to Kurds and overcoming the most acute Kurdish grievances while maintaining Turkish territorial integrity, was mostly dismissed as pro-Kurdish propaganda by the assembled journalists. Perhaps the hostility we encountered reflected the impression that we were interfering in Turkish internal affairs, as well as recommending policies that seemed similar to what the imprisoned PKK leader, Ocalan, had been proposing as a solution to the conflict. In 2012, thirty years after this 1992 press conference, which responded negatively to our recommendation of internal self-determination, a highly placed advisor to the Erdogan government told me in confidence that the Turkish leadership was waiting for the right moment to release Ocalan from prison and seek a political solution along the lines we advocated.

Much has happened since 2012, including the alliance between the governing AKP and the far right, ultra-nationalist MHP, making such a promising option to resolve finally this century old conflict appear far less relevant at this time. I have learned over the years not to trust such appearances, which means that anything positive or negative could happen in relation to the Kurdish national movement without much forewarning.

Leaving Turkey in 1992, I felt that I learned quite a lot in a short period about this important Cold War NATO ally, which at that time possessed such a dreadful human rights record. It was one more learning moment in which I realized that 'the free world' was only as free as geopolitical priorities prescribe. In Turkey's case it was shielded from inter-governmental criticism and censure in this pre-AKP period to the same extent that its failures have been highlighted during the latter stages of AKP governance. As well, the efforts of civil society and human rights NGOs seemed to have little political traction. This experience of Turkey then was strikingly different from the Turkey that has emerged since 2002, displacing secular political elites, shifting the locus of political power from the urban cities in the West to the countryside and interior of the country, and not sufficiently noticed, shifting geopolitical motivations in the NATO West from overlooking Turkey's human rights deficiencies to highlighting them. The Turkey of 1992 was self-consciously Kemalist, secular (in the anti-religious French tradition of laicism), run by modernizing elites from the western cities of the country, with the elected government constrained by the notorious Turkish 'deep state' that intervened periodically via military coups and issued warnings that amounted to ultimatums whenever the elected government crossed the red lines that these unaccountable military and intelligence elites attributed to the unquestionable authority of Ataturk. Invoking the authority of Ataturk should not be confused with applying the ideas of this great Turkish leader, nor with the likelihood that Ataturk's ideas of coercive nationalism and dogmatic secularism that were in control of the country throughout the 1930s would continue to be affirmed by Ataturk, had he lived longer. Ataturk died in 1938, and it remains unknowable whether he might have adapted Turkey differently to changes at home and in the world. Throughout his period of political leadership Ataturk showed himself to be a great innovator who might well have altered the country's trajectory in the post-1945 period of decolonization and self-determination or the post-1978 world of Islamic resurgence.

All Roads Lead to Istanbul

I came to Malta in September 1994 for a small pre-conference organized by the Diplomatic Academy at the University of Malta. It was devoted to the World Order Models Project and was itself a side event tied to the annual meeting of the International Peace Research Association. I arrived in an innocent mood of professionalism. By the time I left Malta four days later I was *emotionally* preoccupied with Hilal Elver who would, the following year, become my fourth wife, permanently changing my life in fundamental ways, and tying me tightly and forever to Turkey.

If most of us think of Malta at all, we think of it as we see it on a map, as a tiny appendage of Sicily that somehow achieved independence and even EU membership, or possibly we regard Malta as one of those several Mediterranean islands that were formerly subject to British colonial rule. Yet for the Maltese, exhibiting national pride far in excess of the island's size and stature, their moments of glory were associated with surviving a sustained bombing campaign and blockade by Germany designed to destroy Malta as a key British naval base in the latter stages of World War II. Even more important for Maltese national pride was withstanding the siege of the Ottoman navy in 1565, which linked the central political drama of Malta to their successful struggle of resistance against their powerful Turkish adversary. It was an emotional and historical bonding, a great victory for the Knights of Malta who had been forcibly expelled by the Ottomans some years earlier from their original Mediterraanean presence on the much larger island of Rhodes.

I accidentally arrived a day ahead of scheduled event planned by Fred Tanner, the Director of the Diplomatic Academy, who had become my friend during his year a short while earlier when he was a Visiting Fellow at Princeton's Center of International Studies. It was Fred who, quite unwittingly, turned my life around by transforming my awkwardly mistaken early arrival into a life changing experience. He asked Hilal, a faculty member at the Academy, to show me around the island for the day, a task she reluctantly accepted, regarding it as a patriarchal request on a par with being asked to prepare morning coffee 'for the boys,' and more time consuming. Worse, at least from the perspective of my making a lasting impression on Hilal, was the fact that I had arrived in Malta with my longtime Swedish partner, Elisabeth, a Swedish peace activist and Lutheran minister, who had become a participant in the WOMP experience.

Hilal was warm and welcoming as soon as we met in the lobby of our hotel. I still remember her country-style blue skirt and captivating smile when we shook hands. She later told me that her main feeling at this moment of meeting was one of relief, that I did not seem to be the stuffy Princeton professor that she had envisioned. We spent the day driving around the island, briefly visiting its exotic communities, discovering that Malta was basically a large rock with almost no vegetation and many rabbits wandering around. We ended the day having dinner together at Hilal's apartment, and meeting Hilal's 14-year-old vivacious daughter, Zeynep, who would become a major presence over the course of the rest of my life. Elisabeth and Hilal became friendly with one another as quickly as I did, but with differently motivating feelings. Maybe my scholarly vanity was stronger than I admit. During dinner Hilal realized that the book she was currently reading was my book, *Revitalizing International Law* (1986). For those so inclined, an early sign of marital 'destiny,' but for me the kind of reassurance I have sought throughout my long life.

When the rest of my WOMP colleagues arrived the next day, as expected, there were changes in the social atmosphere as most of those who came were my friends, including Peri Pamir. Peri was my earliest and best pre-Hilal Turkish friend with whom I had been intimate from time to time during the preceding decade, and who immediately connected with Hilal, exchanging lots of negative gossip about Elisabeth, I later learned, and undoubtedly some about me, which I never learned. When it came time to leave Malta, I was sad to go. The attraction to Hilal had become so strong and yet geography, our age gap, and the fact that we both had existing live-in partners made the prospect of future romance more the stuff of wet dreams than an incipient plan for any shared future. As I was happily to discover, the reasonable can sometimes be displaced by the desirable even here, where the emotional quest seemed at first foolhardy. In practice because we both wanted it to happen, the future unfolded as if prearranged, attaining fulfillment almost effortlessly as in a dreamlike trance. But first I heeded the practical imperative. I needed to resume teaching as the Fall Princeton semester in 1994 was about to begin, and I didn't want my habit of coming too early or arriving too late to become part of my career profile.

After Malta

As I dutifully resumed life in Princeton, I continued to think about Hilal, but it seemed a remote and harmless emotional indulgence that would soon fade, a casualty of both time and space. What drew me to Hilal, aside from her vivacity, spontaneous naturalness, and our instant rapport, was both physical attraction and the instinctive sense that we could be together without losing the magic, feelings that have now been validated by more than 25 years of marriage, not without its lapses, but always with the kind of restorative resilience that keeps a relationship alive and growing. Our early interactions expressed friendship without any overt acknowledgement of attraction. We both are rather shy when it comes to disclosing feelings. This all changed when one evening a month or so later back at Princeton. I attended a small university dinner for Christopher Hitchens following his talk, and drank too much wine, perhaps because I always found Christopher's brand of sardonic brilliance rather sterile. In the spirit of full disclosure, Hitchens made no secret of finding my attempt at journalism tedious (we shared this loveless past refracted through our mutual connections with *The Nation)*. When it came to alcohol, Christopher would rarely be outdone, but that evening I put on a pretty good show of my own. I weaved my way back from the Faculty Club where such dinners were usually held, to my office in the basement of Corwin Hall. While walking I was struck by the fullness of the moon and felt my heart bursting. It was still the era of the Fax Machine, and in my half drunken stupor I wrote a moonstruck message to Hilal, who to my delight, responded quickly in a similar spirit. Her message was sent to my home fax where it was immediately found by Elisabeth, and not surprisingly caused an explosive reaction. After some angry exchanges, we managed to reestablish our connection at least on the surface before she returned a few days later to Sweden to her job as minister of a Lutheran church near Stockholm.

What followed was due to the enabling virtues of a globalizing academic life that would not have been an option for those in my parents' generation or even now for most university people with limited travel opportunities. I was giving a lecture at Boston University dealing with the legacy of the Nuremberg Judgment, and Hilal had come to Boston, this time traveling with her Turkish partner, who gave her a longer leash than romantic prudence would recommend. We met after my talk for dinner and spent time together in ways that confirmed my feelings of a special magnetic attraction. We came close enough to trade romantic kisses and long embraces on Boylston Street, ignoring the gentle rain falling on downtown Boston. A week or so later, we arranged to meet in the lobby of the Waldorf Astoria Hotel where the American Society of International Law (ASIL) was holding its Annual Meeting. Hilal had in the meantime visited San Francisco with my rival. I waited nervously for several hours at what I thought was our appointed meeting place. Finally, emotionally exhausted, I gave up. I succumbed to my insecurities, and with a pounding headache dragged myself off to the Museum of Modern Art a few blocks away where I wandered aimlessly among the paintings, many of which were familiar to me from past viewing. It is hard to remember, but this was before cell phones became more common than house keys, and we had no way of communicating. We did manage to heal the wounds of what I had interpreted as a definitive withdrawal after her undoubted realization that it was unrealistic to carry our infatuation any further. But in point of fact, Hilal had been on time, waiting as impatiently as I, but on another floor of the hotel set aside especially so that people could conveniently find each other during the ASIL meetings!

A short time later, I was invited to be a speaker in Frankfurt, Germany at an event honoring Juergen Habermas, who was retiring from Frankfurt University. This event coincided with the 200th anniversary of the publication of Immanuel Kant's *Perpetual Peace*, and I persuaded Hilal to meet me there. After all she was interested in peace! And I was in love. It was a notable occasion adorned by an array of glittering performers including Habermas, Martha Nussbaum, and David Held. A huge audience came to listen to the main event. This might seem surprising, but this was Germany and unlike America, celebrity academics had large public followings.

Not long after Frankfurt, I met Hilal for a couple of days in Rome, a city she loved and where a decade earlier she had studied Roman Law at an Italian university. I stopped in Rome on my way to Belgrade for yet another conference. We enjoyed sharing Rome together, and the chemistry seemed so right that the obstacles that seemed insurmountable after Malta soon melted away as if mid-summer ice sculptures. The only remaining uncertainty was assessing the views of our respective children, and in her case, her parents, including a Turkish mother of imperious reputation. If this went well, a big if in my mind, then all that remained was the messy task of dissolving our existing involvements with as little hurt and friction as possible.

The children turned out to be easy, almost too easy! In my case, Dimitri and Noah were instantly won over by Hilal, and given their undisguised disapproval of Elisabeth, embraced my new relationship with three conclusive words—'She is great!' I was not sure about how Zeynep responded to this marital prospect except that I knew she was not fond of the man I replaced. I also realized because of her young age and attachment to her mother that our marriage, and with it, my encroachment on space that had been almost exclusively hers, would pose a threat to Zeynep and a challenge to me. Quite likely, the most formidable of these threats was that we were planning to live together in Malta, and then probably move to the United States. And in the period ahead there were times when sharing living space and competing for Hilal's attention aand affections did cause tensions of rivalry, but mostly we managed to be a congenial threesome. I did my best to keep our rivalry within safe boundaries, and usually succeeded, but not always.

As was natural in such a situation, I worried that Hilal's Turkish family would find me unsuitable for many reasons, including what I then regarded as my advanced age (approaching 65) accentuated by the gap between us of almost 24 years, as well as by the discrediting fact of my prior marriages, my American residence, my infidel status as a non-Muslim, not to mention my habitual insecurities. By then, I realized that Hilal's sense of family was exceptionally strong, which is typically the case in Turkey. I believed she would not move ahead with our future without definite signs of approval from her parents, brothers, and daughter, and so my worries grew and grew as the plane approached Istanbul. With a personal resume like mine, even without requiring a green light from Hilal's family, I was anticipating a gracious rejection just as I was preparing to walk down the ramp from the landed plane. In truth, I might have rejected me, myself, if I had been asked for an objective appraisal. On this return to Turkey I was filled with fear and trembling.

But when I deplaned in Istanbul, I found Hilal waiting with open arms at the point where arriving passengers enter the airport. This instantly overcame my anxieties, but still did not dispel my demons. It was not only my anxiety about how I might be received by Hilal's family, I felt some pain, sorrow, and a bit of guilt about abandoning Elisabeth after seven or eight years of connectedness in both Princeton and Stockholm, including my year of residence in Sweden as Visiting Olaf Palme Professor (1991-92). We had many memories, compatible worldviews, and happy experiences together, but never managed to develop those deep spiritual and emotional connections that are needed to make a relationship flourish after initial passions subside.

Even these dreary preoccupations disappeared as soon as we departed from the Ataturk Airport for the Princess Island, Heybali, in the Sea of Marmara, a few miles from Istanbul's shoreline. It was a perfect beginning for my best ever romantic journey, made extra special as our original Malta meeting also took place on an enchanted island. Heybali prohibited cars, relying on carriages to get around. We stayed together for the night at the Heybali Palace Hotel, which most appropriately was a favorite choice for honeymooning couples.

A day or so later, having returned by ferry to Istanbul, my testing time began in earnest, and a new tidal wave of anxieties swept over me. We met Hilal's father who was warm and friendly, making me feel almost at once relaxed in his company, somewhat reminding me of my own father's social style. He had spent much time in America, adored his daughter, and seemed to view me favorably as a potential long-term partner, although somewhat awkwardly as he and I were almost the same age. I never lost my sense of deference to him as he was Hilal's father and I, her romantic companion. Age gave way to status.

A few days later we met Hilal's two brothers, Haluk and Aydin, for lunch at a kebob restaurant in Istanbul, and the meeting was casual, enjoyable, and as reassuring as my earlier meetng with her father. We then went on the day long drive to the Elver summer home in a small community of houses fronting the beach at the resort city of Kusadesi, not far from the great Roman ruins at Ephesus. I was not invited to stay as a house guest, but was dropped off at the Kismet Hotel, picturesquely situated overlooking the sea and elegantly appointed, where we would later often come to play tennis, and watch the sunset from the outdoor bar with its spectacular harbor view. Hilal was not ready to introduce me to her pious mother who was the only religiously devout member of the family. I had been discreetly (mis)identified as her American *girl* friend whom she was showing around during a first visit to Turkey. So handled, I thought this might be the civilizational roadblock I had been fearing ever since I boarded the plane for Turkey. This renewed anxiety exerted a strain I didn't reveal. With this unresolved issue, we proceeded on our planned trip around the Western part of the country ending up in Istanbul a week or so later. Before leaving we agreed to marry sometime after Hilal came to Princeton when her teaching finished at the end of November, yet still I had not been approved by the family authority figure on such matters, Hilal's mother.

On the plane back to the States I wondered if we had made too hasty a decision, especially as we were proceeding without even a nod of reluctant approval from Hilal's mother, whose influence, as for most Turkish families, seems decisive on such matters. I was also contending with my own past. After all, my three earlier marriages each ended in a divorce that I was responsible for having initiated, suggesting that when marrying previously I had not looked beyond the immediacies of attraction and rapport, failing to take proper account of what makes a relationship work over time when the radiance of conquest and adventures of courtship give way to routine and competing agendas. Hilal and I had had only a brief experience of one another, and never lived together for longer than a weekend prior to my whirlwind visit to Turkey. I was confident that Hilal was not afflicted with neurotic moods, and would not challenge me emotionally in ways that Florence and Mary Morris had, but I wondered about how she, almost 24 years younger, would find me down the road after I passed my 70th year and projected a declining physical capacity, and probably serious health issues before long. Since we met, I had felt no impediments arising from our age difference, but what of the future? Some 25 years later, there is no doubt I have slowed down and have reached the age where, to my chagrin, people increasingly make way or get up to give me a seat in crowded busses or trains. Fortunately, so far, my inner age has trailed far behind. My work habits and intellectual commitments have kept me from depression or a sense of irrelevance, but how could I have known that this would be the case? And I imagined that Hilal must have worried about whether she might be marrying an incipient invalid rather than a robust partner. Maybe partly to divert attention from the possibility of my likely impending physical decline, I taught Hilal how to play tennis, squash, and ping pong until she became so good that she was winning most of our matches, although we remained competitive enough to make it still fun, even good exercise, even through my late 80s.

Our wedding was as simple and ecumenical as we could make it, and took place the day after Christmas 1995. The minister, Sue Anne Morrow, Princeton's Protestant chaplain, prepared an appropriate marriage ceremony, a sensitive Christian celebration of this union of Muslim and Jew. Several of our friends were present in our Princeton livingroom where the ceremony took place, reading poems that we chose to express our love and wider hopes. I had two disappointments: Hilal refusing to kiss me after we uttered our vows, exhibiting the customary reluctance of her Turkish generation to express physical affection in the presence of others, and the absence of my son, Dimitri who was far away, engaged in making an excellent documentary film in Cuba.

After our marriage we returned to Malta for the rest of the year, living together with Zeynep in a seaview Sliema apartment across the harbor from the capital city of Valetta. Zeynep was a baccalaureate high school student very much involved with the active local teenage partying scene. Our social atmosphere in Malta was surprisingly animated and dominated by Zeynep's friendships with girls and boys in her local private school. She was an early and adept explorer of what social media had to offer. Hilal and I developed friendships with several leading personalities on the island, including Guido de Marco, who had been a UN diplomat and President of the General Assembly one year, and then President of Malta. After his retirement from public service, Guido as a private citizen published his idealistic plan for strengthening the UN. Guido left behind a visionary legacy, and for me his death meant not only the loss of a good friend, but the passing of the best that Malta had to offer itself and the world.

Malta was quite extraordinary in many ways. Its stately palaces exhibited the affluent and royalist aspirations of the Knights of Malta, while bearing daily witness to the continuing influence of the Catholic Church. Tangibly, this meant no divorce or abortions, except of course for the rich, who could arrange to have the Vatican annul unwanted marriages or travel abroad to divorce and have abortions in more permissive European cities. The Libyan influence in Malta seemed strong, including the ownership of some of the best hotels on the island. Money laundering was a lucrative source of wealth as Maltese banking competed with European financial institutions and also earned foreign currency by adopting extremely permissive registration requirements for international shipping. I enjoyed my leave from Princeton in this new and exotic habitat, finding café hangouts nearby, working on a variety of writing projects, and maintaining a loose connection with the Malta Diplomatic Academy at the university. My notable local accomplishment during the year was not my occasional public lectures, but a victory in a year ending tennis tournament sponsored by Academy. After the year in Malta, we moved to Princeton where I resumed teaching, but with a plan that contemplated retirement, and a move to California, but in this period from 1996 to 2001 I also came to know Turkey better by spending each summer in the country.

Turkey: Engaging Politically

More than in my past involvements with Vietnam, Iran, South Africa, India, the Philippines, and even Israel/Palestine, when it comes to Turkey the political was marginal to the personal, yet far from absent. The personal core is, of course, Hilal, her family and friends, as well as my children and my life experience since my mid-60s. The political core arises from my sympathetic attitudes toward the Turkish version of religiously tinged politics and the affirmation of a government that takes advantage of its sovereignty to fashion its own national future while being attentive to international cooperation, ecological stability, human rights, and the relevance of equity and solidarity with vulnerable peoples' struggles for basic rights, including constructive views on regional and global peace and security. I felt these desirable developments were happening in Turkey during the early Erdogan years, especially as compared with the prior Turkish political profile of the 1990s, and in contrast to the autocratic rigidities of other major states in the region. My appreciation of what the AKP leadership seemed to be achieving during its early years of leadership was neither shared nor appreciated by Turkish economic and social elites that had been running the country ever since the founding of the Turkish Republic by Kemal Ataturk after the first world war. Observing such intolerant attitudes made me realize there was such a thing as 'secular fundamentalism' that could be as dogmatic and suppressive as its religious analogue.

It may not be familiar to many that Turkish secularism derives from its French variant, which is self-consciously anti-religious, as distinguished from its American variant, which is pro-religious while opposing identifying the governing process with a particular religion. Both forms of secularism have their strengths and weaknesses as the contrasting roles of religion in the governance of these two societies exhibits. There is also a stark difference between the degree of religious homogeneity in Turkey due to Muslim identity pertaining to more than 95% of the population compared to the religious pluralism and factionalism of the United States where even the dominance of Protestant affiliations is associated with vast denominational differences often reflecting class differences more than religious beliefs.

My views created social distance and some tense moments due to my failure to affirm the four corners of the secularist consensus that was unrelentingly anti-AKP, and even more intensely anti-Erdogan. This antipathy existed from the moment the upstart party unexpectedly gained and retained control of the Turkish government in 2002. Most of these hard-core critics refused to revise their negative assessments by giving credit for the impressive record of achievement during the first decade of Erdogan's leadership. I admittedly lacked the everyday experience of the society, hence did not have first-hand experience of the victimization claims made by friends or concrete incidents involving encroachments on basic civic freedoms. To a degree this deficiency was offset by being freed from the rigidities of the pro and con intense polarization that has dominated Turkish political discourse for the past 20 years to the detriment of more objective assessments of the achievements and short-comings of the governance experience in the country.

On a less overtly political plane, my enthusiasm for the writing of Orhan Pamuk was treated with annoyed derision by many intellec-tual Turks in our social circle, who castigated him for opportunistically writing for foreigners and indulging in shameless self-promotion in the world publishing market, dismissing his Nobel Prize in Literature as ill-deserved as compared to several other Turkish writers. Pamuk's *Snow*, presenting the Islamic 'other' rather sympathetically, was a book I found illuminating and openminded, but brought sneers to the faces of Turkish friends who dismissed it as trashy, and only of interest for those who are unfamiliar with Turkish society. Again, some of this anti-Pamu-kism is due to dismaying anecdotes related to reportedly unpleasant per-sonal encounters, to his torrid romantic life, and above all, to a hostility by most Turks toward anyone who dares criticize their country while abroad. In this regard, lots of public enmity came Pamuk's way after he commented on repression in Turkey and placed blame on Turkey for the Armenian massacres of 1915 in an interview done while he was visiting Switzerland.

In both of these sensitive domains, I did my best, most of the time, to keep my views to myself without ever assenting to opinions with which I disagreed. My occasional skeptical questions made even my silences strike our friends as partisan, and what blew my cover al-together were a few articles I wrote by request in *Zaman*, the first-rate newspaper of the Fethullah Gulen group then allied with the AKP, al-though later its embittered and dangerous adversary. My friendship with Ahmet Davutoglu, then Chief Advisor to the Prime Minister and Foreign Minister, further confirmed for militant oppositionists my posture of political incorrectness. Most Turks accepted my social presence out of deference to Hilal, but several stridently objected to my views, causing occasional fireworks.

After 2011 Erdogan definitely became more authoritarian and tactically clumsy, mishandling the Gezi Park demonstrations and es-pecially grossly over-reacting to the 2016 coup attempt. This gradually pushed several of Erdogan's most prominent AKP political associates to the sidelines, and shifted my view closer to those of critics and the opposition, although only some of our friends noticed the change, and wanted to keep me targeted as 'an Erdogan lover,' or in Hilal's gentler words of explanation, 'Richard has a soft spot for Erdogan.' Saying this to a committed Kemalist would not be so different from telling an Israeli that 'Richard has a soft spot for Hamas.' So however much my life in Turkey and love for the country and its people developed over the years, I met with disapproval in some circles. Despite this, most of our Turkish friends and acquaintances valued the common ground that lay beneath the surface of political differences. They were not only accepting, but loving, and this made friendships in the country special and abiding.

It is odd in some ways. With my earlier engagements with Vietnam, Iran, and Israel/Palestine I was criticized, sometimes harshly, for leaning too far to the anti-American or anti-Israel side, while when it came to Turkey my effort, at least in my mind, was to understand the complex realities as well as I could, which meant leaning toward the almost vacant center in polarized Turkey. Almost all anti-AKP folks treated my 'neutrality' as situating me in the AKP camp, given the raging debates that dominated the Turkish political scene after 2002.

Social Cleavages and Political Polarization

Even before Hilal introduced me to 'a Turkish life,' with a small Istanbul apartment, annual visits, and a growing number of Turkish friends and experiences, I had a rather strong interest in Turkish politics. While the visit in 1992 under the auspices of the Helsinki Citizens focused on Kurdish aspirations and grievances, my pre-Hilal involvement with Turkish political issues was somewhat more extensive. I had written and spoken about the Armenian massacres of 1915 more in the spirit of solidarity with what I conceived to be a victimized people rather than on the basis of extensive historical knowledge. I had been uncritically willing to endorse Armenian claims of Turkish 'genocide' without doing the homework that should always precede uttering such an incriminating judgment. Rereading what I had written I fault myself most of all for not distinguishing between the legal, political, and moral condemnations of genocide. It should be evident that the crime of genocide could not have occurred in a *legal* sense in 1915 as even the word 'genocide' did not exist until 1944. As the Nuremberg Judgment of the Tribunal evaluating German crimes in a World War II context explained at length, there can be no crime unless delineated by a *prior* law. I also wrote sympathetically of the Kurdish struggle for self-determination, and later regretted that

I had not clearly drawn the crucial distinction between state-shattering self-determination and the satisfaction of self-determination claims within the boundaries of existing states, which is essentially a plea for the collective rights of equality and autonomy. Finally, I had contributed a chapter on the Turkish deep state in pre-AKP Turkey to an edited volume on the nature of the state in international relations that I continue to regard as expressive of the realities of the late 1980s and early 1990s.

My personal and political engagements with Turkey consisted from its outset of a series of encounters, exposing me over a long period to a very different kind of society, culturally rich in tradition, welcoming to strangers, and constantly negotiating the wavering line between tradition and modernity as it plays out in political and social realms, with particular relevance to mosque, nation, market, family, and state/society relations. I became acutely conscious of both the intense polarization that dysfunctionally divides the country not only with respect to religion, but also in relation to class and geography, as well as the human capacity to transcend these socially constructed boundaries if other forms of compatibility are present. Hilal never challenged the secularist mind-set directly but was no less receptive to those on the other side of the wall than I was, only more socially tactful.

Turkish social life touches fuzzy limits based on ethical uncongeniality that assumes a political form. I feel no obligation to listen respectfully to a fascist or racist rant or to respect such distasteful views of how to organize the collective sides of human experience. I remember a couple of unpleasant social events at Princeton where I engaged acrimoniously with apologists for apartheid South Africa. These encounters convinced me that debates between sharply opposed views on such litmus issues may provide a perverse form of entertainment for an audience but it left me feeling extremely dissatisfied and sometimes physically nauseous. For the last 30 years or so I have declined every invitation I received to engage in debates or hostile media exchanges that had no prospect of becoming a dialogue or even a conversation, including with such high wire trapeze artists as Bill O'Reilly, Megyn Kelly, and Alan Dershowitz. I was sometimes told by friends that there is no such thing as bad publicity, but I valued serenity and peace of mind more than public visibility. Despite the value of listening to the other side, nothing useful or enduring is ever learned by taking part in acerbic confrontations.

Thus, it is not a matter of my refusal in all instances to build a firewall between the political and the personal. I could not, on my side, maintain a friendship with a dedicated Trumpster or someone who swung their weight toward neo-fascism out of fear or hatred of refugees, or migrants fleeing from disaster. I did come to realize that for some anti-Erdogan Turks any positive acknowledgement of the achievements of the AKP or the leadership of Erdogan is for them an anathema as defining as are those red lines of Trump and fascism for me. I can say this abstractly, but I do not accept it existentially. These two political cultures, despite sharing this condition of toxic polarization, are not the same. I know of no one within my social circle who admits to supporting Trump or Trumpism although, if political leadership was limited to foreign policy, I am not all sure that the country or the world would have been better off had Hillary Clinton been elected president in 2016, considering her support for regime-changing intervention, her seeming readiness to raise geopolitical tensions with Russia to a level where Cold War II would have been a likely outcome, and her supplicant attitude toward the international excesses of Wall Street. I am reminded of the contempt displayed toward me by liberals after I acknowledged voting for Ralph Nader, a third party candidate, in the 2000 elections that elected George W. Bush as president. The vote was not close in New Jersey where I was living at the time, but would I have made my vote count if I lived in Florida or somewhere close results were anticipated?

After the Iraq War I did lean toward the view, which I continue to hold, that the two main political parties continue to have a consensus on key issues of foreign policy, militarism, and capitalism. I couple this sense of convergence with the belief that significant differences between the two parties do exist with regard to the impact of their social and domestic policies on the lives of the poor and vulnerable, as well as the quality of the judiciary and diplomatic corps and respective engagements with multilateralism and the UN. This has led me throughout my life to vote consistently for Democratic Party candidates in national elections, but accompanied by the almost invariable feeling that I was choosing 'the lesser of evils.' Before I die, it would be exhilarating to vote in a national election for someone I felt really good about. As a presidential candidate, Obama came closest, but his brand of mainstream internationalism worried me during his 2008 campaign, my worries being borne out during the eight years of his presidency.

In some respects, in the last five or so years tensions have eased in Turkey as many earlier supporters of the AKP have themselves become distressed and alienated, and second opponents somewhat fatigued, by Erdogan's autocratic style and long tenure. AKP opponents, on their side, have became readier to admit that there is presently no responsible and unified opposition in the country capable of mounting a successful electoral challenge. This mood changed somewhat after the 2019 CHP victory in the crucially important election of the mayor of Istanbul. The prospect of the surprise winner, Ekram Imamoğlu, emerging as a formidable opponent of Erdogan and potential challenger of AKP leadership is reviving political debate in the country as are the policies toward the region pursued by the current Turkish leadership, especially in relation to Syria and Libya.

In this period I deeply appreciated Hilal's book [*The Headscarf Controversy, Secularism, and Freedom of Religion*] published in 2012 by Oxford University Press, analyzing the headscarf (hijab) ban in Turkey through the optics of law and human rights, producing a strong critique of the prohibitions imposed on headscarf wearers from these perspectives. What was baffling to me, although perhaps wrongly so, was the strong resistance by leading Turkish publishers that she approached concerning a Turkish translation. The explanation given by Turkish publishers was that the arguments pro and con relating to the headscarf ban were already so familiar to Turks that making the book available in Turkish would arouse little interest, manifestly apolitically contending that no Turkish market for Hilal's assessment existed. My experience in Turkey suggested that such reasoning was completely wrong. The truer explanation of this reluctance arises from the unwillingness of secular elites to accept what amounts to the moderate and responsible self-criticism that emerges from a legal analysis that regarded the headscarf ban as an interference with freedom of religion and freedom of expression. There is little doubt that the headscarf ban as applied was interfering with the human rights of a large number of Turkish women. I was reminded of the Turkish negative reactions to Pamuk's *Snow,* which also reflected in my view Turkish resistance to self-scrutiny, rather than the dismissal of the book because it was superficial and trashy, and allegedly written for foreigners. Both Hilal's treatment of the headscarf controversy and Pamuk's humanizing of Islamist lives were threatening to both the ideological left and Kemalist conceptions of the Turkey they fervently affirmed while leaving little political space for dissent or pluralism of belief and social practice.

In important respects, I found the prevailing forms of the opposition mentality deeply anti-democratic and intolerant. I remember one intelligent neighbor of Hilal's family vacation house in Kuşadasi telling us rather proudly that his son's vote should be counted as seven times more than that of those backward and uneducated persons living in Anatolia. Only thus, he argued, would it ever be possible to avoid the dumbing down of Turkey's governing style that he believed resulted from allowing the vote of every Turk to be counted equally. In such a view, democracy was intended essentially to serve as a periodic endorsement of a Kemalist political status quo, a vindication of the established social and economic order, and this should be interpreted to mean that political participation should not be extended to the whole society, and those religiously inclined should be confined to a lower caste status, and ideally kept from exerting influence in the political arena. This informally worked for Kemalism until the AKP came along in 2002 to explode the myth that *exclusivist* democracy was authentic democracy. As was to be expected, when the AKP began after 2002 to dominate Turkish elections and alter the bureaucracy in its favor, there were allegations that the party in power was unfairly using its leverage to the disadvantage of Kemalists. In effect, the claim being made was that religiously tainted AKP political manipulations were responsible for creating illegitimate forms of exclusionary and majoritarian democracy.

Along similar lines, I would mention the pre-AKP acceptance by this dominant portion of Turkish society of the custodial role of the armed forces, along with foreign policy subservience to NATO, and especially Washington's priorities. A decade before the AKP came along I was told by a Turkish friend that it was only the military that prevented a reactionary Islamic tidal wave from sweeping across the country. And when the tidal wave did indeed arrive, despite endless precautions, in 2002, the buzz I encountered in the cafes of Istanbul was that it was only a matter of time before the military stepped in, and this would be a desirable ouster of AKP governance to preserve the Turkish republic as constructed by Ataturk. There was a feeling of bitterness and disappointment by the most outspoken Kemalists, when a coup didn't happen, maybe as early as 2006 or so, combined with ongoing admiration for the military. I was pleasantly surprised in 2016 when, in the immediate response to an attempted coup that came out of a seemingly blue sky, even many of Erdogan's fiercest critics welcomed its failure. Several years after these events, given Ankara's repressive over-reaction there may have been second thoughts, but I have not heard such sentiments articulated. Rather, the feeling expressed here is that the years of AKP governance have transformed the Turkish armed forces to such an extent that it no longer is capable of making positive contributions to the Turkish political scene even with respect to foreign policy, and as such is not seen as either motivated to or capable of launching a coup. I am

not convinced that this is an accurate reading of the situation, and I suspect that if the military leadership surprised the public with a coup that
brought the old elites back to power, few tears of regret would be shed
on Baghdad Street, a prosperous stronghold of White Turks in Istanbul.

This self-segregation of the Turkish less religiously inclined community was brought home to me by a trivial, although telling, social
incident that occurred a few years ago. A moderate journalist couple in
Istanbul had known of our friendship with the Davutoğlu family and
called Hilal to ask if this then emergent AKP leader would be willing to
accept a dinner invitation at their home. After Hilal's reassurance that
she thought that the Davutoğlus would welcome such an invitation, it
turned out that they were free on the particular evening of the dinner
and would be glad to come. The journalists seemed happy about this,
yet somewhat nervous. The journalist wife called Hilal on the morning
of the dinner in a near panic, asking what kind of food to serve that
evening as they never before eaten in the presence of a woman wearing a
headscarf. It so happens that Sare Davutoğlu (Ahmet's wife) is a highly
respected gynecologist who runs her own clinic. She is sophisticated,
friendly, and worldly, despite her affirmation of an Islamic lifestyle, and
as we expected, she was as socially adept and forthcoming, while also
being intellectually informed, as anyone in the room that evening, except
possibly her own husband.

This anecdote reveals a disturbing absence of interaction and perception even among open minded Istanbulians. Such separateness helps
preserve stereotypes and invidious comparisons that are the props needed to sustain hostile and hierarchical forms of polarization. It made me
also more critically self-aware of my American experience. I never felt
patronizing toward Turkish society because I had experienced at an early
age a racist and almost unconscious version of self-segregation while
growing up in New York City, which then prided itself on being culturally light years more open-minded than the vast interior of America, let
alone the South. It should be understood that self-segregation is almost
never *mutual* and is always *hierarchical*, with the self-segregating group
regarding itself as superior, with higher living standards and more genteel neighborhoods, which is surely the case in Turkey, although as in
America mingled with class issues, which are almost always reflections
of racial categories. Such hierarchies are informally enforced by social
norms that are often not consciously affirmed. The 'self' that is doing
the separating and makes its neighborhoods, restaurants, social spaces
off limits, except for servants and workers, exhibits its dominance in

everyday life, creating for itself a sense of the normalcy of its implicit claims of what might be called 'societal ownership.'

The major cities of Turkey in the Western part of the country retain elements of this self-segregated past despite two decades of AKP governance that have blurred such boundaries, which are again reflected in changing class relations. This gives rise to trends toward voluntary desegregation, usually associated with market considerations, most noticeably in Turkey's numerous shopping malls and selected restaurants/hotels, a development sometimes critically commented upon by displaced Turkish elites who speak disparagingly of an 'invasion' that makes them 'uncomfortable,' without their pondering the past humiliations endured by those who dared manifest their religious identity.

Racial self-segregation was taken for granted in the upper West Side of Manhattan in the 1940s where I grew up and endorsed subconsciously by white elites living in this supposedly most cosmopolitan northern American city. From early childhood such separateness, which always came with an unspoken coding of superior and inferior, never struck me as ethically justifiable, socially desirable, or justified by appeals to street safety. Perhaps my friendship with Willis, our longtime African American household helper, grounded my views in friendship and affection, giving me early in life the strength of will to distance my attitudes from those of my mildly racist and homophobic father and his friends. It is interesting that in the later years of ghetto riots, sociologists speculated that New York City avoided the worst outbreaks of racial violence, because there was at least visual contact due to the dependence of both whites and blacks on subways to navigate the city. Lack of such eye contact was invoked to explain why the car culture of Los Angeles experienced much worse racial tensions and violent outbreaks than did New York because of the stronger adverse stereotyping, yet both cities conveyed in distinct and harmful ways to resident and visitors the socio-economic realities of systemic racism. Social distancing may slow the spread of disease during a pandemic, but it is what enables 'good people' to overlook deep injustice until forced to face unpleasant realities in times of turmoil.

In apartheid South Africa I encountered a comparable reality where the only regular visual interracial interaction for whites occurred when they were dealing with their black servants who were technically required by law to return home to the African-only townships. In practice, these servants were generally allowed, even instructed, to sleep in tiny rooms in their white employer's household, again to satisfy the practical convenience of their white masters who sought the benefits of live-in servants. In effect, this was an instance of exceedingly limited 'unlawful' voluntary desegregation, ignored by the state for classist reasons so as not to inconvenience the white overlords.

Although I have been critical of Turkish pushback against the electoral majorities of the AKP as creating doubts about the virtues of democracy, I now raise the same question in my mind as I witness in the United States Trump's headlock on 40%+ of the American voting public. To me this does raise questions about enfranchising society as a whole under present historical circumstances. And looking around the world, I take note of free elections resulting in the leadership of such autocratic and dangerous leaders as Modi, Bolsonaro, Duterte, and others. Little wonder that the most admired thinkers in ancient Athens lost faith in democracy. Yet to limit the vote to the wealthy, the educated, social elites, and religious leaders is to opt for exclusionary paths that have led to Hell in the past. The unfolding tragedy of the human condition is that under planetary scale threats, democracy as a mode of governance is failing almost everywhere, and no alternative on the political horizon holds out much hope of doing better. Arguably, the failure is less of democracy as a system of governance that of its rigged deformation by special interests and bankrolled donor-driven parties and candidates. On more hopeful days I wake up believing surges of support for a social and ecological revitalization of progressive versions of democracy, while currently out of sight is hovering just over the horizon.

Ahmet Davutoğlu's Visionary Democratic Politics

In this period of AKP leadership in Turkey Recep Tayyip Erdogan was the dominant figure, adored and admired by many, feared and rejected by many, the voice and the face of Turkey so far in the 21st century. Erdogan is a complex figure who evolved during his long tenure as supreme leader, moving away from a more inclusive governing style to an increasingly autocratic and arbitrary approach to governance. As with other autocrats dependent on a degree of electoral support, Erdogan seemed to be conscious of his *legacy* at times, both with respect to the glories of the great Ottoman sultans, the long shadow cast by Ataturk's founding of republican Turkey, and the problematics of Turkish deference to U.S. foreign policy and NATO that was a legacy of the Cold War. At other times when challenged from within and without he displayed political tendencies that seemed pragmatic, even *opportunistic*, associated with holding the reins of power tightly without much attention to ideological perspectives. This blend of legacy and opportunism makes the image of Erdogan's leadership confusing, and given the fact that he has been in control for so long, there seems to be a growing feeling in Turkey as of 2020 that it is time for a change.

There are some alternative leaders that begin to show promise as challengers of the Erdogan status quo. I found the most congenial and interesting of these alternatives to be Ahmet Davutoglu, partly reflecting my long friendship with him that has allowed me to be more familiar with the political perspectives he favors and confident about his exceptional strength of character, intelligence, courage, integrity, and dedication to a Turkey that builds on an inclusive past, combining the Ottoman and Ataturk heritages, with a commitment to an inclusive present that is pluralist, protective of human rights, and attentive to the needs of the people and the reputation of the nation.

I learned a great deal through these years from Davutoğlu. I was immediately impressed by his intellectual brilliance and inter-civilizational approach to knowledge when we met in Malaysia some 30 years years ago. Then, thoughts of a career for him in politics would have seemed fanciful, even absurd. At the time I met Ahmet he was a young professor of international relations, and although I envisioned a bright academic future for him, it never even occurred to me that he would become a leading political figure in his country as well as its most distinguished public intellectual. We reconnected after Ahmet returned to Turkey a few years later. Ahmet had created a free educational curriculum for graduate students throughout the country. The work was organized by a small extremely modestly funded foundation facility. The faculty was cobbled together by Ahmet who acted as the primary lecturer in the most ambitious course offerings on a range of topics related to world history, civilizational studies, and philosophy, East and West.

Ahmet was the director and intellectual mastermind of this fledging academic initiative that grew in scale and reputation year by year. He invited graduate students from around the country to come to Istanbul for advanced courses in world history, philosophy and culture, and comparative religion that were taught intensively on weekends. It was a truly innovative learning community that was not constrained by Western ideas of specialized graduate education in the humanities and social sciences, and its faculty, especially Ahmet, also gradually became an informal brain trust and meeting place for important Turkish personalities who formed the nucleus of the AKP. Such personalities included Abdullah Gül who was to serve as President of Turkey between 2007 and 2014, after having been Foreign Minister (2003-2007). Gul gave

Turkey strong and coherent AKP leadership that for a long time seemed to many observers equal, or almost so, in its overall balancing impact on the country to that provided by Erdogan.

Each year I was invited to give a talk on world issues at Davutoğlu's foundation. After my remarks and discussion with the very engaged and bright students, a small invited group would walk to a nearby large mosque for an arranged and tasty traditional Turkish dinner in the mosque restaurant. A religious atmosphere certainly existed, but it was backgrounded, not made explicit in conversation or ritual. In fact, Ahmet's intellectual guidance and erudition was decidedly inter-civilizational and ecumenical, stressing the relevance of global and regional history, as well as the richness of diverse cultural and religious traditions.

In lectures and discussion Ahmet was clear that he believed that republican Turkey had made a huge mistake by educationally and politically suppressing the study and cultural appreciation of Turkey's Ottoman past. He felt strongly that Turkey could not move forward as a country unless it incorporated and claimed cultural ownership over its long historical past as a proud legacy, and even more significantly as a vital part of its current national identity. Only then could Turkey achieve an adequate sense of the unity of its past with its present, which he convincingly believed necessary to build a strong, independent, and inclusively democratic and appropriately modern Turkish future. I was persuaded by Ahmet's assessment of these issues, which, while new to me at first, seemed sensible, enriching, as well as allowing Turkey to move into the future with an empowering awareness of its extraordinarily rich past. I was somewhat aware that this viewpoint was inconsistent with the Ataturk priority given to shaping a modern Turkey, which Ataturk had believed required a repudiation of the Ottoman mentality that he associated with pre-modern traditions and values, including religious constraints on politics. Ataturk by thought and action sought the replacement of Ottomanism by a Europeanized model of secularism that would encourage the dynamic development of science and industry. Iran directly imitated Ataturk's development model, although within a monarchist framework and strategic entanglements with Britain and the U.S., leading to a much more drastic nationalist and religious pushback than anything that ever happened in Turkey.

Ahmet never linked his approach, often wrongly characterized by critics as 'neo-Ottomanism,' to an explicit criticism of Ataturk's leadership. At the same time, as far as I can remember, Ahmet also refrained from mentioning Ataturk at all, which struck me as a non-confrontational way to challenge the continued blind adherence to Kemalism, which certainly seemed to be the hegemonic ideology in my early pre-AKP years in Turkey. This hegemony was reinforced by pictures of Ataturk, and only Ataturk, in all public buildings, public squares, parks, as well as in most shops, homes, banks, and other private sector settings. It remains true, despite the supposed one-man show of Erdogan, that the only image of a Turkish leader publicly and privately displayed, aside from campaign posters, is that of Ataturk. Despite constant and understandable accusations of a cult of personality, the absence of Erdogan's pictures (except in the course of election campaigns) is notable, yet rarely noted. I have posed this question to several Turkish friends, who either shrug unknowingly or say, unconvincingly coming from them, that Islam frowns upon images of humans and other beings, but if that were the case, I would have expected an AKP campaign to discourage the presence of Ataturk pictures, at least in public buildings. This has not happened and deserves more nuanced commentary than it has received.

As the funding base of Ahmet's foundation expanded, he also organized a series of annual international conferences that gathered intellectuals from around the world in a stimulating multi-civilizational setting to focus on themes of global interest. These events took place in a vibrant and free intellectual atmosphere, pluralist in spirit and substance. I felt privileged to be invited year after year as a speaker, followed by being asked to be among the contributors to a conference volume later published.

My first decade of experience in Turkey made me feel that the ascent of the AKP in 2002 was very beneficial for the country. The government was energetic, doing many exciting and positive things for Turkey at home, in the region, even in subsaharan Africa, and elsewhere in the non-Western world. Turkey was dramatically increasing its regional and global reputation and influence. I was very impressed by the quality of leaders and advisors gathered around Erdogan. In addition to Davutoğlu, others whom I came to know, respect, and like in a variety of settings were Abdullah Gül and Ali Babacan, a brilliant economic advisor, as well as Ibrahim Kalin who later became Erdogan's key foreign policy advisor. Turkey was genuinely making the most of two sets of opportunities: unleashing economic growth by extending its orbit of involvement to the Arab world, and to Africa and Latin America, all the while expanding foreign investment and raising the living standards of the bottom 20% of the Turkish population, as well as pursuing an independent role as mediator and promoter of peaceful relations in a variety of surrounding regions and sub-regions where Turkey had geographic, cultural, and historical connections. This diplomatic outreach included the Balkans and the Caucusus, as well as such Middle East hot spots as Israel/Syria and Iran. In all these settings, Turkey's underappreciated role was to act as a pro-active peacemaker and to provide auspices for dispute settlement that were neutral so far as geopolitical ambition or ideological orientation was concerned. I would venture the somewhat unconventional view that no country has made a comparably constructive effort within its region, broadly conceived, to generate peace and prosperity in the period since the end of World War II, and no region stood to benefit more from the success of this effort than the Middle East. It is a tragedy for Turkey, and the Middle East generally, that the dynamics of geopolitical interventions from outside the region and internal turmoil doomed these laudable efforts.

Why, then, did these larger Turkish ambitions fail to produce enduring and intended results? Such a question deserves detailed scholarly inquiry. Here I would offer two tentative explanations. First, there was a play of forces in the region that no one grasped correctly, including Turkey, although its leaders tried more diligently than others, and consistently sought to promote conflict-resolving outcomes without any signs of focusing their efforts on promoting political Islam, or more narrowly, expanding Sunni supremacy in the Arab world. The Arab Spring in 2011 seemed at first conducive to the fulfillment of these Turkish hopes and aspirations, coupling democratic fervor with an affirmation of cultural and religious identity. Turkey was the first important country to show its enthusiastic support for these unexpected developments. In a later phase these achievements of the Arab popular risings were variously reversed by strong counterrevolutionary currents that reestablished authoritarian rule in some countries and produced devastating, violent civil strife in others.

The second line of explanation is the regional play of geopolitical forces that after the Cold War led to American efforts to exert hegemonic control both for the sake of securing oil supplies at affordable prices and to uphold the security interests of Israel and Saudi Arabia. These American interventions and regressive alignments accentuated the counterrevolutionary backlash of Arab regimes of corrupted elites that felt extremely threatened by democratizing demands and their unpopular dependence on U.S. security support.

In this period, then, I not only experienced a sense of personal fulfillment by way of marriage and married life together in Princeton, followed in 2002 by our move to Santa Barbara with summers in Turkey, but also a feeling of political excitement as a result of being in close contact with several of the personalities driving forward the AKP leadership of Turkey during the first decade of the new century. I regarded the Turkish political role to be the most hopeful, innovative, and constructive series of political and economic developments currently going on anywhere in the world. Ahmet bestowed on me a challenging invitation to organize a meeting of foreign policy and international relations experts of my choosing from around the world not long after he took control over the Turkish Foreign Ministry in 2009. I worked hard to produce a result that would not be disappointing. It turned out to be a stimulating and enjoyable gathering held at the Four Seasons Hotel splendidly fronting the Bosporus. I successfully arranged the participation of many outstanding academic and diplomatic personalities from around the world, some of whom were personal friends.

The event had one piece of bad luck. Davutoglu's own participation was very limited due to the fact that the conference unexpectedly coincided with a potential breakthrough concerning a Brazil/Turkey initiative in 2010 to find an agreed solution to regional tensions flowing from Iran's nuclear program. Rather than having its efforts applauded, Turkey was chastised by Washington for not 'staying in its lane' (geopolitically) by trying to promote a positive outcome to a regional crisis that has persisted and intensified during the next decade. In my view, it was the United States that should have returned to its lane and allowed the Brazil/Turkey initiative to go forward rather than blocking it. Nonetheless, our conference on the Bosporus was a big intellectual success, producing some excellent discussions of regional and global issues, but regrettably there was no follow up, wasting its potential, diminishing its impact. I was given a leadership role, including sitting next to Abdullah Gul, then President of Turkey, at a farewell dinner on a cruise vessel on the Bosporus. What I didn't expect was to be asked in the middle of the dinner by the Turkish coordinator of the events, Bulent Aras, to make some extemporaneous remarks as the dessert course arrived. I was not prepared and probably did not rise to the occasion, but neither did I disgrace myself, uttering a few gracious platitudes about accomplishments and hopes related to what had transpired and what we might hope for in the future.

In this period, I was also given significant roles in several high-profile events in Istanbul. I was invited to speak at conferences associated with the Turkish/Spanish leadership of the UN Alliance of Civilizations

Project that was seeking an affirmative alternative to the Huntington conflictual scenario of 'a clash of civilizations.' The discussions brought together prominent personalities from the region, most of whom were more hopeful than realistic, as it turned out. I tried in my presentations to address the interplay between nationalism and geopolitics in coping with inter-civilizational tensions.

In 2011 I was asked by Davutoglu to form and then serve as chair of the First Istanbul World Forum. I invited an outstanding group of progressive intellectuals, especially from developing countries, who welcomed this chance to visit Istanbul, and participate in a semi-official parallel event to the important UN conference devoted to the least developed countries being formally hosted for the first time by Turkey.

In the end, without trying, I had become rather visible in Turkey as an American supportive of the drift of Turkish diplomacy and its worldview. This visibility was almost totally an outcome of my friendship with Ahmet, who invited me to play these somewhat publicly visible roles. At first, this visibility was not particularly noticeable except within Turkey, but as the polarization sharpened in the period after the failed coup of 2016, I became controversial in the Turkish diaspora.

At the same time, I was trying to process the significance of some disquieting political developments. I confronted growing evidence that the earlier polemical attacks on Erdogan were being increasingly validated by his resort to an autocratic governing style, signaling a shift from genuine earlier attempts to provide inclusive leadership to a more exclusivist or majoritarian style of governance with particularly repressive consequences for the critical voices of journalists and academicians. This shift antagonized especially those few liberal intellectuals and social democrats who had stuck their necks out earlier by acknowledging the positive results achieved in the first eight or nine years of AKP leadership. I tried my best to avoid altogether abandoning my position of qualified support for the AKP, still appreciative of what had been achieved both within the country, the region, and even the world, and yet I could not deny that there were disturbing domestic trends that were increasingly worrisome. I felt that my claim of being a truthful witness of controversial global situations was being tested. I truly didn't identify with the hostility to Erdogan and the AKP that seemed to represent a shared consensus joining the odd pairings of displaced Kemalists, the old (Marxist), new (pro-Kurdish; anti-authoritarian) Turkish left, and Hizmet/FETO followers and sympathizers.

In the wider trajectory of my life experience, I think Turkey has provided a valuable learning experience in several respects. The main line of dismissive and critical response of those that are offended by my views, and these include several friends, can be reduced to several contentions: 'You don't live here, so how would you know' and 'As an outsider you just don't realize how bad Erdogan and the Turkish government is on a daily basis.' And maybe out of politeness they only muttered under their breath, 'and you don't even speak Turkish!' implying 'how would you know what's really going on?'

I realize that there may be some truth to these comments, but also that they are self-serving as they do not take into account their own strongly partisan sentiments that lead to one-eyed perceptions, seeing only the bad in the present setup and forgetting the good, or failing to acknowledge the gross policy failures in pre-AKP Turkey or by other actors in the region. As an admitted outsider, but with some strong inside attachments and considerable experience in assessing foreign political developments, I think that the detachment of the informed and partial outsider has certain definite advantages in depicting controversial political realities, including a more balanced capacity to identify whatever strengths and weaknesses may be present, given the simplistic tendencies of polarizing perceptions. Such a semi-detached outlook is also more often willing to make illuminating comparisons with the Turkish past and with respect to conditions in other countries of comparable scale and tradition, although the strong Turkish national pride dislikes comparisons.

Such comparisons were uniformly resented by Turkish critics of the status quo who consider their own fall from grace as not comparable to what has been happening in Egypt and Iran. I regard the two countries as comparable, sharing cultural depth, historic experience, and size of population and territory and sufficiently similar to that of Turkey to make comparisons helpful provided differences are also taken into account. The response I have received from Turks, which I find unconvincing, is the claim that Turkey has progressed so much further constitutionally, institutionally, and economically than either Egypt or Iran to an extent that makes comparisons misleading, even insulting. Nevertheless, I continue to find these comparisons helpful. It encourages an awareness that the intense international campaign to discredit Turkey falls between the ultra-hard line of the West toward Iran ever since the revolutionary events of 1979, but even more pronounced since Trump became president, and the 'see no evil' approach to the crackdowns in Egypt because the 2013 military coup was geopolitically convenient, ideologically congenial, and pleasing to Israel, Saudi Arabia, and the United States.

Such a comparison also serves to remind Turks that despite the encroachments on human rights, especially since the 2016 coup attempt, there remains greater openness in Turkish society and even its media than elsewhere in the region, particularly in contrast to Egypt and Saudi Arabia. This less severe encroachment on democracy is that much more impressive if we take under consideration the fact that Turkey has real bases for nervousness about its internal and external security. Among these concerns are the continuing subversive potential of the Fethullah movement, the various terrorist spillovers from regional conflicts, continuing combat operations involving the PKK operating from Iraqi mountainous areas, Israeli and Saudi hostility, and the seeming receptivity of important political elements both within the country and internationally to a destabilization of Turkey, especially if it led to regime change. The tepid international reactions in the West when it briefly seemed as if the 2016 attempted coup against the government of its NATO ally had succeeded was a telltale sign that unlike explicit support for friendly governments subject to internal threat, as was the Shah's Iran in 1979, regime change in Ankara would not be opposed no matter how it came about.

Beyond these features of the post-coup atmosphere, without downplaying the excesses of the Erdogan leadership since 2011, especially with respect to the freedom of journalists and the dismissals of university faculty and civil servants, it is important to appreciate the continuing, if declining, electoral popularity of Erdogan and the AKP, the absence of responsible or credible alternatives, and the impressive material progress with respect to the bottom 40% of Turkish society, which deserves inclusion in any evaluation of the protection of human rights in the country. These positive factors are somewhat offset by a deepening economic crisis and a sense of what might be called 'Erdogan fatigue,' the feeling in Turkey that it is time for a change, a feeling powerfully confirmed by the crushing defeat of the AKP candidate in the rerun of the election in June 2019 of Istanbul's mayor, hailed inside and outside of Turkey as the beginning of the end for Erdogan and his governing coalition. The new opposition parties headed by former AKP ministers, Davutoglu and Babacan, are injecting much needed political critiques into the Turkish body politic.

I have come to believe that it is part of a liberal and self-serving tacit conspiracy rooted in the individualist capitalist ethos to overlook social and economic rights achievements when appraising the records of countries. I would now argue that without considering social and economic rights, which include poverty, homelessness, and safety nets, it is misleading to rank states' human rights by reference only to 'freedom' and 'political and civil rights.' Such rights are crucial, to be sure, but pertain at most to the upper 20% of society, and thus seem to bear less on the legitimacy and democratic credentials of an inclusive society as a whole than do economic and social rights. I find myself in disagreement with many liberal friends who (rightly) condemn the human rights failures of countries such as China and Vietnam do so without ever acknowledging their extraordinary achievements when it comes to poverty alleviation and the progressive realization of economic and social rights, which compare so favorably to the records of their liberal models of constitutional democracy in many Western countries. This is not to say that I don't acknowledge that suppression of political and civil rights also diminishes greatly the overall quality of a democratic political order, and thus has a wider effect on wellbeing than is assessed by considering only the effects on those whose political and civil rights have been curtailed.

My outlier views on Turkish political developments in the AKP period are emblematic of my struggle. They are maintained at a social cost, are discredited by opponents, first by being exaggerated and misunderstood, and then by being rejected. Hilal has sometimes objected to my efforts to consider both the pros and cons of the AKP record, and herself struggles to find a balance between her secularist background and her sense of political Turkey, which has so far not generated credible alternatives to Erdogan.

In some ways I find parallels with my attitude toward Trump and Trumpism, again a willingness to consider pros and cons, although the pro side increasingly requires an act of will on my part. Due to the extent that Trump has weakened the bipartisan consensus on foreign policy and has resisted the worst warmongering, he deserves credit although there is no evidence that he knew what he was doing. An anti-Russian Democratic president might be worse for the world, although a reelected Trump would be horrible for America, for human rights, for persons of color, and for the future of democracy in the country, as well as his being a dangerous risk taker and bluffer when addressing global and regional challenges, who has given a bright green light to Israeli expansionism and many hugs, physical and political, to autocrats around the world.

The Attempted Coup of July 15, 2016

For Hilal and myself this day started in a normal way, or almost so. It was the first time we had come to Istanbul from our summer home in Yalikavak on the Bodrum Peninsula since arriving in Turkey in June. We came to Istanbul after a short plane ride to take part in a conference at Koç University devoted to Syrian Refugees and the European Migrant Crisis scheduled for the next day, at which I was listed as the keynote speaker. To ensure we would arrive on time in the morning we were put in a hotel the night before on the European side of the Bosporus in the Kadikoy neighborhood. Before dinner we were strolling in the neighborhood along streets lined with crowded cafes filled with young people casually celebrating a warm mid-summer night. We stopped at a Greek restaurant and ran into friends who invited us to join them. As we neared desert after enjoying excellent food, the manager came to our table and discreetly advised us to head home as a coup was underway. He told us that the bridges over the Bosporus were occupied by army personnel and tanks opposed to the government, and that gunshots had been heard.

We followed this advice, harboring intense feelings of apprehension and curiosity. I think that our room was on the seventh floor of the hotel, but it may have been higher. Before long we heard the terrifying noise created by F-16s breaking the sonic barrier while flying at low altitudes, over and over again, close to our hotel, obviously trying to cause panic in Istanbul. We did feel frightened and helpless. While this dynamic continued, we watched TV, trying to get as much sense as possible of what was happening, feeling that this was history-in-the-making. At first, representatives of the coup were before the cameras reading victory statements and reassuring the public that order would soon be restored. After that came the dramatic Erdogan Facetime message urging his supporters and those loyal to Turkish constitutionalism to go out onto the streets and city squares, and gather at the Istanbul Ataturk Airport to protest against this attempted coup and overthrow of an elected government. This broadcast was the turning point, with Erdogan reaching Istanbul an hour later on a plane from the southern Turkish city of Marmares, having apparently narrowly missed a kidnapping or assassination attempt while there with his family on vacation.

Erdogan thanked the Turkish people massing at the airport for their support, and the coup ended as quickly as it began, with signs of national unity being expressed by the main political parties, including those opposed to the AKP, even the Kurdish HDP. What followed was first a sense of relief, coupled with angry accusations directed at the Fethullah movement, immediately called a terrorist organization and insultingly labeled 'FETO.' We had a few anti-AKP friends who questioned the official explanation of events, expressing their belief that it was 'a theater coup,' staged by the government to create pretexts useful in its quest to accumulate even greater power for the supreme leader. However most Turks, then and subsequently, have accepted the broad contours of the official version, including the leaders of the various anti-Erdogan factions, albeit not all their members.

There was an encouraging display of national unity in the days immediately following the coup, even including large posters of Ataturk at AKP demonstrations to suggest that all Turks, whether of the party in power or the Kemalist opposition, were together in safeguarding the country from this takeover. I found this early display of unity after years of polarization to be an impressive sign of the extent to which Turkish society had matured. I admit to being surprised, remembering how many had waited hopefully for a coup in the early AKP years. This change of attitude in the country, although arguably temporary, has never received the commentary or analysis it deserves.

Soon a new phase of recrimination and purges started, partly fueled by genuine fears that the FETO forces still had the capabilities to mount a second coup attempt, especially if outside help were this time forthcoming, and partly out of vengeful feelings toward those deemed to be disloyal by being associated in any way, even intellectually and passively, with FETO. The extent of the resultant purges was unjustifiable, featuring the imprisonment or dismissal of thousands of government employees, especially in the police, judiciary, and armed forces, but also in state educational institutions and the media. It was clearly an over-reaction, even while acknowledging that there were genuine substantial security threats present, and hence prudent for the government to believe that these threats might materialize if the government appeared to any degree vulnerable. Taking all circumstances into account, the Turkish state overreacted, but in a manner that is common among states confronted by internal security threats that cannot be clearly identified and removed.

Many in Turkey took note of the long record of CIA involvement with and support for the head of FETO, Fethullah Gülen, the enigmatic and apparently absolute leader of the movement. Turks found it suspicious that the CIA had lobbied twenty years earlier for Fethullah's 'green card' residence permit when he sought refuge in the United States, managing to overcome opposition from the FBI and State Department. It was also evident that the liberal democracies in the West did not voice strong support for the democratically elected government of Turkey during the coup in July. This was somewhat shocking considering that Turkey had long been a key NATO member and was governed by a government with strong ties to Europe and North America. As the coup attempt unfolded, the liberal democracies seemed to adopt a wait and see attitude, not dissimilar to their response to the Sisi coup three years earlier in Egypt that got rid of a government that was at odds with conservative Gulf forces, Israel, and indirectly, the United States. In Turkey, under very different circumstances, the coup attempt failed, but the lack of any show of solidarity by its NATO partners definitely shook Turkish trust in the value of the alliance and of its relations with the United States, stimulating explorations for new international alignments that have continued up until the present in an ebb and flow rhythm. As might be expected, an action and reaction cycle ensued, with each Turkish step toward realignment stimulating assertions that Turkey could no longer be counted upon within the NATO framework.

Of course, in situations of this sort, ordinary citizens hear many contradictory interpretations, the air is full of conspiracy conjectures, and most people have little hard evidence to know what is true and what is false, which make most fall back on predispositions. The reality of the events of 2016 remain shrouded in the mists created by partisan readings, ranging from a U.S. deep state conspiracy that backfired to conspiracy theories about 'a theater coup' arranged by Ankara to mobilize national unity and portray Erdogan as savior of the nation. As yet, there seems as yet no definitive reconstruction of the events on that fateful night except. That said, we were witnesses to what was undoubtedly to became a major revolutionary moment in Turkish history as well as permanently weakening the foundations of Turkish relations with the United States and Europe.

At first the political crisis centered on the Turkish demand that the United States hand over the accused FETO mastermind, Fethullah Gülen, to Turkish authorities for criminal prosecution. This request was refused by Obama's Washington, either because of concern about what this leader might reveal with regard to U.S. connections with the events or because the evidence justifying extradition provided by the Turkish government was insufficient, or maybe some combination of the two. Soon other issues emerged, involving differing priorities in the Syrian War as between ISIS, the Assad regime, and radical Syrian Kurdish forces, as well as clashing views about relations with Iran and Russia.

At the same time, some fence mending has also taken place since 2016, making the future orientation of Turkey quite uncertain with respect to its alignment and governmental outlook, especially whether it inclines more toward Moscow than Washington in the near future, although their combat involvements on opposite sides in Syria and Libya makes the Russian option currently problematic for Ankara.

What I Learned (or Thought I Did)

Being close, over this 20+ year period, to Turkish developments gave me both a love of the country and a recognition of its deep fissures and uncertain future. Knowing and feeling deep personal ties to those on both sides of these fissures makes me care fervently for the future of Turkey with heart and mind. It is potentially such a promising country in its many dimensions, so much so that it could provide the inspirational basis for a positive future throughout the region, and yet the country might implode at any time, possibly victimized by the tensions within being magnified from a variety of potential regional and global interferences or from some kind of economic crisis giving rise to fiscal collapse.

For me Turkey has been a learning experience from beginning up to the present moment, and undoubtedly for the rest of my life. I have watched this talented and dynamic people struggle to restore their past and create a future that fulfills their potential. This struggle over Turkey's furtue is far from over. It is ongoing, and its outcome may tell a great deal about the future of the region and even the world. The next phases of Turkish political development remain to be determined and vulnerable to an array of positive and negative influences. I retain the hope that the Turkish future will unfold to become as glorious as its best past days. On a personal level, I hope that I will be accepted in Turkey as an engaged friend of the Turkish people and their great civilization and that this will be will be the standpoint from which my opinions emanate, and are judged.

Must Read -- Princeton Emeritus Prof Richard Falk's revealing resurrection of
THE Robert Mueller's senior thesis at Princeton, of which Falk - now happily
based in Santa Barbara - was Thesis Advisor. In The Nation: thenation.com
/article/robert...

Saul Mendlowitz   Mary Kaldor   Gerry Spence

Edward Said   Georges Abi Saab   Eqbal Ahmed

Yasser Arafat

Imam Ruhollah Khomeini

Nelson Mandela

Miguel d'Escoto Brockman

Palestinian Resistance

Human Rights Expert Raji Sourani with Richard Falk in Gaza

Fernando Henrique Cardoso, former President of Brazil with H. & R.

Richard Falk and Ahmet Davutoglu, 26th Prime Minister of Turkey

PART FIVE

EXPLORATIONS OF A CITIZEN PILGRIM

"The world is too dangerous for anything but the truth
and too small for anything but love."

—William Sloan Coffin, Jr.

My professional and political life evolved along increasingly converging paths. I felt that I was learning to understand the world better on the basis of my scholarly and teaching activities and learning to act more knowingly as my life journey unfolded as an engaged citizen, or what is more often called 'a public intellectual.' I learned by stages to trust the heart as much, or more, than the head, yet always seeking harmony between the two while leaving space and time for the soul, that is, for spirituality to intervene and transcend with energies beyond my control. I came to trust the synergies that resulted from such receptivity.

Graduating students or younger colleagues sometimes asked me a question that I have periodically asked myself—'What should I do with my life so that it will have an impact?' I was even asked a few times, 'How can I become like you?' As I have retained some of my adolescent insecurities, I would be slightly embarrassed by such queries, while thinking, yet not saying, 'God, forbid.' I responded awkwardly, sometimes turning the question back—'This is a personal question that only you can answer, perhaps helped by watching and listening to others, but in the end you alone live your life.' In recent years, somewhat more confidently, I would say at least this—'Try to discover that what you enjoy doing as making your life satisfying to yourself will usually help make it satisfying to others. Also, those who enjoy what they are doing, and how they are living, tend to be more persevering, which often leads to greater effectiveness, empathy, a sense of fulfillment, and seem less vulnerable to burnout and cynicism. Joy, play, and dreams are essential ingredients of effectiveness, satisfaction, and sustaining love.' Indirectly, I guess, these musings on the interplay of the political, intellectual, and personal set forth an approach to living well, while acknowledging the torments of the contemporary world. It is about being open to the ethical, emotional, aesthetic, and spiritual dimensions of life, as well as being unafraid to indulge moderate hedonistic impulses, and by trial and error keep discovering and rediscovering balances that work.

As I reflect on these musings, I am struck by my white privilege of living for nine decades free from acute pressures of deprivation, oppression, depression, and illness. In this primal sense, my life choices seem a great luxury that I took for granted until I became self-aware enough to realize that I have been unduly fortunate. Having lived without the urgencies of material needs, health challenges, and adult tragedies befalling loved ones allowed me the head room to dwell on desires, responsibilities, even fantasies. I am aware that very few among us enjoy such freedom to follow their dreams, and among those that are so fortunate, very few are spiritually alert enough to seize the opportunity. Instead most of us plod mindlessly ahead on impersonally prescribed roads seeking prestige, affluence, and societal respect, and if lucky, the satisfactions of family life and cultural diversions.

I remain unsure what enabled me to take some advantage of these primordial freedoms, that are outside the orbit of canons of good governance, yet at the core of a fulfilled life.

Maybe in my case a slow process of maturing is part of the story. I grew up without the pressure of ethnic and tribal traditions or congenial parental models. This caused me to drift aimlessly for many years until strong enough to clear my own path. By the time I awakened enough to feel, think, and act for myself, I became more alive to the pleasures of the mind/body/heart, as well as the stifling restrictions of organized collective life as further constrained by societal patterns of conformity.

My friend, Bill Coffin, one of the great religious personalities of the last half of the 20th century, had a great gift of finding illuminating and catchy phrasings to comprehend the human condition by way of simple binaries that make us see more clearly what is vital and how it relates to our freedom to act in the world, both physically and emotionally. In this vein, his insistence on wakefulness to injustice and attentiveness as guided by love is concisely expressive of an emotional imperative: be encompassing in the affirming acceptance of otherness in a spirit of empathy and equality. Speaking from my public and private experience, love is not love unless differences are conditioned by an overriding ethos and spirit of equality tinged with non-judgmental empathy, recognizing the universal entitlement to human dignity. W.H. Auden ended one of his finest poems with a similar sentiment, 'We must love one another or die.'

Yet love without tangible commitments to try to alleviate the suffering of others is a New Age dead end. 'Taking the suffering of others seriously' as my friend, Upendra Baxi put it, became my mantra, rescuing me from self-satisfied complacency that could have been my fate after discovering my comfortable niche in academic life. Somehow, instinctive reactions against the cruelty, violence, oppression, and inequality in the world in the course of teaching and scholarship needed to be complemented by acting in the lifeworld. Over the years, I reminded myself of the graffiti I saw on a Seattle wall: 'Thought without action equals zero.' I was morally ambitious enough to want my gravestone to justify the inscription, 'Greater than Zero!'

The historical trajectories of many global trends as my life nears its end makes me wonder if any among us made a difference in the sense of overcoming the bio-ethical-ecological crisis that threatens the human future, no matter how hard we tried.

CHAPTER 16

Intellectually Engaging the World: Fears, Desires, and Hopes

"A people without vision perishes."

A Profile of Intellectual Activism: Ideas Beget Deeds

I am not sure when I began to worry seriously about the human future as an object of personal reflection and as a subject of scholarly inquiry. The seeds may have been sown during my university experience of literature, religious thought, and philosophy courses taken during my last two years at Penn, especially writing about Kafka and Rilke, and meeting the challenge of composing 'my religion' in weekly papers on such assigned themes as human nature, good and evil, and transcendence. My worldly interests were shaped shortly thereafter in response to the legal theorizing of the McDougal/Lasswell experience at Yale, which was then followed by adopting a progressive worldview during my years at Ohio State as a fledgling member of its law faculty. Two poles of academic/advocacy engagement were greatly influenced by concerns about global governance and the menace of nuclear weaponry, as given concreteness in my life by two dedicated individuals who became the closest of friends, Saul Mendlovitz and David Krieger. These friendships were linked to my close collaboration in projects that each devoted their lives to achieving. In Saul's case, what I came to call 'humane global governance' was the core of the project he led, having the unprepossessing name of the World Order Models Project or WOMP. In David's case, the work devoted to the abolition of nuclear weapons was carried on under the auspices of the Nuclear Age Peace Foundation (NAPF). Needless to say, neither laudable goal was reached, indeed their attainability receded further, raising a subversive question in my mind—were these '*worthwhile failures*'? I believe they were. We must be willing to keep failing if we are to hold onto hopes of sometime succeeding.

Saul pushed hard the idea that the war system was a doomsday machine that could only be safely managed by a world government. For Saul, nuclear weapons were just the most menacing manifestation of warfare, a terrifying symptom but not the disease. All through my life I have wrestled with the arrangement of this sense of priorities—between war as the primary challenge versus nuclear weapons as the apocalyptic menace that must be given priority in time and attention. At times I felt one way, and at other times the other way, while realizing that the two goals are interconnected in multiple ways. Part of the human ordeal is the uncertainty surrounding relative risks that pertain to choices of this sort. Realists rely on countervailing power to contain the risks, while humanists insist on international law, the UN, and negotiated disarmament agreements. These humanist aspirations that I share lack political traction without the emergence and establishment of a supportive transnational community, and this has yet to happen in my lifetime. As a result, the national communities that underpin realist thought help us grasp, in part, why the flawed structures of internationalism remain impervious to criticism or efforts at globalizing reforms.

These concerns gave rise to my long collaborative relationship with Saul and later David Krieger, the founding President of the Nuclear Age Peace Foundation. Both were dedicated-for-life crusaders who never deviated from their respective obsessive interpretations of what was the most immoral and unsustainable feature of the political arrangements currently governing the world. They each resisted making any concessions to the overlap beyond saying 'yes,' of course, war and nuclearism are connected. Saul believed that if we eliminate war the threat of nuclear weapons would be addressed along the way, and coupled this with the belief that this goal could only be safely reached and maintained if a world government was established. David was just as convinced that the urgency of the nuclear danger cannot be postponed until the deeper, longer process of removing war from the political landscape becomes a viable undertaking, and was convinced that only a denuclearizing process embedded in a universal treaty regime containing monitoring and enforcement capabilities could spare humanity an apocalyptic future. Neither was receptive to more comprehensive approaches that addressed war and nuclearism at the same time. I was engaged in both endeavors rather centrally, heading the North American participation in Saul's global scholarly network and being chair of the board of the Nuclear

Age Peace Foundation for almost a decade and continuing to serve as its Senior Vice President.

Saul and David are warm and sincere, intelligent, informed, and totally committed to their particular visions. Saul was an excellent entrepreneur of ideas with a fundraising talent. As a result, he was able to initiate the ambitious World Order Models Project. Saul never wavered in his conviction throughout his long life that war was the problem and world government was the solution. He never managed to produce scholarship that matched his intelligence or his passionate convictions. Instead he hitched his wagon to World Peace Through World Law, a detailed conception of a much-enhanced United Nations, a form of world federalism or world government set forth as a comprehensive revision of the UN Charter. It was co-authored by Grenville Clark, a successful Wall Street lawyer with a high social standing who wanted more from life than money and prestige, and Louis Sohn, a refugee from Poland who became a professor at Harvard Law School, a specialist in the United Nations. Clark and Sohn realized that there are few among us who believe such global governing schemes are practical or desirable alternatives to world order as administered by sovereign nation states. Their approach never appealed to me. It was too legalistic and apolitical from my viewpoint, seeming to assume that political traction would follow naturally if a strong rational case for overcoming a state-centric world system could be made. I have never believed that political arrangements would be responsive to rational calculations, even if convincingly argued. I was more inclined to endorse and support ideas of popular struggle and inherent conflict as aspects of the human condition that connected dramatic changes in political structures to eruptions from deep below the surface of societal normalcy, usually bursting forth with unanticipated fury. In this regard, I felt that order and stability came from elites and rulers, while drastic economic and social changes came from the mass discontent mysteriously mounting revolutionary challenges to the established order.

In his wish to bring the Clark/Sohn vision to political reality Saul persuaded Harry Hollins, a disaffected Wall Street WASP and devotee of Grenville Clark, to find the funds to make world government happen. Harry, a good natured and humble man, was convinced by Saul's enthusiasm and Grenville's social stature that it was possible to widen dramatically international support for world government, but to do so required the ideas and proposals to be endorsed and championed outside of the United States and the West. The basic idea of the project was to stimulate transnational scholarly inquiry into the requirements of a

PUBLIC INTELLECTUAL

world peace system, which these leading academicians thought would lead indirectly in the Clark/Sohn direction of global governance. Saul was a smart enough salesman of ideas to know that he could not peddle the Clark/Sohn plan as the pre-agreed solution if he wanted to recruit first-class academic participants from non-Western backgrounds. There had to be an openness, an invitation to dialogue, and the promise of give and take.

After many discussions the project saw the light of day in the form of the World Order Models Project infelicitously known as WOMP. After traveling the globe, Saul managed to gather leading public intellectuals from a variety of national and regional settings around the world to ponder the future of world order. The meetings continued for more than almost three decades, devoted to a variety of thematic concerns (e.g. world economy, UN, war, human rights, technology, development, international law, global commons, environmental protection, population growth). On the basis of these discussions and research papers, each main participant agreed to produce a book that set forth a vision of an attainable and desirable future. These books were published during the 1970s in a series called 'Relevant Utopias for the 1990s.' Skeptics often asked 'relevant to what?' And even the avid supporter would have dispensed with 'relevant' and substituted a less optimistic title such as 'Toward a Peaceful, Just, and Ecologically Responsible Future.'

Although the books emerged, the 1990s are long gone, and even a friendly critic is tempted to describe the endeavor as 'Irrelevant Utopias for the 1990s.' But come to think of it, are utopias even supposed to be relevant? And if well-conceived, are they ever really irrelevant if the imagined future manifests a compassionate and creative political consciousness?

I learned from my WOMP experience, despite never sharing Saul's hopes for its substantive outcome. My own contribution to the project was titled *A Study of Future Worlds*, published in 1975. I had become worried by environmental pollution, population pressure, resource availability as competing with war as threats to human wellbeing. This influenced my contributions to WOMP, and led me a few years earlier to write *This Endangered Planet: Prospects and Proposals for Human Survival.*

Saul stubbornly pushed his ideological agenda, claiming authority on his humorously self-anointed role as 'superchairman' of WOMP, but other participants were not hesitant to assert their contrary visions of the future. The ten core participants had their own alternative agendas, and not one of us posited world government as the likely or desired outcome. Despite some tense moments in the public meetings, friendships formed, and Saul more than the rest of us separated conviviality from intellectual and ideological disagreements, which sometimes ran deep. WOMP was in some sense ahead of its time, and might have had more impact if undertaken after the turn of the century, the end of the Cold War when greater public awareness existed of global governance challenges arising from global warming and economic globalization, which were not being met adequately by governments of states or by existing networks of international institutions.

What WOMP participants favored for the future mirrored the tensions that then gripped the world as well as the diversity of perspectives as to how to promote human wellbeing. I learned by being exposed to these self-confident public intellectuals from foreign countries, especially those from the global South. In the WOMP contexts, the principal regional directors were each articulate and dedicated to a set of priorities that reflected their social and political location in the world as well as their personal outlook. This meant that the Western and Soviet preoccupations with war/peace issues connected with the dangers that the Cold War would produce a catastrophic third world war were not nearly as widely shared as I had previously assumed. China was represented by Paul Lin, a scholar teaching in Canada but aligned with the Maoist revolutionary movement that came to power on the Chinese mainland in 1949, decades prior to the modernization embrace that came in the late 1970s under the guidance of Deng Xiaoping. Lin advocated the interplay of peace and development, with less concern about human rights and democracy, but sharing Moscow's hope for great power stability.

The WOMP participant from India, Rajni Kothari, was primarily concerned with economic development in a democratic context, with an eye turned toward regional cooperation. In contrast, the leader of the African group, Ali Mazrui, ardently favored a post-colonial African indigenous identity, a recovery of sub-Saharan traditions repressed by colonial rule, including a sense of militarized virtue and cultural pride. The Japanese participant, Yoshikazu Sakamoto, wanted above all to encourage a belief in democracy and the power of social movements to bring peace and fight militarism to the world. Sakamoto sought to restore Japanese national pride by affirming a non-imperial indigenous worldview that was peace-oriented and apologetic toward the rest of Asia, making amends for the cruelties and militarism of imperial Japan.

Finally, the Latin American team emphasized the goal of participation in world order, which promoted the collective empowerment of
their region, which entailed lifting the burden of U.S. hegemony that had
made Latin America a forgotten continent, virtually unacknowledged in
global settings. Those representing Latin America in WOMP believed
it imperative to foster a robust form of regionalization that excluded
North America, allowing the countries of the region to have independent
voices beyond their national borders. As I write, Latin America remains
a forgotten continent in most settings.

What is most striking in this sketch of the spectrum of views that
dominated the WOMP experience was the apparent disregard of Saul's
advocacy of world government as the indispensable path to take. This
governmental and global approach had little resonance for the rest of us
in the project, so little that no effort was made to engage with such views,
even for the purpose of refuting their claims. This opposition to the in-
stitutionalization of authority at a global level reflected the persisting, if
increasingly dysfunctional, attachment of peoples and elites throughout
the world to identities forged on the anvil of national values and experience. To some extent, as a Westerner and friend, I was a link between
those hoping for rapid economic development, social justice, and regional solidarity, and the war/peace priorities of the West. My contribution
did envision some degree of global transformation and the importance
of mechanisms of 'central guidance' to coordinate and realize stability
in what I vainly hoped would be a disarming and demilitarizing world.
In WOMP, I felt true to my progressive outlook that was then evolving
in the course of my academic and activist opposition to the Vietnam
War. At the same time I felt comfortable assessing world order potentials
with respect to taming the war system in every conceivable way. In both
settings my activism was complemented by a primary commitment to
academic scholarship, somewhat setting me apart from most other scholars and activists who did one or the other, but rarely both.

My engagement with anti-nuclear advocacy had the same blend of
scholarly concerns and activism. It was built around my friendship with
David Krieger and work with his foundation, the Nuclear Age Peace
Foundation (NAPF). In his more serious roles as advocate and foundation head David was as quiet and measured as Saul was flamboyant
and insistent. David's political identity included supporting progressive
causes. Whereas WOMP was self-consciously global in scope, NAPF
was rather local, with its funding and activities rarely occurring outside
the city limits of Santa Barbara. While a junior military officer David had

become an early resister of the Vietnam War while living and studying in Hawaii. He had developed a visceral dislike of nuclear weaponry and the shadow it cast over political normalcy and human destiny.

As with Saul, David had an overarching and unwavering goal: the abolition of nuclear weapons within a short and unrealistic time horizon. This focus gave coherence and meaning to his work, and infused his deep devotion and slanted his writing and reading of poetry. His continuous stream of writings over the years never strayed far from the need for actualizing the political and ethical agenda of nuclear disarmament, and the politics of its promotion nationally and internationally. Unlike Saul, who was a long-time faculty member with respect for scholarly work, David was skeptical whether academic study could do much for the world other than fill library shelves with unread books. David was more of a believer in nonviolent lawful activism, journalistic endeavors, poetry, and denuclearizing steps taken by existing institutions. Saul, despite an intense emotional engagement with a peaceful future for humanity, never strayed far from the Ivory Tower where varieties of Hegelianism held sway, joined by special faith in those charismatic ideas whose time had come. Both David and Saul shared an unshakable faith in the correctness and relevance of their respective visions. Neither was politically radical, although they were both, if pressed, critical of capitalist excesses. They were children of the Enlightenment, believing from the depth of their being that facts and evidence, clear public reasoning, emotional commitments, and a certain level of pressure from benevolent wealthy citizens could make political leaders in the end do the right thing. They had confidence in the willingness of political and even economic elites, if sufficiently pushed from both below and above, to accept the need for the changes that they advocated with passion. Such an affirmation of the reform potential of the existing political system was coupled with cautious and somewhat detached support of and minimal involvement in movement politics asserting more structural agendas relating to socio-economic justice.

In all these respects, I had a different understanding about how drastic change comes about, placing my hopes and commitments in eruptions from below that contain revolutionary energies and put forth radical demands. Admittedly such eruptions have historically generally fallen short of expectations for change even when successful in overturning the old order. Nonetheless, in this fundamental sense, although not without a growing ambivalence, I placed my faith in people, social movements, and substantive democracy rather than in elites and their organizational frameworks. I did do my best to encourage shifts in public opinion achieved through education and progressive journalism. Putting the point more concretely, I felt the anti-war movement was more effective in challenging the Vietnam War than was the Council on Foreign Relations when it finally realized it was a lost cause, although both played distinct roles, one from above, the other from below. Neither realized that underlying structures needed transforming.

I failed to achieve the clarity and continuity of focus achieved by Saul and David, or their degree of vocational and ideational concentration of energy. I was more wedded to the intellectual life and scholarly endeavor, was mostly comfortable with the insularity of university communities, and only secondarily, in the spirit of civic duty, ventured belatedly into policy-oriented domains. I never overcame my dislike of the incrementalist preoccupations in Washington, with the here and now of governance and the ups and downs of various political personalities clinging to the greasy ladders of public sector ambition. I was drawn to philosophical, ethical, activist, and spiritual ways of engaging with the world, and studied on my own, the dominant currents of European thought. I remained attracted to the writers I had encountered long ago as a student, including Martin Buber, Kierkegaard, Sartre, and Camus, and later attracted to Dostoyevsky, Tolstoy, and Nietzsche, and still later to Derrida, Fred Dallmayr, and Davutoglu, among others.

Academically, this diffuseness on my part played out by my engaging with many different issues over the course of my career. I would develop a certain understanding of a topic, write about it for a while, then move on as new issues attracted my interests. I rarely abandoned earlier substantive interests, but took breaks to inquire and explore elsewhere, and then when an occasion presented itself, I happily reverted to earlier interests. With this intellectual profile, I find myself difficult to pin down, which has in some ways limited my impact in any given area while widening it overall. Like William Blake's 'fool' I have persisted, but whether I have become 'wise' as did his fool is a question only others can answer.

With this background, my intellectual and political postures may seem somewhat detached and independent. I became uncomfortable and felt out of place when walking along elite corridors of power as at the Council on Foreign Relations or the American Society of International Law, yet there I was, in my first twenty years as a university teacher. After feeling pleased to be invited to these elite parties, I would soon feel unappreciated, marginal, and somewhat alienated, and began silently sulking on the sidelines, never entirely jumping ship but rarely participating.

Because of my Princeton credentials and continuous intellectual engagement with smart colleagues, I could have connected more closely with such mainstream viewpoints if I had wished to do so. These mainstream arenas reflected my sense that I would often learn more from enemies than allies. In my courses I assigned readings that were distasteful, driven by ideas I found unacceptable and even regressive. I studied the writings of Kissinger, Brzezinski, Morgenthau, Bull, Waltz, Aron, and others, despite fundamental disagreements, because I wanted to understand what the political elites were hearing and heeding.

One result of my rather distinctive way of being in the world was to make many friends, but few, if any, protégés. That said, I seem to have influenced my share of students and others, often to my surprise. I receive moving feedback quite often from students whom I have almost forgotten, who get in touch years or even decades after our time together to tell me how much my course(s) and career has meant to them. At the same time those who entered my academic orbit invariably plowed their own fields and harvested their own crops. If I am at all relevant to how their lives worked out, it is as a fertilizer and non-toxic weed killer, rather than as a persona to be emulated or served.

If I have an ethical/political anchor, or at least can identify a consistently pursued cluster of concerns, it is to be alert to instances of severe injustice and planetary dangers. This helps explain my attention to human rights, and later ecological ethics, that I extend to include the suffering of animals and a caring relationship to nature as animated by lived experience and a reverence for pagan divinities. It also relates to my interest in the wellbeing of strangers, transgressors of social norms, and unborn generations. I acknowledge that these interests are intellectual and quite abstract, and are beset by contradiction. How can I support the struggle of the Uigher minority and yet oppose confronting China for fears of a new cold war or worse? Also, my values and beliefs should lead me to be a vegetarian, yet despite a couple of determined tries, I found it too difficult to remain steadfast, partly due to travels and social situations where it seemed awkward, or worse, to insist on my dietary commitment. This gap between what I believe necessary and desirable on a species level and what I do as an individual is a constant reminder of my 'normalcy.'

I admit that my witness has been at a distance, although not always at a safe distance, as I have ventured close on several occasions to active killing fields around the world. On reflection, I consider myself an 'intellectual worker' inside and outside of the academy, bearing witness through solidarity and writings with all those victimized by the brutality of states and violent societal adversaries. I tend toward being non-judgmental toward the means of resistance chosen by those subjected to severe forms of repression and denial of elemental rights. I did avail myself of my comparative advantage as a scholar/journalist to call attention to various forms of wrongdoing, and in this role was probably more effective than if I had volunteered to work in hospitals or refugee camps, which would have involved addressing the suffering of victims concretely. I retain an ambition to write something worthwhile on the right of resistance in international law and constitutional practice.

The Accursed American Exceptionalism

For me, 'American exceptionalism' is more a curse than a blessing. I instinctively recoil at the claims of American Exceptionalism that has hidden and suppressed the flaws, insensitivities, and criminality of my own political culture ever since the beginnings of this extraordinary country. The truer, more paradoxical, assertion is that almost anything you can say, right or wrong, about America was, is, and will be true, but so will its opposite. For me that exposes the myopia of being either self-congratulatory or self-negating—although recent patterns of U.S. behavior at home and abroad have increasingly rejected the guidance of our better angels, warranting a rogue state status or even the designation of 'negative exceptionalism.' This becomes a testing moment for citizens of conscience to step out from the shadows of resignation and passivity. Unless the underlying structures of predatory neoliberal capitalism and global militarism are challenged from below by a movement not beholden to the established two-party hegemonic control of political life and its accompanying bipartisan consensus on foreign policy there will be no hope of arresting the decline and fall of the United States at home and internationally.

I place assertions of American exceptionalism in the same category as claims derived from the Bible proclaiming Jews as 'the chosen people' of God. Often the same people who make claims of exceptionalism consider it anti-Semitic to point to Jewish influence in the media, Hollywood, and finance or to complain about Israeli lobbying and money pushing American foreign policy in directions that do not serve national interests or that point to leverage exerted on political figures who receive pressure-laden huge donations from ultra-Zionist billionaires. Without

the humility that comes with the recognition of the paradoxes and contradictions that are deeply embedded in the human condition, arrogance
and hubris are almost certain to produce exploitation and domination.
Insofar as collective virtue is a correlative of collective vice, Jews cannot
claim at once the superiority of being 'chosen' and yet simultaneously
angrily fend off contentions of Jewish manipulation of government and
society by money and influence as anti-Semitic tropes. This instance of
having it both ways disturbed me long before I became a critic of Israel
and Zionism in the context of the Palestinian struggle for basic rights.

Having so acknowledged this impenetrable nature of social and
political reality, how then can I justify aligning myself with partisan
causes? Of course, one evasive response would be to explain that this,
too, is a paradox, and in many ways it is. Derrida has made many aware
that making decisions involves unavoidable leaps of faith. This blend of
commitment and doubt is, I believe, the bedrock of progressive politics
that is both dedicated to change, hostile to dogma and extremism, and
amenable to admitting and correcting mistakes. To act confidently in
the face of radical uncertainty as to effects and outcomes exposes some
fundamental dilemmas of the human condition. It also helps explain why
our beliefs, values, and DNA, along with subconscious drives, shape
our behavior even more than do knowledge of what is possible, class
position, and a claimed reliance on science and rationality. In recent
years I have tried clarifying my own views of coping with the tensions
between uncertainty and engagement by learning as best I could from the
profound reflections of Jacques Derrida on these matters.

Forms of Engagement

In searching for ways of being-in-the-world I have naturally been
drawn to the spheres of action where concrete choices between alternatives of 'for' or 'against' are enacted. In making these choices I have often
found that I partially close my mind to counter-narratives to avoid being
immobilized in the treacherous domain of either/or. I have struggled to
retain values associated with decency and innocence to avoid extremities
of behavior arising from 'the end justifies the means' kind of mentality.
In working through such difficult issues I have both tried to be engaged
with struggles of the day, and not just as an interpreter, but as a partisan
and activist, yet remaining deeply concerned with 'the long game' of life,
its meaning, our destiny and potentialities as a species, including ecological and spiritual imperatives that appear to project a destiny of doom
unless a new civilizational consciousness humanely responsive to these

challenges somehow displaces what is now threatening the sustainability of life as we know it and makes horizons of species extinction no longer confined to the orbit of science fiction.

I do my best to see reality from the perspective of personal, social, and political adversaries, and thus sometimes disappoint friends and students by seeming indecisive or hesitant when it comes to denunciations of opposed views. I believe that in many instances partisanship and compassion are complementary, not at odds. For me this is the difference between a humane and an inhumane foreign policy. Part of the disorienting troubles of the world is the relentless insistence of so-called political realists that the world operates more in accord with the logic of their inhumane calculations, although these are somewhat constrained in the nuclear age by considerations of prudence.

In my scholarly work, from the beginning, I have above all tried first to understand all sides and only then to point fingers of assessment and judgment at behavior that significantly departs from moral and legal norms associated with peace, justice, historical circumstances. and practical experience. My encounters with authoritarian regimes in the Philippines and South Korea, with apartheid South Africa, wartime Vietnam, revolutionary Iran, repressed and resisting Palestine, polarized Turkey and the United States have all been addressed or alluded to in prior chapters. Here I propose to discuss my evolving ideas of the evolution of the global order, especially the incorporation of ecological perspectives in the late 1960s and my sense of normative and spiritual dimensions supplied by law, morality, religion, history, and culture.

Not far in the background is my concern about the contemporary workings of capitalism, especially since the collapse of socialist alternative imaginaries in the period since the end of the Cold War. When ideological alternatives disappear from the horizon of political relevance, the dominant ideology tends to fill the vacuum while accentuating its own flaws. To me, Margaret Thatcher's TINA (there is no alternative) was the most depressingly influential observation in the period at the end of the Cold War. In the case of capitalism this development since the fall of the Berlin Wall in 1989 means giving in to materialist greed that shows up in social reality as the widening inequality of income and wealth, and an ethos of winners and losers displacing a win/win economic playing field that demonstrated an inclusive sense of societal responsibility for the wellbeing of all. Other developments reinforced the impact of the end of the Cold War on the next phase of global capitalism, generally associated with 'neoliberal globalization.' These developments, including the weakening of organized labor, digital workplace realities, and the rise of AI and robotics. They have contributed to what seems to be a severe moral crisis afflicting current and near future phases of capitalism, manifesting itself in grossly dysfunctional forms of inequality that generate insecurity, alienation, demagoguery, and scapegoating, which are, in effect, evasions of the moral and political challenge of creating decent work and humane societies.

Arguably, as well, the Soviet failure reflected an ideological rigidity that had denied legitimacy and political space to alternatives to the official version of state socialism, which had the effect of pushing the practice of socialism toward unsustainable rigidities and bureaucratic ineptitude. China, despite serious mistakes and human rights violations, seems up to now to have incorporated enough market-driven thinking to make its type of socialism work as a spectacular engine of growth, influence, and stature at home and throughout the world, although replete with its share of contradictions.

After the Cold War

Without examining the post-Cold War political realities in detail, it seems clear that the verities of the Cold War era have lost their ability to offer reliable guidelines for either thought or action in the third decade of the 21st century. Several converging developments have complicated the process of assessment in rather radical ways. First, it has become evident that the militarization of the governance process in the United States, coupled with the over-investment in military hardware over a lengthy period, has undermined prospects for a peaceful world order and revealed that when in tension, capitalist priorities take precedence over values associated with democracy, human rights, ecological stability, and even human survival. Such a priority is exemplified by pushing arms sales to countries with abysmal human rights and democracy records or treating the rainforests of the world as subject to territorial sovereignty rather than as a global commons. It also leads to perceiving many political conflicts through a militarist optic, which has led to tragically destructive results.

Secondly, with the collapse of fascism and Communism, the absence of political challengers has pushed neoliberal globalization to its predatory utmost, and has contributed to the rise of a series of illiberal democracies exhibiting autocratic tendencies in many of the world's most important countries—indeed to such an extent that a feared return of fascism is no longer a paranoid delusion. Ideological totalism invites political decline and eventual collapse as was the experience of totalitarianism in Germany and the Soviet Union, and has begun to haunt the yet incomplete American narrative.

Thirdly, this hierarchy of priorities, as punctuated by the recent surge of ultra-nationalism in key countries, has made it impossible for a system of world order based on the national interests of sovereign states to create cooperative mechanisms to meet severe environmental and ecological challenges of global scope with prudence, equity, empathy, and rationality.

Fourthly, global inequality, needs-driven global migration, the search for authentic forms of identity, and militarized ruling bureaucracies have generated a demagogic backlash that has decisively weakened, if not deformed, the humane character of even long entrenched constitutional democracies. Such autocratic behavior habitually includes looting the public treasury and a variety of forms of corruption among political and economic elites. Under such conditions the implicit social contracts between state and society lose their legitimacy.

Fifthly, the rise of democratically elected autocrats inclined toward the practice of demagogic geopolitics has increased the risks of ecological catastrophe and species decline, and even extinction. This disturbing tendency is greatly abetted by leaders who substitute their own gut feelings for the warnings and guidance of scientific communities. Such developments have greatly eroded public confidence in the political elites of many countries, undermining trust in national and global political leadership from either ethical or rational perspectives.

As result of these considerations, present political arrangements, especially nationally, regionally, and internationally, are neither ethically acceptable, politically legitimate, nor ecologically sustainable, creating an unprecedented challenge to the political, moral, and cultural imaginations and practices of all, leaders and citizens alike, to imagine and work toward the realization of more durable and desirable political arrangements across the wide spectrum linking the local to the cosmic by way of the national and global.

Global Governance without World Government

When I started thinking as a young scholar and citizen about how to make the world safer and more congenial in a global setting in which the interplay of intense conflict and nuclear weaponry created dangers and dilemmas never faced before, the specter of global anarchy, that is, state-centric world order, seemed to block all realistic hopes for the kind of drastic global reform that I believed necessary. It made me realize that such ends could only be achieved if stronger global institutions able to act effectively in deference to global and human interests, rather than *national* interests, could be brought into existence in a hurry. Yet I remained keenly aware that the strength of nationalist ideologies and global hierarchies meant that it would be difficult, if not impossible, to gain political traction for such global reforms under present circumstances, especially if seen as erasing or even weakening primary loyalties to sovereign states or as regulating geopolitical actors. It was this set of perceptions as guiding my work that set me apart professionally from those in my academic specialties of international law and international relations. In this regard, my academic marginalization preceded my political marginalization, although the two spheres overlapped in the minds of others, and sometimes in my own. I never considered myself as idealist or utopian, although far from antagonistic to such traditions of thought, but rather as a humane realist alive to a postmodern agenda of secularist challenges, prefiguring the end of modernity as it had evolved in Western Europe and then spread throughout the planet, with the explosion of the first atom bomb over Hiroshima in 1945.

I also believed, for reasons explained earlier, that world government was an idea whose time had *not* come, and *should* not come as long as the global system exhibited the present degrees of hierarchy and with no *world* community embodying a robust global ethos based on shared values existed. True, an architecture of human rights treaties exists, reinforced by international institutions and dedicated NGOs, but such a shared framework remained dependent on self-enforcement, and never produced an authentic sense of global, or even regional community. Europe tried hard to create a regional community, but under stress during recent decades, the weakness of even this bold European Union experience was revealed. At best, world government was a rationalist solution of a highly emotive set of political issues and economic interest that on behavioral levels appealed only to Enlightenment true believers who happened to be inhabiting the highest tier of the global hierarchy in the West, and honestly believed that mental constructs of world government could overcome even the most formidable of political obstacles and popular resistance. And there were some among Western elites who believed that a world government built as a replica of the U.S. constitutional order would provide safety and security with the need for only minimal economic adjustments, hence maintaining Western hegemonic, classist and racist privileges. Such a scheme would also bring Americans and their admirers the satisfactions of a world order that looked and behaved in a manner resembling the United States.

In my view such projections of the national self should not even be perceived as utopias but discarded as narcissistic dystopias. I believe that a world government, whatever theorizing proceeded it, would never become a political project or if it did, would almost certainly veer toward global tyranny that reproduced military and material hierarchies. Given existing levels of inequality and distrust, there was no prospect in my mind for accepting a world government that would improve the human condition, except possibly in the midst of a mood of despair that might arise after a global apocalypse—and even then, I would not be hopeful. More likely than some effective form of humane global governance would be the emergence of an incredibly inhumane network of arrangements managed by and for the benefits of small surviving elites.

What, then, might balance this immobility of global political arrangements with the urgent need for effective international law and implementing institutions at the global level? In the end, overcoming the conundrum involves an appeal to reason and survival. It does not necessarily require any drastic reconfiguration of the political environment or adopting the dangerous idea that a humane government can be properly established prior to the emergence of a sustaining ethical and political community. Of course, the existence of the UN and the universal human rights framework offer starting points, an awareness of roadblock, and a plenitude of learning venues. It is a starting point because it provides a complex and durable institutional recognition, supported at least nominally by all governments on the planet, of the need for capabilities and norms that can serve the *human* interests as well as protect *national* interests, assuming their potential compatibility. It is a roadblock because the permanent members of the UN Security Council show no disposition whatsoever to reduce the scope of their geopolitical discretion or compromise their impunity. Unfortunately, the political will is more absent than ever that might allow the UN to function in a more autonomous manner. This would require curtailing the institutional and funding leverage of its geopolitically dominant members, especially in relation to peace, security, human rights, environment, transnational business, and development.

The UN and human rights arenas are learning venues, allowing us to appreciate from their study that from the organization's inception. it emerged from two competing visions of world order, a war prevention imperative in the Preamble of the UN Charter and a geopolitically realistic operating framework set forth in the Charter itself. Over time, as might have been expected, the Preamble has been nullified and forgotten, and the Charter has been operationalized as a brake on UN undertakings rather than becoming a problem-solving capability. When a consensus exists among the Permanent Members of the Security Council the UN can serve as a virtually unaccountable instrument of geopolitics. Illustratively, the UN could not act in either Syria, Yemen, or Kosovo because of a geopolitical split nullifying actions by the right of veto, while the Security Council was able to act as a geopolitical instrument in the first war against Iraq (1992) and regime changing intervention in Libya (2013). In both of these cases, skeptics were disappointed by the UN performance, not because it was ineffective, but because it became a vehicle for achieving certain states' geopolitical goals that ignored the limitations of the legitimating UN mandate authorizing the use of force for limited purposes.

By the end of the second decade in the 21st century it seems evident that despite many valuable contributions to various aspects of human betterment, the UN is too weak and wrongly constituted to serve consistently the peoples of the world as a mechanism for the promotion of human and global interests with regard to the most daunting challenges concerning peace, security, justice, and sustainability. Given the rise of ultra-nationalist governments in all parts of the world, the immediate prospect is for the UN to be reduced to the kind of 'talk shop' that, as its most cynical critics always alleged, seemed to many its principal function—although it should not be overlooked that the UN retains its role in symbolic politics, showing the failure of the United States to gain legitimating support for its geopolitical ventures, including the 2003 aggressive attack on Iraq or the insistence on sanctioning Iran. Until there is a reversal of the political tide at the national level, it is foolish to expect a strengthening of global capabilities at the UN with respect to crisis management, global problem-solving, and long-range planning. At the same time, the world needs a robust UN, and those who are working toward global community-building should respect the potential of a reformed UN to serve better the needs of humanity.

There are only two paths toward the sort of sustainable future that avoids world government while creating a strong enough mechanism to uphold the most vital of human interests with a global scope. The first path involves a more enlightened conception of self-interest at the level of sovereign states than has heretofore prevailed in international society. In particular, ever since 1945, if not before, governments would be better served by accepting the discipline of international law and procedures for the peaceful settlement of disputes rather than relying on military superiority, coercive diplomacy, and geopolitical leverage to pursue their preferred outcomes. In other words, I would christen as *the new realism* in world affairs adherence to international law as reasonably interpreted and at least partial demilitarization. The still prevailing 'old realism' based on weapons, deployments, deterrence, and coercive diplomacy maintains a zombie grip on the behavior of political actors when it comes to matters of national security.

The second path is more populist, depending on the disruptive emergence of an ethical, ecological, and spiritual consciousness that produces a transnational movement with the limited goals of improvising the necessary and effective means to address environmental, security, justice, and economic concerns in ways that are equitable and as non-coercive as possible.

Both approaches, which could be complementary, are committed to producing a sustainable, and to the extent possible, a humane geopolitics, in an historical period during which the destructive capabilities of war create unacceptable security dilemmas and great powers have lost the ability to manage change and sustain order. This new frame for geopolitics would seek to establish more equitably regulated arrangements for trade and investment and support a needs-based and environmentally sensitive approach to economic development than what continues to be assessed by such gross measures as economic growth. Creating a decent life for people in their homelands while respecting limits on the carrying capacity of the earth, is the overriding challenge of contemporary world order and should be the shared goal of global leadership, as well as the foundation of national politics oriented toward an ecologically sensitive, expanded conception of security at all levels of social interaction from the local neighborhood to the global village that shifts its emphasis by stages from 'national security' to 'human security.' China, among major states, is the only country orienting its development strategies toward soft power ascendancy on the global stage, and for that reason alone it threatens its geopolitical rivals, above all the United States.

Toward Human Rights Revisionism

Twenty-five years ago, at the opening of a human rights conference in Kuala Lumpur, I was invited to meet with the then president of the country, Mahathir Mohamed, with three or four of the other speakers, who were all from Asian countries. At soon as we entered the room, the Malaysian leader turned to me, glaring, and asked in a somewhat condescending tone, 'Why do human rights advocates from the West always come to our countries to lecture us about our failures with respect to political rights and yet never discuss our progress with respect to economic and social rights?' Mahathir added that economic and social rights are of much greater relevance to the great majority of people everywhere, especially in the countries of the South. I replied meekly to this formidable leader, often criticized for his autocratic style, that his objections to this Western approach to human rights were reasonable, and that I shared his critical reactions to the arrogance of leading Western human rights NGOs. Actually, this brief exchange has stayed with me over the intervening three decades and has made me more sensitive to the accuracy and relevance of such an observation.

I have noticed, for instance, in the frequent recent criticisms of China, Vietnam, and Turkey, the entire appraisal of their human rights experiences is reduced to a focus on the extent of freedom of expression and the range of related political freedoms associated with dissent and opposition to government policies, while little else is considered. Of course, as suggested earlier, I regard these freedoms as vital for the quality of political life that are integral to my own life, and I join in lamenting their denial, but such encroachments generally affect only a tiny minority largely perched near the top of the social and economic pyramid. To give further credence to this negative assessment of human rights as promoted by the West, instances of dramatic progress that some of these governments have made in meeting the material needs of the poor are totally ignored in the overall appraisal of their human rights records. As an instance, the justifiable British pride in the quality of their political democracy is understandable, but what is not, is to forget the inconvenient truth that one of five living in Britain is food insecure on a daily basis and the figures are not very different in a series of other 'affluent' and 'enlightened' countries.

Additionally, in the case of Turkey, the government deserves praise for dealing humanely with almost four million refugees, mostly from Syria, a number that would break the democratic back of any European or North American country. Similarly, the neglect of extreme poverty and homelessness in America is on a scale that should make the country a human rights pariah, but in fact, even liberals neglect the plight of these materially deprived segments of the citizenry while delivering self-satisfying denunciations of political and civil rights in non-Western countries.

There are a number of explanations for this refusal in the West, and especially in the U.S., UK, and elsewhere, to extend the human rights imaginary to economic, social, and cultural rights. For one thing, such rights are not part of the basic ideological consensus around the idea of political legitimacy, which is essentially based on liberal individualism, free elections, and the rule of law. As is often expressed by liberal apologists, a decent society is one where all are given the opportunity to improve their lot, including access to education and health care, but are not necessarily guaranteed social protection in the event of failure or disability. Of course, this ties in with neoliberal versions of capitalism that became dominant after the Soviet collapse, and the disappearance of any more socially responsible rival. From a neoliberal perspective, it is the market, not the state, that should determine the distribution of material goods and services. This implies 'a right' to fail. Such an exclusion of compassion for losers in the games of life is reflected in the underlying policies, practices, and beliefs of the capitalist state. It is what makes capitalist views of political legitimacy often inhumane in their impacts. This has been manifested in some of the harsh national responses to desperate migrants seeking sanctuary in more affluent countries. The pressure exerted by migrants may admittedly strain national capabilities yet calls for more empathetic treatment than walls, barbed wire, and confinement in miserable conditions. It seems obvious that some kind of hybrid and multi-tiered world system is the answer, combining the dynamism of capitalism with needs-based socialist empathy, and with both infused by policies of responsible ecological sensitivities.

In these respects, in my work and beliefs, I have come to view the essence of human rights as meta-legal, the manner in which a given political order formally and existentially treats minorities, the poor, and the otherwise vulnerable. I would hope that the main human rights NGOs would adopt this kind of orientation rather than devoting most of their resources and energies to the protection of political and civil rights. Admittedly, this shift in priorities would require a kind of depoliticized funding support that might be almost impossible to arrange. As a consequence, many Western civil society actors tend to treat the torments of poverty, joblessness, and homelessness as matters of marginal concern, if relevant at all. Both clusters of rights deserve respect and compliance. It was an unfortunate byproduct of Cold War ideological rifts to convert the unified approach of the Universal Declaration of Human Rights (UDHR) into two separate human rights covenants reflecting the supposedly opposite normative identities of the capitalist West (the

International Covenant on Civil and Political Rights) and the socialist East (the International Covenant on Economic, Social and Cultural Rights). I believe a return to the spirit of the UDHR should become a goal of human rights activists, especially giving policy relevance to Articles 25 and 28 of the Universal Declaration, calling for a standard of living meeting the material needs of everyone and an international order that is so attuned as to satisfy the whole range of norms encompassed by human rights standards. In some respects, the Sustainable Development Goals (SDG) as articulated by the United Nations moves ambivalently in this desirable direction, yet without any pretension of imposing legal obligations. Furthermore, in this era of surging nationalism, it is naïve to expect significant progress along these lines anytime soon. More critically viewed, SDG goals partake of a disturbing trend to treat international undertakings, including carefully negotiated Agreements on major issues, as essentially *voluntary* undertakings rather than as binding legal commitments.

I have come to the view, with some help from Mahathir's provocation, that a legitimate state is one that attends to the entire spectrum of human rights, including their economic, social, and cultural dimensions. As such it rejects the idea of political legitimacy formulated by George W. Bush and others at the end of the Cold War to the effect that the sole form of a legitimate state is one based on what was called 'market-oriented constitutionalism.' Rather, it raises this disturbing question: from an inclusive human rights perspective, is there presently existing even a single legitimate state in the entire world? Posing the question highlights the ideological and ethical morass of our struggling postmodern, pre-ecological world.

Beyond Instrumental Rationality:
Spirituality, Religion, & Ecological Ethics

What most obviously separated me from my academic colleagues at Princeton was the *normative* character of my scholarly work, much more so than my *political* alignments or even my activist engagements. The associated activist sympathies and manifestations, most of which followed from this sense of the world, did widen the gap between myself and my departmental colleagues, especially as my endorsement of the Palestinian national struggle became a matter of public controversy. This orientation toward compassion for victims of suffering, especially victims resulting from American foreign policy, or interest in drastic forms of global reform that involved non-incremental changes in the structure of international relations, or the sense that our own leaders should be held accountable under international criminal law were essentially at odds with the prevailing knowledge paradigm, and were rejected in policy domains as 'idealistic.' In other words, according to the academic norms that dominate current scholarship, what philosophers term 'epistemology,' or the study of knowledge, excluded values and visions from the study of political behavior. In contrast, my endeavors as teacher, scholar, activist, commentator, and citizen, and above all as 'public intellectual' were premised on what I would call 'a moral epistemology,' that is, connecting all forms of knowledge to values at stake and a commitment to consider knowledge as relevant only if it advanced human well-being. I am aware, of course, of contradictory views of human wellbeing and realize that principled conservatives, and even reactionaries, are motivated in ways that can resemble my brand of moral and political engagement. I can claim no inherent superiority for my views over theirs except through the relative political magnetism of such competing visions.

My own professional development proceeded from the embedded assumption that international law with respect to peace, security, environment, and human rights offers potentially beneficial guidelines that should be not only respected by the strong as well as the weak, but of benefit to both. In this respect I remain bothered, as earlier discussed, by American Exceptionalism in its various forms, invariably relying on double standards, condemning others for doing what we do and usually claiming a right for the United States to act internationally without accountability.

These issues crystalized in my thought and practice during the Vietnam War. It was in this period that I began to contend that American policies violated international criminal law, and that proper implementation of the law would hold American leaders accountable. I admit that there is a problematic element to contending that American behavior in Vietnam was unlawful in various ways. Above all there were others equally qualified, and usually with a higher societal status, prepared to argue that these contested practices were lawful. The haunting problem is 'who decides?' in an authoritative manner. Part of the weakness of international law is the absence of trustworthy institutional mechanisms that are regularly available to pass judgment on what is legal and what illegal. My efforts were in the form of appeals to other legal specialists and to the citizenry. But who am I to claim any special authority for my views? It generally ignored my inability, shared with all others, to pronounce authoritatively on what the law allows and disallows. True, the World Court and International Criminal Court exist, but lack the mandate to decide really crucial issues, and have no capability to moderate, much less pass judgment on, controversial geopolitical behavior or even to counteract the misconduct of even smaller states. This contrasts with struggles by opponents of such controversial U.S. Supreme Court decisions as *Roe v. Wade* or *Citizens United.* In this domestic setting the authoritativeness of a legal decision is inherently provisional, and never finalized on a national level even in sovereign states with established and respected constitutional structures.

I was also convinced that in an increasingly interdependent world the constraints of international law, as I understand them, were consistent with national interests of the United States, if properly contextualized to take account of the dangers of World War III, nuclear weaponry, ecological vulnerabilities, and the practical benefits of building a humane world community. As the feedback from my academic and policy colleagues and friends revealed, for most of them I had clearly gone too far. It was perfectly acceptable, especially in the latter stages of the Vietnam War, to contend that this particular war was a serious *mistake,* and that it should be brought to an end as soon as possible, and that a more constrained view of the president's war powers should be legislatively enacted as a policy priority.

In fact, this pragmatic turn against the Vietnam policies became almost a national consensus in the early 1970s. Influential realist opponents of the war, including George Kennan, Hans Morgenthau, and somewhat later, George Ball, and even later, Robert McNamara, based their opposition on this kind of paleo realist reasoning that this particular war involved an imprudent use of American military power in a non-strategic context. Such a setting made it more difficult to project sufficient American power in the combat zone, and weakened global capabilities where major strategic interests were at stake. This conclusion was reached because the Vietnam escapade was declared to have eroded public and elite confidence in U.S. capabilities to achieve battlefield victories at acceptable costs or to stand with its allies when they were facing threatening challenges. This failure was accentuated in the Vietnam context by a loss of support at home for such a military approach to Cold War foreign policy. A large portion of the citizenry came to believe that the sacrifices of American lives and resources were unacceptable, considering that the American homeland was not at risk and none of its important allies was under attack.

What never became acceptable in the mainstream and elite circles, however, was to reject the war policies or militarism because of the devastation and suffering inflicted on the Vietnamese people or to point to the criminal character of the war policies as a sufficient reason to justify their repudiation. Again, it was acceptable in the American mainstream to insist that the war was too costly in lives and treasures, that it harmed the geopolitical reputation of the United States as a prudent and effective global alliance leader in the context dominated by the Cold War. It became unacceptable for criticisms of the war to cross normative boundaries that signified its wrongfulness, questioning the good faith and motivations of those political and military leaders who carried out these war policies, and most of all, crossing over to support the political strivings of the adversary—in effect, saying that Communist-led Vietnamese nationalism deserved to prevail over the geopolitics of the Cold War. The trampling of Vietnamese rights of self-determination and the refusal to respect the legal insulation of liberation struggles from armed intervention made the American attempt to keep a client Saigon government in power a policy that lost even mainstream support as it became clearer that the military mission was not succeeding. Criticisms of policy became quite acceptable, while criticisms of underlying structures of sovereign authority and militarism were not.

In contrast, the mainstream focus of policy debate on the Vietnam War in its terminal phase was concentrated upon whether the commitment to protect the Saigon regime was ever feasible, given the overall historical circumstances, the corruption of the South Vietnamese elites, and the allegedly questionable counterinsurgency tactics relied upon, given the nature of the conflict. Everyone wanted to learn from the Vietnam debacle, but its pragmatic and establishment critics wanted to avoid future mistakes while its normative critics sought to avoid similar commitments entailing military interventions in foreign countries against emergent nationalisms, especially when reinforced by emancipatory rights if the struggle was being waged against colonial rule or apartheid regimes.

There was widespread acceptance that there was much to learn from the Vietnam experience, but given the opposed objectives of critics, it is hardly surprising that the policy recommendations veered in opposite directions. The Council on Foreign Relations was interested in upholding the *continuity* of America's global engagements in the Cold War Era, while the Pentagon and think tanks seemed to be thinking about how to maintain their budgets while reshaping future global security policy. Pentagon thinking addressed tactical issues with the objective of avoiding past mistakes in future combat situations of a Vietnam character. The overall idea was to find better ways to sustain support from the domestic society for lengthy overseas military ventures that were deemed part of the global security mission of the United States.

In contrast to such hawkish views, I argued in favor of future adherence to Charter norms prohibiting recourse to aggressive force and military interventions in foreign societies. I believed that this would prevent future such wars, either to prevent regime change or to achieve it. This was my position then and it remains so now when the nature of the adversaries has shifted, as at 2020 non-state actors seem to pose the largest threat to the established global order. I wanted to prevent such wars, while the political class in Washington wanted to make them winnable. Without question, I was defeated in the domain of policy debate. In fact, since Vietnam the relevance of international law in the setting of American foreign policy has been further manipulated and marginalized, a process made notoriously explicit in the responses to the 9/11 attacks that relied on obviously contrived 'legal' justifications put forward for torture and the violation of territorial sovereignty whenever the imperatives of counterterrorism so decreed.

From this somewhat vocational focus on international law, I politicized my concerns by reference to ethical and historical conceptions of legitimacy as the test of international policy. In this process of putting forward such ideas, I came to appreciate more fully the darker sides of international law, including its treatment of territories occupied by native peoples as empty and subject to sovereign acquisition by the Doctrine of Discovery, legalization of colonialism, aggressive war conquests, and exploitative economic arrangements that produced unjust enrichment for the developed countries of Europe and North America, and their venture capitalists. I believed that law devoid of moral purpose and political implementation could serve unacceptable policies, as was the case domestically in all autocratically governed states. These realizations led me to turn more and more to considerations of justice, and the idea of justice-driven law. As an aside, I reread the thesis of Robert Mueller that I supervised more than a half century ago when he rose to national prominence in his role as Special Counsel and was struck by his congenial idea, as a Princeton undergraduate, that when legal outcomes can be reasonably read in more than one way, it is appropriate to have recourse to how such distinct interpretations of law relate to the questions of justice at issue. Quite interestingly the question that Mueller's thesis dealt with was whether the World Court in The Hague should pass judgment on the lawfulness of apartheid in what was then called South West Africa, now Namibia.

On the broader canvas of what has been called 'peace and global transformation' I indulged a visionary epistemology that was guided by what seemed *necessary* and *desirable* imperatives rather than by what seemed politically *feasible*. My earlier work up through the 1970s emphasized a kind of rational approach to these issues, calling for 'a central guidance system' in world affairs that deliberately fell short of advocating global constitutional or governmental solutions. It was a thin line that sought to separate what was functionally imperative from utopian conjectures that lacked prospects of achieving political traction. I adopted a perspective that gave concrete expression to what might encourage a shift in analysis and prescription from the prism of national interests to that of global and human interests.

My 'midlife academic crisis' forced upon me the acknowledgement that what I was proposing was no more likely to circumvent a variety of obstacles than those of world federalists whose work I demeaned, perhaps overly, in the process of finding and fashioning a voice of my own. At least world federalists had developed a transnational network of cooperative associations that put forth ideas and proposals. My type of advocacy, as epitomized by my longish book *A Study of Future Worlds* (1975), gained a few favorable reviews but found its permanent resting place in the remote stacks of major libraries without creating political waves.

During my involvement with developments in Iran, I came to appreciate the political importance of religion and spirituality in achieving change under certain conditions that could only come from popular movements acting outside the law. In such situations the existing political elites are rendered irrelevant due to their own reality being rooted in a discredited and unpopular established order. This reorientation reflected my disillusionment with Marxist solutions as historically victimized by the Soviet experiment as well as by my alienation from the elite atmospheres of Princeton and the Council on Foreign Relations as potential sources of progressive change.

It also was clear from the post-Shah experience in Iran that political Islam did not offer a positive path forward in the post-colonial atmosphere of the Arab Middle East, but neither did its secularist and monarchist rivals. I had hopes for Turkey during the first years of Erdogan's leadership because it seemed to combine attentiveness to the needs of the Turkish population as a whole, post–Cold War independence, and a peace and justice approach to the region and the world, but then it veered off course domestically and with respect to foreign policy.

My Search for Spirituality without Religion

I came to appreciate in very concrete form, especially in Iran and somewhat in Turkey, how religion and spirituality had mass appeal, and how a firm cultural base in tradition and values gave rise to conceptions of reality less reflective of the priorities of particular territorial states and their supportive nationalist ideology, which promised security and identity in exchange for loyalty and sacrifice. Many of my secular friends, especially those on the Marxist left but also those with negative experiences of religion in their personal or societal experience, were convinced that religion should be unconditionally repudiated, claiming that it was responsible for much of the extremism and social regressions being experienced around the world, and although critical of the Shah, fearing that Islamic governance would be worse.

I never came to such a conclusion, although after the Iranian Revolution took several wrong turns from the perspective of progressive and humane politics, I appreciated more the skeptical attitude of the anti-religious humanists. In some ways my evolving attitudes toward Iran resembled my political judgment of Erdogan's Turkey. I was both impressed positively by some of Iran's achievements and critical of other aspects of its governance. All along, I was strongly opposed to various efforts to destabilize and confront Iran with a variety of coercive threats inconsistent with the UN Charter and the sovereign rights of every state that is a member of the United Nations. I continue to believe that respect for the dynamics of national self-determination is the preferred normative foundation for state-centric world order in the post-colonial era. In sum, the best path to world peace, at present, is geopolitical deference to the politics of self-determination combined with a rejection of regime-changing interventions.

I reach this conclusion not only for ethical reasons, but with a realist appreciation that militarist approaches to foreign policy of geopolitical actors have lost their effectiveness in most post-colonial contexts even while augmenting their destructiveness and human costs. The fact that China and Asia understand this, and the U.S. and West do not, helps explain China's rise and the West's decline.

An Academic Retreat

Out of the ferment of the period and my own wanderings, personal and political, I tried to put forward an approach to religious relevance that recognized the potential but also the dangers embedded in the great world religions. The result was a book with the title *Religion and Humane Global Governance* (2000) that drew a central distinction between the inclusive and exclusive features of the great world religions. By this distinction I meant to express approval for that notion of religious doctrine that incorporated everyone into 'the human family' and regarded those of other faiths or non-believers as equally worthy recipients of rights and social protection, as well as salvation. I expressed a corresponding disapproval of vertical religious constructions that privileged true believers at the expense of everyone else, a hierarchy that has fueled holy wars and religiously inspired violence through the ages. My approach insisted that humanity needs an inclusivist religious mobilization as part of the struggle to construct a better human future, centered on the reality of an emergent global community, while at the same time discrediting and constraining exclusivist religious approaches for the sake of civilizational and even species survival. Putting the distinction as simply as possible: The inclusivist adherent of religion and spirituality is a citizen pilgrim, the exclusivist militant tends toward being an arrogant and aggressive adherent of religiously framed tribalism.

This political memoir is, above all, a depiction of identity, both as revealed through practice and belief, and as the springboard of aspiration and imaginative knowing. In particular, I have thought about my life as partly the quest to become a citizen pilgrim in search of a spiritually endowed future and partly the assumption of responsibilities I associate with being a public intellectual. This future seeks to realize human potentialities for living together in various settings in peace and with justice for all, which explains my encounters as a public intellectual with a variety of strident defenders of the status quo. From this perspective, in my academic work I have tried to interpret and act upon a sequence of global challenges as they became salient in the course of my life. At times, these interpretations led me to engage in public space as a public intellectual and in some instances, as an activist. As an intellectual my engagement was sometimes partisan (Vietnam, South Africa, Palestine), sometimes pushing for balance in opposition to polarization (Iran, Turkey), and only in the American context to offer a critical voice reacting against the foreign policies of the Federal Government and the structural deformities wrought by systemic racism, militarism, and predatory capitalism.

At first, I tried to shape my sense of being a citizen and engaged intellectual around the values and hopes that sustained my life and work. In this regard, with a rather uncritical outlook, I favored racial and gender equality at home and a law-oriented foreign policy that included respect for the principles, procedures, and norms of the UN Charter *as reasonably interpreted.* I thought of the Nuremberg Judgment as creating a foundation for assessing the legitimacy of the future behavior of all states and not just as an imposition of punishment on the military and political leaders of the defeated side in a major war. I thought of political participation as meaningfully channeled through national identification and the procedures of government. In effect, I was a law-oriented nationalist who regarded states as juridically equal and rival Cold War ideologies as morally equivalent. I did regard fascism, most monarchies, and all oppressive tyrannies as unacceptable and illegitimate.

I believed claims of 'world citizenship' to be usually well motivated by a universalist outlook, yet foolish and politically misleading. I thought of Gary Davis's self-dramatizing travel documents, such as issuing a world citizen passport to himself, as largely a publicity stunt. How could there be citizenship without a globally ethical community and effective forms of governance? Effectiveness need not involve government or institutions as many cohesive native communities have illustrated by their reliance on tradition, custom, and shared values to achieve coherence and establish respected normative boundaries as to what is permissible. Despite the proliferation of international institutions and the existence of the UN, there is as yet no coherence and little shared sense of community or legitimacy at the global level. Additionally, there are generally weak feelings of belongingness at regional and civilizational levels.

As well, meaningful participation in international arenas continues to be dominated by governments sovereign over bounded territories, and for important matters there is little public transparency and no accountability. Vital existential identities are clustered around national, ethnic, and religious communities that may clash over their differences but overall are capable of achieving meaningful forms of coherence, cooperation, and above all, feelings of belongingness and loyalty in ways that the UN and globally and regionally oriented identities disappoint and fail. These qualities of communal coexisting are missing at global levels and only nominally present at regional and many sub-national levels of coexistence.

In Conclusion

I discovered in work, activism, and even play that ideas, however compelling to the likeminded, do not affect behavior unless grounded in political reality. As I grew older, I felt that the scope of political reality did not accommodate the character and scope of postmodern challenges in the domain of my persistent concerns with militarism, predatory capitalism, nuclear weapons, environmental sustainability, climate change, global migration, and human rights. In this respect I felt discouraged by political trends that seemed reactionary and dysfunctional, and more recently, reinforcing the most dangerous features and regressive forms of a state-centric system of world order. Such negativity also made sustainable peace based on justice and a spirit of equality seem unattainable for many unresolved conflicts around the world, of which the Israel/Palestine struggle has had the most personal resonance for me. Mainstream politics in the countries I knew most about seemed caught up in whirlpools of distraction and systemic disorder, while the progressive politics I was waiting for, receded over the horizon of plausible expectations.

The descent of my personal stature from a fairly high pedestal followed a parallel trajectory. Throughout the Vietnam War I was treated as a legitimate and even promising young scholar, invited to many establishment venues, sought after by liberal politicians seeking to become president of the country, and viewed as a responsible participant in many elite political arenas. Such prominence was short lived. It quickly faded in my 40s, principally at first as a result of my being (mis)characterized as a champion of the revolutionary movement in Iran, and could be pronounced dead after my criticisms of Israel attracted national and international notice. For the last 25 years, I am barely tolerated even within familiar settings, such as the Council on Foreign Relations or Princeton. At this point even lax gatekeepers would be alert enough to keep me out if I were foolish enough to seek the sorts of entry achieved without resistance, and with much encouragement, in the aftermath of the Vietnam War.

And yet, at the political margins, I find myself praised in recent years beyond my reality as someone who is brave and principled with respect to Palestine/Israel, geopolitics, and international law. In effect, as my mainstream credibility declined and disappeared, my life at the margins gained resonance, influence, and respect. The pattern was self-reinforcing, as I received no attention or invitations from establishment venues, while being flooded with positive feedback from the adversaries of imperial geopolitics. This shift in identities continues. I believe the quality of my writing and speaking has not declined, but its zone of relevance has contracted, shifting to the margins and overseas. Twenty years ago, I could write opinion pieces with a reasonably good expectation of their publication in mainstream media venues. Now it would be an exercise in futility, such a waste of time that I do not even bother making submissions. Instead I content myself with producing posts for my blog and doing at least one foreign interview per week. Of course, the picture is mixed. For the last dozen or so years I have been annually nominated by the Nobel Peace Prize and find myself listed by a Norwegian Nobel NGO watch group, initiated by Fredrik Heffermehl, as among a small group of persons worldwide whom his organization deems deserving of such recognition, and was even declared deserving of the prize in 1973 as a preferred alternative to the actual recipient, Henry Kissinger.

I am not unhappy about this self-marginalizing dynamic that has overtaken my scholarly life, my identity as a public intellectual, and my comings and goings as an engaged citizen. In some senses I am again as alone as when growing up in an unhappy household, but in others I have discovered solidarities that are warm and sustaining even if disconnected from the power-wielders of our country/world. I suppose this trajectory combines the wider political trends away from my beliefs that have created more politically conservative world elites, as well as my own choices that have moved toward a more radically progressive worldview. No matter. Throughout, I was never guided by concerns about pleasing this or that established order.

CHAPTER 17
Transformative Proposals

The fact that I was born on Friday the 13th may explain why, for me, this chapter may be the most important, and yet for most readers it could be read almost as a time out. There are additional reasons why I take this chapter more seriously than any other. I had an academic colleague, Giles Gunn, an erudite man of letters and more, who wrote suggestively about 'ideas to live for' and 'ideas to die for,' which was his way of signifying how significant is the life of the mind for someone who spends so many of his waking hours staring at a computer screen, and in his earlier life sitting calmly at a desk looking at an often chilling typewriter keyboard or blank page. Actually, until I was 60, I did all my writing, even student letters of recommendations, with a pen and long yellow pad. For many years I was spoiled by my lovely and wonderful Princeton secretary, June Garson Brennan, who smiled with sparkling eyes even when angry with me, which was quite often, especially in re-action to work piled on at the last minute, reflecting my lifelong struggle with deadlines. Even growing very old has not made me more realistic about taking on more than I can comfortably handle. It's one of the few things I cannot blame on age! Performing under such pressures has had mixed results over the course of many years.

In any event, I make no Hegelian claims that ideas are what shapes history or ordains change, least of all mine. What I am saying is that the examination of ideas, or conceptual understandings of issues relating to teaching, lecturing, and political engagement, were my moments of greatest intellectual gratification, giving rise to transient feelings of creativity and excitement, perhaps illusions to live by but real while they lasted. The transforming potential of ideas depends on whether they are sufficiently responsive to the surrounding atmosphere without being submissive. I wonder why my ideas, seemingly responsive to rational, scientific, and ethically grounded realities, seemed to lose relevance just as their validity was being confirmed by political and ecological developments. Instead of my ideas being taken more seriously, I felt that my strivings were more and more out of touch—but why? Was the best explanation a recognition that the advertising genius of capitalism, as adapted to the wizardry of social media, controls not only our lives, but our collective imagination, with its seductive consumerist corruptions? Or were my disappointments a reflection of that same mixture of greed and societal disregard that allows extreme wealth to coexist with economic stagnancy, middle class frustrations, and rampant homelessness?

The ideas I associate with my own work over the years have a common feature that I only noticed when I started to write about them. They are all, in some core sense, motivated by what I would call 'normative ambition,' that is, seeking to make the world more humanistic while becoming more ecologically oriented, often relying on innovations in international law and international relations to carry forward the vision. That said, I am sympathetic with several revolutionary horizons, for instance, replacing capitalism with a more equitable and empathetic economic system built on socialist values or relying on nonviolent geopolitics and far less militarized national security systems for the collective protection of the peoples of the world and their natural surroundings.

In the twenty-first century I have offered no sweeping proposals that even I consider of interest or relevance at the present time. As earlier explained, I do not regard world federalist thinking as generally constructive, because it doesn't address the absence of community (in its primary senses of belonging and participating) in the non-territorial frameworks beyond the borders of existing sovereign states.

I am aware that denouncing capitalism is an irresponsible gesture without having some idea about an alternative framework for world economic development that could be realized and would have an improved capability to address the material needs of the peoples of the world while being protective of sustainability, ecological wellbeing, and considerations of justice. In this sense, because of the immensity of the challenge and the magnitude of the risks of failure, I presently favor continuity with maximum increments of reform based on fairness, sustainability, and community. This approach is based on the belief that more humane, less predatory versions of capitalism are within political reach. They could be established in ways that would greatly mitigate the sharp edges of unregulated markets, exploitation, and gross inequality, yet retain the benefits of competition, creativity, and decentralization, which have made market-based economic order in the modern world resilient despite its shortcomings, turning out to be more durable and desirable than such radical alternatives as state socialism and fascism. Over the course of the last 50 years China confirms the remarkable materialist potential of a modified capitalist framework intelligently adapted by state policies to market opportunities. There is much for the West to learn from this Chinese experience, putting aside the disturbing array of humanistic failings that have accompanied its unprecedentedly rapid soft power rise nationally, regionally, and internationally.

As suggested throughout, I am not sympathetic with ideas that propose 'world government' nor do I advocate new structures for the world without envisioning how we get from here to there without high risks of making matters worse. I keep repeating this mantra because I am so often (mis)described in scholarly settings as an advocate of world government no matter how many times I pronounce myself an opponent. Because I am critical of geopolitics as practiced by the United States and other leading states, and favor a normatively oriented globalism, there are mainstream temptations to situate me as a wooly-headed idealist who wants to centralize power and authority in a world state structure of some sort, thereby ignoring the firmly entrenched statist/geopolitical character of world order.

My actual ideas are more modest, contributing to how we think and act normatively to make the world a more humane dwelling for ourselves and future generations, co-existing more harmoniously with natural surroundings. I have long believed we need more robust and attainable institutional capabilities at regional and global levels, and favored such initiatives as the establishment of the International Criminal Court, the convening of civil society tribunals to address issues that neither states nor the UN were will and able to address, and suitable regulatory mechanisms to monitor denuclearization, prohibitions of chemical and biological weaponry, and to verify a nuclear disarmament treaty if the political will ever materializes.

Andy Strauss and I conceived of such a global legislative organ as a democratic outreach that would open spaces for alternative dialogues on global problems to those associated with the outlook of geopolitics, statism, and global economic policy. Such an institutional voice more responsive to the priorities, grievances, and hopes of people could be expected to produce an understanding that departed from the inter-governmental declarations and musings of NATO, the UN, the World Economic Forum, as well as the G-7 and G-20, and hundreds of other statist, geopolitical, and market-oriented venues.

For the decade between 1985 and 1995 I had taken part in an exciting civil society event, called the 'UN of the Peoples' in Perugia, Italy.

It was intended to dramatize the differences in agenda and priorities between the 'UN of the States' meeting in New York City, and those who assembled in Perugia to put forward proposals and concerns rooted in the concerns of the diverse mix of peoples constituting the population of the planet. As might have been anticipated, those present who made the largest impact at Perugia were expressing the torments of the vulnerable and repressed; also deeply respected were those who represented indigenous peoples as the guardians of the earth. Such bottom up orientations contrasted with the top down preoccupation of governments that dominated venues controlled by sovereign states and economic elites.

What I want to express here is the degree to which the life of the mind in and out of the classroom and library involves shaping ideas in new ways that reflect aspirations, experiences, challenges, and grievances yet with a mindfulness toward the realities that are shaping the human condition in this historical period. In my case, the cartography of the ideas for which I want to take some credit flow directly from teaching, studying, and engaging. The word legacy seems too portentous, but in thinking back over my academic life and my more active engagements as a citizen, these are the ideas that I want to remember myself by and invite sympathetic others to join with me. These ideas seem of continuing relevance to ongoing challenges yet are not so well established by now as to be morally and politically integrated into governmental policy frameworks or scholarly perspectives.

Contra Ecocide

In the course of my long involvement with Vietnam starting in the early 1960s, I became concerned about many aspects of the war, including counterinsurgency tactics that relied upon the destruction of parts of the environment used by the Vietnamese adversary to hide their movements, establish safe base areas, and plan their low-tech ambushes and attacks. I became informed about these issues as a result of articles in *Scientific American* by Arthur Westing, who later became a friend, and Bert Pfieffer. These authors very graphically and persuasively depicted environmental warfare in Vietnam as an integral, yet unacceptable, part of the American military approach.

It was not until the early 1970s that I began to think that what these tactics were doing to the environment and natural surroundings had important similarities to what genocide did to people. The analogy led me to think of the word 'ecocide' as descriptive of these tactics, and as justifying their criminalization in the form of a distinct treaty, both for the sake of jurisprudential clarity and to raise public awareness about a proposed limit on combat tactics. By this time, I had become very broadly concerned about the dangerous impacts of modern industrialism, and the lifestyles it generated, on the environment and ecosystemic foundations of life on earth. As described earlier I became ecologically preoccupied in the course of 1968-70 doing research and writing for a book later published with the title, *This Endangered Planet: Prospects and Proposals for Human Survival.*

I am not sure if I originated the use of the word 'ecocide' or unconsciously borrowed it. I later learned that at about the same time as I was doing my writing on these themes, a Yale anti-war biologist, Arthur Galston, was also attacking American tactics in the war, and calling them 'ecocide.' I do not attach importance to who most deserves credit for the word, and it seems most likely we both hit upon the word independently of one another. My effort was to develop the idea of ecocide as the basis for the criminalization of environmental warfare. My 'weapons' were scholarship, journalistic writing, and participation in professional conferences.

Another influence that moved me in the same direction was the presentation of a paper in Stockholm at a side-event on 'War and the Environment' held in conjunction with the historic 1971 UN Conference titled 'Stockholm Conference on the Human Environment.' Our civil society mini-conference, a side event at the large inter-governmental gathering, was partly organized by several of us as a protest against the success of the United States Government in keeping war off the inter-governmental agenda, undoubtedly anticipating a wave of criticism directed at its tactics in the Vietnam War. It was my paper in Stockholm that first articulated the crime of ecocide in the atmosphere of a large international conference. I developed a proposal in the form of a very preliminary text of a hypothetical treaty prohibiting the crime of ecocide. The idea received some attention at our conference and subsequently through the years. Among those who were interested in these issues included Westing and Pfeiffer, and in recent years, the crusading activist Polly Higgins, who died prematurely in 2019, inspiring many to take up her commitment to criminalizing ecocide until success is achieved.

In the course of the Gulf War of 1992, Saddam Hussein deliberately set on fire a series of Iraqi oil wells to create a thick cloud of smoke that enveloped the battlefield with the presumed objective of obscuring it and preventing accurate targeting. Since it was done by an enemy of the U.S. and a country of the global south, the Iraqi moves did cause a legal backlash much more formidable than what had followed from the Vietnam experience. I took part in a large quasi-official conference in Washington, with some participation by U.S. officials, which would have been unthinkable in the Vietnam period. This confirms a pattern that becomes obvious once articulated: the political preconditions for lawmaking that relates to military tactics cannot get very far without enjoying the approval and backing of relevant geopolitical actors.

Unfortunately, this flurry of interest in environmental warfare never led to the creation of a constraining legal framework beyond the very abstract prohibition in a single provision of the Environmental Treaty that is too vague to be of practical relevance. What I mainly learned is that leading states, even if a commitment to law and morality is sincerely present, give a high priority to retaining freedom in wartime to employ whatever weaponry or tactics might be deemed militarily effective in some future combat situation. Debates about nuclear weaponry and more recently drones, reinforce this tendency to forego the protection of the environment in wartime so as to retain maximum combat flexibility.

What I have found encouraging in recent years is the attention being given to various civil society efforts to criminalize behavior of governments and corporations that are doing serious damage to the environment. Environmental activists, especially in Europe, are now calling rather insistently for the establishment of an Ecocide Convention modeled on the 1973 International Convention on the Suppression and Punishment of the Crime of Apartheid. Activists taking part in recent civil disobedience actions in Britain directed at stopping fracking operations have also expressed their underlying motivations by reference to the prevention of ecocide.

I believe it is crucial to move beyond the understandable, yet anthropocentric, focus on genocide to the moral awareness that intentionally destructive acts that disrupt natural ecosystems can also be a severe crime against all of nature (including humanity) that needs to be suppressed and prevented. Because ecocide threatens the strategic behavior of states and the commercial activities of corporations and their financial backers, it has not yet been possible to gain enough political traction to induce important governments to propose a lawmaking Ecocide Convention. In this period, the morality of prohibiting ecocide is dependent on a social movement building wider and deeper public understanding and support than currently exists. I feel that my work on ecocide has had a continuing resonance in environmental scholarship and activism, and represents an academic and activist contribution, which exemplifies a belief that

scholarship is to be valued or not as it relates to concrete issues bearing
on human wellbeing and ecological sensitivity.

The Nuremberg Obligation

In 1969, especially after the My Lai disclosures by the famed in-
vestigative journalist, Seymour Hersh, there developed a strong public
interest in whether the tactics the U.S. relied on in the Vietnam War involved war crimes. It is important to recall that political leadership in the
early stages of the Vietnam War was on the liberal side, meaning that it
wanted to be seen as acting in accord with international law if that could
be achieved by some strained interpretation of the relevant legal norms.
Typically, this leadership was pragmatic, seeking legal rationalizations
upholding its contested behavior rather than exhibiting any willingness
to alter battlefield practices deemed effective in deference to international law. In other words, twisting the law to serve the president is not just
a post-9/11 phenomenon, it was happening whenever preferred combat
tactics collided with actual or recommended legal constraints.

The My Lai massacre in Vietnam in 1968 was the grossest of war
crimes, entailing the deliberate execution of a large number (estimates
ran from 347 to 510) of helpless Vietnamese civilian villagers, primarily
women and children, in a non-combat situation. Yet when Lt. William
Calley, the officer in charge of the events producing the atrocity, was
indicted, a furious nationalist backlash occurred, especially in his native
Georgia. It was claimed that he was a lowly officer being scapegoated
for following the general orders of his superiors issued in difficult battlefield circumstances. There was a national outcry against his prosecution
coupled with a bureaucratic refusal at the Pentagon to look higher in
the chain of command to affix criminal responsibility. Calley actually
become more known in America as a war hero than as a war criminal,
which suggests how deeply the American ethos of impunity and exceptionalism runs. This was not a fact-induced shift but reflected a national
mood that placed patriotic sentiments above the law, and outside of it.
Probably, it was also the case that Calley received no training on avoiding inflicting harm deliberately on innocent civilians, and that the real
nexus of responsibility for battlefield criminality of this extreme variety
was at higher civilian and military command levels.

During these years I and others wrote about these and other wrongs
associated with the Vietnam War, believing that the law of war needed to
be revised in light of the kind of warfare that occurred in Vietnam. As the
war dragged on for more than a decade, American soldiers themselves

began speaking out against the war, making agonizing confessions in public venues about their own wrongdoing, including arguing that their combat experience was itself reason enough to end the war. It led some prominent figures in the legal community, none more respected than Telford Taylor, a former Army general and one of the young prosecutors at the Nuremberg trial of accused Nazis, to point out the violations of international law in Vietnam, and the related shortcoming of international law, given the changing character of warfare, its tactics and technology.

My interest in Nuremberg increased, especially while working with Robert Jay Lifton and Gabriel Kolko on an edited book, *Crimes of War: Indochina* (1971). We divided work by sections reflecting our respective specialties. My assignment, not surprisingly, was to prepare the international law section, while Robert did the psychological section, and Gaby put together the diplomatic/political side. While preparing my section of the book, I was particularly struck by the message sent to the German people by Franklin Roosevelt early in World War II, asking German citizens to collect evidence that could be used after the war to prosecute the German military and political leaders for their criminal conduct. In effect, FDR was suggesting that ordinary Germans had a moral duty that took precedence over their loyalty to the state as law-abiding and patriotic German citizens. I found this suggestion intriguing, and its logic more broadly applicable, including to the role of civil society as a check on unlawful government war-making. And if not a legal *duty,* at least a legal *right, to act nonviolently in opposition to a war reasonably perceived to be unlawful.*

It occurred to me that, given the gravity of what might be at stake in the future, there was a relationship between individuals and the state that could provide a legal foundation for civil resistance to a state guilty of the commission of international crimes of the kinds prosecuted and punished at Nuremberg in 1945. This led me to develop this line of thinking in some talks at several law schools, and then more symbolically at a controversial commemorative conference on the 40th anniversary of the Nuremberg Judgment held in the city of Nuremberg. There I introduced the idea of the 'Nuremberg Obligation' in the exact same physical venue as those historical events had taken place involving the trial and prosecution of the surviving German political and military leaders believed responsible for war crimes. I recall some unpleasant protesters angered by the conference, who carried accusatory posters and shouted angry slogans as we entered the meeting hall. They were protesting the 'victors' justice' of the 1945 Nuremberg trials and they seemed belligerent enough that I was glad to find myself safely inside the building. The large auditorium was filled with European legal specialists and a variety of persons concerned about how Germany fared after the Nazi experience.

The Nuremberg Obligation as a normative justification for civil resistance never caught on under that label, although individuals of conscience have been willing to go to prison to stop aggressive wars, dangers associated with nuclear weapons and the doctrines developed to govern their possible threat or use, and a variety of environmental issues ever since 1945. In the United States this process reached a climax during the latter stages of the Vietnam War. I testified in many cases where the government was prosecuting anti-war activists. I relied on variously modified versions of an argument that citizens who believed the war was initiated and waged contrary to international law had a reasonable basis for holding such beliefs, partly as evidenced by expert opinion, and should be permitted to avoid being forced by law to participate in such a war. In an important case, *Sisson v. United States,* prosecuted in a Federal District Court, a Harvard student put forward this argument, which was accepted by the most influential lower court Federal judge of that era, Charles Wyzanski. I was a witness on the international law aspects of the case. My friend Howard Zinn (famous as the author of *A People's History of the United States*) was the other witness. Howard spoke with his customary wit and wisdom of the distinguished history of civil disobedience that had failed to achieve any legal enactment throughout American history. We felt very encouraged by this judicial victory, which was also a triumph for conscience over the diktat of the militarized state and struck a psychological and legal blow against the continuation of the Vietnam War.

I believe that the Nuremberg Obligation remains a relevant idea. It works against feelings of helplessness by citizens in the face of a belligerent state that manipulates information to deceive its own citizenry and evades any aspect of international law that interferes with the pursuit of strategic interests, especially if the use of force is involved. It legitimizes what might otherwise appear to be lawless behavior and represents a populist check on the abuse of state power, adding a dimension to the constitutional framework of checks and balances, which is at its weakest in wartime. As America, in particular, has become what might be called an 'illiberal plutocracy,' it might serve to energize the citizenry on the basis of such an appeal to civic virtue. Such an exercise of civic responsibility can operate as a kind of brake on dangerous and unacceptable policy choices in war/peace contexts. It may be that the revitalization of democracy depends on precisely the spread of such activism as one way to neutralize the frightening mega-state capabilities to use digital technology to exert excessive control on its citizens while still maintaining a semblance of legitimacy behind the electoral façade of democratic and ethical accountability, as well as the appearance of fidelity to the rule of law. It can be also conceived as a complement to misuses of government secrecy that have generated the contemporary role of 'the whistleblower,' a form of civil disobedience from within the sinews of government, given historical relevance by Dan Ellsberg's release of the Pentagon Papers, and more recently by Edward Snowden's disclosures of the secret arrangements that underlie the surveillance state. It a sad commentary on the political culture of America that Snowden had to seek asylum in Russia while Calley was treated as a national hero.

Nuclearism

Ever since I was a law student in the 1950s, I was conscious of and worried about the dangers of nuclear war and believed that nuclear disarmament was essential to avoid a catastrophic future. I regarded this dark cloud hanging over the world as a primary concern, and early in my university career participated in various activities that reflected an anti-nuclear outlook, preferring the risks of disarming to those of living with 'the bomb.' At Princeton, I came into contact in the 1960s with so-called 'war thinkers,' some of whom even regarded the West as needing nuclear weapons so as to display its willingness to fight what was being described as 'limited nuclear war.' Herman Kahn, whom I knew personally, had written his massive tome, *On Thermonuclear War,* while spending a year at Princeton just before I came, and epitomized what I regarded as an obscenely carefree attitude towards the horrors of a future war fought with nuclear weapons. Kahn used his considerable cerebral firepower to normalize nuclear weapons as an irreversible dimension of strategic thought and warfare in the modern world. Henry Kissinger was a far less histrionic version of this strain of thought, rising to public prominence by writing a book under the auspices of the Council on Foreign Relations that entertained positively the possibility of developing doctrine and weaponry for the nuclear defense of Europe against intimidation and a possible attack by the Soviet Union, which was then presumed, seemingly wrongly, to enjoy military superiority in any European war fought without nuclear weapons. That is, a dangerous myth was promoted by these war thinkers that nuclear weapons were *necessary* for the security of Europe, and since the myth served bureaucratic and private sector interests, it was widely believed and rarely challenged.

I collaborated again with Robert Jay Lifton on a book that ended up with the title *The Political and Psychological Case Against Nuclearism.* Robert, already in the 1970s a leading psycho-historian who combined the study of private pathologies with the excesses of political behavior, had received the National Book Award for his interviews and psychological assessments of survivors of the atomic attacks on Japan in 1945, and held views on nuclear weapons similar to mine. I had in the course of our collaboration felt that the term 'nuclearism' captured what we were trying to express, namely, the lethal interplay of a perverse version of national interest politics emanating from a nuclear weapons establishment and the psychological attachments of most self-styled 'political realists' to weapons of apocalyptic magnitude. In this sense, to identify the nuclear weapons policy of the United States with respect to possession, doctrine, and potential use, 'nuclearism,' as tantamount to a political disease or syndrome that had dominated the minds and poisoned the hearts of political elites in the United States, was intended as an indictment of the nuclear consensus that prevailed. A similar syndrome, less intensely asserted, seemed prevalent in the other nuclear weapons states. Underneath the willingness to rely on such apocalyptic weaponry was a deeply embedded, possibly fatal, human flaw—privileging *political* survival over *biological* survival. Such a hierarchy was not consciously or explicitly endorsed, but it expressed itself by the unwillingness to make genuine efforts to overcome the menace of nuclear weapons, and even more so later on, by evading the gravity of global warming inducing climate change, and promoting demonic slogans such as 'better dead than red,' which peace activists then reversed.

I believe the terminology of 'nuclearism' calls attention to the ideological and emotional elements that make it seem virtually impossible for the leading nuclear weapons states to contemplate participation in a serious nuclear disarmament process, however reliably verified. Even declaratory attempts to delegitimize reliance on nuclear weapons is resisted as evidenced by the 2017 Declaration of the United States, France, and the United Kingdom of unconditional opposition to the UN Draft Treaty of Prohibition of Nuclear Weapons. It is the firmness of this commitment that makes nuclearism such a serious threat to the future of humanity. Any objective examination of world history since 1945 would conclude it has been good luck more than prudence or rationality that explains why nuclear weapons have not been used since the atom bomb was dropped on Nagasaki on August 9, 1945. Martin Sherwin brilliantly documents this past dependence on luck in his definitive history of the early decades of the nuclear age, *Gambling with Armageddon*. I have continued in the last stage of my role as intellectual and activist to work against nuclearism, both through publications and by support of the Nuclear Age Peace Foundation.

Humane Global Governance

A focus on 'global governance' has become very common during the last decade or so, replacing 'globalization' as the primary explanatory concept of how to conceive of political order on a world level. The attractiveness of 'global governance' is that it calls our attention to the ordering of relations among sovereign states and with respect to geopolitics, transnational capital, and trade flows without embracing the sovereignty- and geopolitically-threatening ideas of 'global government' or the static abstraction of 'world order.' Governance can involve any means of ordering relations, linking very different kinds of actors as in complex inter-governmental networks and a variety of regimes that stabilize many routine transnational activities including communications, transportation, commerce, tourism, and have become very global in scope, law-oriented, and non-territorial in character due to applications of digital technology. In this regard, 'global governance' is comprehensive in its ambition to explain how order can be maintained *without government*.

My innovation, in line with my normative preoccupations, is to add the word 'humane' so as to give attention to the importance of developing desirable types of order and stress the pervasive relevance of ethics and human rights in designing global reforms. Global governance as a concept would be quite compatible with a global tyranny so long as it maintained tolerable levels of order. Humane global governance evaluates the quality of order by reference to world order values, including the minimization of war, violence, and political repression and the maximization of ecological responsibility and human rights, including economic, social, cultural, and environmental rights, as well as global justice in its many domains. It also attaches a positive value to policies, practices, and procedures that contribute to ecological sustainability and climate justice.

The World Order Models Project (WOMP) might have received better press if it had identified its undertaking as 'Toward Humane Global

Governance.' Such naming would have emphasized the idea of process and change, and also the insistence that global political arrangements be held to ethical account as well as promote stability and order. I find the distinction crucial, yet I have to admit that it has not caught on in either academic or journalistic writing. As with so many of my life goals, I ask myself 'why?' and feel that the real explanation has to do with the absence of 'global community,' meaning that people, and especially elites, extend their ethical concerns at most to 'humane *national* governance' and the interests of transnational capital. It is noticeable that recently, especially in the Middle East, there have been some strong indications of non-territorial allegiances, especially Islamic affirmations of the *ummah* (community of Muslim believers) recalling the analogous secular distrust of the territorial and nationalist sovereign states constructed in the European model by the influential anti-colonial Algerian writer, Franz Fanon. These deviations from the political consensus on the limits of community suggests the shortcomings of state-centric global governance. These shortcomings include the absence of any alternative conceptions of world order with a wide enough public appeal to constitute a political project. So far, basing community on shared humanity has not proved to be *politically* relevant, although I find it significant that such an inclusive vision is found embedded in the sacred thought of all the world's great religions, and has been exhibited during the COVID pandemic by the statements of the UN Secretary General, Antonio Gutteres as well as by ecologically sensitive thinkers who see whole as taking precedence over the parts.

Citizen Pilgrim

Of all my normative ideas, the notion of 'citizen pilgrim' has probably fared the best, being rather widely used by those who do not want to confine their identity to either national space or to the historical present. It is used here as an apt co-metaphor for my own life journey alongside public intellectual. It is globally and species oriented. I initially adopted this terminology as a way of distancing myself from nationalists on one side and 'world citizens' on the other. As previously discussed, my objection to proclaiming oneself a world citizen is that to be politically relevant falsely implies that a 'world community' exists as an existential reality. It might have been reasonable to hope for such a development when the UN was established back in 1945, but the evidence is overwhelming that in the intervening decades, such a hope has not materialized. Indeed, in recent years there has been a trend toward hyper-nationalism that makes even the more modest notion of 'international community' mostly a thwarted wish, not an emerging reality. Many of us who deal with world issues are lazy about language, and do refer to 'the world community' as a matter of convenience, giving the false impression that there already exists a community of global scale that accurately manifests the collective identity of individuals, governments, and other actors. Yet if international political behavior is scrutinized with a critical eye it becomes obvious that 'world community' and 'global identity' remain empty vessels when it comes to resolving concrete issues bearing on security, human rights, and economic policy.

I was first drawn to the notion of citizen pilgrim by a lecture I heard in the 1970s by a theologian who was talking in an interesting way about St. Paul's views of religious faith as set forth in The Letter to the Hebrews. There were two distinct ideas that I found relevant to my concerns despite the great difference in our motivations for calling attention to scripture. First, St. Paul's emphasis on faith as belief in what cannot be presently seen or proven, and secondly, his identification of the pilgrim with someone searching for something better than the world as it now is, what was called in the New Testament, 'a heavenly world.'

I found these formulations suggestive. I wanted a way of talking about political participation and citizenship that was alive to normative potential, but also recognized that this was a sentimental illusion given prevailing modes of political consciousness and the way world was presently structured. 'Citizenship' conveyed a commitment to active participation while 'pilgrim' signaled the primacy of a journey based on the pursuit and attainability of what didn't yet exist, but could be brought into being through a sufficiency of vision, commitment, and nonviolent struggle against the established order. This established order continues to be based on war, inequality, racism, and oppressive patterns of governance. Such a pilgrimage may seem a utopian quest, yet its aspirations are realistic if the human future depends on achieving a sustainable, globalized, and equitable future, including radically reformed relationships between human activity and the natural environment sensitive to the carrying capacity of the earth. The political consciousness of the citizen pilgrim is infused with this sense of creating livable and benevolent future worlds that are guided by a sense of peace-with-justice.

It was my good fortune to work alongside the Irish political figure, Sean MacBride, who exemplified a citizen pilgrim many years before the term occurred to me. Sean was the son of Major John MacBride who fought against the British in the Second Boer War and was executed as a consequence. He was an Irish revolutionary, whose wife Maud Gonne was the romantic idol of the great poet, William Butler Yeats. My contacts went back to the 1960s when Sean headed the International Commission of Jurists in Geneva. I had been asked to be an expert witness in a trial of 35 South West Africa (now Namibia) nationalist leaders back in 1966 as a result of my involvement in the World Court case decided a year earlier. Not surprisingly, South Africa refused to issue me a visa, and the lawyers in the case turned to MacBride to appoint me as an Official Observer of his Commission at the trial. Sean, drawing on his father's experience of siding with the Afrikaners in the Boer War, persuaded the Prime Minister to grant me a visa, which led to my second sustained contact with apartheid. Then in 1982, after the Israeli attack on Lebanon, when a British MP formed a commission to investigate Israeli war crimes, Sean served as the Chair of the commission, and I was invited to be deputy chairman. During the factfinding mission to Lebanon, I served as acting chair as Sean had become ill, but we worked together in London on the report after we returned. Finally, Sean headed a civil society Nuclear War Tribunal convened in London in 1985, and I was asked to be one of the four judges. In all three of these highly controversial undertakings at the outer edge of what liberal democracies tolerated, Sean modeled for me what it meant to respect and take the integrity of law and morality seriously, independent of political identity. He was very rooted in his Irish experience, and yet above all dedicated to the pursuit of justice. For his efforts he was, I believe, the only person who received both the Nobel Peace Prize and the Lenin Prize in a period when Cold War passions were polarizing identities for almost everyone. I was fortunate to have Sean MacBride teach me what it meant to be a citizen pilgrim, leaving an inspirational imprint that has stayed with me.

Legitimacy Wars

I first became interested in the distinction between 'legality' and 'legitimacy' in the context of my membership on the Independent International Commission on Kosovo. This Commission, largely funded by the Swedish Government, was given the assignment of assessing the NATO War of 1999, which justified its military attack on the Serbian military presence in Kosovo as necessary to protect the people of Kosovo from abusive control and threatened crimes against humanity by Serbia. There were credible apprehensions in the period leading up to the Kosovo War that there would be a massacre of the sort perpetrated by Bosnian Serbs in Srebrenica in 1995 against several thousand Bosnian male Muslims. At the same time, there were allegations that this concern over the fate awaiting Kosovars was hypocritical, given Western indifference to the ordeals inflicted on the Palestinians, Kurds, Kashmiris, others. Chomsky attacked the NATO War as an instance of what he called 'military humanism.' Chomsky insisted that lurking behind the humanitarian rationale was a geopolitical motivation to demonstrate that NATO was still needed and useful despite the end of the Cold War. I found myself moved by the credibility of humanitarian concerns leading to protective action, yet uncomfortable with supporting an intervention under NATO auspices without a wider mandate from the UN as required by international law. I worried, with what proved to be good reason, about the precedent being set.

In the Commission there were a range of views represented, including a politically attuned chair, Richard Goldstone, eager to avoid any sharp criticism of NATO's tactics. These views were strongly reinforced by the ambitious author and political figure, Michael Ignatieff, who made no secret of his connections with White House advisors, which he claimed gave his views added weight. Michael at the time enjoyed a positive reputation in Washington because of his journalistic endorsements of a U.S. foreign policy that he dubbed 'empire lite.' To overcome tensions on the Commission, with the able support of both Carl Tham, the Swedish Vice Chair and former cabinet member, and Mary Kaldor, an energetic comrade who had long been among my closest friends, I proposed distinguishing between the 'legitimacy' of the intervention based on moral and political considerations relating to human rights from the 'legality' of the war. NATO's attack on the Serbian presence in Kosovo could not reasonably claim the cover of 'legality' because the intervention was a non-defensive use of force that was not authorized by the UN Security Council. I nonetheless understood, and worried at the time, that this distinction would likely be misused as a precedent for future undertakings that were neither legal nor legitimate. I didn't have to wait long for these worries to materialize. The Kosovo precedent was widely relied upon to justify the regime-changing intervention in Iraq a few year later.

The idea of 'legitimacy war' was stimulated by making this distinction between legality and legitimacy but with an entirely different set of issues in mind. It had occurred to me as a way of conceptualizing soft power efforts to attain political justice in ways that neutralized the advantages of oppressive military superiority. In this central respect the legitimacy of a war involved the struggle between adversaries for soft power control of the discourse on matters of law which included morality. Discourse control went a long way in determining which side of a conflict would gain sympathy and generate solidarity in the ongoing political struggles. It recognized the impact of soft power on the internal and international balance of forces. However, the reality of how most violent political conflicts end in the 21st century has not been absorbed by most foreign policy analysts nor is it reflected in Western government policies. As mentioned before, and of supreme importance in understanding the currents uses and limits of military power, the weaker side militarily has nonetheless controlled the outcome—in short, has won—many of the most salient wars fought during the last 70 years *for political control of a society.*

A spectacular early illustration of this challenge to the core belief of 'political realism' was provided by Gandhi's nonviolent movement seeking political independence for India in relation to the British Empire. This stunning reversal of realist expectations has been repeated in a series of anti-colonial wars that brought independence to Indochina, Indonesia, and Algeria among many others. As indicated in Chapter 9 this new balance of forces in many, but not all, combat situations, was powerfully reinforced for me by the Vietnam War. In Vietnam, American military superiority gave way in the end, not by being outmaneuvered militarily, but in light of Vietnamese political perseverance and global support that produced a remarkable victory of a materially and militarily feeble David over a geopolitical giant Goliath.

I found hope for the Palestinian struggle in this way of reinterpreting power in relation to violent conflict, thinking that the Palestinians could achieve justice through soft power dominance based on the empowering realization that the history of the last century was decisively on their side, and that this outcome could be achieved both normatively, in relation to the right of self-determination, and politically, with respect to the soft power weight of global solidarity as correlated with Palestinian nonviolent resistance. As a result, the balance of forces could potentially shift in favor of Palestinian rights so that *a just peace* for *both* peoples could emerge, enabling mutually respectful and peaceful coexistence given content by implementations made in the spirit of equality. As at this writing, such a hope may seem absurd, yet it continues to stimulate the only credible imagined future of a just and peaceful outcome for both Israelis and Palestinians. It would be capable of ending the apartheid regime and starting an era of peaceful coexistence and bi-nationality based on equality and human rights. Of course, it entails scaling back the

Zionist project from 'a Jewish state' to 'a Jewish homeland' co-existing with 'a Palestinian homeland.'

Regardless of the predictive accuracy of this idea of Legitimacy Wars, the concept seems exceedingly useful in identifying a shifting calculus with respect to the diminished and restricted role of military power as an agent of change and control. Such an idea also corresponded with my lifetime effort to demonstrate the relevance and importance of law and morality to achieving conflict resolution in the contemporary world. Bureaucratic resistance to an appreciation of the limits of historical agency now enjoyed by military power has to do with justifying bloated military budgets as well as reflecting the foreshortened militarized imagination of bureaucrats disciplined in the American setting by the onset of a permanent war mentality after 1945. The exaggerated militarization of security has led many 'disputes' to be treated as 'threats,' and caused threats to be magnified beyond their true proportions.

Geopolitical Crime

While being concerned with the turmoil in the Middle East and North Africa (MENA), I was struck by the historical allusions chosen by the most extremist adversaries of the status quo. Ayatollah Khomeini complained bitterly about the imposition of European-style territorial sovereign states that led to artificial divisions of the Islamic region, which had been kept together by the Caliphate. Osama Bin Laden voiced similar resentments, particularly as it concerned the rupturing of the *ummah*. Even ISIS echoed these sentiments by using the slogan 'the end of Sykes-Picot' when establishing their short-lived caliphate. Additionally, the region was deeply affected by facilitating the establishment of Israel as a Jewish state, which forcibly and deliberately displaced over 700,000 Palestinians despite the opposition of the majority resident population and most of the states in the region. Although there was a global moral climate in the aftermath of the Holocaust that was sympathetic with the Zionist Project, its realization amounted to the imposition of a settler colonial entity at the historical moment when European colonialism was being morally and politically successfully challenged by strong nationalist movements around the world.

Here, then, is the underlying anomaly. While colonialism was dying throughout Asia and Africa, it was making its last expansionist surge on the collapsing ruins of the Ottoman Empire. It was the diplomacy of over a century ago that inflicted on the region a series of structures that could be maintained only by coercive forms of governance. Great Britain and France betrayed wartime promises to Arab leaders of a unified and independent Arab nation, instead planning via secret diplomacy for a colonial division of spoils throughout the region designed to foil the self-determination visions of Woodrow Wilson and the Americans to use the peace diplomacy after World War I in dealing with the remnants of the collapsed Ottoman Empire.

In the end the Europeans didn't quite fulfill their colonial ambitions and were forced to settle for a favorable compromise known as 'the mandates system' that gave the UK and France most of what they sought by way of control but without the benefit of a colonial imprimatur. It consisted of granting full administrative authority over the governance process of the post-Ottoman artificial states that had been delimited by Britain and France in their negotiations with each other while disguising this political reality by presenting it as a new kind of international trust arrangement containing a vague promise to prepare the populations put under their control for eventual independence at some undetermined time in the future.

This colonial diplomacy coincided in the Middle East with the pledge made by the British Foreign Secretary to help the Zionist movement establish a Jewish homeland in Palestine. The Balfour Declaration in 1917 was carried forward in the Mandate System in the form of the British mandatory authority over Palestine. Britain administered mandated Palestine in accord with their divide and rule strategy that they had long relied upon to sustain control over their colonial possessions around the world at minimum costs of blood and treasure.

What struck me was that for a hundred years the inhabitants of the region, instead of being liberated from Ottoman Rule, were then subjected to a much worse fate than previously. The new regional grid of territorial states ignored ethnicities and traditional communities, and subjected the region to territorial delimitations suiting the convenience and serving the strategic interests of European colonial priorities. To do this at a time when anti-colonial non-European nationalist passions were rising required coercion to sustain order, and when the colonial powers were eventually forced to give way, led to coercive and oppressive forms of statism replacing colonial patterns of coercion. The realities were further complicated by the growing importance of the region's immense oil reserves. This stimulated geopolitical and private sector transnational encroachments which took a post-colonial form, leading to the creation of corrupting relationships with national elites that kept their own populations under rigid controls and relied for regime security and prestige on arrangements with geopolitical actors, often their former colonial oppressors.

It is against this background that it occurred to me that there were reasons to hold diplomats and leaders accountable for wrongs inflicted in such a manner—in effect, to treat what was done to the Arab World after World War I as a series of 'geopolitical crimes' for which accountability should be imposed retroactively, at least in symbolic form. In effect, whenever disregard of collective identities and basic rights results from negligent or manipulative diplomacy, and mayhem and pronounced injustice results, there should be available mechanisms entrusted with investigating political accountability, and in gross instances, criminal accountability.

Admittedly, it is unlikely that governments would accept such a framework of accountability with respect to their diplomatic activity, and yet there is value in articulating geopolitical crimes. It helps to create a broader understanding of why certain forms of prolonged and intense conflict erupt, and makes it difficult to establish governing arrangements based on legitimate forms of political community. Such geopolitical crimes could also be articulated in various regional and global settings through civil society tribunals operating in the manner of the Permanent Peoples Tribunal (PPT) in Rome or the 2005 Iraq War Tribunal in Istanbul. The PPT Tribunal was a continuation of the pioneering initiative of the Bertrand Russell Tribunal made during the Vietnam War. This Tribunal, although disregarded and derided by mainstream media and elite public opinion, documented a record of war crimes that neither governments nor the UN System were prepared to address, much less document or act upon. Such civil society initiatives fill a normative and institutional vacuum resulting from the failure of geopolitical actors and the UN to uphold the norms and procedures of international law.

Concluding Observations

These six ideas are proposals for how to address the reality of living together on the planet. I heard one of Jacques Derrida's last lectures in which he compellingly argued that the most basic challenge facing humanity is how to live together on the planet in a better way. Of course, the word 'better' is viewed differently by those who claim to be 'realists.' I write 'claim' because reality is itself being tested in ways that seem to pose a bio-ethical challenge that has never before threatened the species *as a whole,* as distinct from particular communities and even entire civilizations—but not the human species, and not the planet as an encompassing ecosystem. Whether this species challenge exists is itself contested, and its true extent is unknowable, but the possession of nuclear weapons and the phenomenon of global warming are threats with risks of unknown and unknowable magnitude, yet appraised with growing alarm by relevant segments of the scientific community. The prospect of a worldwide famine in the aftermath of nuclear war is believed likely by experts as is the possibility that the planet becomes uninhabitable by humans if global warming passes certain unidentified tipping points.

To some extent, these normative ideas arise from preoccupations that have shaped my life to undertake direct engagements with the most controversial issues of the day. These issues reflect the specificities of time and place, and most particularly situate me here in the United States as reacting to national issues of global scope. I would put anti-war scholarship and activism during the Vietnam War in this category, along with my recent criticisms of Zionism and Israel, not for their existence, but for their pronounced insensitivity to the rights and grievances of the Palestinian people, and an increasingly unwillingness to compromise or accommodate, which in the name of security will over time generate insecurity.

There have been other issues that have attracted my attention as teacher, scholar, and activist that have not been discussed, including opposition to the apartheid regime in South Africa, to India's and Lebanon's political development, or support for the basic rights of various captive nations such as Tibet, Western Sahara, East Timor, and Catalonia, as well as prolonged advocacy for the basic rights of indigenous peoples, and their humane treatment as long-subjugated nations.

These deeper normative impulses toward living together in better ways on a planet with limited carrying capacities overlap with issues associated with conflict resolution and human rights. I consider these normative proposals or ideas concerned with living together on a planetary scale to be both better responses to the present and improved ways of addressing the future. At stake throughout is the ancient inquiry into the human condition. It is a matter of whether to view our individual and collective beingness as shaped by largely unconscious aggressive and destructive drives, once so influentially depicted by Freud, or whether the becomingness of humanity is a work-in-progress with no fixed attributes. I subscribe to this latter view, which suggests the practical validity of struggling to achieve the best possible future and, with such an awareness of future uncertainty, a *responsibility* to engage actively, and not to give up by escaping, scapegoating, cynicism, and various forms of denialism or extremism. The great underappreciated benefit of the uncertainty surrounding the human future is that it is capable of creating and sustaining genuine hope-through-struggle as well as the possibility of achieving the desired changes.

When I try to link these normative proposals with my personal struggle since adolescence to achieve an authentic identity, I am struck by two sets of considerations. First, to some extent I have depersonalized the struggle by fashioning my own positive models, for instance, the notion of a citizen pilgrim, that are in part nothing more authoritative than a private 'invention' dependent, to be sure, on inspiration based on experience and the example of others. And secondly, that the absence of either positive models or a rooted identity as I entered adulthood led me to endow my professional life almost from the beginning with a normative (legal, moral) dimension satisfying to me personally yet marginalizing my work with respect to dominant professional and societal trends. Further in the background, but still relevant, is my ongoing unconscious drive not to act and think as a top dog in the manner of my mother's family. I leaned toward solidarity with those who were vulnerable and victimized if they fell within the purview of my professional or citizen pilgrim gaze.

It is this gaze, more distinctive than fingerprints, that helps determine who we are and what we become.

PART SIX
QUIXOTIC OR PROPHETIC: SEEKING LIGHT

In this final cluster of chapters I attempt to audit my life experience at a strange historical moment, a time unlike any other in my 90 years on the planet. Despite this, our daily life continues to revolve around interpersonal involvements with friends and family that sometime expose sharp edges of judgment and dissent, but more often heighten bonds of solidarity, satisfaction, affection, and love. Occasionally, a seemingly trivial incident discloses the often obscure interface between the private and the public.

Not so long ago, I was at dinner with close friends, and the conversation turned toward Noam Chomsky who had recently celebrated his 90th birthday and yet showed no signs of slowing down intellectually or with respect to an energetic public life of travel, influential and provocative commentary, and support for those marginalized by the cruelties and dysfunctions of our world. I had been impressed by the romantic tenor and warmth of Noam's relations with his Brazilian wife during a visit to Santa Barbara for a scholar/activist workshop on nuclear issues. When asked by one of our guests about their age difference I guessed that Valeria was in her late 40s, which may have been quite wrong as I often am about such matters. More than one woman at the dinner table reacted with scorn, calling the relationship 'wrong' and 'weird.' I disagreed, saying I found them exceptionally tender and loving toward one another, which was what I had experienced.

My comments made no impact on our guests and led to the abstract rejection of such a possibility, repeated in a somewhat cynical, even angry tone of derision. I felt that some of this hostile reaction was directed toward me for endorsing such a conventionally incorrect sort of late life relationship. In the unspoken background was the socially constructed reality that the Chomsky option was available only to men, especially men of fame or power, and it was unthinkable that a younger attractive man would attach himself to a woman in her 80s or 90s. Maybe also, my endorsement of the Noam/Valeria connection seemed self-serving given my age, and the fact that Hilal is so much younger. In my defense, I would say that throughout my life I have always looked with a favorable eye upon relationships that work, however strange the nature of the liaison may seem if looked at from outside. Behind this feeling is my experience that so many conventionally correct relationships do not work, and that it is rare to find intimacies that outlast sunbursts of romantic intensity. When we do come upon success stories, they should be celebrated rather than assessed by abstract criteria. At the same time, I am quite aware that all societal patterns pass through patriarchal filters, which although evolving, continue to privilege men, and changing filters happens slowly, unexpectedly, and only through struggle from below. Age discrimination is far less damaging than the suffering endured by those with serious disabilities, socially deviant life styles, and ethnically targeted minorities.

Shifting from interpersonal complexities to the deficiencies and dangers of public order serves, in part, to replace emotional vectors of experience by more rational concerns about war, poverty, pollution, racism, and the age old litany of wrongs embedded in economic and political structures, which result in struggles between rich and poor, urban and rural, secular and religious, and left and right. In this regard public life is interpreted from conflictual perspectives, whether winners and losers in neoliberal capitalist circles or class conflict in Marxist traditions. Such polarized assessments tend to withdraw attention from globalism, altruism, and cooperative win/win relationships at the very time in world history when exploring the potential for achieving such harmonies on all levels of social interaction seem increasingly tied to prospects for a benevolent human future.

At present, as the world is struggling with the coronavirus pandemic, the United States, still the dominant actor on the global stage, is led by a sociopathic autocrat while being challenged from within by massive protests against systemic racism and socio-economic injustices that have lit fires around the world. This is happening at a time when America itself is threatened by economic adversity, geopolitical confrontation, infrastructure deterioration, and ecological instability. While each person's life is inherently contingent, in this set of mask-wearing and social-distancing circumstances we develop an hourly existential reckoning with our mortality, as well as having to decide whether inclined to heed health experts, gut feelings, or congenial politicians. Such polarizing responses climaxed in early October 2020 when Donald Trump tested positive for the virus, and was hospitalized, shattering his posture of invulnerability, and making us wonder even more intensely about what kind of post-pandemic reality we will confront, whether, as in my case residing in Turkey and America, or wherever one is situated.

Not too far removed from the crises dominating public conscious-ness at present are the temporarily sidelined urgencies of climate change, biodiversity, nuclear weaponry, geopolitical tensions, militarism, predatory economic arrangements, hunger, poverty, and migration. These urgencies cannot be deferred without incurring heavy costs, heightened risk levels, and possibly disastrous consequences. When this array of conditions is taken into account it does not require a wild imagination to entertain severe worries about whether these convergent world order crises can be effectively managed and contained. In some sense, without foreseeing the dramatization of these recent challenges through the onset of infectious disease, moral outrage, economic dislocation, civil strife, and war. My work and academic commitments have long been motivated by the expectation and fear that a day of reckoning for the future of civilization as we know it and possibly even human survival was only a matter of time. Whether *this* is the early dawn of such a day of global reckoning is so far unknown and unknowable. It is possible that a planetary recovery scenario is lurking just beneath current horizons of perception, which might seem liberating, yet itself may soon give way to a new interlude of world order complacency. Despite the statistics and graphs of futurists human destiny remains locked almost totally in a black box, and the acceptance of radical uncertainty intelligently moderated by a precautionary ethos is our only sensible guide to the future. One positive aspect of this uncertainty is that the future is not foretold, and there is no excuse for writing off the struggle to overcome present challenges as futile and self-defeating. In effect, neither passivity, complacency, nor determinism are rational options.

With such reflections in mind, I am led to wonder whether my dual journey as public intellectual and citizen pilgrim should be dismissed as a jousting with fantasy or vindicated as a canary singing in her cage who not only warns, but for those with decent hearing, is singing a love song designed to awaken humanity to fulfill the ethical, ecological, and spiritual potential of the species before it is too late. Seeking a balance between imagining and worrying is what my journey as teacher/scholar, advocate, activist, and citizen has been about, and I would not alter my engagement with life fundamentally if given a second chance. The journey has no end point, it is a process of becoming, my way of being in the world and with others, self-vindicating if guided by good will, spiritual devotion, and love, self-destructive if not. The process is best measured not by results but by endeavoring, and above all, by persisting. I acknowledge that the goals I most ardently advocated have not been reached in the course of my lifetime, and indeed now seem less attainable than 50 year ago. But was it wrong to try? As Samuel Beckett insisted, we should judge one another and ourselves by the moral quality of our failure, and by our courage to keep trying to do better, in his words, 'to fail better.'

I need to keep reminding myself that this self-affirmation, and accompanying practice, would have been impossible without exceptional good luck with health, race and class privilege, professional opportunity, adult family life, and abundant gifts of love, intimacy, and friendship.

I emerged as a public intellectual in the primary sense of taking my concerns beyond libraries, journals, academic lectures in the latter stages of the American War in Vietnam, that is, not until the late 1960s when I was in my mid-30s. It was not a matter of doing civil disobedience or protest marches, although these modes of expression were never excluded, but it mainly involved raising my voice in the public squares close to home and wherever opportunities arose. My early opportunities included testimony before Congressional committees, being an expert witness in anti-war trials, membership in international commission tasked with global policy issues, and writing controversial opinion pieces in mainstream venues. Once I became better known as a public intellectual critical of the hot button issues, my mainstream access soon dried up, and I redirected my energy to other modes of public engagement. Despite the exclusions from MSM, my sense of commitment as an active participant in the political debates of the day increased over time. My views became more appreciated and known outside my own country than within it, and so my activism gradually assumed a more internationalist character, with a geopolitical focus on the Middle East since 2000, with especial attention given to the interplay of developments in Iran, Turkey, and Israel/Palestine.

In expressing views in public arenas my academic background in international law and international relations was often treated as the basis of my credibility as a commentator on world affairs. I tried my best to bring to bear progressive readings of international law, human rights, and UN authority to bolster challenges to war-mongering and geopolitically motivated U.S. global intrusions on the independence of sovereign states and the human rights of their populations. As a public intellectual over the years I gave particular attention to two principal international concerns: (1) unconditionally opposing all geopolitical forms of intervention in the internal affairs of sovereign states, including by covert means and by way of national sanctions; (2) unconditionally opposing nuclearism, including the possession, deployment, threats, development, and strategic doctrines justifying threat and use assigned to nuclear weaponry.

These views occasioned some blowback in academic and establishment settings. I sometimes remained an invited guest, but no longer seated near the head of the table. For instance, the American Society of International Law (ASIL), the leading professional organization of the bearing of law on the conduct and content of foreign policy, had early in my career besieged me with speaking invitations and opportunities for leadership roles within the organization. These disappeared later on when my views were regarded as controversial and anti-establishment. Of course, there was an interactive element. I no longer expected or sought recognition in such elite settings that brought together international law experts with high profile lawyers representing large companies, financial institutions, and legal advisors to governments. Yet I do not regret my earlier exposure to these professional/political venues. I never fully subscribed to mainstream expectations, and despite Princeton credentials, was never regarded as a completely trustworthy team player. This suited me fine.

As long as I was within the boundaries of 'responsible' dissent I seemed valued in elite communities, partly to make credible their claims of openness to diverse viewpoints. When I unwittingly started crossing red lines by urging criminal accountability for the leading perpetrators of the Vietnam policies or questioning the legality of American Cold War covert CIA interventions and political assassinations or upholding the claims of the countries in the Global South to exercise sovereignty over their natural resources at the expense of foreign investors, my welcome mat was gradually and often unconsciously withdrawn. When I made clear that I opposed the Shah of Iran when faced with an internal movement of opposition or leveled criticism at the Zionist consensus on Israel I fully realized that my political and professional future would be jeopardized.

In sum, being a public intellectual was not the outcome of a calculated plan. It came about through a series of spontaneous efforts to carry my views on crucial international issues in political settings beyond their normal academic and activist confines. It produced lasting friendships and valuable learning experiences, but also created adversaries, which sometimes led to making me a target of smears and denunciations. It brought me into contact with many people from around the world, broadened my horizons, sharpened my alignments, and taught me over time the ever evolving contours of my political identity.

CHAPTER 18

The Citizen Pilgrim as a Public Intellectual

An Illustrative Challenge: The Council on Foreign Relation

The reality of living as a citizen pilgrim is a sequence of concrete occurrences that test conscience, and create tensions between being politically correct and being a conscientious citizen. In effect, do I go with the flow or do I cry 'foul' in the face of wrongs in spheres of my concern? Being a public intellectual is an individual stance, a standing apart from the crowd and expectations of conformity when it comes to following the path chosen by leaders. A small incident occurred in the late 1960s when I put myself in the crossfire of the elite Council on Foreign Relations (CFR). My challenge was rebuffed, and I was chastised, but it left me with a better understanding what it meant to be a public intellectual and why that was my calling. There is an irony present as the CFR is a very private network, verging on secretive, yet playing influential roles in shaping the views of the political class and providing the talent to staff the institutions of government when it comes to foreign policy and international intelligence operations, with a special interest in its economic and ideological dimensions.

In my early years of CFR membership back in the late 1960s I was somewhat surprised to be valued beyond my worth. It seemed that the CFR was out of step with the anti-war mood of the country, and to retain influence and credibility, it needed to alter its image. It was in this impersonal sense that I seemed valuable as a new member who possessed a publicly visible anti-war and critical approach to American foreign policy. I provided a token of balance to its public profile as the Council staff openly realized its need to move beyond a pro-government consensus if its policy pronouncements were to have traction in the post-Vietnam political atmosphere. The elitism of the Council, and its policy ambitions, were more pronounced than those of the ASIL, making little claim to base membership on merit or humanitarian contributions, but rather on access to power, wealth, and social status, especially recruiting from Wall Street professions, retired diplomats, intelligence officials, and high-ranking military officers, as well as a sprinkling of Ivy League professors and think tank stalwarts. As a matter of presumed identity, the Council prized connectivity—connections and discreet access—and avoided public controversy except to back the mainstream bipartisan consensus. For this reason the critical stance associated with public intellectuals was viewed as an anathema from deep state or CFR perspectives. It recalled for me my experience with Carl Kaysen—a consummate insider—during the Vietnam War who condescendingly advised me to refrain from public criticism of the war, and express my doubts privately to high and mighty policy makers. It was precisely this critical role as public antagonist and informant that led me toward affirming public intellectuals such as Chomsky, Said, and eventually Ellsberg, and then emulating their example as best I could.

One day while at my desk in Princeton, I received a message that William Bundy was being proposed as the new editor of *Foreign Affairs*, which immediately struck me as a terrible idea, and contradicted the CFR claim that it was adapting to the anti-war political atmosphere produced by the failure of the Vietnam policies. I was aware that Bundy had a senior position in the State Department at a crucial time during the Vietnam War, and was specifically in charge of the secret bombing of North Vietnam. My opposition increased when I discovered that Bundy's appointment came about, not through normal selection procedures, but as a result of a conversation between David Rockefeller, then President of the Council, and Harvey Bundy, father of Bill and of LBJ's Chief of Staff, McGeorge, and himself a prominent Boston lawyer, at halftime of the annual Harvard/Yale football game. What I learned was that Harvey told David, 'Bill is leaving the government, and needs a job.' And Rockefeller responded along the lines of saying that Bill would be qualified to fill the vacancy at the *Foreign Affairs*, and proposed the appointment. At this point, acting on my own, I wrote a letter indicating my objections to the Bundy appointment, and asking for its reconsideration. I later persuaded Richard Barnet and my Princeton colleague, Richard Ullman, to join me in objecting to the appointment on the merits.

What followed was an object lesson in elite coherence. As a member of CFR my letter was treated respectfully. A meeting of the Council's Selection Committee was convened to which I was invited to present the rationale for my objections. After the meeting, my plea was rejected, at which point I appealed to the Board of the Council, and the issue became known to the membership as a whole. In the weeks that followed I received dozens of hostile letters, mostly denouncing my initiative as 'left-wing McCarthyism.' Even one from George Kennan, whom I considered a friendly acquaintance, telling me that if I was dissatisfied with the way the Council worked 'I should start my own club.' And even an apologetic message from the nationally respected journalist and former LBJ acolyte, Bill Moyers, who was an absent member of the Selection Committee, indicating his sympathy with my objections to Bundy, but saying in the end that he could not oppose the choice because the Rockefellers had been so loyal to him over the years.

In this period, when I was receiving this pushback, Bill Bundy called, asking if he could come to Princeton so that we could discuss his appointment over lunch. At first, my secretary, aware of the controversy, thought the call was fake or a friend's joke, and seemed reluctant to put it through, but I told her to go ahead. It was authentic, and I agreed to have lunch. I actually was curious about the man. Our lunch was uneventful, Bundy seemingly appealing to me as part of the same political class, and assuring me that my articles would be welcome at *Foreign Affairs* during his editorship. I declined, explaining as civilly as I could, why I opposed his appointment. Bill got the job. Somehow the walls of Council secrecy were breached, and the story of these events was covered in the mainstream press as an example of an unusual breakdown of elite decorum.

In subtle ways the Council exacted its 'pound of flesh' at my expense, I retained membership, but was never again asked to be a speaker or even invited to join a study group that issued policy papers under Council auspices. Still, I continued to pay my dues, staying a member over the course of the next 40 years, and occasionally attending a few meetings at which visiting foreign leaders gave off the record talks

Navigational Options for the Citizen Pilgrims

The citizen pilgrim is not necessarily drawn to the public sphere. He or she can embark on very private life journeys dedicated to involving the arts, witnessing, service, and reflections. I was not so inclined. It was not just my inclination to talk truth to power, although this played a part. What motivated me most was the impulse to act in solidarity with progressive initiatives on a wide range of issues. As a result of being situated in the United States, I found myself confronting U.S. foreign policy from time to time—sometimes politely by testifying before Congressional committees or sometimes more militantly by speaking at demonstrations or supporting by petitions and visits struggles against injustice whether in Vietnam, Palestine, or South Africa. As an academic I tried to interpret complex and controversial development in a manner that usually went against the grain of conventional wisdom. This was most evident in my various activities relating to Iran, Israel, and Turkey.

In subtle ways that Council made me realize that I had breached decorum, and although retaining membership, I was never again invited to be a speaker or even part of a study group that issued policy papers. Still, I continued to pay my dues, staying a member over the course of the next 40 years, and attending a few closed meetings with visiting foreign leaders if I could be conveniently in New York City.

For many years I have tried to identify what it meant to be a progressive citizen in a democratic society, given my sense that the boundaries of political engagement should not be tied to narrow nationalist and tribalist worldviews. I preferred thought, feelings, values, solidarity, and action that reflects the *common good*, or a 21st century blend of *human* and *global* interests expressive of the fears and hopes of our time arising from inclusive identities. More spontaneously, I was drawn to the liberation struggles waged on behalf of 'lost causes' and historic grievances (slavery, abuses of native and colonized peoples), and later in life, to the defense of nature and the wellbeing of animals and their habitats. When attaining political maturity I became far more receptive to the tales of 'losers' than the plaudits of 'winners.' This reflected my discomfort with the way capitalism in practice tore societies apart, inducing the twin evils of embittered resentment and moral complacency.

The Dilemmas of Political Participation

As with advocacy of 'world government,' I found assertions of 'world citizenship' premature, misleading, bland, although well-intentioned. At first glance proclaiming oneself a world citizen seemed a welcome escape route from political identity, community, and problem-solving by tropes of patriotism given specific content by reference to national benefits, burdens, and ambitions. The problem I find with asserting world citizenship can be succinctly expressed as its lacking substance, or more pointedly, that it is 'illusionary' so long as there exists only a phantom *world community*. We often speak of 'world community' to suggest the collective activities of governments at the UN and elsewhere without thinking about the nature of a true community, which to exist depends on shared core values and genuine feelings of commonality. In reality, global venues are beset by clashing interests, priorities, and perceptions of entitlement. Everything suggested by invoking 'American exceptionalism' is illustrative of the provincial limits of 'community' by the leading sovereign state.

My effort to find the right path to reformulating citizenship without succumbing to mere wish fulfillment, was to trust my conscience and struggle for what is right and just as I see it, hoping that at some future time the struggle will make real what is appropriately identified as *world community* exhibiting genuine bonds and shared values joining transnational and global political actors. Even should this happen, the imagery of a pilgrimage seems valuable to retain, suggesting that the human condition atrophies whenever it lacks horizons of aspiration and pursues static destinations. There is no destination or resting place, only the ceaseless search for a better future that is kinder, more satisfying, with less suffering brought about by hunger, war, disease, greed, oppression, and various cruelties.

Citizenship in the time of Trump takes on a more rudimentary national challenge: how to preserve the republic in the face of its devastation by the Republicans that has made the risks of a slide into fascism and ecological collapse greater than at any time in my lifetime. Trump and Trumpism has exposed also the acute structural weaknesses of American constitutionalism as of 2020. Checks and balances, supposedly guarding the country against abuses of power, have been disturbingly neutralized, exposing the opposition political party as itself a captive of predatory capitalism, and revealed a citizenry partly enraged, partly naïve, and almost totally alienated, seemingly effectively pacified despite periodic outbursts of rage. The U.S. fared worse than any other major country during the COVID-19 pandemic, exhibiting the features of a failed state in the context of world health, failing miserably to protect its own citizenry or cooperate with other governments, defunding and withdrawing from WHO while demeaning UN attempts to fashion a global approach, and forfeiting the last fragment of any claim to provide constructive world leadership in response to global crisis conditions that impacted upon the lives of people everywhere. The commodification of the quest for a vaccine is an obscene confirmation of nationalist sociopathology at its worst. Treating the search for and dissemination of vaccines as a form of global commons as China and a few other countries have promised to do—gestures toward a sense of species identity and world community that should embarrass Washington—yet so far only seems to produce further withdrawals from a posture of global responsibility, mixing tribal nationalism with geopolitical truculence.

In the background, but only for the duration of the pandemic, are the challenges posed by ecological instability, nuclear weaponry, and torments wrought by global inequality and autocratic governance. On one side, we hear the plaintive plea of Greta Thunberg, 'listen to science and the scientists before it's too late.' On another side, is the data-driven foolishness of Steven Pinker advising the world that human beings have never had it so good while the planet goes down in flames. And rising above this cacophony of voices are the rants of autocratic demagogues such as Trump, Modi, Bolsonaro, Duterte.

Cosmopolitanism

Ever since reading Karl Mannheim as a graduate student I have been aware and partially sympathetic to the rebukes directed at those who champion cosmopolitan values and world citizenship. I also understand related efforts to draw sharp distinctions, as Michael Walzer, does between 'thick' and 'thin' identities, suggesting that nationalism and tribalism remains thick while civilizationalism and cosmopolitanism seems thin, almost vapid, and hence quite marginal to political engagement and human experience.[i] I am also aware of those mean-spirited nationalist and communitarian jibes that intend to draw humanist blood: 'those who love everyone, love no one' or the dagger directed at the heart of ethical conscience, 'America, love her or leave her.'

There are solid reasons to be wary of facile cosmopolitan identifications: as diversions from taking responsibility for local and national injustices as in New Age forms of self-indulgence; as utopian ideas without political traction, and hence a waste of time and energy; as disregard of the psychological need of 'the other' to create a sense of local community and enjoy the satisfactions of patriotism; as an idealistic façade behind which lurks geopolitical ambitions and agendas such as the vain proclamations of 'liberal internationalism' or American exceptionalism; and lastly, as the anthro-political/DNA reality that human attachments have always asserted the primacy of the *part* (family, neighborhood, church, nation, civilization) as distinct from the *whole*, making the sum of the parts *less* than the whole. My abiding world order claim is that present historical circumstances incline toward catastrophe

---

i See Michaek Walzer, *Thick or Thin: Moral Argument at Home and Abroad* (2016).

unless policies and practices at all levels of social interaction behave and believe in ways that make *the whole greater than parts*, thereby reversing the course of all of human history.

These considerations should not be ignored, and persuasive reasons exist why I could never accept an either/or posing of the question, opting instead for what others called 'rooted cosmopolitanism,' rather close in spirit to the writing of Kwame Anthony Appiah. When it comes to law and basic rights, the prime focus should be the human being and local communities, as complemented by nation, ethnicity, religion, gender, sexual orientation. The recognition of this ethical imperative is essential to the whole undertaking of 'human rights,' starting with the recognition of 'human' in the name itself, which stipulates that a person only needs to be a human being to satisfy the fundamental precondition for an entitlement to the legal protection of basic rights.

However, as a practical matter, the implementation of human rights is almost totally dependent in the modern world on the policies and practices of the governing institutions in sovereign states. It is this conjuncture between the universal and the particular that gave me a clue as to how to overcome the dilemma. There is no need to choose between nationalism and cosmopolitanism as both have a role in the realities of our world, and we must not forget in the process to do our best on behalf of the wellbeing of the animals and non-human creatures with whom we share a natural habitat. Although some have talked of animal rights, I view the relationship as more a matter of our duty than of their right. As with the care of children, love of and care for animals can become the source of deep satisfaction and attachment, as it has been for me throughout my life. Few pleasures have been more satisfying for me than in my 90th year in the midst of the Turkish COVID lockdown watching four kittens daily grow to cathood from the miraculous moment of their birth.

In this era of an emerging consciousness of Anthropocene responsibility for both the despoiling and the caring of the planet, it is now widely understood, although also resisted by ultra-nationalist forces, that only a *global* and *species* outlook with an eye to the future can adequately address an agenda of fundamental and increasingly urgent ecological and world order challenges. Such challenges start with climate change, but extend to nuclear weaponry, migration, biodiversity, contagious disease, extreme poverty, racism, militarism, and spiritual malaise. That is, for the first time in human experience, problem-solving bearing on wellbeing and survival depend on a cosmopolitan interpretation of social reality and political responsibility, encompassing biological, ethical, and spiritual dimensions of consciousness, as well as physical behavior.

Yet there are several formidable reasons not to switch from nationalism to cosmopolitanism all at once without pausing to consider whether and how the gaps in between can be filled. As is evident, there is now absent a cosmopolitan political community that can act effectively on behalf of the common good, or even identity what exactly this should mean in different contexts. In this sense, we must grasp the unpleasant truth that the UN is, at best, a hybrid actor responsive primarily to geopolitical pressures and the interplay of national interests, with residual attention devoted to human and global interests—nor indeed possesses the capacity to enforce the wide range of human rights treaties which it had managed to bring into being.

State-Centric World Order

Beyond this concern with short-termism, and related escapist and denialist behavior, there is the reality of a state-centric world order increasingly governed by a variety of ultra-nationalist postures in many leading countries. Finally, we need to ask whether cosmopolitanism can take account of the unevenness of material conditions, accentuated by multiple forms of global inequality, distrust, and enmity, which make it almost impossible to achieve consensus even if a mandate is framed in cosmopolitan terms. Against such a background, it will be difficult to avoid exploitative hierarchies in whatever world order emerges from the interactions among intense pressures for adaptation, the entrenched practices and policies of established structures, and the contradictory impacts of networks, digitization, automation, AI, and cyber connectivity.

The Need for Long-Term Thinking and Policy Formation

The question of questions is not whether cosmopolitanism is a species of utopianism, but rather whether the only positive future, given present conditions and challenges, is best described as 'a necessary utopia.' I have believed for at least the last decade that either utopia or dystopia are the futures that we confront, and it will not be nearly enough to repair a badly broken system. In this spirit, I advocate 'a politics of impossibility,' which entails a rejection of the customary notion of politics as 'the art of the possible' and relies upon an entirely 'new realism' anchored in *necessity, will,* and *struggle* rather than *feasibility, passivity,* and *complacency.*

Put differently, a politics of impossibility considers 'feasibility' in relation to imaginative potentiality rather than what seems attainable, given the character of existing political and economic arenas in which public policy is now being shaped and implemented. In effect, if it is imaginatively possible as consistent with human capabilities then it is in my usage 'feasible,' and given the nature of the global challenges, 'necessary' for a humane and ecologically prudent future. Not only the connectivity of 5-G, but the positive and negative potentials of robotics and artificial intelligence must form integral aspects of this new realism, either generating a creative and compassionate global community or producing a worsening of global militarism and hastening the bio-ethical-ecological collapse of the Anthropocene Age.

Most of the likeminded people I befriend do not see the world around them so starkly, being content to fret about and react to immediate woes. I am not alone in harboring these concerns but somewhat lonely without many comrades dedicated to what might be called 'long-termism.' Yet I am stuck on this island of my foreboding, unable to avoid the psychological backlash that my ways of knowing and feeling unleash. This long-term loneliness contrasts with the solidarities that exist in relation to even my most controversial responses to immediate challenges, including clearing up the mysteries and evasions still surrounding 9/11 and adopting a progressive approach to achieving a sustainable peace for the peoples of Israel and Palestine. Yet even though I have loving comrades in these struggles around the world, this loneliness may be the fate of a citizen pilgrim. It seems to come with prevailing circumstances in the last decades of my life, a reflection of a world without a transformative revolutionary populist movement that is at once national, transnational, planetary, and anthro-ecological in its worldview.

As a citizen pilgrim I look to the feared and desired future as a guide to engagement in the present, even as the political participation of most individuals continues to be primarily confined to national space, concerned with present political, social, and economic arrangements. We live and die in the present, acting in such arenas more as public intellectuals than as citizen pilgrims but we dare not neglect the future. I have decried what so often has felt almost like a choiceless democracy with respect to the concerns that have animated my life. For the past 25 years I have spent part of each year in Turkey, never seeking the status of citizen, but identifying as a kind of partial expatriate with its trials and tribulations. In the first two decades of the 21st century I have tried to sustain the visionary urgency of the near future while continuing to take suffering and international criminality seriously as existential dimensions of the present.

I have found that this positioning is only rarely shared with others, who regard me as either unrealistic, even utopian in the sense of irrelevant, and contrarian or even perverse by sticking to positions that are viewed as abrasive by seemingly likeminded friends and colleagues. I found students more receptive, although occasionally antagonistic, to my mixture of necessary utopianism, anarchism, and progressivism.

Given this understanding, I would rather die a misunderstood 'utopian' or 'contrarian' than be remembered as someone who embraced the false consciousness of dysfunctional patterns of thought, values, and action for supposedly realistic and politically correct reasons.

CHAPTER 19

Personal Hot Spots: A Credo

"I never was a Plan B sort of guy."

—Earl Newton, character in the film *Mule*

"Some men see things as they are and say 'why?'
I dream of things that never were and ask 'why not?'"

—George Bernard Shaw

Against Algorithms

I have for most of my life been a quietly ineffectual rebel against many prevailing ways of conceiving reality, yet my life as lived was nevertheless blessed, not wasted, even precious. This posture of passive, yet determined resistance, began early in my childhood, rebelling against the attitudes I encountered in my own home or in my family. Even my tender and humane Dad reflected the conventional thinking that back then viciously stereotyped (even in sophisticated West Side Manhattan) all forms of deviation, whether political, cultural, social. He castigated those who were impressed by the appeals of Communism, and even those who exhibited socialist sympathies were derisively referred to as 'parlor pinks,' gay people as 'fairies,' 'negroes' as untrustworthy, lazy, and inclined toward crime. For me, even as a kid, these insinuations seemed suspect, and only much later did I come to appreciate that these epithets condemning 'difference' and 'otherness' had dire social consequences for those targeted, and indirectly for the rest of us. When still young, overexposed to adult companionship, I sat quietly most of the time but with skeptical ears, occasionally asking a simple question, knowing it to be provocative—'What is your evidence?' for these harsh judgments demeaning persons for who they were or what they believed. Similarly, but now in the digital vein, I have recently heard more and more about algorithms controlling how we experience social reality, which result from feeding conventional mapping into software programs that are increasingly being used beyond consumer sales and political preferences to give marketable structures to the story lines of TV series, that is, feeding us 'processed entertainment' as an add-on to fast food, and more detrimental to our health. In this sense, our individuality, and healthy deviance, is being suppressed by these covert forms of indoctrination, making us treat the conventional as the normal, and by extension, as the proper way to understand and engage with markets, and even the world.

We are all to varying degrees subject to algorithmic manipulation, whether we realize it or not.

The uplifting Japanese film *Shoplifters* explores the same mismatch between the patterns of living together that society endorses and those that work existentially for people brave enough to defy convention. In this exploration of family life by the Japanese author and director, Hiorkazu Koreeda, the sense of belonging, bonding, and need is given priority over respectability, genetics, wealth, compliance with law, and similarities of blood type. The family of misfits, petty criminals, prostitutes, and money-grubbing retirees is seen as far preferable to the cold formalities of Japanese bourgeois life where material needs are achieved by socially acceptable behavior while emotional needs are virtually overlooked.

I find guidelines from life coach industries to be almost totally irrelevant, and on balance even harmful by drawing one away from one's responsibility for one's own choices and decisions.

I fear that this emergent tyranny of algorithms, robots, devices, artificial intelligence, and political correctness in the digital age purporting to address our desires, fears and needs is the technologically contrived destiny awaiting humanity. It seems likely to erode the life of the mind, heart, and soul, draining life from that remnant of spirituality, awe, and mystery that has struggled to survive the onslaughts of modernity.

Moral Correctness is More than Political Correctness

The empowering response to political correctness is not its opposite. In liberal societies we partly arrive at what is correct to overcome a legacy of past abuse and suffering without any willingness to confront such exploitative structural issues as the militarization of the state and predatory capitalism. Identity politics may fracture the sense of societal community, but until African Americans resisted as African Americans, whites barely perceived the crimes by whites African Americans had experienced, much less acknowledged them. Rather, they were almost erased in the public imagination, and always understated in the historical record. My own upbringing along Manhattan's Central Park West exhibited these qualities of dormant or unconscious racism, which persisted despite my childhood attachment to an African American gay household helper who had a superior intellect, an infectious comic sense of the world, an affectionate disposition, providing a role model during my teenage years. Yet it was not until much later when, as an adult, I finally read Toni Morrison's *Beloved* and experienced trusting friendships with African Americans that I began to acknowledge my own mental infrastructure of racist attitudes and ignorance about the terrible legacies of slavery afflicting current generations of black people, making me ashamed of my insensitivities and ignorance of what might be called deep structures of racist beliefs and social practices. I have also been aware of the tendency by those who are white, male, and liberal to tell those who are economically and socially victimized how best to pursue their goals, as if we defectors from oppressing classes knew more about their experiences, preferences, and the route to amelioration than its victims. After her education was over I became friends with an African American Princeton graduate student, Sherri Burr, who later became a successful law professor, and seemed on my wavelength socially and culturally. I invited her to a concert of Paul Winter's music at the cathedral of St. John the Divine. We went and I enjoyed it very much as I knew I would, having heard Winter's music previously and knowing him personally. But Sherri did not. She reminded me that Winter's music suited white intellectuals' listening preferences but had no resonance for someone of her racial background. So admonished, I meekly admitted my insensitivity, and tried in the future to be more mindful when such situations arose. I am pleased that we remained friends through the decades. In retrospect, the incident was a teaching moment for Sherri and adult education for me.

I fear maybe I have been also sometimes insensitive to Jewish fears and anxieties associated with a heritage of persecution and in face of this, pride in Jewish tradition and identity. I admit a failure on my part to understand sympathetically the willingness of most Jews to privilege their individual and collective security and wellbeing over almost every other concern. In the Jewish case, the Holocaust has deservedly received enormous attention, but it has also been manipulated to insulate Zionism from justifiable criticism as Norman Finkelstein so effectively demonstrates in his book, *The Holocaust Industry*. The mantle of anti-Semitism has been maliciously and pragmatically (mis)used, especially after 1945, to hide the extent of Israel's criminality and cruelty toward the Palestinian people. This has resulted, somewhat deliberately and certainly opportunistically, in confusing the actuality of harm and historic hatred toward Jews, the crux of true anti-Semitism, with the recognition that Israel's behavior toward the Palestinian people is as unacceptable as were the policies and practices of apartheid South Africa to Africans. We should never seek to validate present cruelty and victimization of innocent others by invoking individual and collective suffering of our past, however extreme. We can undoubtedly better grasp the causes of such unjust behavior, and exhibit empathy toward both past and present victims. Reproducing the evil done to us or those with whom we identify is still evil, a retrograde learning curve, which unfortunately is a common thread running through history, and certainly such rationalizations of wrongdoing are not peculiar to Jews.

Outliving My Generation

An early memory was riding in the back seat of my Grandma Eva's limousine with George, her lifetime family chauffer, behind the wheel as we drove down Park Avenue from her spacious Fifth Avenue apartment directly opposite the Metropolitan Museum. Even in her early 90s my grandmother's mind remained sharp enough to play competitive bridge at a nearby club. She never mellowed, retaining her acerbic brand of charm until her final breadth. My recollection from that drive was her pointing to one luxury apartment building after another, repeating this same phrase three or four times before we reached Saks Fifth Avenue to purchase my annual birthday present: 'she's gone.' The impression that lingered after almost 80 years is that she had outlived her generation, which primarily meant in her case, her habitual bridge partners. In the process her life, never joyful, had become sad and lonely. For once, perhaps the only time, I could feel her pain, a welcome relief from fending off her jabs intended to put me in my place, intimidating the shy and insecure boy that I remember being, perhaps the model for my own mother's similar assaults on my self-esteem.

Maybe academic people live longer these days. In any event, although I have lost many friends since this century began, many remain. Also, my continuing activity as scholar and activist has brought me a stream of new friends and moving to Santa Barbara in 2002 helped enlarge my social circle. Perhaps, too, social media and the memes of the digital age reduce the significance of age and even generational differences—or perhaps not. The evidence now available is inconclusive.

Although losing many cherished friends including Eqbal Ahmad, Edward Said, Gloria Emerson, Rajni Kothari, Martha Gavensky, Rani Jethmalani, Ali Mazrui, Yasuaki Onuma, Yoshi Sakamoto, Burns Weston, and Steve Cohen as well as all my close blood relatives other than children and grandchildren, I have not yet experienced social loneliness. I have written a large number of memorial essays in recent years, which of course reminds me of my own mortality, an intimation of the death warrant issued to all of us as soon as we are born, yet periodically doubted deep inside, as most of us want to live forever. Sometimes I even daydream that this impossibility can happen, but hardly admit such an absurdity to myself, much less acknowledge it to others. Now there are apparently genetic engineers working in secret labs, letting it be known that immortality might someday become achievable, at least for a chosen few, and even before the end of the present century. Of course, my situation is far from bleak, given a loving life partner and loving children, and contrasts with my grandmother's plight rather than resembles it.

It also reminds me that I would like to die with hope on my lips. Now the future, if conceived as an extension of the present, paints a bleak picture. The miseries of climate change, global migration, famine, autocratic governance, militarist geopolitics, and diminishing biodiversity seem unlikely to be alleviated within my life span and will more likely worsen. Only those with confidence that technology and statistics will overcome these underlying problems when they become serious enough challenges to the wellbeing of the elites retain the false consciousness of optimism. I am bemused and disturbed that the gifted popular writer, Huval Noah Harari, anticipates that coming generations, having supposedly solved the mega-problems of famine, disease, poverty, and war, will become increasingly absorbed by such tasks as achieving continuous happiness, overcoming mortality, and acquiring the godlike powers of constituting reality itself. Aside from the traditional mega-problems, the Malthusian checks on human wellbeing, Harari seems to forget the profound unmet ecological and digital age challenges of living together and with nature.

In my present frame of mind, I will die an agnostic about the future, priding myself on an ability to live with eyes wide open, yet struggling for what is right almost every day. Enlightenment rationality tells me that we are a doomed species faced with growing threats of extinction, or at least the collapse of civilizational standards, and lacking an adequate *species will* to survive and flourish in a humane and ecologically responsible manner. My spiritual self delivers a quite different metaphysical message: the strength of an emergent politics of *impossibility* that gathers enough traction to produce transnational movements and global projects dedicated to transformative outcomes that move mainly in humane directions.

The Personal is Not (Necessarily) Political

Of course, there was an important insight contained in the consciousness-raising slogan 'the personal is political,' referencing the personal impact of everyday discrimination and exploitation that reflects the particular political determinants operative in each society. Over the years I tried to give my students the sense that their commitment to human rights is most clearly revealed and realized by how they treat the diverse persons who daily cross their paths. Such guidance applies to all of us, at all times and throughout life. We can express the same homely thought differently: the most important decision each of us makes with respect to human rights is how we treat and feel toward one another, and especially toward those who have serious disabilities or are different in color, gender, sexual preference, ethnicity, age, appearance, and belief. Somewhat related, in a manner that challenges especially those with the credentials of privilege, that our humanity depends on taking the suffering and vulnerability of others seriously as vectors of political engagement. The current failures of empathy, highlighted by Trumpism, toward those seeking entry to or residence in the United States exemplifies this tendency of fear, manipulation, and opportunism to occupy most of the political space, leaving us as peoples without compassion for those acting out of desperation who are then punished a second time because they are provocatively depicted as threats, even 'invaders.' Such empathy doesn't mean to suggest that as long as national spaces are a primary source for feeling community bonds, humane restrictions and enlightened discouragement of migration may become necessary and even desirable. In effect, those with resources, livelihoods, human rights and healthy living space have a species responsibility to those that lack these essentials of human dignity. Indeed, if the root causes of displacement and migration are exposed, they often implicate the past behavior (colonialism, unjust economic arrangements, intervention, carbon emissions) of the very countries that are presently erecting exclusionary walls of various kinds.

My priorities here are different. I want to affirm that my love of partner and children is essentially, although not entirely, distinct from my political commitments. By 'not entirely' I mean that if some common ground of belief and perception is not shared, it strains love even among those with the closest blood and love relations. If Noah, Dimitri, Hilal, Zeynep were Trump lovers or immigration haters, it would impinge upon my feelings of trust and intimacy, not extinguishing these bonds, but weakening them in damaging ways, requiring awkward silences and evasions so as to avoid total breakdowns of social relationships. I am reminded of brothers I knew in the Philippines and parents and children in Colombia who gather as families on holidays with the strict understanding that their contradictory political allegiances will not be mentioned.

Despite some differences of assessments and tactics, I have been fortunate to have never faced this kind of challenge in any close family relationship. Also, I admit that I have at times wished for more, for solidarity and fervent support, and even some curiosity as to my views from my children and partners rather than mere tolerance and respect.

My Private Imperative

Sharing my life with Hilal for the past 25 years has been my core personal reality and a most fulfilling experience. Our marriage has had the ups and downs customary in any long relationship, yet the ups last much longer and are more intense and deeper than the downs; they go higher than the downs go lower. We have lived through the ebb and flow of all sustained human experiences of exceptional daily intimacy, leaving only a few faint emotional scars.

With children, feelings seem more stable, partly because adult children have their own lives to live and partly because in the highly individualized world of America their separate lives generally only touch ours at times of celebration or crisis. When Noah, over many years, faced one self-generated crisis after another, I came to feel myself his emergency cash machine, but only a marginal influence on how he chose to live, although he is more traditional than others, except possibly Zeynep, in affirming family affinities. With Dimitri, his lifelong interest in secrecy and practice of covertness is a source of both fascination and distancing, and often meant that I was exposed only to the surfaces of his evidently rich inner and outer experience. Bonding with both Dimitri and Noah through our shared love of sports was a feature of my life as a parent while they were growing up, and even afterwards, overcoming to some extent the familial downsides of my public life, frequent traveling, my failing marriage to their mother, and my unsteady romantic life until Hilal came along.

I feel that at the end of my life, I have had extreme good fortune in my personal life. This fourth and final marriage with Hilal has flourished for me, evolving in many life-affirming directions, at first romantically and then as a pervasive and intimate partnership, with lots of give and take that for me retained its romantic edge. Although our children and many friends seem to be okay with lives lived without a core love relationship, I have always felt unhinged without such an emotional anchor.

Although I have not been as close to my children as I would have wished, it makes me feel fulfilled to affirm their life choices, their human decency, and their clarity about good and evil. Beyond this, Dimitri has been an exemplary parent to an extraordinary child, Juliet, my grandchild, who with grace and abundant talent embodies all of the qualities that bring the deepest satisfactions and strongest admiration, both privately and more publicly. Experience has a cunning way of disappointing expectations, but as of now Juliet's future seems a bright star in the firmament of my personal awareness. Actually, I see Zeynep more than either Dimitri and Noah, and feel alternatively very close and somewhat distant, both true emotions reflecting deep compatibilities yet also strong differences in style and maybe substance.

I also have been blessed by my Canadian family, for whose achievements I can take absolutely no credit. The trials and tribulations of life have made me far less attentive than my feelings of devotion, love, and admiration would suggest. In reality I have enacted the role of a remote, divorced and distant parent and grandparent who never took the trouble to establish a sustained loving presence, and thus is at best (dis) regarded as a benign, yet ghostly reality. Chris and Judy, as with their children Sarah and Matthew, have been highly successful in fulfilling the highest expectations of family life, achieving personal goals that reflect their values of decency and dignity, and satisfy their modest yet satisfying worldly affinities.

Pilgrimage and Quest

Looking back, I have had unusual good fortune at crucial points in my life, many privileges, early career opportunities beyond what I ever expected or deserved, as well as openings to power and maybe wealth that tempted me, but not enough to pursue. I am thankful that I was never been put in situations where I was under severe pressure to act strongly against my conscience. I admit to being occasionally tantalized by the low hanging fruit of ambition and reward offered to compliant Princetonians. Whether with my mother's rich family, or at Princeton, or with early contacts with the U.S. Government and aspiring politicians, it never struck me as worthwhile, or even temperamentally possible, to file down the sharp edges of moral conviction to the point that where I could offer myself to the established order as a dutiful and competent sycophant. True, I had some slight unacknowledged envy for those who did manage to ingratiate themselves to the high and mighty, and were rewarded with the seductive perks of high public office. Among those in academic life with the required ability, worldview, and personality, whom I came to know, I would put such high fliers as Richard Holbrooke, Zbigniew Brzezinski, and Joe Nye in that category, but not such principled academically prominent conservatives as Sam Huntington, Ken Waltz, and Robert Gilpin. It was not just my conscience linked to an evolving sense of self that cast frequent vetoes, but my inability to remain content for very long in any organized collective setting, whether country, institutional workplace, religion, and even at times family. For better and worse, during my entire adult life I swam on my own and often against the current, sometimes with regret, sometimes clumsily, and despite my modest abilities as a swimmer, my emotional stamina and poise has mostly carried me safely to sandy beaches. There is no good way to assess the costs of these life choices to shun the mainstream and find my fair share of enchantment on the margins, but especially when it came to Israel and a rejection of liberal Zionism, I was conscious of enough visible pushback to believe that the road chosen imposed rather high opportunity costs, but never led me to lose a single hour of sleep.

My attitude and actions during the 2016 U.S. primaries, during which I favored Sanders over Hillary Clinton as the Democratic candidate, were emblematic of why I found so few true political comrades over the years within the halls of academe. What mattered to my liberal friends, including most left liberals, was how best to beat Trump combined with their realization that Trump's election would arouse finally several dormant viruses in the American body politic, including racism, xenophobia, unregulated individualism, regression on reproductive rights for women, give rise to renewed discrimination against gays, and loosen inhibitions on many forms of gangster behavior. It was also persuasively argued by my liberal friends that judicial and cabinet appointments would be of better quality if made by Hillary Clinton, and that Democrats would govern in more inclusive ways than their Republican counterparts. My priorities in foreign policy favored political disengagement in the Middle East, nuclear disarmament, ending sanctions against Cuba, Iran, and Venezuela, and the embrace of nonviolent geopolitics as the foundation of global leadership. If nonviolent geopolitics went forward in collaboration with China, that stressed ecological values, a bio-ethical vision of human identity, a strengthened UN, and renewed respect for international law, it could make one readier to believe that a peaceful world is within human reach.

Musing along these lines privately made me wonder from time to time whether conventional liberal perspectives were not too nationalistic in some respects and for foreign policy, too beholden to the bipartisan consensus as sculpted by the deep state. I admit that during the 2016 campaign I often wondered whether Trump might be an *internationally* less destructive presence in the White House than Clinton (remember her notoriously chilling remark about Libya and Qaddafi after the 2011 regime-changing intervention: 'We came, we saw, he died.') Trump turned out to be far more disruptive, actually embracing many tropes of fascism especially domestically, than I anticipated. Yet, we have no way of knowing whether Clinton might have been as bad, or even worse, given her confrontational and militarist inclinations when it came to foreign policy. And I have similar fears with respect to Biden, especially internationally, should he succeed in becoming the next U.S. president.

As a still aspiring citizen pilgrim, my journey goes on despite the perils of navigating without much guidance from a flickering North Star. I have never been motivated by pretensions of 'making a difference' or 'making change happen.' My credo is reducible to 'do the right thing' as consistently and stubbornly as possible, which meant trusting my conscience even if impractical and discrediting, accepting marginalization and frustration, somewhat offset reputationally by being admired and excessively praised, especially in international settings where affinity with my views prevailed, and always hoping for the best.

I remain beset by big questions such as 'Who am I?' 'What can be done?' 'How will it end? When?' Yet what I can say about myself with some pride is that along the way I have enjoyed life as a precious gift while managing to stay mostly true to what I believe, and sharing my understanding of the restorative pathways to the future with those who would listen. Mistakes and discouragements along the way, yes, but without any betrayal of ideals, values, persons. If given the chance I would not only choose the same paths again but try to find them sooner and walk faster. And if given another chance I would hope to be luckier with the tides of history moving in my direction. In this imagined second life I would like to swim more often with the current, and yet not forget that in my former life I had the blessings of genetic and socioeconomic gifts that set me apart, and my only lifelong wound was the absence of the reassuring comforts of maternal love, even affection. Yet I found love along the way. Having Hilal as my loving, imperfectly perfect, partner for the past 25 years is the blessing of blessings, unforeseen until it happened, yet I am proud that I recognized this way of consummating my life quest for love very soon after we met in that unplanned and unexpected encounter in Malta.

I conclude with the fervent public hope that the several revolutionary pathways traveled by citizen pilgrims will be more often and urgently chosen by my sisters and brothers throughout the world, and so widened in scope, extended in meaning, and deepened in influence. We may not overcome but let us pledge, as an invisible global community, to die trying!

At the end, I feel able to claim in good faith, 'I kept trying.' And that is what my life was mostly about.

Index